Durable Solutions

Durable Solutions

Being

Papers given to the Family Justice Councils' Interdisciplinary Conference for judges, directors of social services, mental health professionals, academia, guardians ad litem, panel managers and other professions, held at the Dartington Hall Conference Centre, Dartington Hall, Totnes, Devon, between 30 September – 2 October 2005, together with a record of the discussions which took place in the plenary sessions of the conference.

Edited by

The Rt Hon Lord Justice Thorpe

and

Rosemary Budden
Barrister

Family Law

Published by

Jordan Publishing Limited
21 St Thomas Street
Bristol BS1 6JS

British Library Cataloguing-in-Publication Data

A catalogue record for this book is available from the British Library.

ISBN 1 84661 003 6

Typeset by Etica Press Limited

Printed and bound in Great Britain by Antony Rowe Limited, Chippenham, Wiltshire

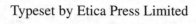

CONTRIBUTORS

Amanda Checkley
Independent Reviewing Officer

Bruce Clark
Head of Looked After Children Division, Department for Education and Skills

Paul Clark
Director of Children's Services, Harrow

Dr Christopher Clulow
Director, Tavistock Centre for Couple Relationships

District Judge (Magistrates' Courts) Nicholas Crichton
Inner London & City Family Proceedings Court

Professor Gillian Douglas
Cardiff Law School

Professor Judy Dunn
Social, Genetics and Developmental Psychiatric Research Centre, Institute of Psychiatry

Katherine Gieve
Head of Family Department, Bindman & Partners

Dr Danya Glaser
Consultant Child and Adolescent Psychiatrist, Great Ormond Street Hospital for Children

Gill Gorell-Barnes
Hon Senior Lecturer Tavistock Clinic; Family and marital therapist; Consultant to Children and Family Legal Disputes and Family Court Proceedings

Dr Cathy Humphreys
School of Health and Social Studies, University of Warwick

Joan Hunt
Senior Research Fellow, Oxford Centre for Family Law and Policy, Department of Social Policy and Social Work, University of Oxford

Professor Charlie Lewis
Department of Psychology, Lancaster University

AP
Parent

Dr Gillian Schofield
Co-director of the Centre for Research on the Child and Family, University of East Anglia

John Simmonds
Director, Policy Research & Development, British Association for Adoption and Fostering

Professor Carol Smart
The Morgan Centre for the Study of Relationships and Personal Life, School of Social Sciences, University of Manchester

David Spicer
Assistant Head of Legal Services, Nottinghamshire County Council

Professor June Thoburn CBE
School of Social Work and Psychosocial Studies, University of East Anglia

Dr Liz Trinder
School of Social Work and Psychosocial Sciences, University of East Anglia

Dr Judith Trowell
The Tavistock Clinic

Lord Justice Wall
Court of Appeal

FOREWORD

by Sir Mark Potter
President of the Family Division

This was the first Dartington conference organised under the auspices of the newly inaugurated Family Justice Council. Having just taken up my appointment as President of the Family Division, it was also my first Dartington Conference. As such, it gave me the ideal opportunity to meet and learn from leading professionals and researchers concerned with marital breakdown and its consequences for children.

The well-chosen theme of the Conference, 'Durable Solutions', resulted in the absorbing papers published in this volume. The oral presentations were of the high standard traditionally associated with the Dartington Conference, as well as the lively discussions which followed.

It is gratifying to see that the Conference Resolutions on domestic violence and family assistance orders have been taken up and are presently being debated as the Children and Adoption Bill passes through Parliament.

We should be grateful to Rosemary Budden, as the conference rapporteur, for collating these valuable materials, and to Jordans for publishing them

Sir Mark Potter
March 2006

EDITORIAL INTRODUCTION

The successful delivery of a Dartington Conference depends upon many contributions. Evidently a conference does not spring from the clouds unplanned. Neither inspiration nor spontaneity are substitutes for careful planning initiated approximately 18 months before we all arrive (given Dartington's popularity we must book our weekend about two years in advance). At the first meeting of the planning group we must choose our theme. The decision is risk laden. What may seem topical at the beginning of one year can have lost its sparkle towards the end of the next. Over the years we have managed pretty well. *No Fault or Flaw* in 1999 was our least inspired choice. The sub-title was *The Future of the Family Law Act 1996*. Between the selection of our theme and the conference itself it had become pretty clear that the Family Law Act 1996 did not have a future.

When we first met to plan the 2005 conference it was Peggy Ray who suggested the theme: *Durable Solutions*. Her idea, perfect in its simplicity, guaranteed the success of the conference. First it was risk free. Second it encapsulates in two simple words what we all strive for at the end of family proceedings whether early on by compromise or at the end of a long contested trial. It is equally true of public law proceedings as of private law proceedings. They are the outcomes most likely to promote the welfare of the children involved in the case.

Subsequent developments owe much to the simplicity and appeal of that message. The planning group felt at once that we were on course and that we had the capacity to deliver an influential outcome. Experts that we approached saw at once how their work related to the message and how it would harmonise with other perspectives.

The enthusiasm of the planning group clearly inspired our contributors. Almost everyone approached accepted the invitation to write. The consequence was a rich meal. Even careful pre-reading did not eliminate the demands on concentration and reflection at the conference. The oral presentations either introduced new ideas or liberated ideas that were still for some of us locked in the texts. The subsequent discussions in the small groups, in the Great Hall, and above all over meals and garden walks, engendered the conviction that we really could change things for the better: changes either in the system or in our practices or in our priorities: achievable changes: enduring changes.

Whether we shall achieve what then seemed so clearly in our grasp depends in no small measure upon this book. Obviously it needs to be widely read and widely discussed. It needs to be debated whilst the ideas are fresh and current. The Family Justice Council may distribute copies to each of its local branches. Jordans will market the title as vigorously as they have marketed its predecessors.

Rosemary Budden is the real editor of the title. She meticulously noted all the discussions in the Great Hall. Thereafter she dealt with all the contributors to ensure that they were satisfied with the text and with her note of their introductions. She has chased the rapporteurs for their notes of the discussions within the small groups. In the end she has delivered to Jordans a manuscript that has required minimal further work so the last word of this introduction should be from her.

Mathew Thorpe

It has been a privilege to be involved both in the conference and this publication seeking to facilitate enduring solutions for children and families. I express gratitude to each of the authors both for their papers as delivered at conference and their subsequent editorial assistance. Malcolm Welsh's administration of the conference was superb. I extend my thanks to all the delegates for their full participation in the discussions arising from the papers and their willingness to submit these for publication. My particular thanks go to the Senior District Judge, Stephen Cobb QC, Elaine Laken and Mark Ormerod for their invaluable assistance in the difficult task of distilling the small group discussions into the readily accessible summaries published here. I echo the sentiments of Lord Justice Thorpe and very much hope *Durable Solutions* and the valuable ideas arising from it will influence continuing discussions to shape and change future practice.

Rosemary Budden

CONTENTS

Contributors v

Foreword *by Sir Mark Potter* vii

Editorial introduction ix

Introductory remarks xv

PLENARY 1: COURT EXPERIENCES AND DEVELOPMENT OUTCOMES

The impact of the court process. What do the children tell us? 3
Dr Judith Trowell

The separate representation of children – in whose best interests? 13
Professor Gillian Douglas

A father's experience of care proceedings 23
AP

PLENARY 2: SMALL GROUP DISCUSSIONS

Small group discussions: plenary 1 29

PLENARY 3: MODELS FOR ACHIEVING SUCCESSFUL AGREED AND ORDERED OUTCOMES
IN PRIVATE LAW CASES

In-court conciliation: brief encounter or permanent resolution? 35
Liz Trinder

**Mediating parental disputes about their children inside and outside the court process:
assessing parents' and children's wishes and attachments in private law** 43
Gill Gorrell-Barnes

Early interventions: an alternative to contact disputes in private law family proceedings 55
Nicholas Crichton

Working with difficult couples in the family justice system 67
Dr Christopher Clulow

PLENARY 4: GENDER, PARENTING AND THE COURTS

Mothers and fathers 81
Katherine Gieve

Father–child relationships and children's development: A key to durable solutions? 87
Professor Charlie Lewis

Parenting disputes, gender conflict and the courts   103

Professor Carol Smart

PLENARY 5: CONTACT IN PRIVATE AND PUBLIC LAW CASES: MANAGING TWO OR MORE FAMILIES

Contact and children's well being in private and public law   115

Dr Danya Glaser

Contact with non-resident parents after separation and divorce   123

Joan Hunt

Contact with non-resident fathers: children's and parents' views   137

Professor Judy Dunn

Making decisions about contact in foster care and adoption: promoting security and managing risk   145

Dr Gillian Schofield

Thinking the unthinkable: the implications of research on women and children in relation to domestic violence   159

Dr Cathy Humphreys

PLENARY 6: PERMANENCE FOR LOOKED-AFTER CHILDREN

Using international comparisons to reflect on permanence options for children in out-of-home care in the UK   173

Professor June Thoburn CBE

Whose Care Plan is it Anyway?   185

David Spicer

The role of the independent reviewing officer – a practitioner's view   199

Amanda Checkley

Permanence for looked-after children   209

Paul Clark

PLENARY 7

Small group discussions: plenary 2–6   221

PLENARY 8: HELPING TO ENSURE SOLUTIONS WORK FOR CHILDREN IN THE LONGER TERM

Adoptive parents and children – support from placement to adulthood   231

John Simmonds

The draft Children and Adoption Bill 243

Lord Justice Wall

The policy context 261

Bruce Clark

PLENARY 9

Small group discussions: plenary 8 267

Issues raised in small groups and discussions 273

The conclusion of the conference 280

DARTINGTON CONFERENCE.
OPENING ADDRESS

Lord Justice Thorpe
Court of Appeal

In opening the last Dartington Conference, *Hearing the Children*, almost exactly two years ago I chose the future as my theme. That was because the creation of the Family Justice Council was underway. I therefore suggested that the 2003 Conference would be the last to be convened by the President's Interdisciplinary Committee and financed by the Department of Health and the Department of Constitutional Affairs. I predicted that the Dartington Conference would be strengthened rather than jeopardised in the evolutionary process. I am relieved to see that that safe prediction has been made good by the events of the last 18 months, which have seen the appointment of the Council and its early achievements. The Council is funding this, its first, Dartington Conference and the papers in your packs justify the claim that the high standards of scholarship achieved at previous conferences have been equalled if not exceeded. However it should be recorded that the vital work of choosing the theme, planning the presentations and recruiting the speakers has been carried out by a working group largely drawn from the Interdisciplinary Committee. Peggy Ray, Katherine Gieve, Clare Sturge, Danya Glaser, Judith Trowell and Gillian Scofield have been the prime architects of what we will discuss over the next 48 hours.

Today we mark a 10th anniversary. The first Dartington Conference, the *Rooted Sorrows* conference, took place on the 22–24 September 1995. Ten years after the event it is easy to regard the Dartington Conferences as a product of the President's Interdisciplinary Committee, and now the Family Justice Council. However that would be to fall into historical error. As I will demonstrate, the President's Interdisciplinary Committee was the child and not the parent of the Dartington Conferences.

Some of the roots of the FJC can be traced to a course developed to train suitable professionals in forensic psychotherapy. It was launched by the Portman Clinic in 1991 and directed by Dr Estella Weldon. The course was entirely innovative and therefore not without commercial risk. So the Portman constituted an advisory group drawn from a wide professional range. They invited Lord Lloyd of Berwick to represent criminal justice. Although not an obvious choice, it was no doubt known that Jane Lloyd, his wife, is a psychotherapist. The Portman approached Elizabeth Butler-Sloss as the obvious representative of family justice. She passed it to me since I had the same qualification as Tony Lloyd. As the Portman course gained momentum Tony Lloyd saw the opportunity for sentencing judges to learn more of what forensic psychotherapy had to offer offenders. He persuaded the Home Office to fund a conference at Cumberland Lodge that brought together specialists from the worlds of psychoanalytic psychotherapy and criminal justice.

What he achieved for criminal justice I wanted for family justice. After all, concepts of child welfare had been heavily influenced by the work of Bowlby, Winnicott and Anna Freud. Anna Freud's most influential publication had been a collaboration between psychoanalytic and legal specialists. Such collaborations need to be nourished and sustained. That I think we did at our first Dartington conference. The subsequent publication of the papers and the discussion has outsold any of our other publications and continues to sell. That is a topic to which I will soon return.

In retrospect the most significant consequence of the *Rooted Sorrow* conference was that it encouraged me to propose to the President, Sir Stephen Brown, the creation of an interdisciplinary standing committee. With his support the committee held its inaugural meeting on 30 April 1996. The first paragraph of the minutes of the meeting record the Dartington derivation. Of the 20 founding members, 12 are still in post and 9 of these 12 are here today. That demonstrates the commitment and gives this conference something of a family feel. So the President's Interdisciplinary Committee was the child of the first Dartington conference and it can thus legitimately claim the Family Justice Council as its grandchild.

This excursion in genealogy has a practical purpose: it demonstrates the value and potential of medico/legal collaboration. Perhaps we now have an opportunity to return to the mental health community and to ask what response they have to social issues and challenges which were unimagined a decade ago. Scientific advances in fertility and embryology, and a general acceptance of an infinite diversity in the composition of families have brought to the courts and the judges challenges which simply did not exist a decade ago. As we formulate our responses we surely need what help we can get. The mental health professions are probably the most fertile source. How then to revive the collaboration of 1995? A number of realities must be faced. First, whichever our discipline we all operate somewhere on the spectrum between hard-worked and over-worked. Second, it is unrealistic to expect innovative thinkers to operate beyond the bounds of their own profession. If lawyers would like the views of the mental health professionals it is for us to take the initiative. Third, original thinkers are in scarce and irregular supply. All the more important, therefore, that we keep open the channels of communication, recognising that there may be nobody with anything to offer at any given moment and also that new ideas are not necessarily good ideas.

In this anniversary year there are signs of regenerating exchanges. Dr Roger Kennedy of the Cassell Hospital published in June *Psychotherapists as Expert Witnesses* and the publication was preceded by an evening lecture at the Institute of Psychoanalysis in January 2004 to which all members of the Interdisciplinary Committee were invited. By way of return, in June of this year Hedley J and Judge Pearlman spoke at the Institute on the work of the judge in the family justice system. There were a number from the Inter-disciplinary Committee there to hear them and their presentations provoked lively discussion. The evenings are chaired by Michael Brearley (yes, the Michael Vaughan of his day) and I am meeting him next week to discuss possible future exchanges. On 8 October Wall LJ delivers The Glover Lecture at the Tavistock Clinic. This is a significant public lecture delivered by an insider and an outsider to the world of mental health in alternate years. As well as the psychodynamic branch of mental health, the outstanding collaboration between lawyers and child psychiatrists is as vigorous as ever, thanks in particular to Drs Claire Sturge, Danya Glaser and Judith Trowell. Doctor Mike Shaw is a recent and generous additional contributor. I am also endeavouring to revitalise our relationship with the psychologists. Jenny Stevenson, a founder member who has contributed valuably to the work of the interdisciplinary committee over many years, is helping in the search for new recruits. Lastly Jordans have proposed a new *Rooted Sorrows*. This is to be not so much a second edition or a revised edition as an endeavour to locate and record the voices of today who can speak with the clarity and the wisdom of the contributors of 1995, such as Dr Clifford York. The search is in the hands of Judith Trowell and Carola, my wife. Suggestions of those who might make a significant contribution would be welcome and also timely, since the editorial work is still at an early stage.

The theme of this conference does not particularly engage that field but that is not to say that it can not generate valuable material for the new edition. We had hoped that Professor Michael Lamb, recently returned from years of work in the United States, would have given a paper, but alas he has had to withdraw for family reasons. He has however collaborated with Charlie Lewis in the preparation of the paper in your pack. The papers and discussion upon which we are about to embark are in the capable hands of our rapporteur, Rosemary Budden, and will in due course appear as the sixth volume in the Jordans series. That vital characteristic of the Dartington Conferences helps us to achieve more than mere ephemeral influence. However as an extension and a strengthening of the Dartington tradition we have agreed that the small groups will be charged with specific tasks and in our final session we may wish to consider the possibility of agreeing resolutions. Resolutions serve as a monument to conference debate and in international family law conferences resolutions are invariable. And invaluable. I would like to see that practice extended to our Dartington conferences.

COURT EXPERIENCES AND DEVELOPMENT OUTCOMES

THE IMPACT OF THE COURT PROCESS.
WHAT DO THE CHILDREN TELL US?

Dr Judith Trowell
The Tavistock Institute

SUMMARY OF PAPER

Dr Judith Trowell introduced her paper by reminding the conference that children want to communicate with us; they want us to be interested in their views. There is a problem for us, however, a conflict we cannot avoid, do we accept that we always give children the right to choose and we endorse what they want.

Dr Trowell suggested there is a risk that we as adults will avoid our responsibility to make the painful and difficult decisions needed. We have to weigh in the balance the child's wishes, their feelings and then review what we believe is in their best interest. Dr Trowell's policy is always to tell the children and young people that she meets that she takes seriously what they say and listen, but she also has to explain that her job is to think about all *the factors and to say what she thinks, but she is happy to tell the court what the child wants her to report. Dr Trowell also acknowledges to the child or young person that they may prefer to say nothing and let the grown ups, the adults, decide.*

It is Dr Trowell's view that sometimes children may feel that they need to be definite about something because they are afraid of offending a parent or being blamed for what happens. She added that if a child has lost one parent, the child will be very scared of losing the parent who is still caring for them and an adult understanding of this must be communicated to the child. If the child is in care, Dr Trowell added that we know that most people want to be able to be where they know, with family, school and neighbours.

Over the years, Dr Trowell has asked the children and young people about their views on the hearing and the process for them; what they think of what has happened, if they wanted something and it did not happen of course, they are angry and upset at the process, but it was important to listen and to try and explain the reasons.

Dr Trowell continued to give some examples of views that children had shared with her together some pictures the children had drawn (not reproduced here).

It is not always easy, and it takes time, but in their play or drawings children and young people usually will share their world with us. We then have to try and understand, and consider how to use this in their best interest.

INTRODUCTION

In the last 20 years or so, there has been a growing recognition of the importance of listening to children's views and wishes. This is a reflection of the changes, which have occurred in how we regard children in our society. The UN Convention on the Rights of the Child, which was ratified by the UK Government in 1991, states that: State parties shall assure to the child who is capable of forming his or her own views the right to express those views freely in all matters affecting the child, the views of the child being given due weight in accordance with the age and maturity of the child (Art12). The Children Act 1989 also includes provision for the child's wishes and feelings to be considered in court hearings, in reaching decisions about the child.[1]

The Children's Rights Alliance for England believes children must be at the heart of all discussions and decisions about contact and residence. They think the only way to make sure this happens is to give primacy in law to children's wishes and feelings. This would require a new clause in the Children (Contact) and Adoption Bill (2004).

Christine Piper (1997) states:

> 'What does not seem satisfactory is that whilst the Children Act 1989 and the Family Law Act 1996 appear to give greater priority to the wishes and feelings of the child, not just in courts but through out related legal, administrative and mediatory processes, our research would suggest that the vast majority of children currently involved in parental divorce do not have their wishes ascertained by any professional, do not know that anybody has the slightest interest in them.'

Children's Rights alliance goes on to state: 'In no other circumstance would it be seen as acceptable for a court to force a person against their will to sever a relationship. We believe forcing a child to have or not have a relationship with a parent violates their integrity and human dignity.'

There are considerable issues here about the conflicts that can arise between the children's views and those considering the child's best interest, to which this paper will return later.

Thoburn & Timms (2003) in *Your Shout!* a survey of the views of 706 children and young people in public care found that 23% had been to court, mainly the young people 12–16 years. They had usually had someone helpful to talk to about the process and about half felt they had been listened to in the proceedings.

In the NCH specialist child sexual abuse project, there was a finding that a quarter of referrals, mainly the younger (under 10) children, were likely to be on the Child Protection Register. Those abused by parent or carer were more likely to be registered than those abused by a more distant abuser. But, referral to the CPS, where again a quarter of cases were included, consisted of older children and young people (over 11 years).

Younger children were therefore more often denied the opportunity for affirmation in court. We know of the difficulties of giving evidence in the criminal court and the rare attendance of children a young people in the civil courts. We know that following disclosure child victims of sexual abuse are often subject to pressure from adults inside and outside the family to retract and that currently the incidence of children disclosing has gone down, although the number of children post-abuse needing services continues to increase. Perhaps, failures in the past to prosecute due to lack of corroborative evidence for young children has influenced both the children, family and professionals. We know from adult survivors of physical and sexual abuse that the abuse was often long standing. We also hear from them that they would have wished to be consulted about the decision to prosecute or not.

Where there is parental relationship breakdown, we also know from young people and older adults that they had views as children, but were not consulted.

A woman in her 40s who had never had any awareness of or contact with her father decided to trace him and over a period made contact. Over a period of five years, they met and spent time together and her view of herself; her discovery of her paternal extended family and her relationship with her father transformed her. Another woman in her 50s adopted as a young child traced her birth family and found a half sibling, her mother having died. Both these women felt it would have been very difficult for their families to tolerate their seeking their birth parent earlier.

---

[1]   *Legal & Ethical Issues in Interacting Children* (ESDS, University of Essex & Manchester, 2004).

If adopted when small then children have little choice until they are free to trace parents if they are around and contactable. Children with learning and physical disabilities also have little choice and usually remain where they are placed if their substitute carers are able to accept and assist their children as they attempt to trace their birth families. Children placed for adoption when older can be asked about contact but in reality this is rarely maintained.

These two were never told anything about their history. They had tried to bring up the topic but questions were not welcome. The law has been changed now children can trace their parents but pressure from the current family can make it hard.

Attempts are made to listen to children and to understand what the court and its decisions mean to them. The judge will decide with whom they should live – mother, father, grandparent, foster carer, new 'adoptive' family – and how often they will see or not see mother, father or grandparents. In addition, there are the consequences of the decisions such as the locality where they live, the school, the outside activities and family friends, all of which may be changed. The children and young people usually understand this process and have a surprisingly good grasp of how and when decisions are made.

Children and young people (45) in court cases were systematically asked why they thought they had come and about half were aware and had an appropriate understanding of the situation. Of the remainder, most had little idea and were not interested in hearing (across the age range) a few had some idea there were 'worries' and something was going to happen. The children were from 3 years to 4 years and came as part of care proceedings, mainly with neglect, some sexual and/or physical abuse and parents with personality disorder, mental illness or learning difficulties.

It was of interest that during the assessment what was noted was a lack of interest or capacity to explore the play materials or the situation, with almost all the children and young people. They did not generally ask questions, play or seek an explanation. A small number of those who understood the process did question and did also use the materials and want to be involved. Again this was across the age range. If the children's use of symbolic play was considered then something more concerning emerged, well over half had little capacity for symbolic activity, they could not in their actual play or in their descriptions of their activity and life at home move beyond the concrete level of thinking and activity. But a third were at the other extreme where fantasy, imagination and pretend had become so vivid they could not tell what was real and what was not. So, whereas the majority were impoverished and lacked ideas, creativity and the possibility of imagining a future with changes, this group were immersed in a state of mind that was full of powerful and powerless images and people and they were also either in control and responsible or very fearful. Most of these children wanted to be 'at home', to play with their friends, wanted the familiar. This did not happen for most of them.

PARENTAL SEPARATION

Parents when they separate, married or co-habiting know only too well that the children are torn, but they long for loyalty, commitment and the support of their children. They want the children to agree with their perception of the other parent and the children know this.

A 17-year-old girl reported in a very distressed state that her mother and younger siblings could not bear to hear the name of the absent father. Mother was often tearful, money was very difficult and mother was often angry. The 17-year-old lived with mother and was supportive but also talked to and saw her father from time to time. If she told her mother there was an angry outburst and mother did not speak to her for some days. Mother wanted her to cease all contact with father but the girl whilst loving her mother also wanted to remain in touch with her father. She was angry, distressed, guilty and resentful but also aware that caught as she was she could not concentrate in school. Her route out to University was threatened and she was very afraid she would mess it all up.

In another family, after the parents split up, the children 9 years, 6 years and 3 years, were fought over, at that time joint custody was awarded and they spent half the week in each household; with mother in one, and father and new partner in the other. Wednesday was the change over day; they went to school from one home and returned to the other. Many things remained constant apparently school and nursery did not change, mother remained in the matrimonial home, father's home was a short drive away. Even so friends, out of school activities, possessions were often in the wrong place.

Seen several years later when the children were 14 years, 11 years and 8 years, the situation was of concern and father was seeking to change the arrangements. The youngest was 'fine': he did not have any worries – wherever he was he spent his time cutting up plants, leaves, flowers, peering down a microscope and drawing, or else on his computer games and Gameboy.

The middle child a girl was flat, withdrawn and deeply unhappy. Whilst with her mother, she had to listen to mother's hurt and resentment; with father she felt she had lost him and resented the new partner. There was also a new baby, half sister that father was entranced by and of whom she was intensely jealous. She was not working at school, was failing academically and hated going.

The older boy was very bright, effortlessly did well but was involved with the police, using drugs and alcohol, taking cars and often excluded.

The passage of time had moved things on for these parents and it does seem that it takes at least two years after the break up (and sometimes five years) for some of the early rage and hurt to settle. Now, these parents could think, still however separately, and contemplate a new arrangement. The older boy wanted to live with father and see mother alternate weekends. The youngest child, the other boy, wanted to live with mother and spend most weekends with dad. The middle child the girl struggled but finally lived with her father and saw mother most weekends.

This solution was still working several years later. The children's views were clear, they should have been asked but they also recognised what they wanted changed and the most important thing was that arrangements could be changed and they did not all have to all do the same thing. Court imposed solutions can lack flexibility, parents can rarely tolerate this, but the children want the arrangements to evolve.

What is being suggested is that during assessments there needs to be particular attention to the process. As well as noticing non-verbal activity, there is attention to detail at a meta level. Rayner (1990) writes that the assessor must be sensitive to the intonational, syntactical and linguistic habits of others, and hear the meaning between and behind words. This involves unlearning the ways of listening conversationally (Schlessinger 1994); that is, we tend to identify with the speaker, we assume the speaker means to make sense and we fill in the elisions/illusions and ignore pauses. This links back to Freud's idea of free-floating attention, that assessors must be free of agendas, their own or others, to allow themselves to be open to listening and to holding on to what is heard and how it makes one feel, in order to think and reflect later, prior to reaching any conclusions. Sternberg (2005) suggests that 'to carry out the cognitive aspects of this complex process the professional needs a certain detachment, an ability to think, evaluate, remember and anticipate. In this way the capacity to become temporarily and partially detached is a pre-requisite of the work.'

This ability to listen is constantly challenged and never becomes easy. An 8-year-old girl whose co-habiting parents separated when she was 2 years stands out. Father very much wanted to be involved and to continue to see his daughter. The parents made more and more allegations against each other and the girl living with mother became increasingly hostile to her father.

When seen for the fourth time she repeated her story word for word like a well-learnt script. The same story was given to the psychologist and the girl could not tolerate questioning or suggestions of other ways to understand events. She insisted on seeing the judge herself and she told him her views in chambers. Her wish was to have no contact with her father of any kind. Several years of supervised contact had preceded this final hearing, which had been proposed, encouraged and supported by professionals. At this stage, the father accepted his exclusion and withdrew; mother and daughter lived together. When aged 14 years, the education authority were threatening action as her school attendance was very poor, this talented girl was dropping out and professionals could do little, she mostly stayed at home in their flat with mother with one 'infection' after another.

But when the parents can also listen it can be different. Back and forth to court, parents of a 4-year-old girl were very hostile. The small girl was dearly loved by both and was well able to appreciate her powerful position. She ordered me around and expected me to do whatever she wanted and provide whatever toy she requested. However, after a while of this dictatorial behaviour, she sat looking down, preoccupied. When I wondered what was going on, she pointed to her socks white with a frill and a ribbon around. She then said everything else is new but these were from mummy and daddy when we all lived together. I said she seemed sad thinking about it and she went on to say she wanted to be cut in half so she could be half with mummy and half with daddy. Later she asked me to tell this to the judge man.

Both parents became quite distressed on hearing and reading the report and did stop trying to exclude the other and work towards an arrangement where she lived with mother but saw father regularly in the week and weekends.

These two cases illustrate how if we can listen and then convey our understanding in such a way that parents can both understand and not feel threatened then sometimes arrangements can be the best possible for the child. But if we cannot do this or a parent has a very strong agenda, then the outcome for the child may be cause for concern.

Clulow C (1996) suggests that 'within one generation we have begun to disconnect the practice of child-rearing not only from the institution of marriage, but also from partnership'. The children are saying something rather different, they have relationships and attachments, they love parents, siblings, extended family, their locality. At any age, their emotional and psychological wellbeing needs this to be recognised. But the parents need time to be robust enough to hear and flexible enough to anticipate arrangement will need to change.

COMING INTO CARE

Children and young people who come into care, on an interim or full care order, have a rather different view of the court and the judge. Frequently, they are very aware of the legal process and that decisions about them will be made by 'the judge'. One 6-year-old girl marched in and said: I must go home, I have to protect my mum. If I am not there who will protect her, 'Dave' (co-habitee) will just beat her up. You must tell the judge I have to go home. She had been caught in the domestic violence and had been physically abused as well as psychologically traumatised by seeing and hearing her mother being abused.

A 12-year-old boy demanded to go home; he needed to be there to take the little ones to school once he had got them up and sorted out breakfast. He just kept repeating he must go home, I had to tell the judge. He could not seem to grasp the other children were also in care, in another foster home. He was in a state of shock following a precipitate removal and it was some time before he could think or listen.

Coming into care often means losing parent or parents, extended family, sometimes siblings, school, friends and outside activities, as very often, foster placements are some distance from their home. A 14-year-old girl, who had been on the run, living on the streets, was placed in a shire county 150 miles from London. She refused to go and her own lawyer contested the placement (the only one with a vacancy), she demanded the judge be told she would abscond or kill herself. Four months later, she was settled there and reported she felt safe and, with a grin, said she could almost like it, could I please tell the judge she wanted to stay and the 'council' had to be told they must pay.

A 13-year-old boy told me the allowance for his clothes wasn't bad and the food was pretty good, could the judge decide he must stay (in a children's home).

Where the young person or child is also involved with the criminal court, there are mixed responses. Mostly, the girls in sexual abuse cases want the alleged abuser punished but when it is their father some are very distressed.

One young woman of 14, nearly 15, was devastated when the court decided her uncle was not guilty. She felt she had failed, not been believed and was more depressed and distressed than she had been throughout. Another girl was glad she had been believed and that her neighbour babysitter was to be punished; but she also missed him, as do many whose father are sent down or given an injunction. When the case was only in the civil court, these girls were often very concerned about what would happen, afraid they would be punished for speaking out.

Reception into care

A family of four children all by different fathers lived with their mother. They were aged from 5 to 12 and there were concerns about neglect, non-school attendance, roaming the estate, poor nutrition and clothing. Mother was a lively, courageous woman who erratically parented well and then opted out. The children were bright but doing poorly. All together they were unmanageable; chaos reigned. Mother's brother tried to help and could impose some discipline but his girlfriend was expecting a baby and they withdrew. Placed in foster care, they all wanted the judge to let them go home.

Mother consented to a range of interventions and persisted with them. When the eldest, now 13, came prior to the full hearing, he was very clear he wanted to be home but he added, 'you shouldn't do this. Dr Trowell, you should not put someone like me from an inner city estate in a nice home and family like that. I got used to all those things, the nice life and now I have to go back. It is not fair it is not right'. He did go home but last heard of was in a Young Offender's Institution (burglary and theft). The third child the other boy asked not to go home and mother agreed. He wanted to stay in the new school and home and in care. He was doing exceptionally well. The two girls went home and mother seemed able to manage them. Should they have been removed on an interim care order? And what of the outcomes? An academic high flyer, an offender and the two girls managing, could all four have had a better chance in life if they had stayed in care?

Many of the children who come into care go home sooner or later. Their parents and extended family do provide a community for those leaving care and thus needs to be recognised. But many children are really struggling and so disadvantaged that substitute care has to be the option.

CHILDREN IN SPECIAL CIRCUMSTANCES

Where children and young people are living in families where there is alcoholism, other substance abuse, domestic violence or mental health problems, the situation is more complex. Child protection issues may or may not be such that removal is required but the parent with residence has concerns, as do professionals. Referrals to consider the most appropriate placement have increased.

A 14-year-old and an 8-year-old living with father and his new partner having lived for the last six years with mother were very distressed and confused. The older girl explained that father had been blamed for everything; now she had been told mother was ill (paranoid psychosis) she didn't know what to think or feel. She wants to see her mum but then gets very upset when mum attacks dad and says strange things. Her younger sister just laughed, giggled, cried and wandered the room. But by the time the case came to court, both girls were settled and had started to learn. They visited mother monthly, she continued to demand they return to live with her but they recognised her difficulties and reported sadly they wished she could be a proper, normal mum. They hoped one day the doctors would make her better but knew that at present she was not right, strange.

Domestic violence, alcohol and substance abuse can be less obvious than mental illness and can be used as weapons. But they do raise real and serious questions about parenting and contact and these questions are rightly being asked more often.

Durable solutions usually depend on a willingness to seek help by the one parent so the children, young people and the other parent have some confidence in the adult's capacity to function appropriately.

A father was violent to his partner, and the children (11, 9 and 3) sometimes were caught in the crossfire. The eldest, a boy, had been accommodated briefly for running away and messing about on the estate. Father was able to recognise he needed to change or lose his family. The father in court agreed to go for help and this he did. The 9-year-old girl reported the judge did a good job, he told my dad. My dad really listened and mostly we don't mind going to see him, its not scary now.

Another father in court was very reluctant to accept his drinking and violence was a problem. His daughter was taken in a taxi for contact and aged 6 years she managed to open the taxi door and wanted to jump out. She stated (as did mother) that she was very afraid and did *not* want to see her father. Contact was stopped.

Where there is personality disorder or addiction, then parenting capacity is often limited or erratic. Treatment programmes are slow, needing both time, commitment and hard work. The timescale for little children is unacceptable but for older children flexible arrangements may be possible in time.

A 3-year-old and her sister were placed with maternal grandparents as mother with a personality disorder became more engaged in the drug culture and the children were neglected. The 3-year-old stated she loved; her grannie (who had done most of the child care) and the placement was working well. The 7-year-old kept running back to mother worrying about mother. She insisted one day she would be back living with their mum and did finally settle in a foster home with contact with mum when mother was able. This child could not settle in a 'permanent' placement. This girl said 'Dr Trowell, grannie brought up my sister really, but mum was OK, it was when she took up with that boyfriend it all went bad. Soon she will come, maybe when I'm 12 or 14.'

Abuse, trauma and multiple losses

A 10-year-old was brought in to be assessed. She was living in a children's home following social services investigation; her teacher had made contact following her questions and comments during a sex education class. She had evidence of sexual activity but the abuser was unclear. Her initials comments had been referring to her father.

The girl sat and sobbed, she was desperate to return home, she wanted to be with father and her brother. If she could not return home she would kill herself. She was insistent and determined. Her mother had died some years earlier and they were alright as a family – dad herself and her younger brother. She was reluctant to talk about anything other than her wish to return home.

She briefly responded to questions about school. She had been doing reasonably well at school, now her functioning was very poor. She looked distraught. She said very little about life at home, what they did, how things were, if they went anywhere. She did finally talk about her mother and mother's illness and death, which she remembered. Some months later, she could acknowledge it might be better not living at home but she was still desperate to spend time at home with dad.

The concerns were such that she went into care long term (on a full care order). Aged 15, she asked to come and see me and talked at length about the abuse she had experienced and requested help for herself. She was clear she could not talk about it all before. Originally, she had no idea that what was happening did not occur in every family. Once removed she missed her father and their time together so much it was all she could think about, it filled her mind. She wondered if she could survive without. Now she realised this is not what happens to everyone, she wanted to go to college, may be work with children, or hairdressing and one day perhaps have a boyfriend although she was very very frightened right now. When I asked what might have helped her to tell anyone, us all about this sooner she was at a loss. But she thanked me for not agreeing she should have gone home.

Thinking about this case one wonders what it was. It was clear she was a deeply troubled girl and had been sexually active. Her account of her mother's death was strange, inconsequential. Father's sister offered to have the children but kinship care in this case did not seem appropriate. Both father and his extended family denied the girl's problems and insisted there was no cause for concern. The girl was independently represented and her lawyer made a good case. The girl asked me to tell the judge in my first report, which I did, repeating her own words, that she wanted to go home but then giving my opinion, which I had shared with her that I did not think she should.

Many of the abused children are in a state of conflict. Often the abuser has also been the carer and whilst they may be desperate that the abuse (physical or sexual) stop, they do not want the abuser to be removed. One child said could the judge be told she wanted to live with her dad rather than her mum, but with no more abuse. On being told this did not seem possible she agreed. But she said you asked what ideas I had about my future!

Another 6-year-old girl missed her father desperately whilst he was in prison. (He had sexually abused her and a cousin who had given evidence.) She reported seeing her father on the pavement whilst she sat on the top deck of a bus and suddenly she was in a panic, her fear was palpable but also her sadness. Her confusion seemed to leave her paralysed.

Many of the children and young people are very fearful and some are very definite that they do not want to see their father or mother or both.

One 11-year-old girl reported her mother hated her. Mother blamed her daughter for the breakdown of her new relationship. The girl had been sexually abused by mother's partner and so now the partner and breadwinner had gone. The girl wanted to remain in care, not return home, mother wanted her back and the professionals agreed. But nine months later, the girl was admitted as an emergency to an adolescent unit deeply depressed and suicidal: home was unbearable. In another similar case, the adolescent girl ended up seriously ill after an overdose. She too had not wanted to be placed back at home, despite it being 'safe'. Emotional abuse and neglect post-abuse is not so rare, involving the non-abusing parent, when the family is fractured and safety from abuse may need to be only one consideration.

A Nigerian boy roamed the streets avoiding being beaten by father. Mother had moved out but had no place for the 10-year-old boy; father remained with the children in the marital home. The boy was placed in a foster home but spent his time moving from parent to parent. Just prior to the court hearing, father died precipitately – a diabetic, he had a heart attack – and so the boy's wish to return home to father could not happen. He was in care on a full care order deeply depressed and guilty he had killed father; did father know he had cared about him really. This boy did finally settle in his foster home, seeing his mother for contact but he needed help over a long period and the snapshot in court was so different from the vulnerable bereft boy after father's death. A committed dedicated social worker made all the difference.

All these children, the little ones who are sad confused and struggling, the primary school children at times very vulnerable and at times arrogant defiant and difficult, and the adolescents who so easily can take off seeming to not need anyone but so vulnerable and defenceless at times, all need responsible concerned adults around them. But they also need to be listened to, not given the burden of responsibility for themselves or others but involved in the decision-making. If what they want is not possible or appropriate, they need an explanation; they need to understand why not. It is distressing and horrible explaining why what they want may not be right for them at this time. Professionals do not find it easy to explain this to children and young people and all too often avoid this aspect of the work.

CONCLUSION

Most children and young people, whatever their age, have thought about their situation and what is happening to them. Some have very clear views, some remain silent preferring not to offend anyone and they stay watchful. Others try to please someone and say what they think a significant adult wants them to hear. All children and young people know some painful difficult decisions have to be made and that they and others will be hurt.

What gets lost is that arrangements will need to change. Young children may be with mother but may want and need to later spend time with father or grandparents. If in foster care, they may move to shared care.

A large family where many children came into state care were placed – some adopted, some in foster care, and some were living independently. One member when she talked of the 'family' wherever they were, she thought about them, hoped they were OK and was definite they would all reconnect one day. The judge had been right, their parents didn't know how to do it but they were all still family.

REFERENCES

Christine Piper (1997) in Ann O'Quigley *Listening to Children's Views. The findings and recommendations of recent research* (York Publicity Services, 2000)

Clulow C *Introduction. In Partners becoming Parents* (Sheldon Press, 1996)

Rayner E 'The Independent Mind' in *British Psychoanalysis* (London, Free Association Books, 1990)

Robert C, Trowell J, Miles G, Usiskin C, Grayson K & Leitch I *Exploring the work of NCH* (Specialist Child Sexual Abuse Projects, NCH, 2004)

Schlesenger H 'How the analyst listens: the Pre-stages of Interpretation' (1994) 75 IJPA 31–37

Sternberg J 'Not simply "doing" – thoughts from the literature on technique' in A Horne & M Lanyado (eds) *Independent Psychoanalytic Approaches with Children & Adolescents* (Routledge, 2005)

Timms J & Thoburn J *Your Shout! A survey of the views of 706 children and young people in Public Care* (NSPCC, 2003)

THE SEPARATE REPRESENTATION OF CHILDREN – IN WHOSE BEST INTERESTS?

Professor Gillian Douglas
Cardiff Law School, Cardiff University

SUMMARY OF PAPER

Professor Douglas set the context of her paper as a summary of the background to a study that she has been conducting with Professor Mervyn Murch into r 9.5 of the Family Proceedings Rules 1991; the provision which allows children to have a guardian ad litem. The impetus for this work has been the expected implementation of s 122 of the Adoption and Children Act 2002 which provides for the addition of private law proceedings to the list of specified proceedings in s 41 of the Children Act 1989.

Where there is provision for a guardian in private law cases, the question for Department of Constitutional Affairs is: 'to what kinds of cases should we extend the use of a guardian?'

The paper seeks to explore the rationale for separate representation and considers the influences of case law, practice directions and the experience of practitioners. Professor Douglas suggests that the decision to direct separate representation usually appears to have more to do with concern for the child's welfare than a desire to hear the voice of the child.

There is little published on the extent of the use of this provision. Professor Douglas drew attention to an article published by two district judges from Leeds who conducted a study of their own cases in response to a view expressed that Leeds may have been over-generous in its use of r 9.5. There is clearly a regional variation as to the use of this rule; however, the overall usage is still comparatively low.

Professor Douglas drew attention to the statistics provided in the section of the paper questioning the reasons for directing that the child be separately represented. She concludes that there are two main situations where r 9.5 is used: firstly where the case has become 'intractable' and lasting some significant time; and secondly where the case is or has become complex for any one or more of a number of reasons, including significant foreign, ethnic or cultural element, mental health difficulties, physical or sexual abuse of a child or care of the child being passed to members of the extended family.

The paper explores how r 9.5 is currently being used. It asks what separate representation adds to the proceedings and sets out the potential advantages and disadvantages. The paper echoes the view of other researchers in suggesting that a guardian may be able to give a fuller picture of the case to the court. The rule is also often used as a last resort where everything else has failed. Some professionals have also suggested that r 9.5 can empower the child and alter the dynamics in the family.

Professor Douglas concluded that part of the need for separate representation of the children may arise because of the inadequacies of the current system, be it classed as 'inquisitorial' or 'adversarial'. She suggested that the planned refocusing of CAFCASS work onto active 'social work' rather than investigation and reporting functions may reduce some of the need for separate representation. She concluded that separate representation is a means of providing a voice for the child – not of hearing the voice of the child.

INTRODUCTION

This paper explores the rationale and use of separate representation of children in private law proceedings and considers its advantages and disadvantages. It also reports on the initial findings of an empirical study conducted by Cardiff University[1] for the Department for Constitutional Affairs into separate representation. The findings reported here derive from the views of professionals. The final report of the study will supplement these with data on the views of children and their parents who have experienced proceedings where separate representation has been ordered.

There appears to be a growing recognition that separate representation[2] of children in private family law proceedings may be desirable in certain cases. Section 122 of the Adoption and Children Act 2002[3] adds proceedings in relation to s 8 orders to the definition of 'specified' proceedings contained in s 41 of the Children Act (and currently confined to public law cases), under which a guardian is appointed to represent the child. Since it is not feasible to extend separate representation to all private proceedings,[4] it is necessary to determine the difficult but key question concerning in which cases and which circumstances such provision should be made.[5] The use of this mechanism must also be slotted into an increasingly 'managerial' approach to children cases, epitomised by 'The Private Law Programme', issued by the former President of the Family Division at the end of 2004.

At present, the appointment of a guardian ad litem under Family Proceedings Rules 1991, r 9.5 is the main mechanism utilised where a court reaches the view that the child's interests cannot adequately be identified or served either by means of the evidence and arguments presented by the parties to the proceedings, or the information provided by the CAFCASS officer in his or her report to the court. In addition to CAFCASS (including CAFCASS Legal) and the Official Solicitor, courts may appoint individual solicitors to act as guardians ad litem,[6] and NYAS, the National Youth Advocacy Service. These are both likely to be utilised where there is either some problem with using CAFCASS officers (perhaps a lack of an available officer or the possibility of further delay) or the judge knows and has a particular faith in the solicitor or has experience of NYAS' services.[7]

---

[1] By M Murch, G Douglas, L Scanlan, C Miles, J Doughty and N Smalley. I am particularly grateful to Nina Smalley for her work in analysing the questionnaire data reported below.

[2] Strictly speaking, being separately represented and being joined as a party to proceedings are two separate things. However, it has been held that, where a child is separately represented, he or she should also be joined as a party (*L v L (Minors) (Separate Representation)* [1994] 1 FLR 156) and the discussion below assumes that both steps have been taken. However, this is not always done, causing problems in obtaining public funding for the child: see C Blackburn 'Rule 9.5 Demystified' (2005) 15, 1 Seen and Heard 19 at 21.

[3] See J Timms OBE 'Current Issues in Relation to the Representation of Children' (2004) 14, 1, Seen and Heard 30 at 37–38.

[4] Cf New Zealand, referred to by the Advisory Board on Family Law, Children Act Sub-Committee, *Making Contact Work* (Lord Chancellor's Department, 2002) para 12.8 and by Thorpe LJ in *Mabon v Mabon* [2005] EWCA Civ 634, [2005] 2 FLR 1011. Sections 6 and 7 of the Care of Children Act 2004, (entry into force on 1 July 2005), impose 'a requirement to appoint counsel to represent the child in all matters involving their day-to-day care that are likely to proceed to a hearing, unless this would serve no useful purpose (for example if the child was an infant so unable to express any views)'. See Judge Peter Boshier, 'Care and Protection of Children: New Zealand and Australian Experience of Cross-Border Co-operation', speech to the 4th World Congress on Family Law and Children's Rights, 20–23 March 2005 at www.justice.govt.nz/family/media/4th-world-congress-family-law-childrens-rights.html.

[5] Concern at 'excessive' use of separate representation has been expressed both in relation to individual courts' use (eg the 'Leeds Syndrome' discussed below) and in recent guidance issued by the President intended to curtail an apparent expansion in use across the country in the wake of her Practice Direction issued in April 2004, discussed below. See J Timms 'The Rights and Representation of Children: Current Developments' (2005) 15, 1, Seen and Heard 24 at 26.

[6] See eg *Re K (Replacement of Guardian ad Litem)* [2001] 1 FLR 663.

[7] See, eg the Court of Appeal's endorsement of NYAS, albeit that in the circumstances it was decided that the Official Solicitor should be appointed instead because of the father's hostility to NYAS' involvement, in *Re A (Contact: Separate Representation)* [2001] 1 FLR 715. In *Re C (a child)* unreported, 16 Feb 2005, CA, (NLJ 25 March 2005, 462) the Court of Appeal granted a father's application that NYAS be appointed as guardian ad litem for the child, on the basis that the CAFCASS officer had reached the limit of his expertise and the child had lost faith in him and so there would be no point in following he usual procedure to approach CAFCASS to supply a guardian instead.

THE RATIONALE FOR SEPARATE REPRESENTATION – 'WELFARE' OR 'VOICE'?

It is suggested here that, perhaps contrary to expectation, it is a concern for the child's welfare rather than a wish to ensure that his or her views are heard, which currently seems to predominate when separate representation is ordered. This may be contrary to expectation because usually, discussions about separate representation start from the assumption that this in some way helps to fulfill the well-known requirement under Art 12 of the United Nations Convention on the Rights of the Child (UNCRC) to 'assure to the child who is capable of forming his or her own views, the right to express those views freely in all matters affecting the child, [such views] being given due weight in accordance with the child's age and maturity'.[8] This Article can be seen as one of the participation, or empowerment, rights laid down in the Convention and as implying a right of children, as Jane Fortin has put it, 'to convey to the courts their own perceptions of … family disagreements'.[9] The United Nations Committee on the Rights of the Child has itself regarded separate representation in this way. In reviewing the United Kingdom's second report on its implementation of the UNCRC in 2002, the Committee expressed concern that

> 'the obligations of article 12 have not been consistently incorporated in legislation, for example in private law procedures concerning divorce, … . In addition, the Committee is concerned that the right of the child to independent representation in legal proceedings, as laid down in the Children Act 1989, is not systematically exercised. …'

It recommended that the United Kingdom

> 'take further steps to consistently reflect the obligations of both paragraphs of article 12 in legislation, and that legislation governing court procedures and administrative proceedings (including divorce and separation proceedings) ensure that a child capable of forming his/her own views has the right to express those views and that they are given due weight.'[10]

The introduction of the European Convention on Human Rights into English law through the Human Rights Act 1998 has given further impetus to the argument that there may be a greater need than hitherto to accommodate children's separate representation in litigation concerning their futures.[11]

HOW MUCH USE IS MADE OF SEPARATE REPRESENTATION?

There are no reliable figures indicating the extent of use of separate representation of children in private law proceedings on a national basis. The only published data on its use come from an invaluable article[12] by two district judges, DJ Clifford Bellamy and DJ Geoff Lord, both of

---

[8] See also art 9(2), which has received less attention, and provides that, in any proceedings concerning the separation of a child from his or her parents, 'all interested parties shall be given the opportunity to participate in the proceedings and make their views known'. It has been argued – surely correctly – that the child is to be regarded as an interested party: A Moylan, 'Children's Participation in Proceedings – The View from Europe' in The Rt Hon Lord Justice Thorpe and J Cadbury (eds) *Hearing the Children* (Family Law, 2004) at 175, citing the UNICEF website in support.

[9] J Fortin *Children's Rights and the Developing Law* (Butterworths, 2nd edn, 2003) 197.

[10] United Nations Committee on the Rights of the Child, *Report on the 31st Session* CRC/C/121 (United Nations, 2002) paras 121, 122.

[11] See Dame Elizabeth Butler-Sloss P in *Re A (Contact: Separate Representation)* [2001] 1 FLR 715, at paras 22, 23. For a full discussion of the potential implications of Art 8 for children, particularly those in the public care system, see Munby J 'Making Sure the Child is Heard: Part 1 – Human Rights' and 'Part 2 –Representation' [2004] Family Law 338 and 427. See also C Blackburn, op cit above, at 19.

[12] DJ C Bellamy and DJ G Lord 'Reflections on Family Proceedings Rule 9.5' [2003] Family Law 265.

Leeds combined court centre, who undertook their own empirical study of the use of r 9.5 in the Leeds area in response to charges of the existence of a 'Leeds Syndrome' of excessive use of r 9.5. They found that in 2001–2, 34 appointments under r 9.5 were made out of a total number of 465 s 8 applications, representing some 7.3% of cases.[13]

The only other statistical data that is available, but is unpublished, is from CAFCASS and the Legal Services Commission showing the number of CAFCASS appointments under r 9.5 made over a given period. These relate to the 10 CAFCASS regions and reveal that there are certainly areas of the country which appear to make much more use of r 9.5 appointments than others – Yorkshire/Humberside, the North West and the West Midlands had the highest numbers of appointments in 2003–4, using r 9.5 in up to around 10% of cases, compared with what we might regard as medium-use areas, such as the South West, the West and the East Midlands, at around 5%, and low use areas such as the North East and East at around 2%.

Finally, the Cardiff research team collected information via postal questionnaires from 420 family solicitors in England and Wales about their experience of separate representation under r 9.5. 75% (315) had been involved in a r 9.5 case, but few had been involved in more than five such cases during their careers.[14] Only 16% had experienced between 5 and 10 cases and only 2% had been involved with more than 20 cases. The same geographical spread of greater or lesser use was found as in the CAFCASS data, with those practising in the 'high use' areas more likely to report having handled more cases.

REASONS FOR DIRECTING THAT THE CHILD BE SEPARATELY REPRESENTED

There is also only limited empirical data on the reasons the court has for directing that a child requires separate representation. If the main motivation is to 'hear the voice of the child' one would expect that the child's age would be a crucial factor, with older children being more likely to be separately represented than the very young. But the evidence is not clear-cut on this point. CAFCASS figures[15] show that in 2004, just under a third (210: 30%) of the children separately represented by their public law teams were aged 10 or over, but nearly half (320: 47%) were aged between five and ten. This age group could arguably be seen as on the cusp of being regarded as 'old enough' to express a view that the court should take into account (but not old enough to represent themselves without a guardian ad litem) and thus as demonstrating a concern by the court to 'hear the voice of the child'. However, if we compare these figures with national statistics showing the age of children whose parents *divorced* between 1989 and 1999, we find that again, the largest group was aged between 5 and 10 with about a third aged over 10, and these patterns have been consistent over the years.[16] The CAFCASS figures probably therefore simply reflect the same pattern rather than any particular emphasis on 'voice' as the predominant motive for appointment. In slight contrast, just on half (60 out of 121) of the solicitors in the questionnaire survey who answered the relevant question considered that the

---

[13]   The authors rightly noted that comparing the number of appointments with the number of applications is a crude device for attempting to measure the degree of exposure to r 9.5 in such cases, but we would agree that it is the best measure available. It should be noted that the Leeds research was dependent upon CAFCASS data to identify the relevant cases. In other areas where non-CAFCASS appointments are made, CAFCASS would not have data on such cases and so reliance on their figures alone would not produce an accurate picture of extent of use.

[14]   86% had been in practice for more than 10 years.

[15]   Unpublished. But note that the data relate only to appointments taken on by public law teams and so do not present a complete picture of CAFCASS activity under r 9.5.

[16]   See HM Magistrates' Courts Service Inspectorate, Setting Up: Report of a Programme of Visits to the Children and Family Court Advisory and Support Service (CAFCASS) (Lord Chancellor's Department, 2002), Annex D, Fig 2.

usual age range for separate representation was 10 and over. They commented that it is more likely to be directed where the child is of an age and maturity to express a view:

'Children are of an age where their views will carry weight.'

'Because the child is *Gillick* competent[17] and disagrees with some elements of the case.'

Bellamy and Lord categorised the cases in their sample according to five main kinds of factual circumstances. The first category was 'intractable' cases where proceedings had been ongoing for an extended period of time with no long-term resolution in sight. This was also the type of case identified by the majority of the solicitor respondents in the Cardiff study as the main trigger for a r 9.5 appointment. In these cases, they reported that parents often become entrenched in their views, locked in a battle that may make them less responsive to their child's wishes and feelings:

'Where courts are faced with serious case of implacable hostility, parents' intractable position means r 9.5 is the only way forward.'

'Children's voices are being lost amongst adults' hostility and inability to prioritise.'

The second category concerned cases with a significant foreign, ethnic or cultural element, especially where there was a risk of, or actual, child abduction. The third involved cases where a parent had mental health difficulties which impacted not just on the parents' ability to care for the child but on the absent parent's contact with that child. The fourth category concerned cases where there was either an allegation of physical or sexual abuse of a child or there had been violence between the adults which had impacted on the child. Drugs and alcohol abuse also featured in some of these cases. Finally, some cases concerned care of the child being passed amongst extended family members, with multiple applications being brought about the child by different such members. One might group these categories together as being 'complex' cases, and complexity was also frequently mentioned in the solicitor survey as a reason for directing separate representation:

'The realisation that some cases are so complex and difficult that a referral to CAFCASS alone and a report will not suffice.'

'Complicated issues – residence abroad, immigration issues and religious issues.'

'Complexity of cases especially where expert evidence from psychologists is required.'

THE CASE-LAW ON r 9.5

The reported case-law suggests that a major motivation for the use of separate representation is to ensure that the child's true interests will be properly revealed to the court. In particular, there is often a concern that they should not be lost in the face of the evidence and arguments being presented by the parents. In other words, the same motivation that led to the introduction of guardians in public law proceedings, applies in such instances – a desire to ensure that a conflict of interests on the part of the parents does not obscure the real needs of the child.[18] A similar

---

[17] One would expect that a child who has this degree of competence should be permitted to instruct his or her own lawyer rather than have a guardian ad litem and there seems to be some confusion amongst practitioners and courts regarding when one or the other is appropriate. For clarification, see *Mabon v Mabon* [2005] EWCA Civ 634, [2005] 2 FLR 1011.

[18] See eg *Re H (Contact Order) (No 2)* [2002] 1 FLR 22 (father suffering from Huntington's disease, which had adverse effects on his mood and personality. He threatened to kill himself and the two children. Mother refused further direct contact. Wall J considered that in a case as difficult as this one, consideration should have been given to the children's being separately represented and, where appropriate, expert advice being sought on their behalf). See also *M v M (Parental Responsibility)* [1999] 2 FLR 737, (the father, partly as a result of a motorcycle accident, had severe intellectual impairments leading to

concern can be seen in cases of 'implacable hostility' between the parents, where the court considers that the antagonism between the parents is such that neither can be regarded as able to put the interests of the child first.[19]

The importance of the welfare rationale can also be seen in a number of cases where it is clear that the court's fear is that one of the parents (usually the parent with residence) may have influenced the child's views and that these cannot therefore be taken at face value.[20] The organisation with the greatest collective experience of representing children, NYAS, has indeed reported that children may be very reluctant to express their opinions because they feel pressured by their parents.[21]

Of course, there are also cases where the court does use separate representation to find out the wishes and feelings of the child.[22] In *Re L (Minors) (Separate Representation)*[23] for example, the Court of Appeal upheld the appointment of a guardian ad litem for three children, aged 14, 12 and 9, who lived with their father, the mother having left home. The father wished to take them back to Australia and the court welfare officer considered that she could not adequately present the children's views to the court. Butler-Sloss LJ noted that there was an 'overall need to ascertain what the children genuinely feel about their future in the present situation'.[24]

THE PRESIDENT'S DIRECTION[25]

Further guidance can be obtained from the practice directions that have been issued from time to time regarding this issue. The most recent, issued by Dame Elizabeth Butler-Sloss in 2004, makes clear that the decision to make a child a party, is only to be taken in cases of 'significant difficulty'. The caution to be exercised in making a direction is spelled out in para 4, which stresses that the court must take the child's welfare as its 'primary consideration', taking due notice of the risk of delay and other adverse factors.

The circumstances listed in the direction reflect both 'welfare' and 'voice' factors. For example, 'where the child has a standpoint or interests which are inconsistent with or incapable of being represented by any of the adult parties'; 'where the views and wishes of the child cannot be adequately met by a report to the court' and 'where an older child is opposing a proposed course of action' are all instances where the concern is to ensure that the child's own point of view is heard. But the other factors turn on welfare matters, such as 'where there is an intractable dispute over residence or contact, including where all contact has ceased, or where there is

---

aggressive behaviour. Three-year-old child separately represented in proceedings brought by the father for parental responsibility and direct contact); *Re W (Contact: Parent's Delusional Beliefs)* [1999] 1 FLR 1263 (father apparently suffering delusional beliefs, but no up to date psychiatric assessment of him available. Children, aged 10 and 11, made parties with the Official Solicitor to instruct a consultant child psychiatrist to report on the effects of contact on them).

[19] See eg *Re A (Contact: Separate Representation)* [2001] 1 FLR 715.

[20] An example of the court's concern may be seen in *Re W (Contact: Joining Child as Party)* [2001] EWCA Civ 1830, [2003] 1 FLR 681. It may be noted that, in the face of the child's continuing refusal to have contact with the father, the latter was permitted to withdraw his application for contact in *Re O (Contact: Withdrawal of Application)* [2003] EWHC 3031 (Fam) [2004] 1 FLR 1258.

[21] E Fowler and S Stewart 'Rule 9.5 Separate Representation and NYAS' [2005] Fam Law 49. Our research with solicitors confirmed this view. As one commented: 'They [guardians ad litem] help to define the issues in a child-centred way where the child can be helped to say what they have been prevented from saying by pressure from a carer or other adults.'

[22] Although one should bear in mind the possibility that the child is uncertain or ambivalent as to his or her 'true' wishes and feelings.

[23] [1994] 1 FLR 156.

[24] [1994] 1 FLR 156 at p 160 C-D.

[25] President's Direction: Representation of Children in Family Proceedings pursuant to Family Proceedings Rules 1991, r 9.5 [2004] 1 FLR 1188.

irrational but implacable hostility to contact or where the child may be suffering harm associated with the contact dispute'; 'where there are serious allegations of physical, sexual or other abuse in relation to the child or there are allegations of domestic violence not capable of being resolved with the help of a CAFCASS officer' or 'where there are international complications outside child abduction, in particular where it may be necessary for there to be discussions with overseas authorities or a foreign court'.

THE ADVANTAGES OF SEPARATE REPRESENTATION

Separate representation may be beneficial to the court, in enabling it to produce a 'better', more informed decision, or to the CAFCASS officer, in enabling him or her to work more effectively in the proceedings, or to the child, in enabling the child to influence the court's decision or to feel that he or she has been respected as a person and involved in the decision.

Judith Masson and Maureen Winn Oakley, discussing separate representation in the context of public law proceedings, conclude that:

> 'Without the guardian's involvement the court would not be able to have an adequate picture of the child's interests. ... Through the involvement of the guardian ad litem it enables the court to have a more complete picture and more active presentation of the child's interests than would be possible of the court only had access to reports from a court welfare officer.'[26]

Our solicitor respondents reflected this opinion:

> 'In cases where the a child is separately represented the issues are usually examined in greater depth, often with expert evidence which can lead to a greater understanding on the part of the parents as to why a particular course of action is being recommended. There is a greater chance of agreement being reached and adhered to.'

> 'Presents matters more independently without being so bogged down in parents issues. It is easier for the court to consider what is right for the child with input from the Guardian in this way.'

It has also been suggested by professionals that appointing a child's guardian ad litem is done as a last resort, when everything else has been tried and the judge (and CAFCASS officer) have run out of other ideas. As some solicitors commented:

> 'Implacable hostility has set in, court proceedings have been exhausted over 3–5 years with no success.'

> 'Usually, after many years of either continued litigation or numerous applications to the court regarding contact, the case reaches a stalemate and the judge has run out of options, patience or both!'

Separate representation enables the guardian to continue to work with the family over a period, extended if necessary, to bring them either to a compromise solution to their dispute, or to acceptance of the status quo. For example, the officer may, as Jonathan Whybrow has identified,[27] investigate allegations of abuse and either shed light on them or seek to bring the person making them to a realisation that they are groundless, from which that person can move on to address the question of contact etc. Or the officer may, as Bellamy and Lord noted, be able to devote additional time and effort, not available within the constraints of investigation and report writing, to help mediate between the parties.[28] It is also a main aim of the Government's

---

[26]   J Masson and M Winn Oakley *Out of Hearing: Representing Children in Care Proceedings* (John Wiley & Sons, 1999) at 117.

[27]   'Children, Guardians and Rule 9.5' [2004] Family Law 504.

[28]   See Bellamy and Lord, op cit at 267, for the view that the extra time devoted by r 9.5 guardians 'is more likely to lead to a better final outcome'. In the solicitor survey, this was a view expressed by those practising in the 'high use' areas but not otherwise. See also The Rt Hon Lord Justice Wall, 'Are the courts failing fathers? Uncomfortable issues to be faced by both' (2004) 14, 4, Seen and Heard 15 at 24–33.

most recent plans regarding the handling of contentious contact disputes, which seek to shift the emphasis of CAFCASS work from report-writing to active engagement with families.[29]

But there is an additional dimension which party status for the child and representation via the guardian ad litem can give, and that is to change the family dynamics and to empower the child. It has been strongly argued by professionals that the CAFCASS officer (or other guardian) has an enhanced status in the eyes of the parents when they know that that person has been appointed by the court to represent their child. The recommendations of the guardian may be more readily accepted by parents, as a 'second opinion', even if they are the same as those previously put forward by a CAFCASS officer when acting as the children and family reporter. The child is said to assume centre-stage in such a case, with the parents more readily persuaded to shift ground and to focus on his or her interests. As one solicitor commented:

> 'It gives more leverage to the judge to press the parents to adopt what is clearly in the child's interests as opposed to their view thereof.'

It is also important to recognise that the 'child's voice' may in fact play a more significant part in the process when the child is separately represented, even if the court's motivation for so ordering was welfare-focused.[30] Of 358 open-ended responses to the solicitors' questionnaires, 137 specifically mentioned giving a voice to the child as a benefit to the child. For example:

> 'The children have been amazed that someone takes their views seriously and will be speaking to the judge for them.'

> 'Children are so often unable to articulate their feelings at short notice, they often sit on the fence or say things to please the parent with whom they reside, and separate representation gives them a greater chance to be heard accurately.'

THE DISADVANTAGES OF SEPARATE REPRESENTATION

In contrast to these positive views, we should also note the possible disadvantages of providing separate representation for the child. First, as has already been pointed out above, there is the likelihood of added delay[31] and cost to the proceedings. Secondly, there is a risk that being directly involved in the case may be stressful to the child, and may even make the child the focus of parental hostility. One-fifth of solicitor respondents to the questionnaire survey considered that r 9.5 can create difficulties for the child, including being embarrassed at having to talk to yet another professional:

> 'The child very often has to meet another professional. ... The signal given to the child is that this is not over and that even worse, there may be something wrong with them. So it can have a negative impact having yet another professional, such as a solicitor, prying into their lives.'

There was also recognition amongst the solicitors that the child can be placed under a considerable onus of responsibility for the outcome of the proceedings. Suddenly, the child 'has to accept a central role in the dispute'. This can serve to cause anxiety as well as to raise expectations where the child may believe that the judge will make a decision based entirely on their view. This appeared to be a double-edged sword in that a manipulative child could use this against the parents whilst a manipulated child could be pressured into repeating allegations or reciting one parent's viewpoint.

Respondents acknowledged that voicing a different opinion to that of the resident parent could 'increase tensions in day-to-day living' or mean that the child may be 'got at' for saying the

---

[29]   DCA, DFES, DTI, *Parental Separation: Children's Needs and Parents' Responsibilities* Cm 6273 (HMSO, 2004), ch 3, especially paras 66–73.

[30]   See also E Fowler and S Stewart 'Rule 9.5 Separate Representation and NYAS' [2005] Fam Law 49.

[31]   But some delay may be 'constructive' if it leads to a better decision or one more willingly accepted by the parties and the child.

wrong thing. Thus, the risk of introducing conflict into the parent-child relationship emerged as a potential problem of separate representation:

> 'It can bring out issues between them and a parent or parents which have not surfaced before. These can then be difficult to get over once the proceedings have ended; it can be a Pandora's Box.'

> 'I fear in some cases it empowers a manipulative child to vacillate and bargain.'

Finally, it is clear that, because r 9.5 envisages that the judge should generally first seek to appoint a CAFCASS officer to act as guardian ad litem, 'too ready' a resort to directing separate representation risks placing an intolerable strain on CAFCASS' resources. Indeed, there are already signs of concern that this is happening. The President issued guidance[32] in February 2005 to attempt to curtail what was described as a 'dramatic increase' in the number of guardians in private law cases.[33] The guidance limits the ability of district judges to order separate representation and requires consideration to be given to transferring the case up to the High Court.

CONCLUSION

The concern, which seems to underpin the decision to order separate representation, that the court will not hear a sufficiently robust presentation of the child's interests unless he or she has independent status, undermines two assumptions or assertions made about private family law proceedings. The first is that the court's role is inquisitorial rather than adversarial. It has been said, for example, that the court is to play an active part in the proceedings rather than act as umpire between the parties.[34] It has the power to set the timetable for the proceedings, control the use of experts, determine how evidence is to be heard and make orders of its own motion. But none of this, it seems, is apparently enough to ensure that the child's interests are adequately identified in every case. Moreover, what may be regarded as the key 'inquisitorial' element – the investigation and report by the children and family reporter – may apparently be insufficient as well. This seems to be a matter not just of resources, although these may well play an important part, but also a question of role and status. It may be that refocusing CAFCASS work onto active 'social work' rather than investigation and report may provide the answer[35] in many difficult cases where, at present, the judge may feel that separate representation is the last chance to produce a significant result. Secondly, as noted above, even if an 'adversarial' model of proceedings is adopted, it seems that this may fail to convey to the court enough of the true picture of the child's interests to enable it to reach the best outcome for the child.[36]

It seems that in their use of separate representation, the courts may have arrived at a broader, more sophisticated understanding of the need to 'hear' the child than is encapsulated in the literal meaning of Art 12 of the UNCRC. Their aim, it would seem, is to ensure that there is *a voice for the child*, rather than to hear *the voice of the child*. On this basis, the age, capacity, maturity or intelligence of the child – factors which would otherwise determine the weight to be placed on the 'voice' of the child under Art 12 – are insignificant. Instead, the child's interests are to be fully explored and expressed from that child's standpoint, and not from that of the conflicted and partial adults.[37] Whether s 122 can provide an adequate mechanism for the

---

[32] Guidance from the President's Office, 'The Appointment of Guardians in Accordance with Rule 9.5 and the President's Practice Direction of 5 April 2004' 25 February 2005.

[33] Of our solicitor respondents answering the question, 60% considered that the volume of r 9.5 cases had increased since the President's 2004 Direction.

[34] DoH *An Introduction to the Children Act 1989* (HMSO, 1990) para 1.51.

[35] But for the view that a diminution in the investigatory role may reduce the number of cases where the child's views are taken into account, see G Harold and M Murch 'Inter-parental conflict and children's adaptation to separation and divorce: theory, research and implications for family law, practice and policy' [2005] CFLQ 185.

[36] Cf Masson and Winn Oakley, op cit, at 248–249.

[37] And see Wall LJ in *Mabon v Mabon* [2005] EWCA Civ 634, [2005] 2 FLR 1011at para 43: 'My difficulty … is that the judge seems to me, with all respect to him, to have perceived the case from the perspective of the adults.'

implementation of this rather fundamental shift in approach to the handling of private law proceedings remains to be seen.

A FATHER'S EXPERIENCE OF CARE PROCEEDINGS

AP
Parent

The title 'A Father's Experience of Care Proceedings' draws attention to two aspects of this issue that are unavoidable; firstly that there is always going to be a limit to just how exemplary, just how representative any individual case is, despite the fact that there can only ever be an accumulation of individual cases, in all their singular complexity. And secondly, that however shareable, one's experience is always profoundly subjective, whatever else it is, a product of one's history and temperament, and indeed gender. My experience of this terrible and necessary business is that, however close the parents may be, they will experience this ordeal in quite different terms. What any so-called family is on the receiving end of in these situations is a set of, in my view, partly unconscious fantasies and assumptions about what a child is, what a child needs, who a child belongs to, and that there is no reason to assume that in any given case these assumptions will be shared by the family in question. The family in question, whether guilty or innocent, is under threat from a group of people whose language is always more powerful; when a social worker says to a mother three days before a court hearing – as was said to my partner – 'how would you like to say goodbye to the baby on Tuesday?' conversation is clearly not what is on offer. Whatever else case work is in these situations it always involves what people do to each other with words, however articulate the parties are. And more often than not, one group is the more articulate; and clearly one of the drawbacks of the less articulate is that they are unable to articulate their grievances about how they are managed by the articulate. All the professionals in care proceedings have learned, at its most minimal, the languages involved in care proceedings; most of the families do not speak these languages. My guess is that field workers in anthropology would have more to tell us about this particular situation than any other group of professionals. As someone trained in child psychotherapy – and as someone who has both seen abused children clinically and supervised the work of psychiatrists, social workers and psychologists involved in child protection work – my experience of care proceedings will not, one would hope, be a common one. There are though, as I will try and show in this paper, things to be gained from having been, as it were, both sides of the line. That is to say, being someone who both speaks the language and has had a version of it spoken back at him and his family.

I need to give you the briefest account of our case so that what I have to say can make some kind of sense. Needless to say I am not interested here in redressing grievances but in seeing what might be gleaned. When my baby daughter was three weeks' old her mother discovered that she had a swollen ankle; she was taken to hospital where it was discovered that she had two fractured ankles and two fractured little fingers. Medical opinion specified these injuries must have occurred over the previous weekend when my partner and I and one other person were present and that they were non-accidental. For the next 10 months we were never allowed to be alone with baby and had maternity nurses in 24-hour attendance; the local authority treating us, the parents, as prime suspects we were involved in four court hearings in which we resisted the removal of the baby. A causation hearing found that one of the three of us was responsible but could not say which. Just before the final hearing the other party confessed to having done it, but an open verdict was passed, the judge would not review his finding. The local authority did not ask for an order. In the first 11 months of my daughter's life, bar the first three weeks, we were involved in care proceedings.

The first and most obvious thing to say about one's experience of such things is their sheer terror. In retrospect part of the terror was the social worker's assumption that one can protect a child by not protecting its parents. It was as if the three-week-old baby was separate and therefore separable from its mother; as though the baby was not being harmed by treating her mother in a persecutory way. This is not, I want to be clear, a plea for non-investigation, but rather a plea for what once would have been called kindness and might now be called psychological mindedness. Professionally one might think that if the mother or the parents have abused a child they are more deserving of concern rather than less. In other words, child protection, if it is to be viable rather than divisive, needs to be called family protection. When D W Winnicott, the paediatrician and psychoanalyst, said 'there is no such thing as a baby' he was stressing the mother-and-baby and father as a unit. No-one doubts that children need protection, but they can also need protection from their professional protectors. My initial experience of social work involvement was that they worked with a perpetrator and victim model, and that it was simply a question of working out which was which and separating them out. Another way of saying this is that there was an attempt to take the then 20-day-old baby into care on the basis of expert (and accurate) medical opinion but without taking a history.

It is my professional experience that, however obscure and difficult to discern, so-called child abuse, like other criminal, sexual and violent acts, comes from a history; or at its most minima, the history of 'perpetrators' tends not to be irrelevant to the acts committed. There may not be simple causalities in play, but there are influences and effects. Many times, formulaically, various social workers would say 'we are hearing you' or 'we hear where you are coming from'; I would say now that in these cases there is nothing more important – despite the lack of resources, training etc – than social workers being sympathetically interested in parents if for no other reason than that the child depends on his parents, even if – and sometimes especially if – he is removed from them. It is perhaps worth remembering that adults who abuse children were once, like all adults, children themselves.

The other professional assumption that seemed to be in play, at least for me – and again this would be a request for psychological-mindedness – was that there is no such things as parental ambivalence; or, to put it more starkly, that if parents abuse their children it means not only that the children need to be protected from them but that the parents therefore cannot also love their children. The abuser – who of course is initially innocent until proved guilty which is itself such a problem for social workers involved – is assumed to be the most malign person rather than the most ambivalent person. If you are not good you must be bad. It is, of course, disturbing to be under suspicion; but what seems most difficult in these potentially dangerous situations is for the social workers to be at once sufficiently vigilant but to also to work with, and thereby affirm the parents' strengths. The mother of a 10-day-old baby, or of a 10-year-old child, is in a very vulnerable state in relation to her child. My experience in this predicament was to be treated – in some ways quite understandably – as guilty until proved innocent; and as someone whose ordinary vulnerability was of no consequence. (Fathers, paradoxically, in these situations probably need to be protected, to some extent, from the fact that they can no longer protect their family from what is happening to them.) If you threaten the parents you are not protecting the child; this, I think, is the very difficult thing that local authorities have to work with. It probably goes without saying that the longer these proceedings go on – at least the longer the legal proceedings go on – the greater the harm done. It is very difficult to look after a child and each other with the background possibility that your child may be taken into care. Everything that is now known about the developmental significance of early attachments – about the long-term effects on parents and children of premature separation – should make foster care very much of a last resort. It is perhaps worth mentioning that people who go into this work with severe (and sometimes unconscious) grievances against their own parents are more likely to be punitive in this regard. Wherever there is a prevailing ethos that children are good/innocent/vulnerable, adults are violent/sexual/exploitative there will be workers who have had bad early experiences. (It is not news that professionals, just like their clients, have a history.) It was part of my experience, I believe, to have been the beneficiary, so to speak, of a complicated mixture of responsible and intelligent social work procedures, and the histories of the individual social workers involved. Being professional over the intimately personal is never simple; and children, whatever else they are, are profoundly evocative of our deepest and most complicated feelings. There are, unfortunately many cases, as everyone in this room knows, in which children need to be taken into care and in which parents are unable to cope with parenting. The gravity of these situations, and the very real danger that many families live under is not to be over or under-estimated. What I now know something about, in a different way, is both what it is like living under a certain kind of local authority surveillance; and indeed what it is like, after the long haul of extremely traumatic court proceedings to live with an open verdict, neither exonerated nor convicted. Both are long stories, possibly unending ones; but for the sake of brevity I want to offer a few brief points for consideration.

The local authority, however they do their job, are in an unenviable position. But I think there are degrees of adversarialness; if the social services cannot get themselves into any kind of collaborative position vis-à-vis the parents they offer the parents an external enemy. The social workers are coming after all with a complicated message which is: what is in your child's best interests is not in your best interests. I think that, in itself, creates panic and confusion. It is as though the very proceedings themselves, the social work investigation, separates out from the child from the family before either the children or the family can begin to emotionally conceive of such a differentiation. We were being talked to by the local authority as though our baby was something other than a member of our family (at its most extreme, as though our daughter was not a party of our bodies). The defences called up to deal with the extremity of this situation – rage, contempt, denial, despair, cynicism and so on – then become part of the problem. This potentially disfigures the family's experience of itself; the ordinary love and hate the family have for each other is transmuted into exaggerated hatred of social services and exaggerated love and protectiveness of each other. And the people who know you and care about you are themselves rendered impotent; so your taken-for-granted resources of family and friends are rendered resourceless. Every local authority intervention creates a new community of the beleaguered; a group of people isolated in and by a trauma that mobilises feelings that are very often unbearable. These are just inevitable consequences of social work practice that is essential; it is, though, worth spelling out the impact on the family and its wider system. It is particularly dismaying when the social services admit of no doubt about what they are doing; as though their vulnerability is also proscribed.

In our case the police, after interviewing us, dropped the case, but the social workers continued to work as ersatz policemen. By that I mean they pressed us, on several occasions to, as they called it, 'confess' (one of the social workers said to me that it would be difficult for me to confess because it would ruin my professional reputation, and so on). Quite understandably they assumed that either we, the parents, were involved in a *folie a deux* or that one of us had caused the injuries and not told the other. Either way, and the logical of this is obvious, they were involved in an attempt to split us up as a couple. I cite this because there is an obvious and possibly unconsidered risk in putting the parents as possible or potential abusers through this kind of experience; under such pressure people are potentially less able to, in the fullest sense, look after their children – hold them in mind emotionally, be fully present in their care for them. It would not surprise me if the pressure at least some local authorities put on families in these terrible predicaments creates precisely the situation that the family is being accused of. How would a family, in this situation, not become abusive? If you mobilise more rage in your clients than they can bear then there will inevitably be consequences somewhere along the line. The long-term effects of these situations, I now know, need to be thought through. The question is; in what way do these investigative procedures help parents to better care for their children? The despair and rage engendered have long-term effects, which means long-term effects on the family if it survives. If you are treated as guilty until proved innocent – a danger to your child until it is established by due legal process that you are not – then damage is done whatever the final verdict in the legal proceedings. It was our experience that the police, and the legal system were far less traumatic – both, I think, in their intent, and in their effect – than the local authority. The legal system made us – made me – feel reassured (or even held) by its clarity, its impartiality and its regard for evidence (the police seemed to be in pursuit of the truth not in pursuit merely of perpetrators). The local authority seemed, in my experience, to be rather more driven by fear and righteousness, and therefore more prone to intimidate than in any sense identify with us. I do not know whether there is a way of doing their extremely difficult job without intimidation, but it does, at least, need to be acknowledged what intimidation tends to produce. Because everyone believes in protecting children terrible things can be done in the name of protecting them. At their best child protection procedures genuinely protect the most vulnerable people in the community; at their worst they are a licence to torment families – and particularly women as mothers – to the core of their being. A mother even suspected of child abuse has already, in her own eyes – her inner eyes – begun to fail as a mother. As a father, in so far as one can generalise, one is more likely to be left with a corrosive rage. None of these feelings end when the procedures have been completed.

And so, by way of conclusion, I want to say something about the aftermath; of the experience of living with a so-called 'open verdict'. Presumably if you are convicted, so to speak, of child abuse, even if the violence was done in a state say, of post-natal depression or comparable emotional stress, you know that when and if you next take your child to the GP or to accident and emergency, you will be subject to significant suspicion and investigation. But if, as we are, you only may be a child abuser you are in a peculiarly ambiguous position, utterly dependent, I would imagine, on the tact, sensitivity, intelligence and professional competence of the professionals you find yourself dealing with. It is clearly, a recipe for a sense of unsafety and could never be conductive to confident parenting. One hopes, as one always does, that so-called good sense will prevail – and indeed most of the things that happen to children are fairly accurately diagnosable – but how, in such a predicament would one know the extent to which one was being what is usually called paranoid? As it happens we are quite robust people, and not unconfident parents; but it is easy to see how someone else in such a situation might be driven mad, might be rendered either stiflingly over-protective of their child, or simply paralysed by fantasies of potential catastrophe. The potential for cynicism, despair or vengefulness as potential self-cures for such a difficult situation is self-evident. The open verdict – which may be legally unavoidable on the evidence available – is an extremely dangerous place for parents – and probably for local authorities – to go on living in. The parents, in a not entirely melodramatic sense, are given a life sentence of 'possibly guilty' and never proved innocent. It turns all the child care professionals that one has subsequent dealings with into part of a potentially punitive child protection team; it means, in short, that the suspicious surveillance never ends. And one can see that there could be a good side to this – that it makes parents unusually attentive. But it also means that what is done naturally, out of love and affection, is also done out of fear and intimidation. It needs to be starkly stated – even though it is self-evident that the child protection work of local authorities is an essential social service – that child abuse proceedings are experienced by the parents as an attack on their capacity for love, care and concern (and not only of their children). This is, whatever else it is, an attack on the core of their being. It seems to me to be important that what psychoanalysts call rationalisations – plausibly reasonable justifications used as cover stories for abusive and/or unacceptable behaviour – are not used by professionals doing this extremely difficult work. Having been through the ordeal of child care proceedings it is hard to see what it would be to recover, or what could be recovered. Only one thing is clear to me; that people who are investigated for child abuse need to be protected and not scapegoated.

SMALL GROUP DISCUSSIONS: PLENARY 1

SMALL GROUP A

PLENARY 1: COURT EXPERIENCES AND DEVELOPMENT OUTCOMES

- Working with children in the court process is as much about listening to children as giving them information. Children of all ages need to be able to make sense of their lives, environment and history.

- The group commended the use of pictures drawn by children as a symbolic and simple way to communicate. Professionals are conditioned to use legal language whilst children have their own methods of communication.

- There is concern at how little of the system's resources are put into understanding the child's perspective. This also varies between private law and public law.

- Is the separate representation of children primarily concerned with the child's rights or the child's welfare? There is a need to progress the system to a model where every family decision is assessed as to what is needed for that family.

- There is a danger that child protection, domestic violence and private law applications can be treated as three distinct arenas with the only people making the connections being the children. There is an argument for increased sharing of information between all those who have a role to invoke other agency procedures.

SMALL GROUP B

PLENARY 1: COURT EXPERIENCES AND DEVELOPMENT OUTCOMES

- There is a wide variety of child protection cases, a wide variety of social work competencies, a wide variety of social work responses, and a wide variety of resources available. This affects the consistency and quality of responses by professionals to cases of this kind.

- In the investigative stages of care proceedings, mothers, fathers and professionals alike have to work with great uncertainty, emotional complexity, and ambiguity.

- Notwithstanding that uncertainty, emotional complexity and ambiguity, professionals need to remain respectful of the family throughout the investigation; if this is achieved/maintained, the process would be more acceptable and understandable to both mothers and fathers.

- The appalling impact of delay was clear from the parents' story in Plenary 1: there is a real need for the courts to list the fact-finding hearing in public law cases at the very earliest stage. This is just as important for the innocent parents as it is for the parents who are responsible for the neglect/abuse of their children.

- It is not appropriate for social workers simply to rely on the police investigation in the context of a child abuse investigation. The police and social services have a different focus for their work: the police are seeking to identify whether a crime has been committed, the social services are seeking to determine whether a child needs protecting. However, the evidence from each will need to inform the risk assessment and child contact plan.

- Nor is it sufficient for social workers to rely on the medical evidence alone in presenting its case on 'significant harm' to the court; the social workers should be considering the wide canvas of material. In this respect, it is important for social workers to take a proper narrative history from the parents; this must be done in an open-minded and respectful way. Training in this respect would be important.

- A 'family therapy' type interview was thought to be helpful in some cases, to encourage parents to speak, though not in cases where there is a significant risk of violence and abuse.

- Following a strategy meeting (at the outset of a child protection investigation) the parents should be provided with a copy of the outline of the strategy plan – including the timetable for investigation – so that the plan can be scrutinised by the parents. This would vest greater confidence in the process.

- Generally, judges should be willing to revisit the factual finding(s) if material new evidence (on the issue of causation) emerges before the final hearing (or even after the final hearing as in *Re K (Non-Accidental Injuries: Perpetrator: New Evidence)* [2004] EWCA Civ 1181 [2005] 1 FLR 285).

SMALL GROUP C

PLENARY 1: COURT EXPERIENCES AND DEVELOPMENT OUTCOMES

There is a clear tension between delivering a consistent service nationally and local democratic practices and the present process for funding – other models need to be explored.

There needs to be more funding for grassroots 'helping services' – recruiting, supporting and training health visitors, social workers etc rather than engaging external experts. There is also a requirement for interdisciplinary training which is properly funded, for all professionals working within the family justice system, including the judiciary.

[*A summary of the discussions and conclusions of Small Groups D and E are to be found in Plenary 9.*]

SMALL GROUP F

PLENARY 1: COURT EXPERIENCES AND DEVELOPMENT OUTCOMES

The first area the group discussed was the question of the time allowed for the children in the process; and the skills of those interacting with them. The following points were made:

- The system was not good at assessing the emotional maturity of the children. How do you get across the child's perception of the world? How should this affect the way we work?

- For the court to understand these issues, someone needed to spend time with the child; and needed the skills to extract the child's perceptions.

- Care proceedings were becoming more attuned to the needs of the child but children in private law cases were in effect, receiving a second-class service in this respect.

- There was a tension between pressure to move cases on and the need for a child focus in the system.

- People in the system were insufficiently skilled at communicating with children.

- Representation was available to help solve the problems of the court but it needed to go further to ensure the involvement of the child, though it was recognised this may not be appropriate for all.

Next the group discussed the problem of uncertainty. All professionals needed to be aware of the difficulties and ambiguities that uncertainty brought, for example in care cases. It was probable that social services were insufficiently skilled in that respect.

On separate representation for children, the group noted that there was no research evidence that separate representation was beneficial. It was not necessary to use separate representation in all cases but it was necessary to find a way of determining in which cases it would be appropriate.

In conclusion, the group identified the danger of not differentiating between process and outcomes. We needed to understand better what outcomes were wanted. There was also an unresolved issue about how far the state should intervene in private law cases and the extent of its duty to children who, on the evidence of Joan Hunt's research, may be as damaged as those in public law cases.

MODELS FOR ACHIEVING SUCCESSFUL AGREED AND ORDERED OUTCOMES IN PRIVATE LAW CASES

IN-COURT CONCILIATION:
BRIEF ENCOUNTER OR PERMANENT RESOLUTION?

Liz Trinder

School of Social Work and Psychosocial Sciences, University of East Anglia

SUMMARY OF PAPER

Dr Trinder introduced her paper as an abbreviated version of fuller research which is to be published consequentially. She suggested in court conciliation was something of a last-ditch attempt to assist parents to reach agreement and to avoid a hearing in a s 8 application.

Dr Trinder explored the ingredients of an enduring solution. These included the production of an appropriate agreement, implementation of the agreement, withdrawal from the family justice system, contact (where appropriate), management or resolution of conflict and contact problems and enhanced parental capacity to collaborate.

She suggested that the child's ability to adjust depends on collaboration between parents. The system should be aiming for high quality contact.

There are currently many different models of in court conciliation at county court level. In her research, Dr Trinder examined the effectiveness of three different models. The research team asked people to participate as they were leaving court and achieved a 68% response rate from those who had used conciliation, resulting in baseline interviews with 250 parents. This was followed up with a questionnaire between six and nine months later to which 175 participants responded. The research was funded by the Department of Constitutional Affairs.

Those surveyed comprised the 10% of the population who were unable to resolve child arrangements between themselves and resorted to the court. The researchers were aware of this but still found the situations more difficult than they had anticipated. The researchers found multiple contact problems, the parents were conflicted, distrustful, often poor and each accusing the other of being unreliable. They often had concerns over each other's care and there were problems with child support in half of cases. When questioned about the adult and child distress and the impact of the dispute on the child, there were disproportionately high levels of distress and parents were measurably struggling.

The conciliation appointment typically lasted just 45 minutes. The focus was on what the contact timetable would be. The outcome was a high agreement rate and in that sense highly efficient. Half of parents reported a full agreement and 75% a full or part agreement. There was a lower satisfaction rate amongst the parents who reached only a partial agreement or no agreement.

When the families were followed up six months later, most of the agreements were found to be still in place; either intact or renegotiated to allow more contact to the party who sought it. In a small amount of cases the contact had collapsed. It was apparent that more children were having contact eight months later than had been having contact at the time of the application, and further that the amount of contact had increased. In 90% of cases the children were having contact. The parents had increased their well-being by withdrawing from the process. The courts appeared to be effective in terms of ordering contact, at least over the short term.

The problem appeared to be that there was no impact on the quality of contact and no impact on the factors that impact upon a child's well-being such as the parents' ability to collaborate or co-parent. The court is effective in achieving agreements but it is almost common sense that this has little impact on how the parents get on. Simply having contact does not mean that it works for the children.

Looking towards an enduring solution, one-fifth of cases were still ongoing at the time of follow up; 40% of cases had needed additional assistance, either more than one 45-minute session, a review or a report; less than a third were simple open-and-shut cases. Even for the cases that do settle, there is a clear gap between settlement and resolution: simply having an agreement does not equate to a resolution which requires the reduction of contact problems and conflict.

Dr Trinder concluded, there is a gap between settlement and resolution, between contact happening and contact working. Education and/or therapeutic interventions are required to run in tandem with the dispute resolution processes (and effective risk management). Families need more than dispute resolution, they need something to address the emotional issues, which echoes the findings of Janet Walker's research on mediation.

In-court conciliation is a form of dispute resolution, typically conducted on court premises in contested private law proceedings. The aim is to reach a settlement, thereby avoiding the need for a contested hearing. In-court conciliation is not a new phenomenon. A number of conciliation schemes were developed in the 1980s (Davis (1988)). Since then the development of schemes has occurred in a fairly piecemeal fashion, with schemes adopting a range of objectives and processes and with some courts having no provision at all (MCSI (2003)). Nonetheless this remains a significant part of the work of CAFCASS and an important means by which the family justice system handles private law cases. In 2004, for example, CAFCASS conducted 38,788 private-law-court-directed dispute resolutions (CAFCASS (2005)).

More recently there seems to be a renewed emphasis on the role of conciliation in private law cases. In 2002 the Children Act Sub-Committee, in its report *Making Contact Work*, recommended that a system of in-court conciliation be made available at first appointment in all courts (para 10.27, 10.41). This suggestion has been taken up subsequently by the Government as part of the Private Law Programme, with the expectation that in-court conciliation will be made available to all courts as resources permit (DCA (2004), Secretary of State (2005)).

In some respects the emphasis on conciliation is something of a puzzle. Socio-legal researchers (and mediators) have always raised questions about whether brief negotiations in the highly-pressurised court environment can ever be fair or produce sustainable or appropriate agreements, particularly in comparison with (out-of-court) mediation. In one of the earliest studies, Gwynn Davis concluded that although the conciliation process could work, '[at] its worst it is a thoroughly unsatisfactory hybrid: a kind of "mediation" without party control, or "adjudication" without the opportunity to give evidence' ((1988): 107). The few studies that have been conducted do bear out some of these points. Compared to out-of-court mediation, in-court schemes tend to produce higher numbers of agreements, indicative of greater pressure, as well as lower levels of satisfaction with both those agreements and with the process (Ogus et al (1989); Davis et al (2001)).

A recent thematic inspection by the MCSI (2003) repeated long-standing concerns about pressure and parental consent, but also added two new process issues that have become more prominent over the last decade: the inadequacy of current risk assessment procedures and the very limited way in which children were able to be heard directly in the process.

Notwithstanding these concerns, in other respects the renewed embrace of conciliation is not surprising at all. Conciliation offers a means of processing large numbers of cases more quickly and more cheaply than by a report or a hearing. The focus of conciliation is entirely consistent with long-term trends in English family law towards rule-based decision-making and settlement rather than adjudication (Dewar & Parker (2000); Davis & Pearce (1999a) and (1999b)). Given the failure to divert large number of cases into out-of-court mediation (Davis et al (2001); Walker et al (2004)), with the rising number of s 8 applications and an increasing sense of crisis within the family justice system surrounding contact, the interest of policy-makers and practitioners in conciliation does make sense.

In this paper I look at what contribution in-court conciliation might make towards producing durable solutions in contested private law contact cases. Is the turn to conciliation simply a rather desperate attempt to do something in the face of mounting pressure, or does it offer a mechanism to resolve at least some disputes in a less conflictual fashion? I start off by delineating what an enduring solution might look like, or on what basis conciliation should be judged. I then draw on a recently completed study of conciliation for the Department for Constitutional Affairs (Trinder et al (forthcoming)) to describe the process and outcomes of conciliation.

WHAT WOULD AN ENDURING SOLUTION LOOK LIKE?

The traditional marker of success within the family justice system has been settlement or agreement rates. This does not, however, give any real answers to the critical question identified by Davis et al ((2001): 272) 'to what extent are things now better?' or, in this context, to what extent conciliation makes contact 'work' for children and their parents or produce an enduring solution.

The messages from developmental research give a fairly consistent message about what supports child well-being post-separation and what might, therefore, be appropriate indicators. It is worth pointing out that the quantity of contact per se is not consistently associated with positive child adjustment. Instead the key predictors of child well-being post-separation are income, the level of conflict between parents and the quality of the relationship with, and parenting capacity of, each parent although probably particularly the resident parent (for reviews see Amato & Gilbreth (1999); Whiteside & Becker (2000); Rodgers & Pryor (1998); Hunt (2003); Dunn (2004)).

Drawing on these messages appropriate targets for conciliation, or the ingredients of an enduring solution, would therefore consist of *all* the following:

- production of an agreement through a fair and non-coercive process with effective risk assessment and risk management;

- implementation of agreements;

- (re)introduction, extension or affirmation of contact, where contact is appropriate;

- cessation of further involvement in the family justice system;

- future informal adaptation of agreements to meet changing needs and circumstances and following consultation with children;

- resolution of parental conflict and contact problems and enhanced parental capacity to collaborate and to focus on the child's needs and wishes.

WHAT TYPE OF CASES ARE DEALT WITH IN CONCILIATION?

The components for an enduring solution listed above do present a significant challenge. Many separated parents, even amongst the majority who make informal agreements, find it difficult to collaborate or to share decision-making (Walker et al (2005)). The profile of families involved in in-court conciliation presents even more of a challenge. In our study[1] the great majority were first time cases, but the range and level of difficulties were considerably greater than those reported in non-court or community populations (Trinder et al (2005)) and very similar to the profile of families involved in the court welfare process (Buchanan et al (2001)). Looking at the sample as a whole it is clear that the parents, and children, were facing significant difficulties, with fraught or tenuous contact, conflicted and distrustful parental relationships, minimal shared decision-making, high levels of dissatisfaction with current arrangements and multiple reported contact problems including children refusing or being upset by contact, lack of reliability, threats to stop (having) contact, concerns about possible harm, neglect and domestic violence and interwoven disputes about child support. Combined with high rates of economic deprivation, it is therefore no surprise that the level of conflict and reported problems translated into levels of adult and child distress well above community norms.

WHAT HAPPENS IN THE CONCILIATION PROCESS?

Faced with such a range of needs, in-court conciliation has remarkably simple goals even if these are delivering via a bewildering range of local processes. Conciliation, focuses on reaching an agreement about when and how contact will occur. How this was achieved varied between the three different models evaluated in our study. In one area, conciliation consisted of a scheduled one-hour appointment in a side room at court where the CAFCASS officer attempted to get parents to negotiate a deal before reporting back briefly to a district judge in chambers. In the second area the negotiation process took place in a courtroom, led by a district judge, with lawyers heavily involved in negotiating on behalf of the parents. In the third area the parents began the process in chambers, retired with the CAFCASS officer to negotiate an agreement before returning to the district judge.

Despite these technical or procedural differences, the broad approach was similar across the three areas. Meetings were short. The median length of the conciliation meeting, as reported by parents, was 45 minutes. Both parents and professionals concurred that the process was overwhelmingly task-focused, where the primary, even the sole, task was to reach an agreement on the timetable for contact.

Earlier research on the conciliation process by Davis & Pearce ((1999a), (1999b), (1999c)) highlighted how courts focus on the future rather than the past as a means to manage the uncertainty of having to deal with large numbers of parents presenting a wide range of potentially unmanageable problems. The future focus of conciliation was just as evident in our study as the following extracts from the qualitative interviews with professionals indicate:

'I think that wherever possible we should be drawing a line under the past and trying to be constructive for the benefit of the child for the future ... close the door on the past and try and guide people forwards to the future.' District Judge

'The ineffective ones [conciliators] allow the parties to take control of the interview, as it were, and let them carry on harping on about what their beefs are about what's gone on in the past. I don't think that is at all helpful, because you are there for the future not for what's gone on previously ...' Solicitor

'I'm against the past on the basis that we don't have space to counsel people in the session, neither is it in my view appropriate .... I can't make a judgement on the past. Can't put things right. I can see that they want to get it all out in the air, but maybe they need to do it somewhere else.' CAFCASS

---

[1]   The research consisted of 250 structured interviews with parents immediately following the conciliation session together with a six months follow up with 175 parents from the baseline sample. The data from the parents was supplemented by qualitative interviews with district judges, CAFCASS officers and lawyers in each of the three study areas.

It is worth noting that screening for domestic violence was minimal[2] and that there was a presumption that all cases were suitable for conciliation, unless there was a very specific reason for this not to occur.

WHAT WERE THE IMMEDIATE OUTCOMES OF CONCILIATION?

The courts were successful at achieving the principal aim of reaching an agreement. The overall agreement rate was high, with nearly three-quarters of parents reporting reaching some agreement and nearly half of parents reporting that they had reached a full agreement on all issues. This agreement rate is considerably higher than the 45–46% agreement rate reported in two recent studies of out-of-court mediation (Davis et al (2001); Walker et al (2004)). The high conciliation agreement rate is consistent, however, with rates of agreement for court-based conciliation reported in previous studies (Ogus et al (1989); Mantle (2001)).

Not all parents were happy with the 'agreements' to which they had apparently signed up, perhaps reflecting some degree of pressure, or at least a perception of limited choice between reaching a settlement or having a welfare report or contested hearing. Under two-thirds of parents were satisfied with their 'agreement'. Non-resident parents were significantly more satisfied with agreements than resident parents.

WHAT WERE THE OUTCOMES SIX TO NINE MONTHS LATER?

In many respects the very brief intervention had quite a marked impact – only a fifth of agreements did not work at all, most agreements were intact or had been extended, most cases were closed with low re-litigation rates, almost all children were having contact, with more hours of contact and more staying contact than prior to the application, more parents were satisfied with the quantity and quality of contact and both parents and children were doing better than at baseline. It seemed that having an agreement, or at least ceasing the court battle, generated its own momentum, at least in the short term. Parents whose cases were closed scored better on almost all measures than parents where the court battle was ongoing or had been resurrected. The other important factor was parental relationship quality at baseline – conciliation appeared to work best with what were the less entrenched cases.

Although this is an impressive list of achievements, albeit sustained only over the course of six to nine months, it does fall rather a long way short of the components of an enduring solution. Conciliation offers a quick fix for only a minority of cases. Under a third of parents were involved in 'open and shut cases' where their case remained closed at follow up after a single conciliation session. The bulk of the remainder required more professional input than a single conciliation session, either in the form of a review, report or hearing before they could be closed. A quarter of parents were involved in cases that were still ongoing or active six to nine months after the baseline conciliation session. Although the re-litigation rate was fairly low overall, the majority of cases did require additional professional input and a quarter remained active.

Although parent satisfaction with arrangements and parent and child well-being did improve from baseline to follow up, overall levels remained low. It is important also not to over-emphasise the positives of having an agreement – only 60% of parents whose cases were closed were satisfied with arrangements at follow up.

Perhaps the most disappointing result, however, is how little impact the conciliation session, the agreement or the adoption of new contact arrangements had on parental relationship quality, shared decision-making and contact problems. At follow up less than a third of parents reported

---

[2]   The fieldwork was conducted before the introduction of the gateway forms.

ever discussing children's problems with the other parent, and only a quarter ever shared major or day-to-day decisions. Only a fifth of parents rated their relationship as quite good or fair, no advance on the baseline position. The impact on contact problems was uneven. Although contact was more firmly established at follow up, most parents reported that overall contact problems were about the same or worse than before the court application. Some specific problems associated with the exercise of contact were significantly higher at follow up, notably reports that children were reluctant or refusing contact and that the other parent was not sticking to arrangements. Concerns about the ex partner's parenting quality did drop since baseline, with concerns about lack of supervision reduced significantly. However, the prevalence of concerns before court meant that even with this reduction, four out of ten parents still expressed concerns about the other parent's parenting at follow up. Similarly, although there was a significant decrease in reports of fear of violence impacting on contact arrangements, this remained an issue for a third of parents, particularly for resident parents/mothers.

DOES IN-COURT CONCILIATION PRODUCE DURABLE SOLUTIONS?

It is too early to tell from our results whether the outcomes of conciliation do endure over the medium to long term. Not all, of course, had a short-term fix, let alone an enduring one. A minority of cases fell at the first hurdle, with a rapid return to court. Others took rather longer to get out of the traps, typically requiring one or two review sessions before exiting the court process. It remains to be seen how long these agreements last. The results were fairly promising in the short term but it is not clear that agreements were capable of adaptation without recourse to future litigation.

There are also doubts about whether conciliation produced a solution to the problems parents and children were facing. It seemed that conciliation was effective at making contact happen but not necessarily at making contact work for children in terms of addressing the concerns that parents had beyond the contact timetable, in reducing conflict or building collaboration. Most cases appeared to be closed, with a timetable for contact set in place, but few parents seemed to reach closure.

This in itself should not come as a shock. Smart & May ((2005):2), describing the Children Act 1989, comment that: 'The legislation has not succeeded in providing highly conflicted parents with the means of changing their behaviour; it only exalts them to do things differently.' This could equally apply to conciliation. The service that parents receive is very brief and is not designed to address relationship issues. Indeed the future focus explicitly excludes consideration of emotions and problems in favour of reason and solutions. While reaching a settlement avoids the possibility of further inflaming conflict, it does not in itself resolve conflict, given the range of issues that parents are concerned about.

Previous studies have also reported little impact on parental communication and collaboration (Pearson & Thoeness (1988); Ogus et al (1989)). It seems that simply providing a dispute resolution process does not in itself have further interpersonal or communicative or therapeutic consequences. Even the typically more extended and less pressurised negotiation process offered by out-of-court mediation, makes little difference to communication or shared decision-making, even where a full agreement had been reached (Walker et al (2004)).

Finally, in some cases even the restricted goal of reaching agreement is questionable without a far more considered approach to risk assessment and risk management.

In sum, for a very brief intervention, in-court conciliation does have a considerable impact but it falls short of providing an enduring solution for children. That is not to say that a welfare investigation or a contested hearing or even out-of-court mediation would necessarily produce a better, or indeed, a different outcome. What might be helpful would be to team a method of reaching a timetable (whether negotiated or imposed) with far greater availability of some form of educational and/or therapeutic intervention, together with appropriate risk management. Otherwise children will continue to be placed in a war zone.

REFERENCES

Amato, P & Gilbreth, J 'Nonresident fathers and children's well-being: a meta-analysis' (1999) 61 (3) Journal of Marriage & The Family 557–73

Buchanan, A, Hunt, J, Bretherton, H & Bream, V *Families in conflict: The Family Court Welfare Service: the perspectives of children and parents* (Bristol, The Policy Press, 2001)

CAFCASS *Annual Report and Accounts. 2004–2005* (London, CAFCASS, 2005)

Children Act Sub-Committee of the Lord Chancellor's Advisory Board on Family Law *Making Contact Work: A Report to the Lord Chancellor* (London, Lord Chancellor's Department, 2002)

Davis, G 'The Halls of Justice and Justice in the Halls' in R Dingwall & J Eekelaar (eds) *Divorce Mediation and the Legal Process* (Oxford, Clarendon Press, 1988)

Davis, G, Bevan, G, Clisby, S, Cumming, Z, Dingwall, R, Fenn, R, Finch, S, Fitzgerald, R, Goldie, S, Greatbatch, D, James, A & Pearce, J *Monitoring Publicly Funded Family Mediation. Report to the Legal Services Commission* (London, Legal Services Commission, 2001)

Davis, G & Pearce, J 'The welfare principle in action' (1999a) 29 Family Law 237–241

Davis, G & Pearce, J 'On the trail of the welfare principle' (1999b) 29 Family Law 144–148

Davis, G & Pearce, J 'A view from the trenches – Practice and procedure in section 8 applications'. (1999c) 29 Family Law 457–466

Department for Constitutional Affairs *The Private Law Programme* (London: DCA, 2004)

Dewar, J & Parker, S 'English Family Law since World War II: From Status to Chaos' in S Katz, J Eekelaar & M Maclean (eds) *Cross Currents: Family Law and Policy in the US and England* (Oxford, Oxford University Press, 2000)

Dunn, J 'Annotation: Children's relationships with their non-resident fathers' (2004) 45 Journal of Child Psychology and Psychiatry 659–671

Hunt, J *Researching Contact* (London, National Council for One Parent Families, 2003)

Mantle, G 'Helping Parents in Dispute: Child-centred mediation at county court' (Aldershot, Ashgate, 2001)

MCSI *Seeking Agreement. A Thematic Review by MCSI of the operation of schemes involving CAFCASS at an early stage in private law proceedings* (London, MCSI, 2003)

Ogus, A, Walker, J, Jones-Lee, M, Cole, W, Corlyon, J, Ingham, T, McCarthy, P, Simpson, B, Wray, S *The Costs and Effectiveness of Family Conciliation In England and Wales, Report to the Lord Chancellor* (London, Lord Chancellor's Department, 1989)

Pearson, J & Thoeness, N 'Divorce Mediation: An American Picture' in R Dingwall & J Eekelaar (eds) *Divorce Mediation and the Legal Process* (Oxford, Clarendon Press, 1988)

Rodgers, B & Pryor, J *Divorce and separation: the outcomes for children* (York, Joseph Rowntree Foundation, 1998)

Secretary of State for Constitutional Affairs, Secretary of State for Education and Skills and Secretary of State for Trade and Industry *Parental Separation: Children's Needs and Parents' Responsibilities: Next Steps* Cm 6452 (London, Stationery Office, 2005)

Smart, C, May, V, Wade, A & Furniss, C *Residence and contact disputes in Court* Vol 2 (Research Series 4/05) (London, Department for Constitutional Affairs, 2003)

Thoennes, N & Pearson, J 'Predicting Outcomes in Divorce Mediation: The Influence of People and Process' (1985) 41(2) Journal of Social Issues 115–126

Trinder, L, Connolly, J, Kellett, J & Thoday, C *A Profile of Applicants and Respondents in Contact Cases in Essex* (London, Department for Constitutional Affairs, 2005)

Trinder, L, Connolly, J, Kellett, J, Notley, C & Swift, L *Making Contact Happen or Making Contact Work? The Process and Outcomes Of In-Court Conciliation* (London, Department for Constitutional Affairs, forthcoming)

Walker, J et al *Picking Up The Pieces: Marriage and Divorce Two Years After Information Provision* (London, Department for Constitutional Affairs, 2004)

Whiteside, MF, & Becker, BJ 'Parental factors and the young child's postdivorce adjustment: A meta-analysis with implications for parenting arrangements' (2000) 14 Journal of Family Psychology 5–26

MEDIATING PARENTAL DISPUTES ABOUT THEIR CHILDREN INSIDE AND OUTSIDE THE COURT PROCESS: ASSESSING PARENTS' AND CHILDREN'S WISHES AND ATTACHMENTS IN PRIVATE LAW

Gill Gorrell-Barnes

Honorary Senior Lecturer, Tavistock Clinic; Family and Marital Therapist; Consultant to Children and Family Legal Disputes and Family Court Proceedings

Gill Gorell Barnes began by explaining her professional background and training to work with children and families. Family system therapy is based on observations and descriptions of the way families interact. This works in the context of people's behaviour and explores how the past may affect this. This therapy has been helping in these disciplines for 25 years but is not alone the answer to court disputes.

Ms Gorell Barnes explained that Dr Trinder's point as to the rational processes the court seeks to impose is central to Ms Gorell Barnes' thinking on the irrationality that the families feel. In contrast to the families who enter court conciliation, the families with whom Ms Gorell Barnes has contact have been at war for never less than three years by the time she sees them and often five years or even longer, usually where a child is being withheld from the other parent. Intractability and irrationality are the two most pressing problems Ms Gorell Barnes faces. She also undertakes work with couples separating where they are referred by solicitors.

The goals Ms Gorell Barnes seeks to achieve in her work are:

(1) to establish co-operation around the children;

(2) for the parents to develop shares views on how to address the child issues. This very much ties in with what Katherine Gieve explores in her paper as to who takes responsibility for the children's lunch boxes etc;

(3) to assist the parents to have a more positive perception of the other's intentions and efforts;

(4) to develop a joint understanding of how the child might be feeling.

A key feature in 50% of the cases Ms Gorell Barnes is protracted irrational or mental health issues although these are not always psychiatrically labelled. This may lead to distorted adult perceptions and distorted child development.

Ms Gorell Barns is unable to recommend contact in approximately half of the cases she sees. It is very sad not to be able to recommend contact and this is usually for one of three reasons: a result of extreme behaviour that are highly distressing to the children, safety issues or a lack of attachment between the child and the parent seeking contact. Ms Gorell Barnes believes consideration of attachment between the child and the parent is under-recognised in the court process. She gave the example of a 5-year-old child who experienced attrition and the deterioration of interest in a person called father. This child had only seen his father at a contact centre and Ms Gorell Barnes had to work with the child on what he thought a 'Dad' was. Where parents separate before a child is two, there is a marked increase in the number of children with no knowledge of their parent.

Ms Gorell Barnes considers that there are five key issues which suggest whether a successful relationship could be established. These are:

- *the way attachment is expressed by the parent seeking contact;*

- *the way in which attachment is expressed by the child;*

- *the capacity of a father to understand the effects of former behaviour both on the child and on the mother's concerns about contact;*

- *the ability of both parents to work towards minimal position of understanding of the other parents' position. This encompasses both how each parent views the other in their mind and what can be done to improve the understanding and perception of the other parent's position;*
- *the child's wish to reconnect.*

There are three change issues which Ms Gorell Barnes tries to build into her work; firstly to empathise with pain of the parent who has been cut off from their child, secondly to increase the understanding of children as unique beings and thirdly to develop each parents' ability to understand and interpret the behaviour of the other.

The paper explores the difficulties very young children experience in retaining positive memories and how family voices may prevent a child doing this. It addresses the affect of domestic violence on children, with particular focus on the need to look at the meaning of violent acts for each child. She gave the example that a father breaking a window in the family home may be seen by the child as an attempt by the father to have access to the children for contact indicating both love and interest in the child, or alternatively it may be perceived as an act of violence designed to intimidate the child's mother. The child's perception of this violence would have a key influence on how the child perceives the parent who carried this out. The extended family may have an impact on which perception of the domestic violence the child holds.

Ms Gorell Barnes concludes by citing the concerns that many parents hold as to care and welfare where the other parent wishes to have contact with very young children. There is an issue for the family justice system as to how to train people other than experts to carry out some of this systemic work with the families who would benefit from it.

BACKGROUND

I have a hybrid background.

I am not formally trained as a mediator, but have worked in child and family mental health in a number of settings for all of my professional life, mainly as a family and marital therapist and also as a researcher. During the 1980s I focussed both clinical work and research on children growing up in stepfamilies at the Institute of Family Therapy, London, and in the 1990s on children and parents going through divorce, a clinical project in the Department for Children and Parents at the Tavistock Clinic, London. I have seen approximately 120 couples or families going through separation or divorce, and interviewed a very large number of children of different ages.

In the last six years I have worked with the courts, acting as 'expert witness' in relation to 20+ families, but also seeing a higher number of solicitor-referred couples attempting to make satisfactory and agreed arrangements for parenting their children during and following acrimonious separation or divorce. I see the children in all the cases where I am positioned as an expert witness, and also see the children in all other cases where the parents agree this would be beneficial either to themselves, or to the children involved (about 50% of solicitor-referred couples).

WORKING TOWARDS NEW ARRANGEMENTS

Where severe disputes over the children accompany or replace patterns of arguing and fighting that precede the break-up of relationships, I have common goals in my own intervention both within and without the court setting. However, these have to be approached and implemented in different ways depending on the context of the work.

Goals

- Moving from 'battleground' to co-operating around parenting the children as the primary task of involvement with one another (and with me).

- Moving from a single oppositional view of the other, to the development of a number of shared views on (a) how disputes around the children can be framed and thought about (b) solutions to parenting put 'on the table', and negotiated.

- A shift in the affective view of one or both parents towards the intentions and efforts of the other.

- A shift in developing joint understanding about how the child might be experiencing some of the emotional aspects of the relationship transitions taking place, the psychological and developmental needs of the child, and the fit between these and current parent–child interactions.

- The development of a new 'post separation story about family', and how parents and children relate to one another (descriptions of behaviours, ideas, and perceptions). This can be as educative, directive, imaginative and collaborative as parents can engage in, and is illustrated by parents, contributions from friends and family who have 'been through it', to current thinking as gleaned from newspapers, from celebrities' lives, 'soaps', plus my own dovetailing of 'professional' and life input.

I have used Dr Liz Trinder and colleagues' (2004 Family Law) paper to help clarify and distinguish in my own thinking some differences between the families she cites as using the court to sort out contact disputes, and the families I am asked to assess as an expert. The main distinguishing feature that appears is the length of time the disputes over contact have continued – the least being 2–3 years, and the most being over nine years.

An important feature to note in 50% of the families I see has been protracted mental health issues in one of the parents. These are not always psychiatrically 'labelled', but show in a variety of ways, complicating potential contact. They may lead the 'other' parent, and sometimes the child or children, to be viewed in ways that are distorted and in the case of children, developmentally inappropriate. The distinction between formal, diagnosed illness, and the unhealthy obsessive behaviour that can develop in the context of protracted contact applications is sometimes hard to make. Hostile pursuit of the other party in the form of abusive texting, monitoring and stalking, lengthy emails, and more worryingly threat of abduction, may not constitute 'illness', but carry their own persecuting weight and distortions for all parties involved.

Assertions of violence by one party (usually the party with residence, but not always), or acts of violence witnessed by the children, are also a feature of 50% of the families I have worked with. A distinction from the families in Dr Trinder's sample may be that the violence has become a core aspect of one parent's narrative about the other, dominating all other stories. Where this is also part of the children's story about a parent, and in some families part of the grandparents' story as well, it becomes harder for a parent seeking contact to create a new niche in their child's affections. Whereas in the clinical process it may be possible both to challenge the predominant story of violence, and to work with a father to create a safer context for the child, the court process does not usually allow time for such developments to be worked through.

In doing a rough and ready analysis of my two groups of 20+ cases seen in and out of court processes, I note that I have an apparent much higher success story with cases outwith the court. Out of 24 cases contact proceeded in all but three, usually because, however bitter or enraged, parents by coming have committed to try and sort working arrangements out. In the Court group I only recommended contact in 50% of families seen (all but one being contact with father). In my view it is a very sad thing not to recommend contact, and the reasons for doing so are usually related to either, 1) extreme behaviours that have become highly distressing to children, and cannot be mediated, or mitigated, 2) safety issues, 3) a failure, or lack of attachment from child or children to the parent seeking contact, or to a combination of these. I believe the third point, the failure of attachment in the child, may be under-recognised in the court process. Whereas a child may have once been attached to a parent who lived with them (however poor the relationship between the parents) their 'internal working model' of a parent may change in the deterioration of secure contact that follows a separation. A child's 'model' of a parent is responsive to input from real life experiences in an interactive relationships, and in young children the attachment to an 'out of house' parent cab become subordinated to a more secure attachment with the parent with whom they reside.

The court, in attempting to assess whether contact should be re-instigated, often allows a flexible interpretation of 'assessment', in which the possibility of proceeding to a supervised contact within the remit of the order, depending on the expert's therapeutic judgement as to the advisability and usefulness of this, can be part of the remit. Usually the allegations against the father by the mother have included violence, and sometimes in addition inappropriate sexualised behaviour, upon which it has not always been possible for the court to make a clear finding. In many of these cases separation between the parents took place before the child was three years old, and contact ceased before the child was five years old.

Whether it is a mental health or a violence issue if contact is proceeded to, supervision of parent-child interaction by the assessing person is in my view an essential feature of maintaining 'safety' in the minds of all concerned: the parent who is anxious about contact, the child themselves, but also for the parent who does not wish to be further 'accused'. Other components of parent-child interaction can then be looked at 'in vivo'.

In assessing whether there is a likelihood of a successful relationship being re-established I explore the following five issues:

(1) the way attachment is expressed by the parent seeking contact: is the attachment primarily directed towards the child or is it towards the former partner (which is sometimes the case)?

(2) the way in which attachment is expressed by the child towards the absent parent;

(3) the capacity of a father to work on understanding the potential effects of former or current bad behaviour, or violence in the parental relationship on the child, as well as on the mother's concerns about his own future contact with the child;

(4) the ability of both parents to work towards at least a minimal position of understanding of the other parent's position (intersubjective understanding) in the service of promoting the child's best interests in developing a relationship with both their parents in the future. [I note that Dr Trinder remarked how difficult her core group of parents found this];

(5) the child's 'wish' to reconnect (how have they held onto the out of house parent in their mind?).

THE FAMILY COURT PROCESSES AND THE 'EXPERT'

The context of assessment for the court, in families where there have been long-standing disputes, involves meeting with parents whose position regarding each other and the children's relationship with the 'other' parent has rigidified often over two to three years or more, in the context of allegations, refutations, affidavits and counter assertions; sworn statements of oppositional positions that have necessarily been taken in order to further a particular goal. The court process itself may become construed as essential to the preservation of some key definition of self as a good or bad parent. By implication the definition of the 'other parent' as good or bad has become part of this self-definition, and the child becomes in part a hostage to these parental self-definitions, often at the expense of their own development. The emphasis placed by the Children Act on the 'child's best interests' can be directly placed before each parent as an alternative position, strengthening the focus on the child but also as a free-standing 'metaposition' neutral to parental parties. The process authorised by the court is both time limited and has cost implications, and is in its construction open to scrutiny by all parties involved. In this pressured transparency there is a therapeutic possibility. The tension created lends itself both to more direct exploration and the posing of different kinds of possibility of thought and action for the parties to consider. Future-oriented questions inviting parents to consider the well being of the children in two years or five years' time; when they are old enough to seek a parent out for themselves, or when a current parent might find themselves in a new role as grandparent, assists in creating a longer term developmental perspective that can take some of the tension out of the current cramping preoccupation with achieving or preventing a goal of imminent contact. The ability of a parent to set aside their own grievances and consider the potentially different positions of their child in relation to the dispute, as well as the possible effects on the child of the dispute, is always a useful indicator of likely future dispute resolution.

THERAPEUTIC CHANGE

The court framework, though not one of 'therapy' as noted, does not preclude possibilities of emotional change developing. Three change issues that I would always try to build into the assessment process include:

- first, on my part an explicit expression of empathic understanding of the pain and passion experienced by a parent who has been cut off from their child;

- second, on the part of the parent seeking contact, increasing an understanding of children as unique beings who, while still dependant and developing, carry their own repertoires of making sense of the world around them, and then seeing where parents' understanding promotes, or hinders their goal of developing contact;

- third, developing each parent's ability to understand and interpret the behaviour of the other in terms of possible mental states underlying the behaviour or at least to develop willingness to attempt this.

These three processes combined with much greater attention to the effects of violent acts on a family system can all play a key part in negotiating successful contact.

LABELLING MUTUAL INFLUENCE

I have found that a systemic approach, in which the mutual influence of the parties involved is openly looked at, makes sense to a family in entrenched dispute.

For a father seeking contact a willingness to understand the child's mind necessarily will include an understanding of how children's thinking is likely to be linked to their mother's thinking (and maybe to the thinking of her extended family). To access the goodwill of his child, a father will necessarily need to take into account the child's capacity to work out father's own intentions towards and understanding of the child's mother. A child's readiness to meet with a long absent father is, in my experience, directly affected by the child's beliefs about how the father himself is holding both the child and his mother in mind. And even after one or two meetings the question of 'how he was horrible to my mum' can arise as a serious concern that has to be addressed.

YOUNG CHILDREN RETAINING POSITIVE MEMORIES

A problem for very young children in this situation is how to retain their own positive memories of their father. Where a mother has emphasised negative aspects of a father's behaviour or intentions to her children, consciously or unconsciously over the years, the children will need to have a legacy of good memories or a source of stories about the good aspects of a father to construct an alternative narrative that will take them through the anxieties attendant upon court proceedings to the meeting point itself. Similarly where a child has directly witnessed violent or verbally abusive behaviour from father to mother he will need a significantly different range of personal experiences of father inside himself to counteract the behaviour he has witnessed and the effects it has created. Many children may have such positive experiences from former living alongside their fathers, or from former contact; but such experiences may not be brought into the open in the child's own home. In the assessment process the complexity of these levels of feeling and knowing about both parents can be discussed in a more neutral way and the ambivalence children may feel towards a direct contact that they may simultaneously construe as disloyal to their mother be voiced.

YOUNG CHILDREN AND VIOLENT ACTS

Following many years of detailed research, which corroborates and amplifies clinical experience we now have greater understanding of the effects of marital conflict on children and their adjustment (Cummings and Davis (2002)). It is important to listen to the way children narrate the effect of specific stimuli in specific contexts (ie doorstep violence, letter box violence or kitchen sink violence); the specific characteristics of what has gone on (ie did father break a pane of glass); with what intention did he break it (violence to objects); did he break a corner cupboard which had mum's treasured tea set in it (violence towards loved objects); or did he break glass to threaten mum with it (violence towards the key loved person in the child's life). It is important to set the responses of children in the specific context of each child, their particular family history and prior histories of violence. The attributed or assigned meanings evolving from former violent episodes will affect the way the child perceives and interprets what is going on at the present time.

For illustration two families where father was seeking contact following a break in direct contact of three or more years are compared – the children aged 7 at the time of family assessment. In each case the mother and father separated when the child was under 3 and contact ceased when the child was less than 5. In each family the children had witnessed violent behaviour from their father towards their mother on more than one occasion prior to and following separation. However, family A and B differed in important aspects.

- In family A father could accept that this acts of violence could have had an effect on the children. In family B father both denied his own actions, and their potential effects.

- In family A father had a good relationship with his own family of origin. In family B father had experienced much deprivation and attachment. It was apparent that his 'capacity to mentalise' (to enter into an understanding of the state of mind of another) had been damaged by his own earlier experiences' (Fonagy (1999)).

The way in which the children subsequently assigned intention to their fathers' violent behaviour also differed in a number of ways; as did the alternative stories of positive experiences of life lived with their father before and after parental separation.

The effect on a child of any particular piece of conflict therefore relates to their former exposure to such episodes and their interpretations of these, as well as the current climate of available understanding they are living within. If we take an example of violence common to family A and B, the breaking of a pane of glass on the front door, Paul, who had been having regular contact with his father prior to this, was able to voice a belief, three years later, that his father had been angry at the time 'because his mother had not let him in to collect the children'. He could retain an idea, which held a positive intention by father to contextualise the violent episode. However a similar episode in family B was interpreted by Roseanne as one only of fear and threat: first, because her father had tricked her on a former occasion by getting her to give him the key through the letter box, following which he had 'burst in and flown at her mother'; second, because of the former episodes of threatening behaviour she had seen from her father to her mother; and third, because her expressed belief was that he might try to kidnap her, a belief based on threats he had uttered in temper on previous occasions. Children also note expressions of fear from either parent as particularly distressing, and whereas Paul's mother did not express fear, but rather anger, Roseanne's mother had acute anxiety attacks following episodes such as these.

FAMILY TALK ABOUT FATHER AND VIOLENT BEHAVIOUR

In reflecting on the goals that guide children's appraisals of violence between their parents, Cummings (2002) concluded that children form representations based on a composite perspective of the socio-emotional climate in the home in turn drawn from their experiences in multiple family systems. Thus what grannies, uncles and aunts say about what is going on can elaborate understanding or corroborate negative perspectives. In Paul's family a robust maternal grandmother took a general position that men could be rubbish (having divorced her own husband) but nonetheless maintained an alternative perspective on Paul's situation, as 'boys need their father when they're growing up'. Roseanne's grandmother not only maintained that Roseanne's dad was a threat to family security, but also gave several instances of how in her view he had never shown much loving to Roseanne, when he was still living in the home, describing episodes where he had smacked her, leaving her granny 'all of a tremble' To this view of the danger of fathers Roseanne added her own experience of watching *EastEnders*, describing her father as 'worse then C. who had put the iron on his wife'. The meanings or truths originally embedded in these family events, long past became hostage to the constructions put upon them by different family members and their narratives about the events repeated over time.

Negative appraisals and expectancies about what may take place in the future evolving from personal and extended family narratives about the past will inevitably fuel a child's negative reactions to a father seeking contact. The emotional arousal created by demands for contact and by court processes exploring earlier painful episodes full of violent emotion, may bring into current consciousness former cognitive negative representations of a father, and may motivate a child to reduce their own emotional arousal through avoidance strategies that help them cut off from painful feeling. Children often escape into other areas of their lives to avoid the topic of their absent parent but again there is variation in the degree to which they do this. Paul said 'I just get on with it…that's what most people do isn't it'; whereas Roseanne said with a greater show of agitation 'I won't look at a photo of him because of the bad dreams.' She refused to open cards or letters from her father or to receive birthday or Christmas presents, stating 'I don't want him to write "Daddy" on it because he was bad to Mummy and made her cry'. What she wanted to do was forget his presence in her life, adding 'Mum's got a new boyfriend now, and I feel safe. I want to get on with being part of this family.'

As we are talking about 'enduring models' I include a family vignette of a successfully mediated contact. This was child focused, used the court as a lever in negotiating fresh positions in entrenched disputes, and illustrates (hopefully) some of the points outlined above.

PAUL AND KELLY AND THEIR PARENTS TED AND ANNA

Paul and Kelly's parents separated when Paul was 3 years old, and contact with their father, Ted, began when Anna was still breastfeeding Kelly who was under a year old. A court order had been made for there to be overnight contact with father. Anna's anxiety about handing over her girl baby for overnight contact was acute and was likely to have been conveyed non-verbally to Paul as well as affecting her ability to calm and soothe Kelly. Neither parent had been prepared for it to be more difficult to effect such handovers, as Kelly got older, rather than less difficult.

> **Comment**: Solomon and George (1999) in a study of infants between 12 and 20 months found that conditions affecting their secure contact with fathers included the conditions of handover and return and the degree to which mother felt under threat from father and the effect this had on her own ability to soothe and comfort her infant.

Anna's experience of being rendered powerless on behalf of her own infant and her anger at having her pleasure in her baby daughter spoiled was powerfully expressed three years later. Her belief that Ted may have been harmful to Anna arose in the earlier context of this long mistrust of enforced contact procedures, and contact was broken off when Kelly was 18 months old and Paul 4½.

At the point of my involvement three years later Paul retained suppressed affectionate memories of his father. These were, however, in conflict with his observation of his mother's continued expressed anger with his father and his own memories of his parents being angry with each other at point of handover. He also feared that his father might have harmed his little sister because his mother appeared to believe this. Anna at this point in the court process alternated between agreeing that she may 'have been mistaken' and also asserting aloud that Paul would not want contact with his father if 'he believed his father had hurt his little sister'.

Discussing the court process

In placing myself in the lives of the children I established why in their minds, we were meeting. Paul thought we were meeting 'because the court said we should meet'. He then introduced the notion of 'justice' into our shared discourse. His mother took this up in terms of 'the judge had asked me [Gill] to get them to help it happen that they would see their dad again'.

> Comment: I have used the 'authority of the law' in different ways in different cases to create a new position from which each party can think. Thus the court process allowed the issue of 'meeting their dad' to be moved outside the personal domain of mother's control and sanctioned a joint endeavour between the children and me.

Paul took this forward in terms of the judge as 'someone who decides if wrong has been done and who decides what they are going to do about it'. On being asked, Paul 'did not think anyone in his family had done anything wrong', but agreed that 'someone might have thought so once'.

Paul described a particular incident on his birthday when he had not wished to leave his mother's house but his father had insisted that the time was 'due to him' and he had to leave the house kicking and screaming. He correctly dated this event to 30 months earlier. Other features of Paul's narrative included his protectiveness of his little sister in relation to his father's care of her. I introduced the subject of difficulty in looking after little babies and Paul allowed us to discuss the possibility of doubt in the attribution that his father had hurt Kelly: 'in looking after babies it might be possible that dad had been rough with Kelly and not meant to.' I then directly addressed Anna's expressed ambivalence contained in the statement that 'if Paul knew dad had hurt Kelly he would not want to see him', and asked Paul if he felt that his mother had given him permission to see his father. He indicated that he was not sure, so I invited Anna to repeat in the room what she said they had discussed in the car. Anna said clearly that 'she knew Ted loved Paul' and she thought Paul should feel he could see his dad whenever he wanted to.

> Comment: The value of such open statements in the court process is that they are spoken in the knowledge that they will become information for the other party: an issue, which is more ambiguous in the clinical process.

A letter from father to the children

Subsequently I invited Ted to write a letter to the children and enclose a range of photos of things they had done together. I suggested that he include an expression of any regret he might feel for harm that had been done to the children by the parental court proceedings as well as assurance of his continuing love for them. The photographs were intended to elicit memories of the times he had spent with them, which I believed might have been suppressed in their minds in the context of the subsequent acrimonious proceedings. The higher authority of the court as a place where things could be sorted out was once again referred to in this letter, as it had earlier been by Anna and by Paul. The combination of the letter and the photos evoked a very personal response from Paul, memories of his own, laughter and some wistfulness. At the end of that meeting he said he would like to meet his dad if I was there all the time. This meeting took place the following week fully supported by Anna. In this meeting the same photos acted as a bridge between the 'taboo' of a past when dad had been a legitimate part of the children's lives, a visual assurance that there had been good times with father, which did not need to be denied and led to a discussion about a shared possible future: 'maybe you could come and help me finish the pond in the garden/come and have a holiday in the caravan again next year.'

> Comment: It is important to note how powerful the taboos against loving memory can become in the minds of children. For all the reasons outlined above the powerful affect aroused by remembered experience in a context where such remembered experience seems to run contrary to the wishes and possibly the well being of the parent with whom the child has residence may make it easier to deny such a parent than maintain the wish to see them as a living reality.

In a subsequent meeting with Kelly, who now wanted to meet her dad because Paul had met him and there had been no negative effects in the mother's household, she was very active in trying to remember what he was like, although the only memory she could produce was that his 'chin was prickly'. My job at this point seemed to be to keep the possibility of a safe father alive in the room, given the three years of uncertainty she had lived through. I checked many times on this reality before I accepted that she would really like to meet her father, double checking on the fact that mother's wishes might still influence her one way or the other, taking into account the 'other' in the child's mind: 'If I am talking to mummy and she asks me about whether you want to see daddy if I am here with you, am I still to say you said "yes".' Thus throughout I took into account the presence of the 'other parent' in the child's mind.

The meeting took place the following week and it was as though it had only been the previous week they had parted, with a warm physical contact initiated and reciprocated on both sides in an appropriate and direct manner. Contact continued initially supervised by me, and then by a local specialist contact centre, and a joint meeting between mother, father, and myself then took place. This is described in some detail so aspects of 'what works for whom' can be discussed.

Meeting between Anna and Ted

I began with some introductory remarks expressing my pleasure that we had managed to meet together and that the parents had been prepared to set aside their grievances to focus on planning for the future. I stated my belief the we could make plans that would be the easiest and the best from the children's point of view, that avoided the children feeling caught in the middle, whether geographically or in their minds, and referred them to the time in my early meetings with Paul, when Paul had showed me a picture where a little child felt pulled in half on Christmas Day. Each parent had prepared a list of issues they wanted to see resolved. In summary the issues that we all wanted to resolve included:

- how contact would take place in the future;
- the amount of time that Ted wanted to be involved in his children's lives;
- how practical communication could best be established between mother and father (telephone numbers, fallback numbers, fax);
- how changes of arrangements could be dealt with;
- how direct contact between the parents could be set up quickly in the case of an emergency, or a need for information;
- and, as I put it, 'things affecting the children's lives where either of them might want the help of the other'.

Summary of key aspects of the progress of the meeting; establishing and building on positive mutual experience

Anna created a positive track by reassuring Ted that she would always promote contact as she could now see that this was for the children's benefit.

Ted responded that he 'did not wish to be inflexible'. Should Paul or Kelly not wish to come on any occasion he would not want to 'push it'.

Anna in turn responded to Ted positively. She asserted that she did not 'bad-mouth him'. She added 'I never have and I never will'. Ted in turn confirmed a similar attitude on his part (both were 'bending the truth' in the best interests of their children).

The build-up of mutually positive reciprocal influence led to a change in tempo in which the parents took over the momentum of the meeting. Anna suddenly confided to Ted 'I have been thinking what it must be like for the children to pass your gate when they go shopping on Saturdays, and to feel that they can't go in. I would like them to feel that they could pop in at any time.' She said she hoped that such a point might be reached. Ted added, 'I would like to see a normalisation of our lives so that we can be civil to each other, then we could risk it.'

I asked 'what a normalisation of their lives would look like. What would it mean in terms of changes of behaviour?' Anna and Ted agreed that the problem was that either of them could become intractable if there was a problem that they had different views about, so it was unlikely that too much informality would develop. Anna expressed her underlying fear that Ted was trying to take the children away. She assured Ted that she was not trying to run the children's lives, and that she recognised that what he wanted was more involvement. Ted reassured Anna that he was *not* trying to take the children away from her: 'I'm there to be their father, it's part of their entitlement to know their father. All I want them to be is comfortable with me in my house.'

Continuing the theme of 'normalisation' we proceeded to discuss overnight stays, holidays, place and timing, taking into account the different ages of the children. We also discussed the freedom to ring one parent when with the other, and added this to a developing 'list of good parenting practice'; 'When you are in one parent's house you can always ring your other parent'.

They then engaged in a long discussion about school issues, which they agreed to resolve together. Anna also raised other issues that if one of the children were ill and did not want to visit would Ted think that it was she that was trying to block contact. She felt that she was often criticised by him and given 'lists of things that she had done wrong'. Ted in turn said that he hoped that Anna did not feel that he was 'steamrollering' her into contact. Anna replied that she did not think that, but she continued to fear that Ted would be 'nagging' her about a list of things that she was doing badly as a mother. Ted agreed that he would *not* do this. He said: 'I am not going to catch the children in any crossfire. It is not fair to them.' (It had taken all of a year to reach this position.) Anna commented humorously to me 'We will never be in each other's fan club!', and I responded that 'nonetheless you each need to hear positive comments from the other inside your own head'. Anna concurred with this, saying 'it may be more important to have such comments inside one's head than to hear them outside'.

In a very helpful judgement, Dame Elizabeth Butler-Sloss from the Court of Appeal, adjudicating on four contact appeals, laid out again factors relating to contact applications. They were a summary of many previous judgements, and drew out the principles on which the restoration of contact in cases where children have been affected by an exposure to high acrimony or violence are based:

> 'The Children Act draws attention to the centrality of the child, and the promotion of his or her mental health and well-being as the central issues amid tensions surrounding adults in dispute. The purpose of contact must be clear, and have a potential for benefiting the child in some way. The risk of promoting direct contact includes the risk of increase of the climate of conflict around the child, which might undermine the child's general stability and sense of emotional well-being. Research indicates that even where children do not continue in a situation where there have been high negative emotional behaviours, emotional trauma can continue to be experienced from preceding high conflict situations.'

In the family B cited briefly earlier, no progress to contact could be made. The possibility of a 'transformative process' in which the qualitative changes in the stories one person (the child) heard and held about another person (her father) could not be made in spite of the work of a third party, myself. The father's attempts to move towards more understanding of his daughter's position came too late in her narrative of repeated frightening episodes to make a difference to her beliefs. Her attachment to him had been overlaid by her fears for her mother, as well as her current positive experience of safety with her mother's new live-in boyfriend.

SUMMARY

Key features for the instigation of successful contact following lengthy breakdown therefore includes in my view:

- The importance of being child-led with regard to developing positive mutual influence in potential contact arrangements, rather than a parent pushing too fast for too much contact.
- The importance for the 'assessor' of keeping old parental patterns of arguments, and fights, at a lower order of importance in the parents' minds than the goal of promoting the best interests of the child in the future.
- The importance of parents being able to respond positively to the children talking about the other parent (positive connotation of the other parent in the mind of the child).

- The creation of a context of safety for a new child-centred parenting pattern to be developed (ie a specialist contact centre where supervision of the contact can be written up as part of the court process).

- The need to remain as a stabilising aspect of the newly-formed post-divorce family system until parents are ready to maintain that pattern themselves, or with the use of local resources.

I would suggest that for this group of families a court service more trained in principles of working with families (not just couples) is essential. This service needs to be interventionist, robust, and developmentally educative. In my allotted 10 minutes I will present possible components of training for such a service, and hope the wisdom of the conference can be brought to bear on how such a service might be developed.

REFERENCES

Byrne, JG, O'Connor, TG, Marvin, RS & Wheelan, WF 'The Contribution of Attachment Theory to Child Custody Assessment' (2005) 46.2 Journal of Child Psychology and Psychiatry 115–127

Cummings, EM & Davies, PT 'Effects of Marital Conflict on Children: recent advances and emerging theses in process oriented research' (2002) 43.1 Journal of Child Psychology and Psychiatry 31–63

Dowling, E and Gorell Barnes, G Working with Children and Parents through Separation and Divorce (Basingstoke, Palgrave, 1999)

Dunn, J, Davies, LC, & O'Connor, T 'Parents & Partners, Life Course & Family Experiences: links with parent child relationships in different family settings' (2000) 41.8 Journal of Child Psychology & Psychiatry 955–968

Dunn, J 'Children's development & readjustment in different family settings' in W Yule (ed) *Child Mental Health in Europe'. Occasional papers No 7* (2001) 17.4 Association of Child Psychology & Psychiatry 154–61

Dunn, J 'Contact and Children's perspectives on parental relationships' in A Birnbaum, B Lindley, M Richards, & L Trinder (eds) *Children and their Families: Contact, Rights & Welfare* (Oxford, Hart, 2003)

Dunn, J, Cheng, H, O'Connor, TG, & Bridges, L 'Childcare Relationships with their Non-resident Partners: influences, outcomes, and implications' (2004) 45 Journal of Child Psychology & Psychiatry 553–566

Gorell Barnes, G, Thompson, P, Daniel, G, & Burchardt, N *Growing Up in Stepfamilies* (Oxford, Clarendon Press, 1998)

Gorell Barnes, G *Family Therapy in Changing Times* (Palgrave: Macmillan, 2004)

Gorell Barnes, G. 'Narratives of Attachment in Post-divorce Contact Disputes' in E Dowling & A Vetere (eds) *Narrative Therapies with Children.* (2005)

Hill, J, Fonagy, P, Safier, E, Sargent, J 'The Ecology of Attachment in the Family' (2003) 42.2 Family Process 205–221

Hunt, J, Roberts, C 'Child Contact with non-resident parents' (2004) Family Policy Briefing 3 (University of Oxford Department of Social Policy & Social Work, Barrett House, Oxford)

Moffitt, TE & Caspi, A Here 'Implications of Violence between Intimate Partners for Child Psychologists and Psychiatrists' (1994) 39.2 Journal of Child Psychology & Psychiatry 137–144

Solomon, J, & George, C 'The Development of Attachment in Separated and Divorced Couples: effects of overnight visitation, parent and couple variables' (1999) 1.1 Attachment & Human Development 2–33

Trinder, L, Connolly, J, Kellett, J, & Taoday, C 'Families in Contact Disputes: a profile' (2004) 34 Family Law 877–881

Trinder, L, Beek, M, & Connolly, J Making Contact: how parents and children negotiate & experience contact after divorce (Joseph Rowntree Foundation, 2002)

EARLY INTERVENTIONS
AN ALTERNATIVE TO CONTACT DISPUTES IN PRIVATE LAW FAMILY PROCEEDINGS

Nicholas Crichton
District Judge (Magistrates' Courts)

DJ Crichton began at the end of his paper where he mentioned that he would meet with a government minister in September to seek funding for the pilot project to be continued. DJ Crichton has now met with the minister. DJ Crichton explained that £350,000 has already been spent on the set up costs of the project and the costs to continue it would be much less. The minister said she would consider the position but has now decided not to continue to finance the project, so sadly the plug has been pulled.

The project was based on the provision of information to parents. The parents attended the first session in groups and began by watching a video. The project had hoped to have real parents and children in the video but this was not possible and actors were used as an alternative. This worked well with the video showing firstly scenes of the parents arguing, with the children in the background; secondly, the day the father left the family home; and finally a scene one month later when the father returns to visit the children, arrives late and upsets the children. The video is stopped at each break in time and a panel of children are invited to comment. Their comments are very telling.

The parents then engaged in a discussion about what they had seen and were given firm advice by the facilitator about their responsibility to meet the emotional needs of their children at what was a very difficult time for the children as well as for themselves. They were then asked to go away and think about the video and then come back to discuss further at a second group session. This provided a robust focus on the emotional needs of children. DJ Crichton had observed the training of facilitators. It was a fascinating experience to persuade women to role play in the part of fathers and vice versa and gave parents an insight into the views and difficulties of the other parent. A third meeting then took place between the parents and the CAFCASS officer.

DJ Crichton thought that it was a pity that the project has been brought to an end and believed that an opportunity has been missed. One difficulty was that a disappointing number of cases came into the project. This was because the project could not be made compulsory. However it was beginning to work for those that did come into the project. DJ Crichton had been concerned as to what different ethnic groups might make of the project. When a Muslim family came into his court asking him to endorse their agreed order he took the opportunity to ask what had been their experience of the process. Their response was that they thought it had been excellent. It had helped them both to understand the emotional needs of children and had enabled them to reach agreement. This had been echoed by a number of anecdotal experiences. Dr Liz Trinder has conducted more extensive research into this but the results will not be publicly available until the research is published in January.

On a more positive note, all may not be lost! Hedley J is seeking to develop a similar project in North Wales using some of the material made for this pilot project. It is hoped the Welsh project will enjoy better support from practitioners.

In really difficult cases, where early intervention is not successful, it is apparent that cases must have the same tribunal if parents are required to come to court several times. Judicial continuity enables the parents to gain trust and confidence in the system.

Finally DJ Crichton wanted to mention a drugs project in which he was involved. Some at the conference had already seen the video from California. DJ Crichton was seeking to establish this project at Wells Street. However as a result of the bad experience with funding in the pilot project he was seeking to secure his own funding for the drugs project. He had raised £40,000 of private funding and the project is to be set up under the influence of a steering group. He hopes to be able to report back in two years time on a more successful project.

THE PAPER

'Emerging social and psychological research had long told the legislature and courts that in most cases children need both parents; and that, if they have more frequent contact, children grow up healthier, better adjusted, more successful with better self-concept. They themselves make better parents. Experience showed that the traditional adversarial judicial process was detrimental to children; it drove parents farther apart at a time when their children needed them to work together to restructure their system of parenting.' (Judge John C Lenderman, Circuit Judge, Sixth Judicial Circuit of Florida)

In 2001 Dr Hamish Cameron, a consultant child psychiatrist who will be known to many of you, asked me to chair a working group whose object was to consider initiatives being taken in other parts of the world in an effort to move away from the adversarial approach to resolving contact disputes between divorcing and separating parents. Two successful conferences were held, the first in March 2002 chaired by Dame Margaret Booth, the second in April 2003 chaired by Joyanne Bracewell J at which Judge John Lenderman from Florida gave a presentation.

In October 2003 the group produced an 'advice' paper which it delivered to the Department for Constitutional Affairs and to the Department for Education and Skills. I do not think that I can do better than attach to this paper a copy of that 'advice' paper. It was the hope of the working group that a pilot scheme based on our proposal might represent a step towards a change in the culture in which these problems are addressed. Too much court time is spent arguing about whether contact should take place every week or every two weeks; whether it should be for two hours or three hours; what should be the handover arrangements; etc etc. It had been our hope that a culture would develop in which courts would expect that, unless there were good reasons to the contrary, children should see their fathers for as much as half of their 'free' time, ie alternate weekends and half of all school holidays. Ideally weekends would mean Friday night to Monday morning, with father collecting from and returning to school, feeding and doing the laundry, helping with homework, as well as providing treats. In suitable cases the children might have contact on one evening per week, father cooking a meal and helping with homework before returning them to mother. Of course there could be many reasons, including work and geography, which might make such arrangements impractical, but if such a norm could be established then it could be adjusted to meet the individual case.

DCA and DfES consulted widely, and DfES took on responsibility for building the pilot project which was to run at the Inner London Family Proceedings Court at Wells Street, and at Brighton and Sunderland county courts. A small steering group was set up, whose membership included Joyanne Bracewell J. A larger design group was set up, chaired by Mavis McLean. Initially only the CAFCASS officer who served on the working group was invited to join the design group. Eventually (with assistance from the then President!) I was invited to join the design group. I was concerned about the weight of departmental civil servants' representation on the group. I asked that one or two more members of the working group should be asked to join. That was denied. I felt that the group should include more people who understood the nature of the work 'on the ground' and its difficulties and, perhaps foolishly, asked that the group should contain more people who 'have the passion'. I was told that the whole object was to 'steam roller out the passion'. Not a good omen!

Throughout England and Wales there are many initiatives involving in-court conciliation. Most, if not all, involve advice and conciliation given for anything between 20 minutes and 1 hour at the door of the court. I am not aware of any research which tells for how long agreements reached in such circumstances hold good. The Early Intervention Project attempts to provide information for parents, together with the time to reflect. The pilot envisaged parents attending two group sessions, meeting with and engaging in discussion with others (both mothers and fathers) in similar situations. They would not attend the same sessions. At the first session they would see a video illustrating children's perceptions and experiences at the time when their parents' marriage or relationship breaks down and their family disintegrates. They would be expected to enter into discussion about their children's needs at this time. In the second group session, to take place approximately two weeks later, they would start thinking about the process of communication and negotiation, and managing conflict. This session includes role play. Finally the individual couple would attend a family resolution session at which they try to come to an agreement which would best meet the needs of their children. At this session they are asked to ask themselves what they want their children to remember from this time in their lives.

In London the two group sessions are run by workers from Relate, and from the Parenting Education and Support Forum. The final family resolution session is run by CAFCASS. In Sunderland and Brighton all the sessions are run by CAFCASS.

The object is to help parents find ways of reducing the conflict between them and to focus on the needs of their children at a difficult time in their lives; and to find solutions for these problems much more quickly than is likely to occur in protracted court proceedings. If at any time during the process parents do reach agreement they can withdraw from the Project. They can present their agreement to be endorsed by the court in a formal court order, or they can agree that an order will not be necessary.

The pilot project was launched as the Family Resolutions Pilot Project in September 2004. It was expected to last for one year. A research element was built in, Dr Liz Trinder being commissioned to undertake the research. She will have the up-to-date figures, but take-up on the project has been extremely disappointing. We had hoped that approximately 1000 cases would come into the project during the course of the year. In fact there have been fewer than 60. I discuss the reasons in a moment. Nevertheless, the indications are that for those families who have gone through the process it has been successful.

As I write this (mid-August 2005) the indications are that DfES will not extend the project beyond the end of September. I am still hoping to persuade them to reconsider, and expect to have a meeting with a junior minister early in September. I believe that we have learned much and that there are steps which can be taken to improve the take-up and to demonstrate more clearly the potential of this project.

I have spoken to those involved with the project at Brighton and Sunderland. The reasons identified for our disappointing showing are common to all three sites:

- Without consultation DfES changed the name from *Early Intervention* to *Family Resolutions*. The working group had involved and had connections with people from various pressure groups who where interested and supportive. When the name was changed they assumed that DfES had changed the nature of the project and they became disillusioned and obstructive.

- DfES had announced that the project would commence in September. In fact it was not ready, and I urged them to postpone. They would not. In particular I was anxious that we should hold events to which solicitors and barristers would be invited in order that we could explain the project and hopefully obtain their support. I had urged this from the outset, but it did not happen save for a hurriedly arranged meeting attended by 10 or 12 solicitors. Without the support of practitioners I could not see how the project could succeed. In March

2005 we did manage to hold such an event at Wells Street at which practitioners expressed interest and surprise that they had not previously been aware of the existence of the project!

- There was a problem with public funding (legal aid). It is a requirement that solicitors refer clients to a mediator before a public funding certificate is granted. Having established that they did not think that mediation was for them, clients felt that the project was offering them more of the same.

- Entry into the project is not compulsory. In Florida parties do not have access to the court process unless or until they have been through the Early Intervention Programme.

- As a result we have never achieved the critical mass that would make the group sessions work as we had hoped. The group sessions have been held in the evenings. We had hoped to hold them at different times of the day to suit parents' differing needs, but to do that we needed more people coming into the programme. Further, it had been hoped that the project would provide a quicker resolution than court proceedings. Again, because we did not have enough people coming into the project, we could not hold the group sessions as frequently as was hoped, and the process has therefore taken longer – sometimes as long as a contested case.

- Relate take a very purist attitude to the issues of domestic violence. The project has sought to screen out serious domestic violence cases. However, there has been a clash of opinion, Relate believing that any instance of violence should disqualify.

- Whether or not they are connected, there has been a fall in the number of applications made to the Inner London Family Proceedings Court, and at the same time an increase in the number of applications made to the PRFD!

After so much work results from the project have been a disappointment. However, there have been significant successes for those who have entered the project. I believe that we have learned and that the set-up costs will have been wasted if we are unable to continue for at least another year. Senior District Judge Waller and his colleagues at the PRFD have indicated that if DfES would be willing to extend the project, they would be willing to transfer cases from the PRFD to Wells Street in order to bolster the number of cases eligible. This, and other suggestions, will be put to the minister at the beginning of September.

EARLY INTERVENTIONS
AN ALTERNATIVE TO CONTACT DISPUTES IN PRIVATE LAW FAMILY PROCEEDINGS – A PROPOSED PILOT

INTRODUCTION

This 'advice' paper on a proposed pilot for the early resolution of private law family disputes is forwarded to the Department for Constitutional Affairs and the Department for Education and Skills, in response to a request from departmental officials. It has been prepared by a pre-planning group representing agencies concerned with child welfare and representation, mediation, child mental health and social research, chaired by District Judge Nicholas Crichton of the Inner London Family Proceedings Court.

A two-stage process is envisaged:

(1) departmental approval is invited in principle;

(2) subject to the above, a steering group will be formed to submit a formal proposal for the pilot scheme.

The pre-planning group was set up in recognition of the success of similar schemes in other jurisdictions – notably Australia, New Zealand, the United States of America and Scandinavian countries, where they have successfully operated for 20 years. The group's aim has been to devise a viable pilot scheme for the introduction and development of this work in England and Wales that will be informed by those schemes.

During the past two years, public seminars highlighting international perspectives on family dispute resolution have attracted significant support among the senior judiciary, Family Bar and Family Law practitioners. The pre-planning group has made particular reference to the process described by Judge John C Lenderman, of the Sixth Judicial Circuit of Florida (see Appendix 1).

Of equal interest has been the family dispute resolution initiative being developed by the Children and Family Court Advisory and Support Service (CAFCASS), in discussion with the Court Service, Lord Chancellor's Department and mediation agencies. Participants have expressed active interest in working in partnership on further development, although funding has not been secured to undertake this. It is nonetheless clear that an integrated scheme would have broad support.

The rationale of the proposed pilot will be to link the understanding from the above and introduce to this jurisdiction a conceptually new, integrated, collaborative, child-centred scheme, to ameliorate post-separation parental discord about children and sustain the child's family ties.

A FLAWED SYSTEM

There is growing momentum among professionals and others concerned with child contact and residence disputes to seek more effective and efficient ways of helping families resolve their differences than is presently achieved by formal court proceedings. It is apparent that the traditional adversarial approach can drive parents further apart at the very time when their children most need them to work together, and that prolonged interruptions in contact are likely to impair a child's relationship with their non-resident parent, to the detriment of both. The principal conclusions reached by the Children Act Sub-Committee of the Advisory Board on Family Law in its report on contact[1] acknowledged the unsatisfactory nature of adversarial proceedings in resolving contact applications; the desirability of promoting alternative procedures for facilitating contact; and the great need for better provision of information to parents.

The courts and difficult cases

The judicial perspective on contact disputes can be summed up in the words of Wall J:

> ' . . . A striking aspect of difficult contact cases is the apparent irrationality of the parents'behaviour . . . The risk in this situation is of course that both lawyers and the judge tend to treat the symptoms and not the illness. It is easy to lose patience ... We are realising more and more that, although the court, as the only body able to impose contact on a reluctant residential parent, undoubtedly has an important role to play, the adversarial court system is not well suited to contact disputes, and the powers of facilitation and enforcement currently available to the court are limited and were not designed to deal with breaches of contact orders.'[2]

Bracewell J further adds: 'Usually these contact cases are publicly funded. They are immensely expensive, they produce very little result; they clog up the courts' (Contact Dispute Resolution seminar, April 2003, see Appendix 1).

Campaigning groups

Consumer groups are increasingly strident in promoting their grievances against the family justice system:

(1) Those concerned with domestic abuse believe that parents with safety concerns are not sufficiently listened to, are not given sufficient information about what they can do and that current procedures are inadequate and can leave children and resident parents in unsupported situations involving risk.

(2) Those who believe the system compounds insufficient contact campaign against what they see as intractable resident parents and ineffective action by the courts, not only for the establishment of contact, but to ensure contact is sufficient to enable non-resident parents to share qualitatively in the parenting of their children.

(3) Children are perceived as having no voice in these disputes.

Despite the polarised views, valid concerns are being expressed and need to be heeded.

The role of CAFCASS

In 2001, CAFCASS took over the in-court dispute resolution work previously undertaken by court welfare officers. CAFCASS believes that past development of this work was hindered by organisations that had their priorities elsewhere; support was lacking and featured insufficient training and wide variations in practice, not always updated by research. Critics often complained that these interventions seemed more concerned with reducing court workloads than with assisting families. In the year to March 2003, CAFCASS practitioners spent approximately 51,000 hours 'intervening' at directions appointments, and completed 42,000 pieces of work. The Magistrates Court Service Inspectorate will publish a final report in autumn 2003 on its

---

[1]   'Making Contact Work – A Report to the Lord Chancellor,' (LCD, 2002).

[2]   'Making Contact Work,' a paper by Wall J for the joint Association of Lawyers for Children, Solicitors Family Law Association and Family Law Bar Association Conference (February 2003).

thematic review of in-court dispute resolution, as currently conducted, but among its preliminary findings are:

- there is a variety of practice
- courts are the customers of current schemes, the family is secondary
- time pressured sessions are of doubtful efficacy
- few examples of practice standards, training or monitoring
- outcomes unclear
- children not included
- no/little client feedback.

CAFCASS is aware that its practitioners have considerable experience and skill in dispute resolution with intractable cases and that this work needs developing to fully utilise and advance that skill. The essential purpose of all such activity is to improve the outcome for the child. The evidence is that the conflict and delays inherent in adversarial proceedings harm the child. CAFCASS and the judiciary believe that there is a link between provision of current in-court dispute resolution and fewer requests for welfare reports. It follows that an improved, more available service is likely to assist more families to find better, longer lasting solutions to their difficulties than at present. In other words, earlier, properly targeted resources should lead to fewer less satisfactory, more expensive proceedings later. Evidence from other jurisdictions indicates that a service improved in this way should lead to substantial economic savings.

The current widespread interest in early interventions schemes can be harnessed to develop high quality provision with multi-agency input and support. With suitable piloting and external evaluation a new, effective service can be established and deployed across England and Wales in an integrated, systematic way.

THE NEW APPROACH

Experience has shown that the majority of parents who are helped in the initial stages of litigation to focus on their children can devise a viable, child-centred co-parenting plan, without recourse to a formal court hearing, despite their animosity towards each other. A properly designed, family-oriented dispute resolution scheme will achieve this by:

(1) promotion of an integrated scheme through a strong partnership between courts and associated statutory and voluntary organisations;

(2) safeguarding children from the risks of domestic violence and abuse and from the adverse effects of their parents' conflict through good quality screening and risk assessment;

(3) providing well-presented relevant information and guidance in planning for shared parenting, as well as ongoing support.

The pilot project represents a major advance from previous practice in conceptual terms. The focus is above all on helping families. The following principles are inherent in the scheme:

- Children need and benefit from positive relationships with both their parents, particularly following separation or divorce. Parenting is more than simply 'seeing' a parent, but is about children benefiting from the significant participation of both parents in their lives.

- Children have the right to a relationship with both their parents where that is safe and in the interests of the child.

- Children should have the opportunity to be heard. [3]

- Most parents on separating can and do reach agreement on the future arrangements for their children, without recourse to the courts, and this should be encouraged as the norm.

- Families need to be properly informed with key information about court processes, principles applied in deciding disputes, support services available, and the needs of children during and after separation.

- Interventions need to be timely and not add to delay.

EARLY INTERVENTIONS

These are the key elements of the scheme (see flowchart). At any stage parents who agree a parenting plan may exit the system.

Diversion to the scheme at application stage

When parents file a private law application concerning children, the court lists for hearing six weeks ahead, sends information about the scheme and makes immediate referral.

Screening for domestic violence/abuse

A court-directed sift of paperwork will be made at the referral stage, and risk assessment will be undertaken when parents are seen. Where appropriate, parents will be referred for prompt judicial findings of fact before further work is undertaken.

Parent information/skills building sessions

Shortly after referral, parents will separately attend two group sessions, that may be set up in conjunction with an external provider, each lasting about three hours:

(1) An information session on research findings and practice experience relating to post-separation contact, court processes and children's needs. The emphasis will be on providing information about co-parenting after separation and will include a video illustrating children's perceptions and experiences. Parents will be given advice on preparing their parenting plan.

(2) A skills session, focusing on strategies for communicating with each other, adjusting to new relationships, negotiating arrangements for their children, and managing conflict.

Family resolution session

This 1½ hour session for individual couples will follow later and focus on making an agreed, time-tabled plan for their child/ren's future co-parenting. Allowance might be made for a second session to complete the discussion and/or for children to participate or have their views represented. This session will be provided by suitably experienced and prepared CAFCASS practitioners. If agreement is not reached, there may be onward referral to a range of services, including extended mediation, child counselling or therapeutic parental work.

---

[3]   Findings from research emphasise that a 'mediatory approach' tends to focus on parental disputes, rather than the needs of children; that children have a desire to be informed and involved in the process; that the consequences of poor parent relationships are extremely difficult for children to manage.

Outcomes

When cases leave the process prematurely; are resolved but need a consent order; or where there is failure to agree, a brief professional report will be prepared for the judge, setting out the position and advising on any areas needing attention/action. If the matter is resolved and a consent order is not required, the hearing is vacated. Where there is no agreement, the matter proceeds to directions and trial in the usual way.

To allow for a realistic evaluation of both process and outcome, the pilot should ideally be for one year and possibly be based in three areas with differing characteristics. Three potential bases have been identified in different geographical locations. These judicially-led pilots will need to be aligned with selected local CAFCASS teams. All first (as opposed to repeat) applications would be referred to the scheme. It is suggested that at least 150 referrals would be needed to enable useful evaluation. Inner London Family Proceedings Court is willing to participate in the pilot, and has approximately 10 new applications each week. It is reasonable to assume that if 10 referrals are made weekly in each of the three areas chosen for the pilot, over a thousand cases could be processed during the pilot year.

RESEARCH AND EVALUATION

External evaluation by an independent researcher is essential. A part-time, or possibly full-time, researcher will be necessary. Expert consultancy will be needed in three areas:

(1) advice on setting up and establishing the project structure, ensuring clarity on project aims and objectives;

(2) assistance in establishing data collection systems and ensuring their satisfactory operation;

(3) analysis of data, sample interviews and preparation of an independent report on findings.

PRELIMINARY COSTING

These figures are suggested approximations for a one-year pilot in three locations (Note: there will be some offset in relation to in-court work already done, but this has not been included in these preliminary figures):

Six part-time CAFCASS practitioners (£28,000 + 19% oncosts + 14% for admin support, accommodation per full-time practitioner)	=	£111,720
Half-time scheme manager (£32k + 19% + 14% full-time)	=	£21,280
Transport and subsistence	=	£7,560
Research consultancy	=	£60,000
Video	=	£9,000
Estimates for parenting information/skills groupwork @ £25 per hour per parent (not inc venue hire, crèche & transport costs). Based on a group of 16 unrelated parents per week (after screening/dropouts) for 3 hour sessions x 2 (note: this will need to go for tender)	=	£110,400

Publicity: 1x leaflet (draft, test, edit, design & print) 10,000 copies   =   £13,000

Above does not include referrals to other services (some of which,
such as mediation & contact, might already be covered in CAFCASS
partnership funding), training/preparation and additional printed
material.

Total   =   £332,960

FLOWCHART: FAMILY RESOLUTIONS PILOT

A new approach to resolving (contact) applications in private law aimed at:

- developing 'therapeutic justice' tools for more effective judicial intervention;
- providing information to help families understand their situation, the processes involved in formal proceedings and their children's needs;
- offering children an opportunity to have a voice in the decision-making;
- providing information on/referral to other services which can assist;
- doing the above at a child-centred pace rather than yielding to court schedules.

*   *Early Interventions Pilot*

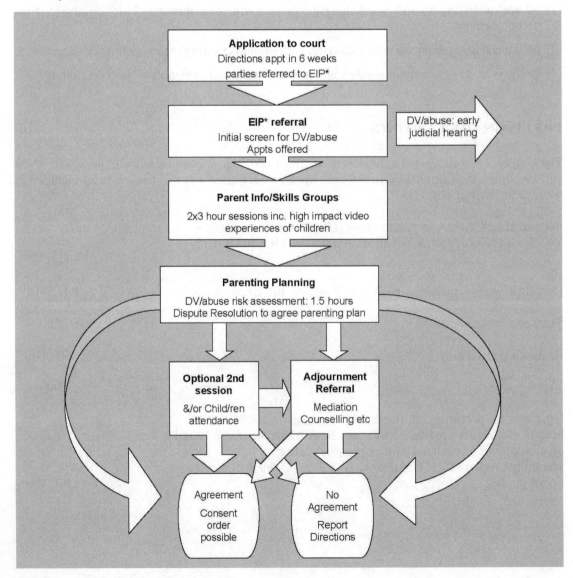

APPENDIX 1

'Contact Dispute Resolution: Early Interventions – Towards a Pilot Project', chaired by The Honourable Mrs Justice Bracewell, DBE, 10 April 2003, at Hardwicke Building, Lincoln's Inn, London

APPENDIX 2
EARLY INTERVENTIONS PILOT PROJECT

Pre-planning group members

District Judge Nicholas Crichton (chair)	Inner London Family Proceedings Court
Dr. Hamish Cameron	Consultant Child Psychiatrist
Audrey Damazer	Clerk to Justices, ILFPC
Diane Elliott	Institute of Family Therapy
Joan Hunt	Family Policy Unit, School of Social Policy, University of Oxford
Brian Kirby	Partnerships Manager, CAFCASS
Ruth Smallacombe	Mediator, Family Law in Partnership
Jonathan Tross	Chief Executive, CAFCASS
Veronica Carter (reporter)	Formerly Chief Clerk, Official Solicitor's Department

Issues for Consideration by the Steering Group

The following questions arose in pre-planning group meetings, but were considered more appropriate for the Steering Group, when appointed, to address:

(1) criteria for selecting the pilot area(s);

(2) what materials to prepare to (a) publicise and explain the scheme to professionals; and (b) inform parents (and children?) about co-parenting planning;

(3) how to secure the support of local lawyers in the selected pilot areas. What are the implications for public funding (legal aid), bearing in mind the present requirement for negotiation before filing court proceedings?

(4) how to screen cases involving a risk to a parent and/or child(ren);

(5) should the parenting education programme comprise two sessions: (i) information, and (ii) skills; if so, should the second session be optional;

(6) should the family resolution session be privileged, or should a post-session report, with recommendations, be made to the court where agreement has not been reached (i.e. non-privileged);

(7) to what extent should children be involved;

(8) what ongoing support should be made available to families in problematic cases;

(9) the creation of a suitable video about family restructuring;

(10) systems design, research and evaluation: the appointment of an expert, also the extent of supervision necessary to ensure Early Interventions protocol is followed;

(11) participating agencies; whether the pilot should be Court- or CAFCASS-led;

(12)   terminology: parent education/orientation; family resolution/mediation; contact/co-parenting; parenting planning/ADR family restructuring, etc;

(13)   detailed costings.

WORKING WITH DIFFICULT COUPLES IN THE FAMILY JUSTICE SYSTEM

Dr Christopher Clulow
Director, Tavistock Centre for Couple Relationships

INTRODUCTION

One thing I have learned from working with couples, difficult or otherwise, is that people undergoing identical experiences will represent those experiences in different ways. Evidence for this is likely to have been provided by differences between what individual members remembered as important from the previous day's small group discussions and the reports of those discussions from their delegated representatives. I am attached to the aphorism that 'it is not what happens to be people that is important but what they think happens to them'. What really matters is not some externally agreed objective reality but the internal constructions of experience that reflect subjective states of mind. A question posed by Professor Judith Masson at the start of the conference as to what lay at the heart of the family justice system – children, parents, families, court systems, the law? – is likely to be answered in ways that reflect professional identities and personal predilection. So here are two points that indicate my position, which may or may not accord with yours, but reflect a reality based on professional experience and, no doubt, personal prejudice:

(1) The family justice system is centrally engaged in shaping emotional experience, whether it intends to or not.

(2) However important the voice of the child is, parents provide the key to durable solutions. Only if they are unable and cannot be assisted to act in that capacity has someone else to step in.

'Durable Solutions' is a problematic title that sits uneasily with the realities of the human predicament, where things are seldom resolved once and for all. Family relationships change, and need to change, if there is to be development. Yesterday's solutions may not work well today and could constitute tomorrow's problems. Families, and those involved with them, are part of an unfolding process. 'You cannot step into the same river twice', the saying goes; things move on, and the very act of stepping into the river alters the flow of the current. The importance of dynamic processes was underlined for me and colleagues who, now some years ago, undertook research into the scope for achieving privately ordered settlements in the context of reporting to the courts (Clulow and Vincent (1987)). We learned about the risks of viewing an individual frame from a film as if it was the whole picture. The hate and violence of today can change into the sadness and regret of tomorrow. Like the earthworms that so fascinated the evolutionist Charles Darwin, dirt can be converted into a fertile tilth that generates and supports growth. So I would replace the title 'Durable Solutions' with something like 'Sustaining Environments', or 'Supporting Frameworks' to address the task we have in hand.

My thesis is a simple one:

(1) The key to finding solutions to problematic family processes affecting children who come to the attention of the family justice system lies in the relationship between their parents. The evidence for this lies not only in knowledge accumulated from practice experience but also from 30 years of research into the effects of divorce on children (see, for example, Rodgers and Pryor (1998)), studies of conflict within intact families (Reynolds (2001)) and longitudinal studies of family transitions (Pape Cowan and Cowan (2005)).

(2) During separation and divorce the greatest threat to joint parenting is the raw feelings generated by the process of uncoupling. Unless the past is put sufficiently to rest, the future will be haunted by its ghosts.

(3) Empowering parents involves helping them to disengage from each other as partners. This involves engaging with the mess of their emotional realities, and not trying to avoid, sanitise or replicate the struggles they are engaged with. We know from child development studies that the engagement of parents with their children's emotional life can have a transformative affect on social and mental development.

(4) This has implications for services and training, raising a number of questions: Where is mental health expertise to be located in the family justice system? Do we need forensic activities in which the parents are commissioners, recipients and beneficiaries (it's not only the professionals who don't understand what's going on)? How can we develop a 'learning organisation' culture for families throughout the life course that enables them to change in ways that rise to the challenges they have to meet? And what sort of consultancy can we offer these institutions in change?

Change involves losses as well as gains. The family justice system exists to help manage the emotional as well as legal dimensions of family change, and this inevitably involves encountering and acknowledging pain.

CHANGE AND TRANSFORMATION

There is a story told of a response given by the American composer, John Cage, to a question posed by a musician friend: 'don't you think there's too much suffering in the world?'. 'No', Cage replied, 'I think there's just about the right amount'. Adam Phillips, a literary psychotherapist who cites this anecdote, argues that the scientific and philosophical stories recounted by Darwin and Freud were principally concerned with our relationship to change: 'They wanted to convert us to the beauty of ephemera' (Phillips (1999), p 7). His book takes Darwin's fascination with earthworms as a starting point for exploring this relationship. Darwin saw their digestive labour as symbolic of the work of transformational change rooted in natural processes. In his interest in transformational change he had common cause with Freud. The potential for loss to be formative, and indicative of lives that have been led, features in both psychoanalytic and evolutionary philosophies. The role of a child's wooden reel (in Freud's famous 'Fort–Da' account of an infant negotiating anxiety associated with loss and separation through play) is linked with the extinction of a species through the thought that the experience of loss has potential to promote development. Darwin persuaded us that without adaptation species become extinct. Freud proposed that without mourning life could not move on. Both were naturalists. They speculated not about life after death, but life with death, death as a part of life, and life as a result of death.

No one here needs to be told that suffering is an inevitable aspect of marital breakdown, and that it involves many minor deaths. These generate anxiety at public and private levels. In the public debate divorce can represent an attack on institutions that are considered to be vital to the security of individuals and society as a whole. It can threaten the well-being of children, incur huge financial costs, and place in jeopardy the principles of justice, morality and a sense of fair play in relationships. Alternatively, divorce is seen as symptomatic of a changing relationship between women and men, a socio-economic environment that is radically different from even fifty years ago and a culture that is tolerant and accepting of doing something about, rather than putting up with, the restrictions and sometimes damage of a bad marriage. Divorce is also likely, in the short term at least, to be a distressing private experience. The knowledge that so many people divorce does little to mitigate the pain for those going through it.

While I want to say something about what we have learned about the nature of anxiety from those who have been influenced by the philosophical traditions of Darwin and Freud, let me start with a vignette from a couple talking about their impending divorce. When they started therapy he thought they had come to repair their relationship, but she used the first session to say she wanted a divorce. Although she loved him, she experienced him as a dangerous person to live with because she felt she was losing her grip on herself in the marriage. She feared her announcement would devastate him and was concerned that they managed the divorce in a constructive way. Her announcement and wishes *were* devastating for him. Over several months they worked at the emotional implications of ending their marriage and reached the point of selling their home – a major symbolic and practical step. In one session he talked about how difficult it was having estate agents tour the house with potential buyers. He described how he felt ejected from a home that he had invested so much in, and told of how much responsibility he had taken for looking after the house. He wanted a strict agreement with her to control the information about the sale leaking out to family and friends, and said that while he had consented to the sale he was not yet ready to go. She acknowledged what a special house it had been, how they had tried to have everything just right – it was like the perfect home. But she felt it had never been quite what he or she had wanted, and the pressure of getting it right had exhausted them both. And she was concerned that they did not delay the sale unnecessarily.

I want to make just three simple observations about this exchange. First, the house was a metaphor for the marriage – something they had jointly constructed but which had failed to come up to the standards that at least one of them was perceived as having set. Selling the house – divorce – was a legal solution to the emotional problem of feeling fused in the marriage. Second, the process of going public about something intensely private raised fears about losing control to others. Third, and following from the other two, the practical and emotional issues they were contending with were essentially inter-woven: the dispute brewing about the timing of the house sale was rooted in how far each partner had come to terms with the marriage ending.

The family justice system encompasses various public responses to private sorrows – legal advice and adjudication, information giving, counselling, psychotherapy, mediation, child protection and so on. These responses, while involving separate roles and activities, are essentially inter-linked and overlapping in relation to the phenomenon they seek to address: change. Change evokes anxiety. It generates difficulties. It takes just a short step to anthropomorphise those difficulties into the label of 'difficult partner', 'difficult child' or 'difficult client', and we usually do that when other people's difficulties make us anxious on our own account.

WHY WORK WITH DIFFICULT COUPLES?

One of the ironies of family research is that we have learned how valuable partnerships can be through studying what happens in their absence. A solid tradition of research has established the value to children of divorcing parents – in terms of educational achievement, behaviour, health and general well-being – of having parents who can work together and keep their childrens' interests in mind. We are now scrolling back to make the unsurprising discovery that destructive conflict within in-tact families can have the same deleterious effects – on children, on the adult partners and on the community as a whole. These costs can be quantified, and exceed by a ratio of 100:1 the public investment in trying to prevent them (Hart (1999)). So there is a prima facie case for working with adult couples to prevent these costs, whether before or after their relationship ends.

We work with 'difficult' couples because we have no choice. People usually seek help, or come to the attentions of services, at points of change in their lives. They may be looking to bring about change or prevent it from happening – often both at the same time. The prospect or reality of change can trigger a crisis because previous certainties can no longer be relied upon, however bad those certainties might have been. Change introduces a combination of loss and gain into peoples' lives. Those most aware of the gains will be anxious not to give ground, as will those who fight to ward off the losses they fear. When you're fighting for your own psychological survival there is every reason to be difficult – and the nature of that difficulty is not just associated with fighting, but also with compliance. Studies my organisation has done with social workers in a social services department (Mattinson and Sinclair (1979)), or with family court welfare officers in the pre CAFCASS days of the Probation Service (Clulow and Vincent (1987)) or on why collaboration between agencies can be so difficult (Woodhouse and Pengelly (1991)) show how a small number of 'difficult' clients can absorb the lion's share of agencies' resources. So-called difficulties are infectious, take us over, fragment our relationships with others and detonate chains of events that beckon us to run in ever-increasing circles away from the still eye of the storm where it might be possible to think about what's going on. Focusing on the emotional dimension of what's happening between the couple, and for the individuals who constitute the couple, has potential to contain forces that otherwise can operate in very destructive ways.

SEPARATION ANXIETY

At the heart of the divorce process is the experience of something coming to an end. Endings involve a mixture of loss and gain, and loss is usually the problematic half of the equation. Loss relates not simply to the legal contract of marriage, but to the many and various connections that bind couples together in partnership. Separation disrupts the ordinary rituals of living together, and the sense of a common history and continuing conversation that is rooted in it. It disrupts sexual activity and a boundary of privacy surrounding the couple. As knowledge of the breakdown becomes public it affects alliances within families, most notably between children and their parents but extending also to others. One household becomes two, with the financial and logistical problems this generates for its members as they manage a new balance between being together and being apart. Networks of friends are restructured, and changes may be required at work. New, and sometimes unwelcome, networks are created as couples are drawn into the machinery of divorce and exposed to the public gaze. The habits of a lifetime are disrupted, a framework for living dismantled and there is the loss of love. These multiple changes, clustering around the central transition of divorce, will impact on a person's sense of identity – 'who am I?' can become an unnerving question when people feel estranged from themselves as well as from others, as if the rolling film of their lives has become jammed into a distorted single frame that is unrecognisable to all around.

The picture is complicated by the reality that most marriages end, at least in emotional terms, well before a physical separation takes place. It is not uncommon for one partner to register that all is not well in the marriage and to attempt to engage the other about this. If the attempt is successful, the marriage can develop. If not, the emotional and practical investment in the partnership may gradually be withdrawn until the 'bank' becomes empty. A cycle of detachment and denial may result in the breakdown of communication until one partner, perhaps years into the process, takes advantage of an opportunity to leave. Leaving, and being left, is an anxious business.

John Bowlby, the architect of attachment theory, heavily influenced by both Darwin and Freud, asserted that separation anxiety is generated by both the fear of separation and the experience of loss. Such anxiety is a natural and inevitable response to the unaccountable and unwanted absence of an attachment figure. While he was principally concerned with the relationship between children and their primary caregivers, Bowlby believed that separation anxiety and the need for attachment continued to motivate behaviour throughout life (Bowlby (1988)). Subsequent work in this area has proved him right, and focused on the relationship between felt security, states of mind and behaviour in relationships.

Responses to current experiences of loss will be patterned by previous attachment experiences. During the course of growing up people develop their own particular strategies for protecting themselves against perceived threats, and these will influence whether and how they seek help from others when in trouble. For those who have a secure history of *consistently responsive* attachment there is likely to be a confidence that others will be available and responsive when needed, and an ability to be available and responsive to others when they, in turn, make an approach. These people are likely to seek out and make good use of help. For those whose childhood experience has been of *consistently unresponsive* parenting, emphasis may be placed on keeping an emotional distance and playing down the importance of attachment. The compulsively self-reliant, care-giving or detached patterning of responses that can follow such experiences are at odds with seeking help. For those whose childhood experience has included *inconsistently responsive* parents, a pattern of bidding for or coercing others into providing care, and reacting to what is offered ambivalently or aggressively, may be the prominent feature of their behaviour. Such features, alongside responses to previous traumas of loss or abuse, may characterise their approach to seeking help. With the rupture of marriage (arguably the most significant attachment formed in adult life) comes a chain of experiences that can resonate with previous losses, focusing the anxieties of a lifetime within a single contemporary process.

PERSECUTORY AND DEPRESSIVE ANXIETY

Divorce involves not only the loss of a partner and all that goes with it, but also a loss of self. It is not only that people have to reconstruct their view of their partners, they also have to rebuild themselves. With the loss of one's 'other half' – be that a 'better' or 'worse' half – comes the loss of that part of one's own identity that finds expression through the person one has chosen to become intimately associated with.

The loss of oneself in another can trigger intense persecutory anxiety. Persecutory anxiety is associated with what the child psycho-analyst Melanie Klein described as the 'paranoid-schizoid' position (Klein (1946)). In this state of mind individuals unconsciously deal with threats to the self by splitting off and projecting into others all that is felt to be bad, shameful or blameworthy in order to try and preserve a core of the self as good and deserving of better. Negative qualities are attributed to former partners and all who might associate with them. Allegations are made and reinforced in ways that amplify complaints and provide a positive feedback loop in the relational system of the couple, further alienating them from each other and themselves in a rage that feels good – in the same way that it feels good to identify an enemy and go to war. By these means a sense of solidity and solidarity may be achieved.

It is not hard to see how well-matched psychological processes driven by persecutory anxiety are to inquisitorial and adversarial systems. Fault-based divorce is a more intelligible concept than 'irretrievable breakdown', and meets the needs of people who feel persecuted, besieged and deeply wronged. Litigation is a means of constructing and conveying, to the individuals concerned, and those around them, a story about how they come to be where they are. The purpose of the story is to retain some semblance of identity and integrity by prosecuting blameworthiness in others and seeking vindication for the self. Court decisions can be received as a form of public absolution and acquittal or, conversely, as a conviction and life sentence. In the nightmare world of monsters and villains to which divorcing parents may sometimes temporarily regress, the concepts of 'fault' and 'matrimonial offence' are eminently comprehensible. As one man in our study of family court welfare work described below put it: 'I think adultery is a crime. Full stop. It's a terrible crime.'

Persecutory anxiety is linked with psychological processes that split off aspects of the self, locating them 'out there' rather than 'in here'. It is essentially linked with a failure in the capacity to distinguish others from self. In contrast, depressive anxiety is associated with feelings about the loss of an actual other person, rather than an aspect of the self located in that person. In what Klein described as the 'depressive position', there is a recognition of the other as a separate person with legitimate agency to behave as s/he might wish. Feelings of sadness, guilt and concern characterise this state of mind, and there is awareness of the part the self has played in bringing about an unhappy situation. Reparation replaces retribution. What has been lost can be mourned. The world becomes a less threatening place; the self a wiser, and perhaps sadder, being.

SOME IMPLICATIONS FOR MANAGING CHANGE

Some years ago I and colleagues at the Tavistock Centre for Couple Relationships researched the work of a specialist team of family court welfare officers (before CAFCASS, when the Probation Service served the family courts, providing a reminder that historically divorce was equated with social deviance). The aim of the project was to explore the feasibility of mediating between parents over contact and residence disputes while preparing court-ordered reports concerning the welfare of their children (Clulow and Vincent (1987)). The research involved us in working with a core sample of 30 families who were the subject of welfare enquiries. By definition, they were a particularly contentious section of the divorcing population (around 11% of the total divorcing population at that time). Three-quarters of the petitioners had used the behaviour clause of the 1969 Act to establish 'irretrievable breakdown', the same proportion had involved one partner taking the decision to divorce unilaterally, and we judged there was ambivalence about the marriage ending in 25 of the 30 cases. All these factors have been associated with high levels of conflict and poor adaptive responses to divorce.

Putting aside the wisdom or otherwise of combining reporting, mediating and therapeutic functions, agreement was recorded in over half of the core sample of cases at the end of the enquiry period. In over two-thirds of these, the parties were judged by the welfare officers to have moved closer to a joint position during the enquiry period. These figures probably overstate the role played by the practitioners in achieving this outcome (the prospect of a court order deterred some couples from pursuing their dispute, some agreements were arrived at to deflect unwelcome attention and some were paper agreements that masked unchanged positions). However, the results were interesting.

We classified our sample of divorcing families into three groups, allowing us to make some assessment of which couples were most amenable to change.

Nominal divorces

The nominal group of divorces contained parents who remained ambivalently attached to each other, unable to acknowledge their relationship as durable or to implement a decision to part. They could absorb a lot of time to no good effect. Not knowing their own mind they pressed others to take responsibility for decisions, and sometimes elicited a therapeutic response from welfare officers that could neither be sustained nor was appropriate to their role.

Long-lease divorces

At the other end of the spectrum were *long-lease* divorces, where the prognosis was equally poor. These parents remained distantly but chronically attached, as if they could never quite disengage from a sense of belonging together. A lengthy history of divorce-associated litigation, highly discrepant accounts of events, a determination and ability to 'play the system', plus a preference for by-passing direct communication, made them unlikely candidates for out-of-court assisted settlements.

Shot-gun divorces

The key indicator of a favourable prospect for achieving agreement was a degree of accessibility in the ways parents approached each other. This was most often found in our *shot-gun* category of divorces (in which one party clearly wanted out and the other felt they had had no opportunity to establish what they wanted), and was partly determined by the situation existing between the parties at the time and partly a product of the opportunities afforded them by their welfare officers. Accessibility implied a capacity, however limited, to hear what others were saying and to take it into account, to press for claims in an assertive but not self-defeating way, and to show a certain amount of flexibility towards the claims of others when circumstances warranted it. Parents were most likely to be accessible when they were far enough removed from the trauma of separation not to feel their lives were in pieces, but not so far removed that patterns of conflict had become entrenched and embittered.

From our experience there are some broad questions that practitioners working with separating families might find it helpful to keep in mind:

What meanings do separation and divorce carry for those involved?

The significance of any change depends not just upon its nature and extent but also upon what it represents for the adults and children concerned. What has been invested in the relationship? How exclusively has it been relied upon and for what kinds of things? How much of a gap will be left? For couples parting early on in their relationship there may be losses about giving up a fantasy of what might have been rather than the experience of what actually was. For older couples, a lifetime of shared history may seem to be at stake, questioning assumptions that had hitherto been taken for granted.

How has change been managed previously?

Highly relevant to the management of loss in the present is how people have experienced and managed loss previously in their lives. Current events provide a hook on which past traumas can be hung, with all the confusions and emotional charge that attend fusing the past with the present. A man in our study of divorce court welfare enquiries vigorously pursued an application for his children to live with him, irrespective of practical and other difficulties that made the proposition unrealistic. When confronted with the impracticality of his proposals he brushed objections aside, saying he had lost contact with a child from a previous marriage and was not going to let that happen to him again.

Why is this change taking place now?

The understood causes and circumstances in which a marriage breaks are likely to be very important, both in relation to the reactions they provoke and the process of adjustment that the changes require. Divorce, unlike most deaths, follows the exercise of choice. Feelings of rejection, betrayal and injustice are likely to be intense for one or both partners. Who is thought to be to blame for what has happened? Was it thought to be avoidable? How does one live with the feelings of physical, sexual and emotional rejection that follow from one's spouse becoming involved with someone else? These questions are relevant to children as well as the grown-ups, and involve emotional work as well as cognitive recognition.

How much forewarning has there been?

The more predictable change is, the more manageable it is likely to be. In our study we learned how devastating sudden and unexpected departures from the family home can be for those who are left behind. Yet we have also observed that when partners cannot bear to know that the marriage is in trouble it may be impossible for them to pick up the signals that herald change. These observations can be applied to the legal and para-legal processes that are set in train following an application for divorce. The more informed people are about what happens if they initiate divorce proceedings, where they can go for different kinds of help and what they can expect to receive in terms of response, the less stressful the experience is likely to be. This is mainly because information is power. Change is best accomplished when people feel empowered in relation to it.

What about the balance of power?

When relationships break down the imbalance of power between partners can sometimes be starkly revealed. The manipulation of assets, physical violence and emotional coercion may be brought to bear by one partner against the other. Many women are fearful of leaving violent marriages because of the repercussions they expect to follow, and threatening attitudes may lead either partner to settle for an arrangement that falls short of what they might be entitled to or what is in their own and their childrens' best interests. Mediators are trained specifically to be alert to such imbalances when facilitating the private resolution of disagreements over post-separation arrangements. The rest of us also need to have this dynamic in mind, and to remember that we, too, have power, and need to exercise care in how it is used.

How will family and friends respond?

The support of family, friends and colleagues has a major impact on the management of change. These people provide a thread of continuity with ordinary life. They can provide encouragement, support, counsel and the vitally needed thinking space in which events can be talked about, replayed and reworked. When divorce involves moving away from familiar people and surroundings an important supply of 'social oxygen' is cut off. Even when no physical moving away is involved, people who are divorcing, and those around them, may enter a conspiracy of silence and avoidance because they do not know whether and how to talk about what is going on. Sometimes family members and friends feel so strongly about what has happened that they may contribute to the polarisation of the parties and become part of the problem.

What professional help is at hand?

Closely related to the social and emotional support of family and friends comes the practical support available to parents and children once a marriage comes to an end. Financial worries can be all-consuming, and information about benefits and entitlements is much needed at this time. So, too, is information about services that can help families manage the transition they are going through. The attitudes of teachers towards children going through family upheaval, and of schools towards them and their parents, can act as helpful and unhelpful influences. Practitioners need to be aware of the part they play, unwittingly or not, in fashioning the experience of divorce. The ways in which divorce is – and is not – ritualised by society, the processes that people go through, their access to rites that help them refashion meaning from experience, will all be relevant to how able they are to integrate their past with their future.

Most of the parents we saw in the study were intensely preoccupied with their own psychological survival. Their emotional and social viability had been seriously disturbed. The roles of parent and spouse had acted for them, as with most people, as life-support systems. Perhaps unsurprisingly, the fight for survival was carried out in relation to partners and children. Shock, fear, outrage, and intransigence were their understandable reactions to the threat and realisation of being dispossessed. 'The argument simply wasn't rational', one mother in our study observed with hindsight, 'I felt I would lose my rights. I think my husband felt the same way.'

This had a clear impact on the welfare officers who needed to survive the verbal abuse and emotional battering that were frequently part of the work. In surviving the impact it was essential for the team to feel supported and together as a group in relation to their role and tasks. Co-working was sometimes helpful as a way of feeling less fragmented by family dynamics. Having a partner to confer with – and occasionally to fight with – helped preserve some balance between partisan interests. Agreements were more likely to be achieved when working in pairs than when working alone. Supervision was also a vital support in managing the boundaries of the task in a world where boundaries were collapsing and being redrawn in sometimes astonishingly rapid succession.

Part of the stress of the work was related to how family experiences resonated with the emotional life of the practitioner. This is particularly true in relation to the highly emotive issues of family dissolution and child welfare, both of which are likely to activate transference and counter-transference responses in the client-practitioner relationship. Members of divorcing families are capable of 'getting under the skin' of those whom they turn to for help, which is a colloquial way of expressing the idea that people can disown feelings and states of mind they cannot bear to know about, projecting them into others where they might be recognised and related to from a safer distance.

There are many different ways in which the experience of divorce can unconsciously engage us as practitioners (Wallerstein (1990)):

(1) There are our responses to marriage, partnerships, separation and divorce, inviting identifications and counter-identifications with the institutions and relationship states they portray and the feelings they generate – betrayal of trust, sexual jealousy, envy, rejection, fear of loneliness and the many other emotions that attach themselves to marriage and divorce. This may be at the near conscious level of evoking disapproval and censure, or at a deeply unconscious level of evoking anxiety states and the fear of annihilation that speaks to, but is not consciously linked with, the client's experience. It is not uncommon for practitioners to find themselves drawn into the persecutor or persecuted role in relation to those they see, as the nature of a client's anxiety is unconsciously communicated through enactments of one kind or another.

(2) Diminished parenting can also engage the practitioner in different ways, inviting anguish, rage, impotence, judgemental responses and fantasies of rescuing the 'victim' child. Alternatively, the desire to be non-condemnatory and even-handed may result in a cool remoteness where feelings of anger or alarm may be more appropriate.

(3) There are also gender factors that may reverberate in the transference, conflating this man with all men, or that woman with the 'other woman', and so infusing the professional relationship with hostile, vengeful or erotic overtones.

Between 1992–1993 I wrote a regular column for *Family Law* entitled 'Only Connect'. The reference was to a line from EM Forster – 'Only connect the prose and the passion and both will be exalted' – that appears in his novel *Howards End*. The intention was to put the power of emotion alongside that of reason in thinking about outcomes in the family justice system, knowing that the force of feeling was the factor that most often accounted for the label 'difficult' being tagged to people and relationships. It was also intended to connect the users and providers of family justice so they might be thought about as part of the same system. In so far as problems can be divided into those of a technical and those of an adaptive nature, separation and divorce falls squarely into the adaptive category, where we all have to be viewed as part of the problem as well as its solution. In one of those pieces (Clulow (1993)) I identified feelings that could make us part of the problem by raising professional anxiety, especially in relation to uncertainty, and some of the defences we used that could make us into 'difficult' practitioners:

- the fear of confusion and uncertainty making us push for false clarity;

- the need to establish the truth overlooking the truth that the same situation can support opposing realities;

- the tendency to deal with the things that can't be known through creating experts who are assumed to know, and can be taken to task for not knowing;

- the opposing tendency to deal with things that can't be known through demolishing all external authorities in the cause of sustaining the conviction that 'no-one knows better than me';

- wishing to rescue and make reparation as a way of dealing with guilt stirred up by having hostile and destructive feelings towards clients, when this might be quite inappropriate;

- responding to feelings of powerlessness and loss of control through increasingly controlling behaviour (unconsciously exporting the helplessness into others).

The list can easily be added to, and contains just some of the responses we and those we see can make in the face of emotional difficulty.

So what happens when the human drama of divorce is played out on a changing public stage? What happens when the roles of the 'Greek chorus' are in a state of flux – as is the case in the family justice system? Family and professional transitions can then become intertwined, and unpredictable consequences may ensue. From the professional network there may be a jockeying for position and power, competitiveness between the players and the temptation to blame others for things going wrong. From the family network there may be pressures to split the professional system, and to recruit different players into alliances against each other.

Because we professionals are (generally speaking) on the side of reason, and are unwilling spectators to the darker side of human nature, there are a number of traps that we can fall into as we try to protect ourselves against the pain and discomfort of those we see. We may be propelled by persecutory anxiety to join that part of the human condition that tends to polarise issues, especially when under pressure and in circumstances that are perceived to be threatening. We may, for example, come to think that the 'gold star' outcome of our endeavours is that those who present themselves for divorce end up being reconciled. If 'marriage' is good, the danger is that 'divorce' will be bad – or, at least, a second best outcome. Of course, we have come a long way from perceiving divorce as social deviance, something to be granted only after a 'conviction' for a matrimonial 'offence'. But there remain questions for those operating divorce procedures about how they view those who are determined to secure their divorce and who are perhaps impatient of practices and procedures that may feel to them at best as irrelevant and, at worst, as infantilising. The attitudes of professionals will contribute to defining the experience of divorce. If part of that experience involves reshaping personal identities it will not help to cast those intent on ending what they have been unable to make work into the roles of failures, second best citizens or awkward customers.

In the same way that we might be tempted to split our responses to marriage and divorce, so too might we be tempted to distinguish between the 'good' and the 'bad' divorce. The 'good' divorce will be characterised by civilised behaviour, reasonableness, a willingness to 'give and take' in trying to find a solution to persisting differences, and an inclination to use the services of mediators in the process. The 'bad' divorce will be conflict-ridden, messy and blaming, with the parties attempting to engage professionals in adversarial approaches to resolving their problems. The invitation to practitioners will be to be drawn into making judgements about behaviour, rather than reflecting upon its meaning in the context of experiences and anxieties that the parties are having to manage. We, as professionals, need the same sort of time for reflection and consideration during the divorce process as our clients if we are not to be drawn into idealising or denigrating ourselves, each other, and those who use our services. Being alive to the psychological processes that affect all of us in the work provides some protection against splitting off and dissociating ourselves from our own experience and that of the people with whom we are working.

My last point is related to the preceding two. The longing for a happy ending which reunites the couple (something that may relate to the 'internal parental couple' that we carry around inside us and that we yearn to reunite), or pursuing the 'good' divorce, may lead us to try and sanitise experiences that involve powerful and messy feelings. Denial, protest and despair are well-recognised features of the road leading out of any significant experience of loss. These responses easily transpose into behaviour. People sometimes do not want to recognise what is happening to them, need to express their rage and hostility to others, and may be unable to mobilise themselves to do the things that they need to do because the experience they are going through impacts so heavily upon them. If we are intent on recasting 'angry tigers into docile pussycats' (Sclater (1999)) we may encourage a purring within juridical procedures that does nothing to prevent the roaring within families from continuing outside, with its predictable consequences for children.

So, to return to the question with which I started: is there too much suffering in the world of divorce, or just about enough? For transformation to occur there needs to be neither too little nor too much pain. Change usually involves distress. Human distress can be messy. We need to accept that as a fact, and then be prepared to get our hands dirty. We cannot clear the mess up, but we can share the load in many different ways. Like Darwin's worms, we need to know how essential the mess may be, and that it has the potential to be converted into something textured and fertile, providing the nutrients for future growth.

REFERENCES

Bowlby, J *A Secure Base: Clinical Applications of Attachment Theory* (London, Routledge, 1988)

Clulow, C 'Containment' (1993) Family Law (June) 359

Clulow, C and Vincent, C *In the Child's Best Interests? Divorce Court Welfare and the Search for a Settlement* (London, Tavistock/Sweet and Maxwell, 1987)

Pape Cowan, C and Cowan, P 'Two central roles for couple relationships: breaking negative intergenerational patterns and enhancing children's adaptation' (2005) 20(3) Sexual and Relationship Therapy 275–288

Hart, G *The Funding of Marriage Support* (London, Lord Chancellor's Department, 1999)

Klein, M *The Writings of Melanie Klein* Vol 3 (London, Hogarth Press, 1946)

Mattinson, J and Sinclair, I *Mate and Stalemate. Working with Marital Problems in a Social Services Department* (Oxford, Blackwell, 1979)

Phillips, A *Darwin's Worms* (London, Faber and Faber, 1999)

Reynolds, J (ed) *Not in front of the Children. How conflict between parents affects children* (London, One Plus One, 2001)

Rodgers, B and Prior, J *Divorce and Separation: The Outcomes for Children* (York, Joseph Rowntree Foundation, 1998)

Sclater, S *Divorce: A Psychosocial Study* (Aldershot, Ashgate, 1999)

Wallerstein, J (1990) 60 American Journal of Orthopsychiatry 337–345

Woodhouse, D and Pengelly, P *Anxiety and the Dynamics of Collaboration* (Aberdeen, Aberdeen University Press, 1991)

GENDER, PARENTING AND THE COURTS

MOTHERS AND FATHERS

Katherine Gieve
Head of Family Department, Bindman & Partners

Katherine Gieve explained that she was struck by the huge contrast between how family practitioners talk in court about parenting and children and how they talk about this in the remainder of life. She suggested that within the family justice system we need to look more carefully at the roles of mothers and fathers, and this paper is written as a response to that need.

The court currently takes an approach of gender neutrality. This does not recognise the substance of relationships between mothers and fathers and their children. In failing to appreciate this, we are unable to address the dynamics which need to be managed when parents separate. It is clear that many families have moved away from traditional role models but the question arises as to the extent to which families have changed and what is the significance of those changes? How much difference is there in the way people look after children?

The call from fathers for contact on the breakdown of their relationship has been high profile. However, Katherine Gieve asks the question as to whether this is a call to continue the relationship that the father enjoyed with the child during the marriage or relationship or whether fathers, who have previously relied on mothers to mediate their relationships, need to establish a more intimate relationship with their children than they have had before.

The paper suggests that taking care of babies and small children is a transforming psychological experience for an adult and suggests that it is still generally women who allow themselves to be shaped by babies and who change their own lives to put children at the centre. On the whole, men do not usually have that role although that sometimes can and do. Questions arise as to what is the primary relationship and how important is this over time for children. There is a distinction between parenting activities, trips and treats which the children enjoy and parenting which is akin to something of the grouting, providing the shape for every day life. The paper suggests that men have not often taken on the same role as a mother.

Where parents are separated, the father is hugely important. Two parents are an absolute minimum for a child. When separation occurs it is important to understand the changes for the mother, in trying to 'keep the show on the road' and support a relationship between the father and the children.

Questions as to how families manage their lives on a daily basis will help to resolve the dynamics that must be addressed in separation.

I want to draw attention to an odd contrast between the way in which families are described and considered within the framework of law, the courts and in government policy on one hand and ordinary life on the other. The language of law and government is the language of gender neutrality: for mothers and fathers, substitute parents; the language of every day life is gender specific, most particularly in the arena of the family. Although the roles of men and women have changed significantly during the last 30 years they still generally play quite distinct roles from each other in family life. The studied neutrality of the court is at odds with what looks like a major sex war if you read the newspapers: 'Mothers to be punished for preventing contact'; 'Batman in tights in Buckingham Palace', and the rest of it.

I believe that we, in the family justice system, need to look more carefully at the roles of mothers and fathers and how they are changing in order to help parents find durable solutions when relationships breakdown.

The present approach of gender neutrality seems to me to do a disservice both to mothers and to fathers in not acknowledging to substance of relationships between mothers and fathers and their children and thus in not confronting the complexity of the changes which are needed when parents separate.

My intention is to raise a series of questions that arise from my day-to-day practice as a children's law solicitor. I hear the narratives both of mothers and fathers in the very difficult negotiations at the end of relationships. These accounts have made me very conscious of tensions between the ways of being a mother and being a father which are often not allowed to come to the surface in the difficult negotiations and in due course judgments about what should happen on relationship breakdown. I hope that colleagues from the psychological professions and from social research will help us with the answers.

A HISTORICAL ASIDE: HOW DID WE GET TO WHERE WE ARE NOW?

There have been dramatic and rapid changes in the shape of the family and particularly in the relationships between fathers and their children.

In *Re G* (1956) the judge said: 'In the case of an illegitimate child the limit of the obligation of the father will be to make financial provisions for the child in order to relieve other people and particularly the general public of that obligation, [that] it is in the child's best interests to know both parents is not at any rate by any means applicable in the case of the illegitimate child.'[1]

The control of a woman's fertility and freedom of movement by shame and by poverty constrained women until well into the second half of the last century. Men were expected to play a marginal role, if any role at all, when babies were born outside marriage. Divorce was rare, causing both shame and poverty. The role of fathers within their families was often not an intimate one.

The radical changes during the end of the 1960s and 1970s have been well rehearsed: the pill, and abortion law reform in 1967 gave women a greater control over their fertility. Divorce law reform in 1969, followed by the Matrimonial Homes Act in 1974, the Domestic Violence Act in 1975, the Housing (Homeless Persons) Act in 1977 and changes to the social security regime transformed the framework in which men and women formed and ended their relationships. Increasing numbers of children were born outside marriage and increasing numbers of marriages came to an end through divorce. Now a significant minority of children are brought up not living in the same household as both parents: 10% of children live with a step parent; 25% of children live in a household with only one parent.

By 1977 the courts were already getting to grips with the implications for children of these new found freedoms and particularly the loss of connection between fathers and their children. In *M v J* the judge said: 'The court should always be slow to deprive either parent of access to a child and should have, when refusing a father access to his illegitimate child, positive and compelling evidence that access is not in the child's best interest, particularly when they have lived together under the same roof.'[2]

In parallel, women's role in the outside world has been transformed. Large numbers of women work whilst they have small children, part time if not full time. Fathers are more involved in the care of their small children.

---

[1]   *Re G* [1956] 2 All ER 876.
[2]   *M v J* (1977) *The Times*, 20 October.

It is difficult to judge what the changes consist in and they are no doubt very different in different households and different classes and groups. There are daily reports in the newspapers about relations between men, women, children and domestic responsibilities. *Guardian Weekend*[3] in an article by Melissa Benn entitled 'When did you last see your husband?' rails against the fact that women have a second full-time job in caring for their home and children. She describes an IPPR study: 'while the public assume a high degree of gender equality at work, most people see the care of home and young children to be woman's responsibility'; and a study supported by ESRC which confirmed that it is predominantly women who take time off to look after sick children, including 60% of women who earn the same or more than their partners. A survey for the Equal Opportunities Commission highlighted a shift in attitudes to fatherhood: the proportion of fathers who believe they should be the main provider while the mother's place is in the home falling from 52% to 20% in the past 20 years. Nine out ten fathers of infants aged between three and 15 months questioned reported feeling as confident as their partner when caring for a child.[4]

It is difficult to know what to make of these figures and in particular the extent to which changes in attitudes have been supported by changes in roles. Does the urgent call by fathers for contact on the breakdown of relationships represent a call for continuity in the relationship they have had with their children during the marriage? Or are they sometimes fathers who have not had a close domestic relationship with their children before, who have relied on mothers to mediate their relationships, and who need on separation to establish a more intimate relationship with their children than they have had before? Does research exist that distinguishes whether parents are more or less able to resolve disagreements about post-separation arrangements according to the kinds of arrangements they had before; and the extent to which arrangements for contact after the breakdown of a relationship reflect the relationships before?

The freedom to have children outside marriage; the freedom to divorce; the changing role of women in paid employment and changes in relations between mothers and fathers and their children are of epic proportions. However great the changes, it does not seem to me that we have reached the point of androgynous childcare. The courts are so bent on agreement and resolution that there is an unwillingness to look at the content of relationships between parents and children. The drive to the division of 'parenting time' and an unwillingness to acknowledge and explore the different kinds of relationships parents and children have and need deprives us of a language for the resolution of differences.

MOTHERS AND FATHERS

The needs of children for succour and support have not changed to fit in with new patterns of adult life. Babies, in my experience, have a clear notion of what they need and set about shaping adults who can meet those needs: they need adults who are available and respond to them. Taking care of babies and small children is a transforming psychological experience for an adult. I believe it is still generally women who allow themselves to be shaped by babies and who change their own lives to put children at the centre. I am not suggesting that men cannot and never take on that role; they both can and do; but it is much more rare than for a woman and in most of the cases that come before the courts men have not adopted a maternal role.

The current language of mothering and parenting suggests more action and less being and availability; the use of language ignores essential elements of the relationship. I accept that men play a greater role in children's lives than a generation ago and see it as a change for the better. The question is whether that new role is akin to being a mother or whether it is more of being a father or whether the roles are really converging. If they are different what is the significance of the difference? Surveys tell us that more fathers are changing more nappies and taking more

3   *Guardian Weekend* 9 April 2005.
4   *The Guardian* 16 June 2005.

children to the park – but the surveys are on the whole event based. Surveys do not ask questions like:

- How often do you notice one football sock under the sofa so that you can find it on Monday morning?

- How often are you within earshot and alert for a child doing home work while you are making tea?

- How often do you think about tomorrow's school lunch box whilst you are on your way back from work?

What mothers/primary carers do is to hold their children in their mind; they are available for them even when they are doing something quite different. They create a shape for the daily lives of their children. There are both psychological and practical aspects to the managing maternal role. These are notions that we are very familiar with in the assessments of parents in care proceedings: they are called bonding/putting the needs of your child before your own needs. They are less familiar now in planning the arrangements on relationship breakdown in private law proceedings. We have lost a positive sense of the importance and meaning of primary care – it is more frequent to find that role described in a pejorative way – mothers as 'gatekeepers' for contact, for example.

My impression is that whilst men have become more engaged as fathers they have not generally taken on a role like mothers: the sort of holding together and shaping the week; drying tears and filling the gaps. For parents who live together, they sort out the balance of these relationships as best they can. There is recent publicity about new mothers rejecting paid employment and focussing on domestic life but equally of much more sharing between mothers and fathers.

SEPARATED PARENTS

Where parents separate, or where in some cases they have never lived together, the character of these specific relationships becomes much more important. The emphasis in government and the courts has been on helping parents to reach agreement. Children's experience of parental separation is made much more painful and damaging if there is conflict between their parents. It seems likely that those who do reach agreement themselves independently do so on the basis of an agreement about their respective roles which probably reflects how they operated together during their relationship. My hypothesis is that as well as helping parents to reach agreement, which is undoubtedly important, there needs to be a greater awareness and openness about the significance of the different roles which parents have played during the relationship. It is often in those differences that parents stumble when trying to sort things out. There needs to be a language within the courts and government which reflects the reality of family lives. This is particularly important when models of shared/divided time are being put forward as a basis for agreement. Parents are being guided to particular kinds of arrangements if they have not reached agreement themselves and some fathers' groups are arguing for ratios of 'parenting time'.

The language of gender neutrality allows respect for the diverse ways in which men and women live their lives; it does not suggest fixed gender roles that would certainly be resisted and rejected by fathers and mothers. But it suppresses a recognition and discussion of how children are cared for day by day. If that discussion were allowed to surface, I suggest that parents would be able to have more fruitful discussions about the lives of their children.

I have recently represented a mother of two small girls aged 4 and 6. The father lives nearby. The father has had contact every second weekend from Friday after school to Sunday 6.30 pm; the children have tea with him every Wednesday; they spend half of each holiday with him and additional times by agreement. The father wanted more contact: every second Sunday night and overnight every Wednesday. This was his second family, he had had to work hard when his first children were young and was now retired and had more time. The mother resisted: she felt that she could not continue to maintain a calm rhythm for the children with such a fragmented week; she couldn't hold things together for them. She worried about their things being in order for school if the girls went to school from their father's. The girls loved seeing their father but came back exhausted and strung out after all their activities. Things only worked, she felt, if the children pottered at home during the time they were with her. They needed quite a lot of pottering time. The parents were advised by an eminent male child and adolescent psychiatrist. He was impatient with the mother's concerns about lunch boxes and homework. The case was heard by a woman judge who found for the mother.

The mother felt she was trying to maintain a pattern to life that she felt the children could manage and which she could manage. The father saw things in terms of shared time and activities; he did not really seem to understand what the mother thought she was doing or why it was necessary at all. This dynamic is one which is replicated in a number of cases I see. The notion of being a mother (or being a parent) has lost out to the language of activity and parenting time.

There needs to be respect and awareness of 'being a mother' not only from the mother's point of view but also because the father needs to understand the extent of what is going on in the day-to-day care of children if he is to have a good relationship with them when he is on his own with them. If you are the person in sole charge of a child even for quite short periods of time you need to understand about being and not just doing.

PARENTING TIME

There has been a lot of activity by Government in conjunction with the judiciary on the resolution of conflicts on relationship breakdown. The Family Law Advisory Board Children sub committee chaired by Wall J (as he then was) published two volumes *Making Contact Work,* one dealing with domestic violence and one with situations where contact was thwarted. The government responded and in July 2004 published *Parental Separation: Children's needs and Parents' responsibilities.* The President of the Family Division issued the Private Law Programme on 9 November 2004 providing a new framework for resolving applications under Part II of the Children Act 1989. In February 2005 and again after the election on 14 June 2005 came the publication of the Children (Contact) and Adoption Bill.

The emphasis has been, quite properly, on how to help parents resolve the arrangements for their children and how best to use the courts and support services, such as Cafcass.

What is absent is any acknowledgement of the range of different roles which parents play and in particular the different roles of men and women. In an effort to avoid accusations of gender bias from the enormously vigorous and effective father's lobby, there has been very little open recognition of the business of day-to-day care; nor the important need to support the parent who has primary care. Nor is there perhaps sufficient recognition of the major task for the non-resident parent in establishing a new kind of relationship. There is a suggestion that all that needs to be done is to recognise the equal importance of both parents and reach agreement on the division of time between them. The Government has resisted proposals for a presumption for equal rights to equal time[5] in every case, but has not really explained why. Some families do divide time equally but the real task is to share responsibility so that that can be done. In most families the management, the gathering together of tasks and the holding on to and organising children is done by mothers; but whether it is done by the mother or the father there needs to be recognition of this real endeavour in exploring the best arrangements on family breakdown.

There is impatience in talking about the needs of adults. However, we need to think about the experience of each parent as well as of the child. Putting the needs of the child first is an

---

[5]   *Parental Separation: Children's Needs and Parents' Responsibilities* July 2004 (para 42).

important maxim but our capacity to talk about families is impoverished if we do not also reflect on the experience of the adults and their needs too. Children and parents flourish and suffer in relationship to each other. We should not ignore half of the equation by holding resolutely onto a focus on children which does not take account of the experience and welfare of adults – if only because children will not benefit from it, but probably for other reasons too.

My bid is that we recognise what goes in to bringing up children and what the parents feel about their roles and relationships. It is not sufficient to divide tasks and divide time. We need to look at how parents create a pattern and coherence for their children's lives and indeed their own lives in caring for their children.

FATHER–CHILD RELATIONSHIPS AND CHILDREN'S DEVELOPMENT: A KEY TO DURABLE SOLUTIONS?

Professor Charlie Lewis
Centre for Research in Human Development, Department of Psychology, Lancaster University

Professor Michael E Lamb
Department of Social and Developmental Psychology, Faculty of Social and Political Sciences, University of Cambridge

Professor Charlie Lewis began with apologies from Michael Lamb, the co-author of his paper. The title to the paper begs the question 'why focus on fathers?' and whether this is a knee-jerk response to the high profile fathers' movement. The statistics suggest otherwise and other factors have brought men to the fore. In 1975, 400 academic papers were written on the subject of fathers, in 1980, this rose to 800 but in 2005, the figure is just 700. This paper outlines four themes.

Firstly, the paper explores men's capacity to parent. Tests measuring the responsivity using the galvanic skin response show that men react to the cries of babies in similar ways to women. When holding a baby, men demonstrate a change in hormones and men may also experience the equivalent of post-natal blues. This attachment is demonstrated even where contact with the child is minimal. While research suggests no distinction between attachment to mother and father in the second year of life, longitudinal studies have shown that fathers often become play specialists and mothers may have the edge in terms of the closeness of their attachments. However, men have become increasingly involved in child-care in the last 30 years, partly in response to the increased maternal presence in the workforce. Thus the nature of parent–child attachments might be changing

Secondly, the paper considers the complex determinants of fathering. Trends show that the better a man has been fathered and the closer his relationship to his own father, the better he will be able to father his child. The more time fathers are able to spend with their children, the closer their relationship will be. Consequently parental employment patterns have an impact on how involved men can become. The influences are transactional; parent–child relationships are dynamic and patterned over time and through different life experiences.

Thirdly, the paper addresses paternal influences which are the crux of the paper. There is a distinction between the pre-school to primary school period and the period post primary school. Maternal–infant attachments predict the outcome of the child when they enter primary school. Although paternal attachments have a weaker predictive power than maternal attachments, maternal attachments have a diminishing influence from the primary school years. Early paternal influences appear to be predictive of the child's adjustment in the longer term.

Professor Lewis moved to the fourth question of what is the clearest parental influence of family relationships on children's development. Research suggests this is parental relationships and any conflict therein rather than the specific interactions between a parent and a child. Cummings et al (2004) suggested there may be a greater influence of 'spousal' discord on men rather than women. We must be cautious about the influence of parental conflict as Goeke-Morey (1999) concluded that children can be influenced positively by 'constructive conflict', potentially learning resourcefulness in response to this conflict.

Non-resident fathers have an influence on children that varies depending upon their parenting style and their life circumstances. Active parenting rather than simply contact correlates with child adjustment; most fathers continue to have close relationships with their children, albeit subject to fluctuations over time. They have an influence on their children's development, which extends from experiences in childhood well into adulthood. For these reasons, we should tailor services for post separation families to foster the father–child relationship. Such services need to be adapted to the child's developmental level and the transactional patterns of influence.

Fathers are in the centre of policy and research debates as never before. Not only have the actions of fathers' groups like Fathers 4 Justice drawn attention to their complaints of unfair treatment following parental separation, but the work of organisations like Families Need Fathers and, particularly, Fathers Direct, have persuaded policy makers in the UK to consider men's roles more closely. In this paper we provide a brief overview of the vast literature on fathers (the reader is directed to Flouri (2005); Hobson (2002); Lamb (2004); and Tamis-LeMonda and Cabrera (2002) for more extended reviews) in order to assess whether the nature of men's family relationships provide crucial evidence for our design and construction of durable solutions to family problems, notably parental separation. Because most fathers in industrial cultures spend less time with their infants than mothers do (Pleck & Masciadrelli (2004)) it has been assumed that they have much less influence on their children. Emerging evidence suggest that, although fathers may indeed have less influence in some respects than mothers do, their impact tends to be both important and enduring.

This paper has four aims. First, we will summarise what the research on father–child interactions tells us about the nature of men's capacity to form and engage in relationships with children. So long have the words 'parenting' and 'mothering' been treated as synonymous that it is important to explore the evidence on the capacities of men as parents. In the second part, we examine three factors which must be considered when attempting to explore the nature of, and variability in, fathers' relationships with their offspring. We argue that to understand a man's involvement in family life we have to consider factors as diverse as his sensitivity to the child and the social circumstances in which his parenting takes place. The third section considers ways of assessing parents' influence on their children's development. We contend that research exploring family processes over time may provide vital evidence regarding fathers' roles in families and, more importantly, their influences. In the final section, we consider men who no longer live with their children, but may still contribute in important ways to their children's development.

MEN'S CAPACITY TO PARENT

There has long been debate about the extent to which men are unprepared for or temperamentally unsuited to parenting. This belief is implicit in post-war psychoanalytic (Bowlby (1951/54); Winnicott (1965)) and sociological (Parsons & Bales (1956)) analyses of the family, but some earlier commentators, such as Cobbett (1828–32), have argued that men and women are equivalently prepared for parenting. The empirical literature tells us that fathers have a clear capacity to engage in parenting and to develop close relationships with their children, even when those children are very young.

One might expect that, because mothers and fathers experience pregnancy differently and women have usually had more contact with young children, they must have different abilities when it comes to caring for a new baby. In fact, however, parents interact with their newborns in similar ways both in the delivery room (Parke & O'Leary (1976); White, Wollett & Lyon (1982)) and in the weeks that follow (Rödholm & Larsson (1982); Parke & Sawin (1977)). Even within the first hours of contact they learn to discriminate their own babies through a number of modalities, including touch (Kaitz et al (1994)). Interestingly, men seem to show physiological changes early in their infants' lives. Around the delivery of their children their levels of testosterone (the 'male' hormone) have been found to decrease while levels of prolactin (the hormone that promotes milk production in mothers) and cortisol increase (Storey et al (2000)). All these pieces of evidence suggest that men are 'wired' to engage in parenting, particularly as they often report having had minimal contact with babies before their own are born (Lewis (1986)).

From the moment of delivery, men have the capacity to 'parent' in the same way as their partners. In many studies with infants and children, no differences have been found in levels of maternal and paternal sensitivity. In one research procedure, for example, a parent is asked to complete questionnaires within a fairly limited time, while their one-year-old sits in a high chair next to them – almost all children in this setting make bids for the parent's attention. In this context, mothers and fathers appear to be equally sensitive to their children's needs (Notaro & Volling (1999)), and in other, more ecologically valid settings, fathers appear highly attuned to their toddlers' and young children's interests during interaction (see Lewis (1997), for a review). Indeed this pattern continues into the school years, where both parents engage in comparable amounts of nurturant caretaking (Russell & Russell (1987)), even though the nature of the parents' input changes. For example, fathers are reported to help children battle with increasing amounts of homework and tend to take on particular roles, often as the family maths or science specialist (Solomon et al (2002)).

However, there is also some evidence that mothers have the edge on fathers in handling their children, even in the early stages of parenting. Some researchers have found that men were less skilled at soothing irritable newborns, even when the children were not their first (Kaitz et al (2000)), that they teased and 'intruded' upon their children more (Frascarolo-Moutinot (1994); Labrell (1994)) and that they expected less cognitive maturity and social autonomy from children than their partners did (Mansbach & Greenbaum (1999)). Within the first year of life, children may develop different relationships with their fathers and mothers. Home observations show that mothers tend to hold their 7- to 13-month-old infants to care for them, whereas fathers tend to do so in response to infants' requests to be held or during playful interaction (Belsky (1979); Lamb (1976b)). Presumably as a result of these differences, the infants in these studies were reported to respond more positively to being held by their fathers than by their mothers (Lamb (1976a), (1977c)). Such sex-linked differences become wider, with men coming to specialise in physically stimulating and unpredictable play especially in infancy and toddlerhood (eg, Clarke-Stewart (1978); Dickson, Walker & Fogel (1997); Lamb (1977c)). This becomes less prominent in the later preschool years (Crawley & Sherrod (1984)), but even in the teenage years the father is often depicted as the family's figure of 'fun' (Warin et al (1999)).

Across many cultures, fathers have been identified as specialists in play with their children. This had led some to argue that men's roles are somewhat less important, because the primary aim of parenting is to nurture children. Why do men appear to be specialists in 'mucking about' with children? The debate has centred on the claim that fathers have a biological tendency to specialise in play or that their playfulness is culturally prescribed, given men's roles as secondary caregivers in most cultures. If studies across the world show that fathers engage in distinctive patterns of interaction, this would suggest a biological imperative.

In fact, men specialise in physical play, not only in the UK and in white US culture, but also in Hispanic (Hossain et al (1997)) and African-American (Hossain & Roopnarine (1994)) families, in southern Europe (Best et al (1994); Maridaki-Kassotaki (2002)), and in India (Roopnarine et al (1992)). In such cultures, the 'preference' for physical play over caretaking occurs despite variations in the employment patterns of mothers and fathers (Roopnarine et al (1992)) and in the fathers' commitment to shared parenting (Hyde & Texidor (1988)).

Data from other cultures and from other family types suggests that the picture is more complex. In some cultures, like the Aka hunter-gatherers in the Central African and Congo Republics (Hewlett & Lamb (2005)), men spend considerable amounts of their time caring for small children. Their involvement is required to ensure the children's very survival in a harsh physical environment. Within some industrial contexts, there is evidence of greater similarity between fathers and mothers, too. In contexts as diverse as northern Europe (Best et al (1994); Lamb et al (1982)), Israel (Sagi et al (1985)), and Taiwan (Sun & Roopnarine (1996)) fathers do not specialise in play roles. So, the different social styles of mothers and fathers do not seem to be the result of biological influences.

WHAT DETERMINES PATERNAL INVOLVEMENT?

As we have argued elsewhere (eg, Lewis & Lamb (2003)) we need to take into account many interrelated factors in order to understand why fathers' and mothers' styles of interaction are both similar and yet show differences. We have suggested that there are three key factors to take into account: paternal 'sensitivity' (examined in part above), the effects of the different roles performed by men and women outside as well as inside the family, and the family system, particularly the relationship between the parents. We will briefly examine these factors here.

Are fathers simply less sensitive than mothers to their children's needs? If so, we might not see the cultural differences reported above, but clearly there are wide variations in the extent and nature of interaction between fathers and their children. Some fathers take primary care of their children (on occasion because their partners openly admit to being temperamentally less able to perform the parenting role), some see their main role as providers (see, eg, Lewis (1986)), and a small minority deny their paternity and/or their commitment.

Because individual differences are so great, explanations of paternal involvement need to consider the interaction between individual and social factors. The data showing the hormonal changes experienced by new fathers (Storey et al (2000)) suggest that physiological changes are markers of investment in child care. But paternal sensitivity does not occur in a psychological or social vacuum. Fathers' interaction skills are related to their recall of their own positive childhood experiences (Cowan et al (1996)) as well as to their current feelings of well-being (Broom (1994)), and the extent of their involvement in infant care (Donate-Bartfield & Passman (1985)), such that, for example, men in impoverished families who live with their babies are more sensitive than their non-resident counterparts (Brophy-Herb et al (1999)). Evidently, therefore, the sensitivity of individual fathers is clearly affected by the time they spend interacting with their children and the roles they perform.

What determines the type of relationship men develop with their children? Clearly, sociological factors, like the employment opportunities for both men and women, have an impact although decisions about divisions of labour are often complex. There is now a large literature on the division of labour inside and outside the home and on the associations between involvement in these two spheres. Researchers have charted the continued rise in mothers' involvement in the labour force over the past 40 years, even when their children are young. Maternal employment is correlated with the amount of paternal care of infants (Hyde, Essex & Horton (1993); Lamb et al (1988)), preschoolers (Berry & Rao (1997)) and even school-age children (Crouter et al (1999)). Evidence from a national British study also shows that, by the early 1990s, fathers were the main carers for young children while their mothers were at work (36% of young children whose mothers work) and that fathers were more common such carers than all other relatives (35% of children) and professional child carers and nurseries (Ferri & Smith (1996)). Similar patterns are evident in the US (O'Connell (1993)).

It seems that shifts in the overall domestic division of labour are not made easily. In the 1980s, Anne Crouter and her colleagues (1987) found that increased maternal employment was accompanied by an increase in paternal involvement in child care and increased *dis*satisfaction between spouses. This could have been because the men were keen to maintain their sporting and leisure pursuits. More recent research has focussed on the early days of parenting, when mothers return to work. This suggests not only that parents express concern at leaving their young children (Deater-Deckard et al (1994)), but also that, when the children are under six months old, their fathers appear to be less responsive to their children when their partners work (Braungart-Rieker, Courtney & Garwood (1999); Grych & Clark (1999)).

To understand the interaction between internal psychological factors and the cultural processes that influence parents' choices about the care of infants and young children, we need to consider the family as a dynamic and interactive system. In 1975, Arnold Sameroff and Michael Chandler wrote a seminal article in which they depicted 'transactional' influences of individual family members upon the others. This concept takes both the family system and the notion of change very seriously. In many respects the research on fathers since then has demonstrated the validity of their argument. Family members not only influence each other directly, but also affect other relationships within the family (eg, Cummings, Goeke-Morey & Raymond (2004)). For a start, positive relationships between the parents predict more positive interactions with their infants (Beitel & Parke (1998); Grych & Clark (1999)) and toddlers (Goldberg & Easterbrooks (1984)). Indeed the relationship between the parents is often vital for the adjustment of family members (Cummings et al (2004)).

Secondly, however, the adjustment of individual family members can affect other relationships. For example, maternal depression has long been associated with long-term negative outcomes in children (Goodman et al (1993)), and when mothers become postnatally depressed, their husbands/partners engage in more positive interactions with the babies than men with non-depressed partners (Hossain et al (1994)). Recent research has shown that paternal depression has long-term consequences too. A study of 13,000 children found that when fathers were depressed eight weeks after the delivery, their children, particularly their sons, were more likely to have conduct problems or hyperactivity almost three years later even when later paternal scores on depression and maternal depression were taken into account (Ramchandani et al (2005)).

Patterns of familial influence thus have to be understood over time. We have long known, for example, that conflict between partners is a key predictor of the child's later adjustment (Davies et al (2002) and that adjustment in children sometimes predicts the parents' later adjustment to the relationship (O'Connor & Insabella (1999)). Such patterns of influence are not always purely reciprocal. Because mothers are the main caregivers and managers of the children in most (but by no means all) households, recent analyses of paternal influence have considered the possibility that they are 'gatekeepers' (Allen & Hawkins (1999)) of paternal involvement. While the evidence for this claim is complex (Zacharostilianakis-Roussou & Lewis (in progress)), it serves to point out that paternal involvement in two-parent households is influenced by a variety of interacting factors.

In this section, we have concentrated largely on households in which the adults are the child's biological parents. In blended families or homes with step-parents, the same patterns are even more apparent. We know, for example, that second partnerships show a steeper decline in reported marital satisfaction (Kurdek (1991)), are more characterised by open conflict (Hetherington & Clingenpeel (1992)) and that the children are viewed as sources of parental conflict both concurrently (Coleman et al (2001)) and at later time points (Jenkins et al (2005)).

DO FATHERS INFLUENCE THEIR CHILDREN'S DEVELOPMENT?

Developmental psychologists are principally concerned about the long-term consequences of earlier events in childhood. Family researchers focus upon whether relationships in childhood have an influence during and beyond this period. The closeness of mother– and father–child relationships has been examined in hundreds of studies, particularly those conducted by attachment theorists who claim that parental sensitivity determines the security of attachments which in turn underpin children's psychosocial development (Bowlby (1969)). There are so many of these studies that their results have been aggregated to reduce the effects of any bias present in single projects. This technique, known as meta-analysis, shows that the association between paternal sensitivity and the security of infant-father attachment is present but is clearly weaker than the same association between maternal sensitivity and the security of infant–mother attachment (Van IJzendoorn & DeWolff (1997)). Likewise, even though attachments to both parents correlate with higher level cognitive skills in toddlers (Belsky, Garduque & Hrncir (1984)), the maternal link appears to be stronger. Children's adjustment in the primary school years is predicted by earlier attachments to their mothers but not to their fathers in the UK (Steele et al (1999)), Germany (Suess, Grossmann & Sroufe (1992)), and the US (Main, Kaplan & Cassidy (1985)). At best, such longitudinal evidence suggests that secure father–child attachments can partly offset difficulties in mother–child attachments (Benzies, Harrison & Magill-Evans (1999); Verschueren & Marcoen (1999)).

Thus, research reliant on what some consider to be the 'gold standard' of developmental assessments suggests that fathers have less impact on their children than mothers do. At the same time, other measures have long suggested that fathers indeed influence their children. There are, for example, associations between fathers' interaction styles and their children's later language development (Magill-Evans & Harrison (1999)), IQ test scores (Wachs, Uzgiris & Hunt (1971); Yogman, Kindlon & Earls (1995)), and more general factors such as an interest in books (Lyytinen, Laakso & Poikkeus (1998)) and school attainment (Hoffman & Youngblade (1999); Lewis et al (1982)). Of course, such findings do not tell a coherent story about how, when, or whether men influence their children.

Longitudinal studies help us to explore such correlations further. When pieced together, the evidence is now clear that paternal 'influences' on children are discernible, but less clearly in the areas of research, like attachments, that have so preoccupied researchers. The data suggest that maternal attachments have clear predictive validity into the primary school years but that maternal influences may wane by the time the child enters secondary school. Several recent reports further suggest that aspects of paternal relationships with children appear to have more predictive power than similar measures of mother–child relationships and that their impact continues into adulthood. Thus, paternal involvement in childhood predicts the children's feelings of security in late adolescence (Grossmann et al (2002)), as well as their social interaction styles (Allen et al (2002)), their adjustment to spousal relationships, and their self-reported parenting skills (Burns & Dunlop (1998); Franz, McClelland & Weinberger (1991)) in adulthood.

Over the past five years, Eirini Flouri has conducted key research exploring these longitudinal patterns in the National Child Development Study, which followed 13,000 children from their births in 1958 up to the age of 33, as well as in studies of current parent-teenager relationships (Flouri (2005)). In several papers, she has found clear associations between paternal factors and later child adjustment, even when possible mediators (eg family structure, gender, maternal involvement, parental mental health, and parental SES) were taken into account. For example, father-involvement at age 7 predicted closeness to fathers and a lower likelihood of police involvement in their lives at 16 (Flouri & Buchanan (2002a)). Closeness to the father at 16 predicted marital satisfaction and lower psychological distress at age 33, while closeness to mother at age 16 predicted only later marital satisfaction (Flouri & Buchanan (2002b)). Flouri's more recent analyses have suggested such other links as those between paternal involvement and teenagers' academic motivation and general feelings of happiness (Flouri (2005)). Perhaps more importantly, she has also shown that paternal 'effects' may be mediated by the children's gender and family social background. For example, fathers' participation is related to daughters', but not sons', educational achievements in adult life, appears to protect all sons from delinquency, and protects sons in impoverished families from homelessness in adult life.

It is difficult to say why such links have been found, but given the centrality of play in father–child relationships, it might be that paternal influences are discernible because of the very differences between fathers and mothers. In Grossmann et al's (2002) study, fathers' play styles in interaction with their three-year-olds predicted the children's adjustment 13 years later. Such data echo Parson and Bales' (1965) and Berko-Gleason's (1974) claims that men might act as bridges between the family and the outside world.

THE INFLUENCE OF NON-RESIDENTIAL FATHERS

How do the patterns we have described above fit families after parental separation, when there is no resident father figure, or (in blended families) new father figures? The evidence shows that children seem better adjusted when they enjoy warm positive relationships with two actively involved parents (Amato & Gilbreth (1999); Hetherington (1999); Lamb (1999), (2002b); Thompson & Laible (1999)). Because children, particularly infants and toddlers, require regular interaction with their 'attachment figures' in order to maintain secure relationships, the absence of regular interaction may weaken infant–parent relationships (Lamb (2002a); Lamb, Bornstein & Teti (2002)). Thus comparisons of children in two- and single-parent families show differences in measures of adjustment, conduct and achievements at school, employment prospects, involvement in delinquency and the ability to establish and maintain intimate relationships (eg, Amato (2000); Hetherington & Stanley-Hagan (1999); Lamb (1999), (2002b); McLanahan (1999)). Flouri (2005) suggests that these associations are found because a minority of extreme or 'clinical' cases help to exaggeration the apparent effects of divorce/single parenthood, and it is clear that the majority of children are not adversely affected, in the long run, by their parents' separation (Emery (1999); Hetherington (2002)). As a result, we need to identify the specific ways in which parental separation/single parenthood influences children's lives so as to identify what makes some children react in an extreme way. Research has identified four inter-related factors.

First, and most importantly, single parenthood has long been correlated with social and financial stresses with which resident parents must bear (Herzog & Sudia (1973)). Such economic stresses or poverty appear to account not only for the statistical associations between single parenthood and child outcomes (McLanahan (1999)), but also for their consequences.

Secondly, single resident parents need to spend more time in paid employment and so spend less time with their children. Thus their levels of supervision and guidance are lower and less consistent than those of parents in two-parent families (Hetherington (2002)). In turn, disruptions in the amount and nature of parental stimulation and attention have been associated with measures of children's achievement, compliance, and social skills. Diminished supervision also makes anti-social behaviour more likely (Hetherington (2002)).

Thirdly, just as conflict between the parents is a strong predictor of children's adjustment in married families, so too is it vital to our understanding of the continuing processes associated with conflict or separation (Johnston (1994)), especially when that conflict is heightened or prolonged by the continuation of adversarial legal negotiations between parents. Kelly (2000) maintains that the 'effects of divorce' are largely the effects of pre-separation marital conflict more than negotiations after divorce. However, Mark Cummings (Cummings et al (2004); Cummings & O'Reilly (1997)) argues that conflict experienced during the separation or divorce is of less concern than that which continues after their divorce. This view is supported by the series of findings that anger-based marital conflict without parental separation is also associated with children's behaviour problems (Jenkins (2000); Jenkins et al (2005)).

Fourthly, separation often disrupts one of the child's enduring relationships, usually that with his or her father. As Amato (1993) has shown, the link between father absence and children's adjustment is complex. His meta-analysis showed no simple association between the *frequency* of father–child contact and child outcomes, largely because of the great diversity in the types of 'father-present' and 'father-absent' relationships studied (Amato & Gilbreth (1999)). Children's well-being *was* significantly better when their relationships with non-resident fathers were positive and when the non-resident fathers engaged in 'active parenting', however. This latter finding has also been reported by British researchers (Dunn, Cheng, O'Connor & Bridges (2004)) who have made clear that active paternal involvement, not simply the number or length of meetings between fathers and children, predicts child adjustment. This has clear implications for the amount and nature of contact with non-resident parents.

Other factors that help predict children's adjustment after parental separation include the children's socio-economic circumstances, the quality of relationships between both parents and their children, and the amount of conflict between the two parents (eg, Amato & Gilbreth (1999)). It is difficult to determine which factor is most important, particularly as repartnering further complicates this picture (Hetherington (2002)), although it is clear that contact with non-resident parents may not have the same positive effect on children when there is substantial conflict between the parents as it is does when levels of conflict are lower (Amato & Rezac (1994)).

In light of these patterns, should we legislate to establish joint residence after parental separations or reopen debates about the efficacy of mediation during the divorce process? The plight of the 'visitation father' has long been bemoaned. Children may well enjoy fun-filled outings with their fathers, but mothers often describe these in negative terms, and many men describe the process as sufficiently painful that they feel excluded from and pushed out of their children's lives following divorce (Wallerstein & Kelly (1980)) or cohabitation breakdown (Lewis, Papacosta & Warin (2002)).

CONCLUSION: FATHERS AND DURABLE SOLUTIONS

In this article, we have reviewed evidence suggesting that fathers play a central role in the lives of most children, even though the father–child relationship continues to be downplayed in much writing on families. Indeed the results of longitudinal studies following children into adulthood suggest that paternal influences can be stronger than maternal ones, although this might reflect the greater variation among fathers rather than any magical ingredient provided by men. Clearly, however, a strong case can be made that fathers should be considered as important contributors to their children's development and thus must be taken into account when we seek to identify durable solutions to children's adjustment to the dissolution of families. In this final section we consider how this might be done.

To begin, we must recognise that there are many cases in which non-resident fathers clearly have poor relationships with their children, usually as a result of their own psychopathology, substance abuse, or alcohol abuse. Likewise, conflictual or violent relationships between the parents prompt consideration because high conflict is reliably associated with poorer child outcomes following divorce (Kelly (2000); Maccoby & Mnookin (1992)), and in these cases there is good reason to limit contact and require supervision. Maccoby and Mnookin (1992) estimated that about 25% of separating families experience high levels of conflict around the time of divorce, but perhaps only 10% of these are severe enough to rule out contact with the violent parent. While the numbers of cases is quite low, allegation of conflict or even marital violence can be powerful tools in legal system, and can lead to dramatically lower amounts of court-sanctioned contact between fathers and children (Sternberg (1997)).

Greif (1997) estimates that perhaps 15% to 25% of children from separated families might not benefit or want contact with non-resident parents, and this, of course, implies that over 75% may well benefit from continued relationships. For this majority of cases, the prohibition of some form of co-residence has been justified by prejudices and beliefs rather than by clear empirical evidence (Warshak (2000)). Writing on behalf of a large group of 'experts' on the effects of divorce, Lamb, Sternberg, and Thompson ((1997); see also Kelly & Lamb (2000)) put forward the view that relationships between mothers, fathers and children would be enhanced by the establishment of parenting plans that focus the parents' attention on their shared interest in children's development. These plans would both maintain the quality of each parent's relationship and allow non-resident parents to maintain central roles in their children's lives. Overnight stays with non-residential parents are especially important psychologically for young children as they facilitate crucial social interactions and the daily activities that enhance child–parent attachments.

The design of such parenting plans can be guided by empirical research on normative child development. The literature on early attachments suggests the need to maximise the frequency of parent–child contact. Thus in early development, frequent transitions would serve this purpose whereas such frequent transitions might disrupt the routines of older children (Kelly & Lamb (2000)).

In conclusion, the research on early social development and analyses of the multiple correlates of parental separation together suggest that better and more durable solutions could be promoted by a shift in current practices. Children benefit from supportive relationships with both of their parents, whether or not those parents live together. Relationships are transactional in their influences and are thus dependent on continued opportunities for interaction. In order to ensure that both adults become or remain parents to their children, post-divorce parenting plans need to encourage participation by both parties in as broad as possible an array of social contexts on a regular basis. The occasional visits to a park, shared meals at fast food restaurants or occasional weekend visits do not maximise the development of parental relationships. Serious attention to the evidence on parenting suggests that close relationships with both parents serve children's best interests.

REFERENCES

Allen, JP, Hauser, ST, O'Connor, TG & Bell, KL 'Prediction of peer-rated adult hostility from autonomy struggles in adolescent-family interactions' (2002) 14 Development and Psychopathology 123–137

Allen, SM & Hawkins, AJ 'Maternal gatekeeping: Mothers' beliefs and behaviors that inhibit greater father involvement in family work' (1999) 61 Journal of Marriage and the Family 199–212

Amato, PR 'Children's adjustment to divorce: Theories, hypotheses, and empirical support' (1993) 55 Journal of Marriage and the Family 23–38

Amato, PR 'The consequences of divorce for adults and children' (2000) 62 Journal of Marriage and the Family 1269–1287

Amato, PR & Gilbreth, JG 'Non-resident fathers and children's well-being: A meta-analysis' (1999) 61 Journal of Marriage & the Family 557–573

Amato, PR & Rezac, S 'Contact with residential parents, interparental conflict, and children's behavior' (1994) 15 Journal of Family Issues 191–207

Beitel, AH & Parke, RD 'Parental involvement in infancy: The role of maternal and paternal attitudes' (1998) 12 Journal of Family Psychology 268–288

Belsky, J 'Mother-father-infant interaction: A naturalistic observational study' (1979) 15 Developmental Psychology 601–607

Belsky, J, Gilstrap, B & Rovine, M 'The Pennsylvania Infant and Family Development Project, I: Stability and change in mother-infant and father-infant interaction in a family setting at one, three, and nine months' (1984) 55 Child Development 692–705

Benzies, KM, Harrison, M.J & Magill-Evans, J 'Impact of marital quality and parent-infant interaction on preschool behavior problems' (1998) 15 Public Health Nursing 35–43

Berko-Gleason, J 'Fathers and other strangers: Men's speech to young children' in DP Dato (ed) *Language and linguistics* (Washington DC, Georgetown University Press, 1975) 289–297

Berry, JO & Rao, JM 'Balancing employment and fatherhood: A systems perspective' (1997) 18 Journal of Family Issues 386–402

Best, DL, House, AS, Barnard, AL & Spicker, BS 'Parent-child interactions in France, Germany, and Italy – The effects of gender and culture' (1994) 25 Journal of Cross-Cultural Psychology 181–193

Bowlby, J *Child care and the growth of love* (Harmondsworth, Pelican, 1951/54)

Bowlby, J *Attachment and Loss* Vol 1 Attachment (Harmondsworth: Penguin, 1969)

Braungart-Rieker, J, Courtney, S & Garwood, MM 'Mother and father–infant attachment: Families in context' (1999) 13 Journal of Family Psychology 535–553

Broom, BL 'Impact of marital quality and psychological well-being on parental sensitivity' (1994) 43 Nursing Research 138–143

Brophy-Herb, HE, Gibbons, G, Omar, MA & Schiffman, RP 'Low-income fathers and their infants: Interactions during teaching episodes' (1999) 20 Infant Mental Health Journal 305–321

Burns, A & Dunlop, R 'Parental divorce, parent–child relations and early adult relationships: A longitudinal study' (1998) 5 Personal Relationships 393–407

Clarke-Stewart, KA 'And daddy makes three: The father's impact on mother and young child' (1978) 49 Child Development 466–478

Cobbett, W 'Advice to Young Men: And (Incidentally) to Young Women, in the Middle and Higher Ranks of Life' in a *Series of Letters, Addressed to a Youth, a Bachelor, a Lover, a Husband, a Father, a Citizen, or a Subject* (London, Henry Frowde, 1928–32)

Coleman, M, Fine, MA, Ganong, LH, Downs, KJM & Puak, N 'When you're not the Brady Bunch: Identifying perceived conflicts and resolution strategies in stepfamilies' (2001) 8 Personal Relationships 55–73

Collins, WA & Russell, G 'Mother–child and father–child relationships in middle childhood and adolescence: A developmental analysis' (1991) 11 Developmental Review 99–136

Cowan, PA, Cohn, DA, Cowan, CP & Pearson, JL 'Parents' attachment histories and children's externalizing and internalizing behaviors: Exploring family systems models of linkage' (1996) 64 Journal of Consulting and Clinical Psychology 53–63

Crawley, SB & Sherrod, RB 'Parent–infant play during the first year of life' (1984) 7 Infant Behavior and Development 65–75

Crouter, AC, Helms-Erikson, H, Updegraff, K & McHale, SM 'Conditions underlying parents' knowledge about children's daily lives in middle childhood: Between- and within-family comparisons' (1999) 70 Child Development 246–259

Crouter, AC, Perry-Jenkins, M, Huston, TL & McHale, SM 'Processes underlying father-involvement in dual-earner and single-earner families' (1987) 23 Developmental Psychology 431–440

Cummings EM, Geoke-Morey, MC, Raymond, J 'Fathers in family context: Effects of marital quality and marital conflict' in M E Lamb (ed) *The role of the father in child development* (Chichester, Wiley, 2004, 196–221)

Cummings, EM & O'Reilly, AW 'Fathers in family context: Effects of marital quality on child adjustment' in ME Lamb (ed) *The role of father in child development* (New York, Wiley, 3rd edn, 1997) 49–65; 318–325

Davies, PT, Harold, GT, Goeke-Morey, MC & Cummings, EM 'Child emotional security and interparental conflict' (2002) 67 Monographs of the Society for Research in Child Development Serial number 270(3)

Deater-Deckard, K, Scarr, S, McCartney, K & Eisenberg, M 'Paternal separation anxiety: Relationships with parenting stress, child-rearing attitudes, and maternal anxieties' (1994) 5 Psychological Science 341–346

Dickson, KL, Walker, H & Fogel, A 'The relationship between smile type and play type during parent–infant play' (1997) 33 Developmental Psychology 925–933

Donate-Bartfield, D & Passman, RH 'Attentiveness of mothers and fathers to their baby cries' (1985) 8 Infant Behavior and Development 385–393

Dulude, D, Wright, J & Belanger, C 'The effects of pregnancy complications on the parental adaptation process' (2000) 18 Journal of Reproductive and Infant Psychology 5–20

Dunn, J, Cheng, H, O'Connor, TG & Bridges, L 'Children's perspectives on their relationships with their non-resident fathers: Influences, outcomes, and implications' (2004) 45 Journal of Child Psychology and Psychiatry 553–566

Emery, RE *Marriage, divorce, and children's adjustment* (Thousand Oaks, Sage, 2nd ed, 1999)

Ferri, E & Smith, K *Parenting in the 1990s* (London, Family Policy Studies Centre & Joseph Rowntree Foundation, 1996)

Flouri, E *Fathering and child outcomes* (Chichester, Wiley, 2005)

Flouri, E & Buchanan, A 'Father involvement in childhood and trouble with the police in adolescence: Findings from the 1958 British cohort' (2002a) 17 Journal of Interpersonal Violence 689–701

Flouri, E & Buchanan, A 'What predicts good relationships with parents in adolescence and partners in adult life: Findings from the 1958 British birth cohort' (2002b) 16 Journal of Family Psychology 186–198

Franz, CE, McClelland, DC & Weinberger, J 'Childhood antecedents of conventional social accomplishments in mid-life adults: A 35-year prospective study' (1991) 60 Journal of Personality and Social Psychology 586–595

Frascarolo-Moutinot, F Engagement paternal quotidien et relations parents–enfant [Daily paternal involvement and parent–child relationships] (unpublished doctoral dissertation, Universite de Geneve, Geneve, Switzerland, 1994)

Goldberg, WA & Easterbrooks, MA 'The role of marital quality in toddler development' (1984) 20 Developmental Psychology 504–514

Goodman, SH, Brogan, D, Lynch, ME, et al 'Social and emotional competence in children of depressed mothers' (1993) 64 Child Development 516–31

Greif, GL Out of touch: when parents and children lose contact after divorce (New York, Oxford University Press, 1997)

Grossmann, K, Grossmann, KE, Fremmer-Bombik, E, Kindler, H, Scheurer-Englisch, H & Zimmermann, P 'The uniqueness of the child–father attachment relationship: Fathers' sensitive and challenging play as a pivotal variable in a 16-year long study' (2002) 11 Social Development 307–331

Grych, JH & Clarke, R 'Maternal employment and development of the father–infant relationship in the first year' (1999) 35 Developmental Psychology 893–903

Herzog, R & Sudia, CE 'Children in fatherless families' in BM Caldwell & HN Ricuiti (eds) *Review of child development research* Vol 3 (Chicago, Chicago University Press, 1973) pp 141–232

Hetherington, EM For better or for worse: Divorce reconsidered (New York, Norton, 2002)

Hetherington, EM & Clingempeel, WG 'Coping with marital transitions' (1992) 57 Monographs of the Society for Research in Child Development (2–3, Serial No 227)

Hetherington, EM & Stanley-Hagan, MM 'The adjustment of children with divorced parents: A risk and resiliency perspective' (1999) 40 Journal of Child Psychology and Psychiatry and Allied Disciplines 129–140

Hewlett, BS & Lamb, ME 'Recent research and emerging issues in the study of hunter–gather childhoods' in BS Hewlett & ME Lamb (eds) *Hunter–gatherer childhoods: Ecological, developmental, and cultural perspectives* (Hawthorne, NY: Aldine, 2005) 3–18

Hobson, B (ed) Making men into fathers: Men, masculinities and the social politics of fatherhood (Cambridge, Cambridge University Press, 2002)

Hoffman, LW & Youngblade, LM *Mothers at work: Effects on children's well-being* (Cambridge: Cambridge University Press, 1999)

Hossain, Z, Field, TM, Gonzalez, J, Malphurs, J & Del Valle, C 'Infants of depressed mothers interact better with their nondepressed fathers' (1994) 15 Infant Mental Health Journal 348–357

Hossain, Z, Field, TM, Pickens, J, Malphurs, J & Del Valle C Fathers' caregiving in low-income African-American and Hispanic American families (1997) 6 Early Development and Parenting 73–82

Hossain, Z & Roopnarine, JL 'African-American fathers' involvement with infants: Relationship to their functioning style support, education, and income' (1994) 17 Infant Behavior and Development 175–184

Hyde, JS, Essex, MJ & Horton, F 'Fathers and parental leave: Attitudes and expectations' (1993) 14 Journal of Family Issues 616–641

Hyde, BL & Texidor, MS 'A description of the fathering experience among Black fathers' (1988) 2 Journal of Black Nurses Association 67–78

Jenkins, JM 'Marital conflict and children's emotions: The development of an anger organisation' (2000) 62 Journal of Marriage and the Family 723–736

Jenkins, J, Simpson, A, Dunn, J, Rasbash, J & O'Connor, TG 'Mutual Influence of Marital Conflict and Children's Behavior Problems: Shared and Nonshared Family Risks' (2005) 76 Child Development 24–39

Johnston, JR 'High-conflict divorce' (1994) 4 The Future of Children 165–182

Kaitz, M, Chriki, M, Bear-Scharf L, Nir, T & Eidelman, AI 'Effectiveness of primiparae and multiparae at soothing their newborn infants' (2000) 161 Journal of Genetic Psychology 203–215

Kaitz, M, Shiri, S Danziger, S, Hershko, Z & Eidelman, AL 'Fathers can also recognize their newborns by touch' (1994) 17 Infant Behavior and Development 205–207

Kelly, JB 'Children's adjustment in conflicted marriage and divorce: A decade review of research' (2000) 39 Journal of the America Academy of Child and Adolescent Psychiatry 963–973

Kelly, JB & Lamb, ME 'Using child development research to make appropriate custody and access decisions for young children' (2000) 38 Family and Conciliation Courts Review 297–311

Kurdek, LA 'Marital stability and changes in marital quality in newly wed couples: A test of the contextual model' (1991) 8 Journal of Social and Personal Relationships 27–48

Labrell, F *Educational strategies and their representations in parents of toddlers* Paper presented at the Fourth European Conference on Developmental Psychology (Sterling, England, 1990)

Labrell, F 'A typical interaction behavior between fathers and toddlers: Teasing' (1994) 3 Early Development and Parenting 125–130

Labrell, F, Deleau, M & Juhel, J 'Fathers' and mothers' distancing strategies towards toddlers' (2000) 24 International Journal of Behavioral Development 356–361

Lamb, ME 'Effects of stress and cohort on mother– and father–infant interaction' (1976a) 12 Developmental Psychology 435–443

Lamb, ME 'Interactions between two-year-olds and their mothers and fathers' (1976b) 38 Psychological Reports 447–450

Lamb, ME 'The development of mother–infant and father–infant attachments in the second year of life' (1977a) 13 Developmental Psychology 637–648

Lamb, ME 'The development of parental preferences in the first two years of life' (1977b) 3 Sex roles 495–497

Lamb, ME 'Father–infant and mother–infant interaction in the first year of life' (1977c) 48 Child Development 167–181

Lamb, ME 'Fathers and child development: An introductory overview and guide' in ME Lamb (ed) *The role of the father in child development* (New York, Wiley, 3rd edn, 1997) 1–18, 309–313

Lamb, ME 'Non-custodial fathers and their impact on the children of divorce' in RA Thompson & PR Amato (eds) *The post-divorce family: Research and policy issues* (Thousand Oaks, CA, Sage, 1999) 105–125

Lamb, ME 'Infant–father attachments and their impact on child development' in CS Tamis-LeMonda & N Cabrera (eds) *Handbook of father involvement: Multidisciplinary perspectives* (Mahwah, NJ, Erlbaum, 2002a) 93–117

Lamb, ME 'Noncustodial fathers and their children' in CS Tamis-LeMonda & N Cabrera (eds) *Handbook of father involvement: Multidisciplinary perspectives* (Mahwah, NJ, Erlbaum, 2002b) 169–184

Lamb, ME (ed) *The role of the father in child development* (New York, Wiley, 4th edn, 2004)

Lamb, ME, Bornstein, MH & Teti, DM *Development in infancy* (Mahwah, NJ, Erlbaum, 4th edn, 2002)

Lamb, ME, Frodi, AM, Frodi, M & Hwang, CP 'Characteristics of maternal and paternal behavior in traditional and nontraditional Swedish families' (1982) 5 International Journal of Behavioral Development 131–141

Lamb, ME, Hwang, CP, Broberg, A, Bookstein, FL, Hult, G & Frodi, M 'The determinants of paternal involvement in primiparous' (1988) 11 Swedish families International Journal of Behavioral Development 433–449

Lamb, ME Sternberg, KJ & Thompson, RA 'The effects of divorce and custody arrangements on children's behavior, development, and adjustment' (1997) 35 Family and Conciliation Courts Review 393–404

Lewis, C *Becoming a father* (Milton Keynes, UK, Open University Press, 1986)

Lewis, C 'Fathers and preschoolers' in ME Lamb (ed) *The role of the father in child development* (New York, Wiley, 3rd edn, 1997)

Lewis, C & Lamb, ME 'Fathers' influences on children's development: The evidence from two-parent families' (2003) 18 European Journal of Psychology of Education 211–228

Lewis, C, Newson, LJ & Newson, E 'Father participation through childhood' in N Beail and J McGuire (eds) *Fathers: Psychological perspectives* (London, Junction, 1982) 174–193

Lewis, C, Papacosta, A & Warin, J *Cohabitation, separation and fatherhood* (York, York Publishing/Joseph Rowntree Foundation, 2002)

Lyytinen, P, Laakso, ML & Poikkeus, AM 'Parental contribution to child's early language and interest in books' (1998) 13 European Journal of Psychology of Education 297–308

Maccoby, EE & Mnookin, RH *Dividing the child: Social and legal dilemmas of custody* (Cambridge, MA, Harvard University Press, 1992)

Magill-Evans, J & Harrison, MJ 'Parent–child interactions and development of toddlers born preterm' (1999) 21 Western Journal of Nursing Research 292–307

Main, M, Kaplan, N & Cassidy, J 'Security in infancy, childhood and adulthood: A move to the level of representation' (1985) 50 Monographs of the Society for Research in Child Development 66–104

Mansbach, IK & Greenbaum, CN 'Developmental maturity expectations of Israeli fathers and mothers: Effects of education, ethnic origin, and religiosity' (1999) 23 International Journal of Behavioral Development 771–797

Maridaki-Kassotaki, K 'Understanding fatherhood in Greece: Father's involvement in child care' (2000) 16 Psicologia: Teoria e Pesquisa 213–219

McLanahan, SS & Teitler, J 'The consequences of father absence' in ME Lamb (ed) *Parenting and child development in 'nontraditional' families* (Mahwah, NJ: Erlbaum, 1999) 83–102

Notaro, PC & Volling, BL 'Parental responsiveness and infant–parent attachment: A replication study with fathers and mothers' (1999) 22 Infant Behavior and Development 345–352

O'Connell, M *Where's papa? Fathers' role in child care* (Washington, DC, Population Reference Bureau, 1993)

O'Connor, TG & Insabella, G 'Marital satisfaction, relationships and roles' in EM Hetherington, S Henderson & D Reiss (eds) *Adolescent sibling in stepfamilies: Family functioning and adolescent adjustment* (1999) 64 Monographs of the Society for Research in Child Development (4, Serial No 259)

Parke, RD, Dennis, J, Flyn, ML, Morris, KL, Killian, C, McDowell, DJ & Wild, M 'Fathering and children's peer relationships' in ME Lamb (ed) *The role of the father in child development* (Hoboken, NJ, Wiley, in press)

Parke, RD & O'Leary, SE 'Family interaction in the newborn period' in K Riegel & J Meacham (eds) *The developing individual in a changing world* Vol 2 Social and environmental issues (The Hague, Mouton, 1976) 653–663

Parke, RD & Sawin, DB *The family in early infancy: Social interactional and attitudinal analyses* Paper presented at the meeting of the Society for Research in Child Development, New Orleans (1977, March)

Parsons, T & Bales, RF *Families, socialization and interaction process* (New York, Free Press, 1955)

Pleck, JH & Masciadrelli, BP 'Paternal involvement by US resident fathers: levels sources and consequences' in ME Lamb (ed) *The role of the father in child development* (Chichester, Wiley, 2004) 222–271

Rödholm, M & Larsson, K 'The behavior of human male adults at their first contact with a newborn' (1982) 5 Infant Behavior and Development 121–130

Roopnarine, JL, Talukder, E, Jain, D, Joshi, P & Srivastav, P 'Personal well-being, kinship tie, and mother–infant and father–infant interactions in single-wage and dual-wage families in New Delhi' (1992) 54 India Journal of Marriage and the Family 293–301

Sagi, A, Lamb, ME, Shoham, R, Dvir, R & Lewkowicz, KS 'Parent–infant interaction in families on Israeli kibbutzim' (1985) 8 International Journal of Behavioral Development 273–284

Sameroff, AJ & Chandler, MJ 'Reproductive risk and the continuum of caretaking casualty' in FD Horowitz, M Hetherington, S Scarr-Salapatek, and G Siegal (eds) *Review of child development research* Vol 4 (Chicago, University of Chicago Press, 1975) 187–244

Solomon, Y, Warin, J & Lewis, C 'Helping with homework? Homework as a site of tension for parents and teenagers' (2002) 28 British Educational Research Journal 603–622

Sternberg, KJ 'Fathers, the missing parents in research on family violence' in ME Lamb (ed) *The role of the father in child development* (New York, Wiley, 3rd edn, 1997) 284–308; 392–397

Steele, H, Steele, M, Croft, C & Fonagy, P 'Infant–mother attachment at one year predicts children's understanding of mixed emotions at six years' (1999) 8 Social Development 161–178

Storey, AE, Walsh, CJ, Quinton, RL & Wynne-Edwards, RE 'Hormonal correlates of paternal responsiveness in new and expectant fathers' (2000) 21 Evolution and Human Behavior 79–95

Suess, GJ, Grossmann, KE & Sroufe, LA 'Effects of infant-attachment to mother and father on quality of adaptation in preschool: From dyadic to individual organisation of self' (1992) 15 International Journal of Behavioral Development 43–65

Sun, LC & Roopnarine, JL 'Mother–infant, father–infant interaction and involvement in childcare and household labor among Taiwanese families' (1996) 19 Infant Behavior and Development 121–129

Tamis LeMonda, C & Cabrera, N (eds) *Handbook of father involvement* (Mahwah, NJ, Erlbaum, 2002)

Thompson, RA & Laible, DJ 'Noncustodial parents' in ME Lamb (ed) *Parenting and child development in 'nontraditional' families* (Mahwah, NJ, Erlbaum, 1999) 103–123

Van IJzendoorn, MH & DeWolff, MS 'In search of the absent father–meta-analyses of infant–father attachment: A rejoinder to our discussants' (1997) 68 Child Development 604–609

Verscheuren, K & Marcoen, A 'Representation of self and socioemotional competence in kindergartners: Differential and combined effects of attachment to mother and to father' (1999) 70 Child Development 183–201

Wachs, T, Uzgiris, I & Hunt, J 'Cognitive development in infants of different age levels and from different environmental backgrounds' (1971) 17 Merrill-Palmer Quarterly 283–317

Wallerstein, JS & Kelly, JB *Surviving the breakup* (New York, Basic Books, 1980)

Warin, J, Solomon, Y, Lewis, C & Langford, W *Fathers, work and family life* (London, Family Policy Research Centre, 1999)

Warren-Leubecker, A & Bohannon, JN III 'Intonation patterns in child-directed speech: Mother–father differences' (1984) 55 Child Development 1379–1385

Warshak, RA 'Blanket restrictions: Overnight contact between parents and young children' (2000) 38 Family and Conciliation Courts Review 422–445

White, D, Wollett, A & Lyon, L 'Fathers' involvement with infants: The relevance of holding' in N Beail & J McGuire (eds) *Fathers: Psychological perspectives* (London, Junction, 1982)

Winnicott, DW *The family and individual development* (London, Tavistock, 1965)

Yogman, MW, Kindlon, D & Earls, F 'Father involvement and cognitive-behavioral outcomes of preterm infants' (1995) 34 Journal of the American Academy of Child and Adolescent Psychiatry 58–66

Zacharostilianakis-Roussou, I & Lewis, C *The maternal gatekeeping hypothesis examined* (in preparation)

PARENTING DISPUTES, GENDER CONFLICT AND THE COURTS

Professor Carol Smart

The Morgan Centre for the Study of Relationships and Personal Life,
School of Social Sciences, University of Manchester

INTRODUCTION

Prior to the introduction of the Children Act 1989 there was, in policy debates, considerable concern over the extent to which legal procedures and legal terminology might contribute to hostility and promote an adversarial attitude amongst parents at the time of divorce or separation. The architects of the Children Act hoped that by affirming the paramountcy of the welfare principle and promoting a policy of negotiation between parents coupled with a non-interventionist approach by the courts, the legislation would go some way to defuse conflict between divorcing parents. The Act was based (in part) on an aspiration that the (re)newed emphasis on the welfare of the child would deflect parents away from hostility towards a joint (future-oriented) parenting project. In refusing to dwell on the past the new ethos also hoped to move parents 'on' in emotional terms, rather than allowing bad feelings to dominate the divorce process. The Act also abolished the legal terms 'custody' and 'access', which were seen to cause a sense of inequality among parents or a feeling of there being winners and losers. These terms were replaced by the terms 'residence' and 'contact', and the new term 'parental responsibility' was introduced to deflect emphasis away from the idea of parental rights. All these measures taken together were meant to emphasise a sense of 'shared' parenting after divorce or separation.

In addition, with the implementation of the Child Support Act 1991 and the setting up of the Child Support Agency, child support issues were separated from the legal processes of divorce, separation, matrimonial property, residence and contact. Although this reform was driven by different principles and developed separately from the Children Act, it was also hoped that in turning child support into an essentially bureaucratic issue, separate from emotional issues or issues of fault, the opportunities for conflict could be reduced.

Yet, more recently, with the realisation that conflict between parents does not seem to have abated, it has been felt that it would help parents to overcome their conflicts if they could be directed towards their children's needs and anguish and so an increasing emphasis has been placed on the voice of the child, in addition to the more conventional welfare of the child principle. So more information is being made available to parents about children's experiences of divorce, and greater consideration is being given to involving the voices of children (if not actual children) in mediation and court processes. All (or perhaps almost all) of these have been welcome measures based on good principles However, the conflict does not appear to be abating; indeed it appears as if it is getting worse and the hostility that is part of the divorce process now seems also to be directed at the system (CAFCASS, the Children Act itself, judges etc) and not just the ex-spouse.

In this paper, I[1] shall examine the extent to which a policy which might be described as one of 'conflict deflection' and/or 'conflict avoidance' in the divorce process can really be successful.

---

[1] Many of the ideas and data relied upon in this paper are the product of joint work. Research with children funded by the ESRC and Nuffield Foundation has been carried out with Drs Jennifer Flowerdew, Bren Neale, and Amanda Wade, while the research on conflict in courts which was funded by the DCA was carried out in collaboration with Dr Vanessa May.

Without being critical of the principles underlying the Children Act, I would argue that experience over the last 25 years indicates that parental conflict is a much harder problem to solve than might have been imagined. Moreover, it would appear that while certain elements of parental conflict seem to be unchanging (eg financial matters), other elements or foci seem to be shifting or growing in significance. Thus conflict over children seems to have expanded in recent years as more fathers are claiming time with their children rather than (or in addition to) moving on to found new families. Moreover, the conflict has become both more political and more focused on gender difference. This emphasis on gender has not been raised by the women's movement as were issues of the impoverishment of ex-wives under old divorce legislation, or the incidence of domestic violence, but has been raised by the various groups which go to make up the fathers' movement in the UK. While I do not suggest that the family law system is neglectful of this conflict, I do suggest that some of the measures that have been or are being taken to deal with the problem seek to marginalise the conflict and/or deflect it rather than recognising that some conflict may be intractable and/or that it may require long-term intervention, or even that in 'solving' one area of conflict there will inevitably be others that emerge as social conditions change. In other words all the steps that we seem to take assume that it is possible to be rid of conflict and, if conflict does not diminish or disappear, we tend to assume that previous policies have been misguided or are ineffectual.

To pursue my discussion I will draw on recent research projects with both children and parents in high conflict cases. In the first section I will focus on the perspective of children and young people and their feelings about enduring parental conflict following divorce. Here I will consider not just how damaging children report the conflict to be, but also how they too wish that parents could find a way of either resolving the conflict or living with the hurt and pain of divorce in a less destructive manner. In the second section I concentrate more on the shape and content of parents' anger when they are involved in divorce proceedings. Arising from this I will suggest that in high conflict cases many parents are quite unaware that their conflict is in any way harmful to their children because they are so convinced of the righteousness of their cause. But I also argue that negative feelings are such a dominant element of the divorcing process that we need to pay more critical attention to the social meanings embedded in these conflicts. Finally I shall suggest that we need once again to be more aware of the gendered nature of these conflicts. Controversially, I suggest that parents do not raise children but that mothers and father do, and that gender-neutral terminology may only obscure some of the problems we face.

THE PROBLEM OF PARENTING DISPUTES FROM THE PERSPECTIVE OF CHILDREN

Parenting disputes can take a number of forms and research suggests that some types of parental conflict are more damaging to children than others (Harold et al (1997); Reynolds (2001); Kelly (2003)). Particularly problematic are forms of conflict which appear to involve the children themselves and those that are without apparent resolution. Thus, it is argued that it is not having rows about everyday matters that is intrinsically harmful to children, but the sort of conflict that can occur prior, during and after a divorce or separation is likely to fit into the harmful category because parents may not 'make up' and they may be fighting over the children themselves rather than more neutral issues. Temporary conflict and hostility is reported by children to be distressing but if this settles down and parents can achieve a relatively civilised demeanour then it seems that children too can regain an equilibrium. But conflicts which endure over a long time, even many years, which are both about and involve the children, and which have no resolution at all, create a major burden for these children (Smart, 2006). Such negative relations might be called toxic because they create an emotionally poisonous environment in which children are required to grow up.

In previous research we have sought to establish children's views on post-divorce family life (Smart, Neale and Wade (2001)). More recently we have carried out further research with a subsample of the same children (60 from the original 117) in order to develop a more longitudinal perspective on children's experiences over time. This second round of interviews also allowed children to reflect upon changes to their circumstances and to take a longer view of the ways in which their families have changed. For a subset of these children a major concern was the ongoing conflict between their parents. Some parents had been divorced (or separated) for 10 or 12 years at the point of the second interview, and yet it was the problem of unresolved dispute that still loomed large for the children.

From this study we drew the conclusion that a core problem for children is that the conflict not only endures long beyond the 'point' of legal divorce but that it becomes a way of life which is sustained years after the family court system has lost interest in the families concerned. What was interesting was that we found that some of the children of these highly conflicted parents sought counselling or were sent for counselling themselves (and sometimes indeed appeared to suffer from adjustment problems), but the parents themselves were doing nothing to address their own ongoing behaviour. Thus while the parents could see that their children were distressed and they were willing, even eager, to have their children 'treated', they could not see that these problems were related to their ongoing behaviour. Thus parents might 'blame' the divorce as if it was the actual separation that generated negative outcomes, but they saw the problem as belonging to someone else or as being located somewhere else. The children however were much more likely to see their parents as responsible for their living conditions and problems. Often they expressed severe regret at the behaviour of their parents:

> **Caitlin (16 years):** I think it's very important [that parents talk to each other] because, if your parents were like constantly arguing with each other or about each other, you'd feel more like your family had gone. Whereas, if they are still talking then it's more, you know, your family is still there even if they are not together.

This quotation from Caitlin expresses the extent to which parental conflict over years isolates children. The sense of abandonment described here is not related to the actual separation of her parents, but to the emotional abandonment caused by their ongoing conflict with each other. Thus children may feel that they 'lose' both parents, not just the stereotypical one parent, after the divorce:

> **Cheryl (12):** I can remember some arguments and I can remember thinking 'Oh my god my parents hate each other' but now I don't think they hate each other; they are friends. But if you argue in front of your children they will think you hate each other.

And some children are often cut off from support from wider kin because the thing that troubles them most (the conflict) they are not able to speak about because it appears to be an act of gross disloyalty. Moreover, it often means a child cannot go to one parent for support if they feel the other parent (or their new partner) is being unfair or uncaring because they know it will ignite more conflict. So these young people have to shoulder their burdens alone, or risk talking to friends and other outsiders. Although they did not express their situation in sociological terms, these children often seem to be talking about a loss of cultural and emotional capital. They lost the support of their parents and the kinds of material, emotional and interpersonal securities which go with it. They saw their parents as impoverishing their lives because they were so intent on pursuing their own grievances:

> **Cheryl (12):** Sometimes I think my mum and dad have been really, really selfish by fighting over us and stuff like that. But you can understand it, but sometimes you get so infuriated by it you could just strangle them both.

These young people were rarely in a position to intervene directly in their parents' conflicts; most felt they had to put up with them until they could leave home. Others took sides and saw the other parent as 'the enemy' too, while yet others withdrew in various ways. Often the most difficult situation was for children who had to continue seeing both parents and who therefore continually lived through the conflict whenever they left one parent to join the other.

In many ways the goals of the children of high conflict parents we interviewed chimed with current policy goals. When asked they almost unanimously said that they most wanted their parents to stop fighting and to just get on with life. They did not expect their parents to be friends, but they wanted them to be 'civilised'. Some children had come to the realisation that their parents had been divorced for longer than they had ever been married and yet still their old grievances were what fuelled their ongoing conflicts. They felt resentful that this conflict had become the virtual motif of their childhoods.

> **Jonathan (9):** Well one of the things I'd like to say to [parents getting divorced] would be that whatever you do; you do what would be better for the child rather than them – because they've had it. They've done what they want, but the child is still growing up. So if they did split up then they have got to make it [work] even when they go to each other. All I'd say is really that do what's best for the child and ask the child.

Jonathan who was only nine at the time of our second interview (he was five at the first interview) very clearly expressed the view that parents should not inflict their problems on their children and that they have a responsibility to put their problems to one side so that their children may still have a good childhood. His moral stance could not be clearer, and undoubtedly this view is much the same as the feelings of many solicitors, judges and mediators. However, what the older children often began to realise was that, although they suffered because of their parents' behaviour, their parents were not necessarily able to change their emotional responses and actions. One of the older 'children' in our sample who had lived with both parents 50% of the time throughout her childhood and into early adulthood (as a university student) made this point:

> **Angela (20):** You know all parents mess up their children whether they intend to or not. And then I have talked to my friends and they say 'Actually no'. Some people have normal parents and it doesn't happen like that and they are just there to support them when they need it. And I'm like, 'Well I never had that experience you know'. ... I think all parents do pass on neurosis to their children even the normal ones. So I think possibly I might be more a product of the way my actual parents are than because they are divorced.

Here Angela puts her finger on a major problem for the family law system. She began to realise that the divorce alone was not the issue for her parents, but simply the kind of people they were – or had become. It probably did not matter whether they were still together or not, they were going to continue in a kind of pathological and toxic relationship with each other in which they involved their children, for as long as they possibly could. Neither parent was able to change the script. It is clear from this that any kind of quick intervention at the time of divorce would have little chance of redirecting these embedded antagonisms and the irony in this particular case was that both of these parents were involved in the counselling and family policy professions.

These children and young people's accounts provide an insight into a much deeper set of problems than just a degree of 'unreasonableness' or 'heightened emotions' at the point of divorce/separation. Moreover, this intractable long-term conflict is much more of a problem for them.

PARENTAL PERSPECTIVES ON THEIR DISPUTES

The second study I draw on here is one on residence and contact disputes in court that we conducted between 2002 and 2004. The first part of the study was based on an analysis of court files in three county courts (Smart et al (2003)) but here I draw on the second stage based on 61 interviews with (34) mothers and (27) fathers who had been to court in 2001 and 2002 (Smart et al (2005)). This interview sample was reached through the court records (with names and addresses accessed only by court staff until consent was obtained) in our three county courts.

As discussed above, the Children Act encourages parents to recognise that they have a joint, on-going responsibility for their children, and to focus on what would be best for them. It also acts as a call to parents to rise above whatever distress or anger they are experiencing at the breakdown of their relationship, and to put their children's interests above their own feelings. Unfortunately it appears that parents are less ready or able to separate events that have occurred during a marriage or relationship from the issue of what should happen to the children. Notwithstanding the importance of creating a clear-cut distinction between adults' issues and children's issues, parents' emotions and feelings rarely followed this admirable logic (Brown & Day Sclater (1999)). We found that parents linked these issues because it was precisely these disputes which generated the breakdown of trust which in turn meant that the erring parent was deemed to be unworthy of spending time with or caring for the children. These parents saw the other parent as wholly 'bad' and hence a damaging influence on their children. In what follows I explore this logic in a number of areas because I suggest that it is important to grasp how deep seated the problems are in order to avoid oversimplifying the issues at stake. The areas I have selected here are financial matters; broken trust; and the impact of new partners.

Parents and the significance of financial disputes

Along with other many other studies (Maclean & Eekelaar (1997); Lewis et al (2002): 29, 39–40; Bradshaw et al (1999); Trinder et al (2002): 33; Herring (2003): 95–96; Davis, Wikeley & Young (1998); Barton (1998)), we found that the parents in our sample felt that child support and contact were interconnected issues. Typically residential parents (most often mothers) claimed that the contact parent (most often fathers) showed their lack of commitment to the children by failing to pay child support, and thus forfeited their right to contact. This feeling, it appears, runs very deep because financial support is taken as a proxy for love particularly where fathers are concerned because the idea that a 'good' father is predominantly a good provider is still a powerful motif for many parents. The father who does not do his duty by his children is seen to be an unworthy figure in their lives and when the courts appear to 'overlook' this deep character flaw if is often found to be quite offensive to ordinary people.

This account by a residential mothers expresses this logic and it becomes clear how the issue becomes a running sore and is not one that she can put behind her in order to 'move on':

> **Ellen**: When Wes left me I was penniless, I feel very disgruntled that the court would not in any way pick up any maintenance issues, 'Oh we will just leave that to the CSA'. I am still waiting for the CSA to sort it out and it is four years down the line. I feel very disgruntled about that because my ex-husband has a 300-acre farm in [X]shire, he has a 4x4 Shogun, she has a Nissan Patrol, they have race horses, they have just bought a brand new tractor. [. . .] I cannot get a penny and I feel that that is another issue that really the court should pick up and sort out. And I feel most disgruntled that time and time again the issue of maintenance was brought up very, very vaguely and just wiped under the carpet. [Residential mother, residence dispute]

The following quote is from a contact father who had gone to court after the residential mother had stopped contact. He argued that he had proved that he had 'earned' the right to contact by paying for the mother's bills through her pregnancy and by providing financial support for their son.

> **Stuart**: But I still kept in contact, paid bills and still had contact with my little boy. Well I did not know he was a little boy then, I was paying some phone bills and things like that right up until the birth. And then we started something with more structure but I cannot remember what the payments were, every week, something along those lines. And when that was working ok I got to see my little boy more or less whenever I wanted. [Contact father, contact dispute]

Stuart's account reveals the moral calculus that many parents work with. If the father is economically supportive he shows himself to be sufficiently decent to merit contact. It is a sign of trustworthiness and good character. These parents' views may be out of step with current family law, yet they hold fast to a moral code in which it is the father's obligation to support his children and, through this economic support, to demonstrate both love and responsibility, while it is the mother's obligation to facilitate the father–child bond or relationship as long as he behaved as fathers 'should'.

The belief that paying child support is a moral duty appears to receive wide support in England and Wales. In 2004 an Omnibus survey reported that 81% of the respondents thought that fathers should pay child support (Peacey & Rainford (2004): 14). 67% of the respondents went further and asserted that a father should pay the same amount of support to his first family regardless of whether he had subsequent children (Peacey & Rainford (2004), 15). In other words a commitment to the duty that fathers should provide economic support for their (first) children runs deep. This finding is relevant to our smaller qualitative study because it puts in context the strength of feeling that parents express when a father fails to support his children, or when a father is supporting his children – yet cannot have contact. We found that the bureaucratic disaggregation of financial support from emotional support was not something that many parents could readily grasp because it simply ran counter to their ethical code. For the parents it was a combined moral obligation, not a disaggregated bureaucratic one.[2] But what is also demonstrated is how these conflicts have the capacity to run and run and cause bitter resentment over many years.

Parents and the significance of broken trust

Another set of issues that could be uppermost in parents' minds was to do with broken trust or vows, and how to come to terms with what was perceived to be disingenuous behaviour on the part of a former spouse. This meant that although parents 'should' be focusing on children, they were actually preoccupied with blame and recrimination. Trinder et al (2002: 38) also found that the way in which the emotions connected with a relationship breakdown were managed by parents affected the quality and quantity of contact. The parents in our sample, for example, could use details of past infidelity against the other parent. In these cases, it seemed as though the dispute was actually about the failed relationship between the parents, and this acrimony spilled over into matters of contact and residence. Thus some parents might have agreed contact, but the arrangements kept breaking down because of their continued bitterness rather than for reasons to do with child welfare.

In the interviews some parents went further and would make a link between 'immoral' behaviour and suitability to parent. This is perhaps part of what Day Sclater (1999: 172) has identified as a part of the divorce process – looking back at the past to make sense of and reinterpret events – and James (2003: 136–137) argues that it is perhaps even too much to expect parents not to do so. In our sample, such revisiting of the past could mean that the parent who had left the marriage was seen as having less of a claim to the children.

> **Jeffrey**: She should have been held guilty of breaking a marriage up; there was not a no-fault divorce *it was her fault totally*. She had no good reason for divorce and she should have therefore kept her vows and the children should have come to the parent best able to look after them – myself simply because I was physically able to look after them and because I had the money coming in, if you like. I had the chance of an income and also because I was not the one who destroyed the damn family and therefore morally they should have come to the person who was not guilty if the court had been involved at all. [Contact father, residence dispute]

These fathers expressed a simple view that the party who was, in their eyes, morally culpable should not benefit from their behaviour. Such views are not supported by the Children Act 1989, but they would not of course have been incongruous with legal policy before the Divorce Reform Act 1969. The fathers who held these views were quite clear that they were the innocent parties and that justice lay in punishing the guilty. This meant that 'losing' the residence of their children added insult to injury and that these fathers could not 'get over' their anger at all easily.

But mothers too, and even entire extended families, could be appalled by the behaviour of one parent, and seek to exclude the erring spouse from contact with their children. In one case from our study of children we found that after the father left the mother for 'another woman', the

---

[2]   Although the Children Act 1989 treats these issues as separate, it is actually confusing for parents that the Child Support Agency, when calculating child support payments, *does* take the amount of contact into consideration (Pirrie (2000)).

paternal grandparents sided with their daughter-in-law and shared their condemnation of their son with their grandsons, even as long as a decade after the divorce. One of the sons explained:

> **Josh (17):** His mum and dad, we always talk about it, me and them two, we talk about how much we all hate her [the second wife]. And they know him, well obviously, he's their son; and they still say, they would never say it to his face because they know it would break his heart, but they still don't know what he is doing with her because, they just can't see it in her, they just can't see what [he sees in her].

In this case the mother made contact difficult (but not impossible) when her sons were young, but by the time they were in their teens they were reluctant to go to see their father on their own account because they shared the 'family moral stance' that he was an unworthy and failing father. The point I wish to make here is that the modern ethos – that such matters should be put aside in order to promote an ongoing relationship between parents and children – is simply unthinkable in this kind of family culture. Again I are not condoning or condemning these values, rather I seek to demonstrate that such a stance (lack of forgiveness) should not simply be approached as a psychological impediment that can be overcome by a few hours of mediation or some kind of shock treatment like the threat of imprisonment.

Parents and the significance of new partners

The third issue raised by many of the parents as central to the conflict was that of new partners. Even quite good arrangements that exist between divorced parents can be disrupted when one of them repartners (Simpson et al (1995): 17, 30–31; Trinder et al (2002): 32; Bradshaw et al (1999): 110–111; Smart & Neale (1999)). This theme of new partners igniting or being the root cause of a dispute also emerged from our interview data. One got the impression from many of the accounts that arrangement might have been running relatively smoothly until one of the parents repartnered, which then caused problems for contact with the children. For example, Kenneth believed that his former wife had become jealous of his new relationship:

> **Kenneth:** Initially when the marriage broke there was not too much [of a] problem with contact, in fact at one stage I felt I was being, I could not cope with the amount of contact I was having. I was on my own and come to terms with that, the problem started when I met someone else within quite a short time I was getting phone calls virtually 10 minutes before I was due to pick them up saying the children are not coming. [. . .] In the end it got to the stage where contact was severed entirely, no real explanation given, other than silly explanations i.e. you are feeding the children vegetarian food and your girlfriend is too young. [Contact father, contact dispute]

Contact parents often saw this behaviour as unjustified, spiteful, and against the interests of the children. Residential parents however spoke of their worry about their children being 'brought up by' or being 'taken over' by a rival parent (cf Trinder et al (2002): 32). In some of the interviews we conducted it was clear that the arrival of a new partner could signal problems as, for example, in the case of a father who second marriage was to an alcoholic. In this case, once he split up with his second wife, staying contact was resumed. So the fears that parents may have about new 'step' parents can be well founded and speak deeply to issues of who they feel they can trust to look after their children.

In other cases, it could be the contact parent who became worried about a new 'step' parent living in the house with their children. This could lead to new conflicts and even attempts to alter residence agreements:

> **Norman:** Then I heard that Ashley had been hit. I was walking past the school and Ashley said 'Dad, dad, dad.' And of course I got over to her 'What is up darling?' 'Lee hit me.' Well it's like rocket fuel that is someone has hit your kid.

> **Interviewer:** That is your ex-wife's boyfriend?

> **Norman:** Yes, so I calmed down, 'Fine, Ashley, leave it with me.' I got in the car straight down to Social Services, told them, [X], 'Right' he said, 'I will look into it.' [Contact father, residence dispute]

We also found that new partners could alter the dynamics between former couples by themselves investing in ongoing disputes and supporting their partner in pursuing further court cases. In some of our interviews which included new partners it became clear that a dispute over residence or contact could become a joint enterprise for the couple, into which both invested a huge amount of energy. The often huge costs (both personal and financial) of these disputes could in turn affect the quality of life of the stepparent's own children or new children born to the couple. The dispute could become a joint project which could entail the stepmother (for it usually was the father's new partner who became so closely involved in the dispute) meeting with a court welfare officer, with solicitors, or even going to court to show solidarity against the former spouse. Exactly how 'helpful' this strategy might be is perhaps open to doubt because such tactics could increase the hostilities between the parents. However, the point is that these cases (like the case of Josh above) reveal the extent to which these conflicts can become 'family affairs', owned by quite a lot of people and not just the biological parents of the children concerned. A lot of people may have a stake in pursuing the conflict and in such circumstances it becomes much more difficult to 'let go' of the dispute.

THE ISSUE OF GENDER

The fathers' movement has put the issue of gender back on the agenda for family law. It is not just that there are calls for equal treatment for fathers with mothers, but some segments of the movement also see the whole family law 'system' as siding with women (as well as being staffed by women or foolish men overly influenced by women). I will not be drawn into the issue of equal treatment and discrimination here because it seems to me to be more important to look behind these surface claims. In practice it would seem that English family law has always been highly conscious of gender difference and has sought to match remedies to the realities of the lives of wives and husbands, mothers and fathers. Thus courts are aware that mothers tend to be the primary carers of children and that fathers tend to work full time and, in practice, opt in and out of child care. The problem is that the forward-looking ethos of current policy, combined with the ideals of equal and/or shared parenting is making such practices appear to be 'outmoded' or problematic. We therefore face an ironic situation in which the (apparently) most desirable outcome of disputes over children (namely shared care) does not reflect gendered everyday practices, but arises from an aspirational set of principles which are compelling but for which there may be limited support.

This reintroduction of gender as a specific element in criticising how courts manage the conflict between parents reflects an interesting social change in which – in the context of divorce or separation at least – the care of children has become re-interpreted as a privilege rather than a burden. Thus mothers are seen as over-privileged because their closeness with children is taken for granted (notwithstanding that the feminist movement has long argued that this very taken for grantedness has been the source of discrimination against women). Fathers, on the other hand, are seen a deprived if they cannot continue to have almost daily care of (or contact with) their children. Even 25 years ago this would have been unthinkable. There is not space here to explore why this shift has come about but it does represent a very real source of conflict between men and women in which attempts at deflection into a focus on children's needs seemed likely to fail. Perhaps what is needed is (in parallel with other measures such as involving children in the process of decision making) is a recognition of the source and basis of this conflict. In arguing this I am making a case for a more sociological understanding of the enduring nature of conflict between parents than the more usual perspective which sees the inability to resolve conflict as a personal failure or a pathology generated within specific relationships. These latter 'causes' may be perfectly valid and do seem to be particularly relevant when practitioners are dealing with parents on a case by case basis. But there is a major social change on going and it seems likely that both practitioners and politicians will be constantly frustrated by the ways in which parents continue to engage in conflict, notwithstanding their efforts, unless we can appreciate the constantly mutating basis for the conflict.

REFERENCES

Barton C 'Third time lucky for child support? The 1998 Green Paper' (1998) 28 Family Law 668–672

Bradshaw, J, Stimson, C, Skinner, C & Williams, J *Absent fathers?* (London, Routledge, 1999)

Brown, J & Day Sclater, S 'Divorce: A psychodynamic perspective' n Bainham, Andrew, Lindley, Bridget, Richards, Martin & Trinder, Liz (eds) *Children and their families: Contact, rights and welfare* (Oxford, Hart Publishing, 1999)

Davis, G, Wikeley, N & Young, R (with J Barron & J Bedward) *Child support in action.* (Oxford, Hart Publishing, 1998)

Day Sclater, S *Divorce: A psychosocial study* (Aldershot, Ashgate, 1999)

Harold, GT and Conger, RD 'Marital conflict and adolescent distress: The role of adolescent awareness' (1997) 68(2) Child Development 333–350

Herring, J 'Connecting contact: Contact in a private law setting' in Bainham, Andrew, Lindley, Bridget, Richards, Martin & Trinder, Liz (eds) *Children and their families: Contact, rights and welfare* (Oxford, Hart Publishing, 2003)

James, A 'Squaring the circle – the social, legal and welfare organisation of contact' in Bainham, Andrew, Lindley, Bridget, Richards, Martin & Trinder, Liz (eds) *Children and their families: Contact, rights and welfare* (Oxford, Hart Publishing, 2003)

Kelly, JB 'Legal and educational interventions for families in residence and contact disputes' in Dewar, John & Parker, Stephen (eds) *Family law: Processes, practices and pressures* (Oxford, Hart Publishing, 2003)

Lewis, C, Papacosta, A & Warin, J *Cohabitation, separation and fatherhood* (York, Joseph Rowntree Foundation, 2002)

Maclean, M & Eekelaar, J *The parental obligation: A study of parenthood across households* (Oxford, Hart Publishing, 1997)

Peacey, V & Rainford, L *Attitudes towards child support and knowledge of the Child Support Agency*, (Research Report No 226) (London, Department for Work and Pensions, 2004)

Pirrie, J 'The child support, pensions and social security bill' (2000) 30 Family Law 199–203

Reynolds, J (ed) *Not in front of the Children? How conflict between parents affects children* (London, One Plus One, 2001)

Simpson, B, McCarthy, P & Walker, J *Being there: Fathers after divorce,* (Relate Centre for Family Studies, University of Newcastle upon Tyne, 1995)

Smart, C, May, V, Wade, A & Furniss, C *Residence and contact disputes in court* Vol 1 (Research Series 6/03) (London, Department for Constitutional Affairs, 2003)

Smart, C, May, V, Wade, A & Furniss, C *Residence and Contact Disputes in Court* Vol 2, (Research Series No 4/05) (London, Department for Constitutional Affairs, 2005)

Smart, C & Neale, B *Family fragments?* (Cambridge, Polity Press, 1999)

Smart, C, Neale, B & Wade, A *The Changing Experience of Childhood: Families and Divorce* (Cambridge, Polity Press, 2001)

Trinder, L, Beek, M & Connolly, J *Making contact: How parents and children negotiate and experience contact after divorce* (York, Joseph Rowntree Foundation, 2002)

REFERENCES

... ...

CONTACT IN PRIVATE AND PUBLIC LAW CASES: MANAGING TWO OR MORE FAMILIES

CONTACT AND CHILDREN'S WELL BEING IN PRIVATE AND PUBLIC LAW

Dr Danya Glaser

*Consultant Child & Adolescent Psychiatrist, Department of Psychological
Medicine, Great Ormond Street Hospital for Children*

CONSIDERATIONS

The fact that the issues of contact needs to be considered implies a less than ideal situation for a child. This situation may well have been preceded by separation, likely acrimony or possible maltreatment. Contact is, by its nature, a more or less happy compromise or the least detrimental alternative for all the parties concerned. It is, therefore, particularly important to ensure that contact arrangements are optimal for the child. As will be described elsewhere, the evidence base for this is not by any means complete and it may therefore be useful to consider some generic principles. The issues discussed here concern direct contact.

THE CIRCUMSTANCES

There are three circumstances within which contact will be required:

(1) during interim care, either under s 20 accommodation or under a (usually interim) care order;

(2) following a permanent alternative placement;

(3) following parental separation or divorce.

CONTACT WITH WHOM

Contact is designed to enable the child to maintain some sort of a connection with one or more important persons in the child's (usually previous) life. These persons include

- the child's parent or parents
- siblings
- grandparents
- other extended family
- previous foster carers.

THE PURPOSES OF CONTACT

In the heat of the decision-making process about contact, its purposes are sometimes overlooked. There are a number of purposes for contact, not all of which will apply in every case. There are often different considerations when the vantage points are those of others in the child's life, including siblings. Those views and interests may not be in the particular child's best interests or they may be in actual conflict with them. There may also appear to be a conflict concerning human rights. It is important to consider those interests which pertain to the particular child. Interestingly, they apply both in private law and care proceedings.

Continuity in the face of discontinuity

The maintenance of contact allows for some continuity in a child's life when the child is faced with a major discontinuity and a relationship has been interrupted. It reduces some of the pain of a separation and reduces the trauma of a sudden move. This applies not only to parents but also to contact with grandparents and siblings.

Maintenance of a relationship

Contact enables the child to continue a relationship during a separation, which at its inception may be intended to be a temporary one, or whose duration is uncertain in the early stages. This too applies not only to parents but also to contact with grandparents and siblings.

Reduced discomfort of divided loyalty and guilt

In the context parental separation or divorce, a continuing relationship with both parents reduces the divided loyalties, which a child often feels towards the parents. In care proceedings, children who may come to sense the benefit of the alternative placement are more able to enjoy this if contact is maintained with a parent who is supportive of the placement or does not criticise it.

Reassurance about parents' well being

Separation for the child often follows parents' own serious difficulties and/or the separation may leave the parent distressed and angry. Children often worry about their parent(s) even when the child does express their concern.

Maintaining a realistic view of non-resident or biological parent(s)

A child separated from their parent is unlikely to have formed a neutral view of their parent. Over time and without regular updating, the view of the parent is more likely to move in the direction of either idealisation or vilification. Contact allows for a more reality-based view to develop.

Links with biological roots and identity

This is relevant for younger children who are placed cross-culturally and becomes important for all children as they approach adolescence. Identity includes the questions at any one time, 'who am I and how do I see myself in relation to others'. While identity is experienced and owned by the child, how others view, and interact with, the child contributes to the child's experience.

Reality of shared parental responsibility

Parental responsibility loses its meaning somewhat for children who are old enough to understand it, when there is no direct contact with that parent.

Shared understanding of past

An understanding of the circumstances which have led to the (need for) separation becomes increasingly important as the child grows older. A meaningful narrative is far more likely to be created between the child and the parent than with the child alone.

Likelihood of later reunion in adulthood

The majority of children who are separated from a significant member or members of their family will find a way of meeting them again sometime during their life. The greater the extent of the separation, the more important this may become in later life. Clearly, continuity of contact will facilitate the maintenance of this relationship. This is especially important for sibling groups of children who were removed from their parents' care.

Maintaining shared past experiences

Sibling contact enables a child to continue to share an important thread of past experiences and weave them into a shared future.

EVIDENCE OF BENEFIT OF CONTACT

As well as these theoretical considerations, there is empirical evidence for the benefit of contact, some of which is summarised here and will be amplified in the following papers.

Private law

Children benefit from contact with their fathers, within which there is a good quality of relationship, this being defined as warm, authoritative, supportive and involved. This is especially important when children live with a, now, single mother.

Conversely, the absence of a father and lack of contact with him has been found to be associated with girls' early sexual activity and with teenage pregnancy.

However, in order for contact to be of benefit, there needs to be good cooperation between the parents. Moreover, the benefit of contact with fathers is maintained when the fathers do not abuse substances and are not involved in anti-social behaviour.

Fostering and adoption

In temporary placements, more frequent contact is associated with earlier rehabilitation. However, both the frequency of contact and rehabilitation may well be associated with a 'good enough' interaction with the child which are considered to be beneficial rather than harmful to the child. Indeed, the level of family dysfunction is the best predictor of level of contact and rehabilitation.

In long-term placements, there is no clear evidence that contact is related to the child's functioning. There is some evidence of increased stability of placements with contact. There is no evidence that contact will invariably hinder the formation of new attachments. Attachments are particular relationships which build up over time when the child lives in proximity and care of the person who will become their attachment person. Security of attachment is dependent on the caregiver's sensitivity to the child's needs especially when child feels threatened, frightened or distressed. A child can form new attachments while previous ones exist.

PREREQUISITES

With such a list of purposes and benefits of contact, the question may be asked as to why contact is not invariably established. The reality is, however, that unless a number of prerequisites are satisfied, the benefits of contact may be outweighed by significant disadvantages which may amount to significant harm.

The most important one is the child's safety. This includes protection from sexual abuse, emotional abuse in the form of blame and being used in a conflict between parents and neglect during staying contact.

Can contact be sustained reliably? If not, the child is likely to be not only disappointed and angry but also feel unloved or guilty for, in some ill-understood way, displeasing their parent.

Direct contact with a parent, or other family member, who does not support the child's placement faces the child with a painful dilemma in which the child's wish (and capacity) for maintaining a simultaneous relationships with different persons is not tolerated by one of those persons. This lack of support may be expressed implicitly in a manner which is difficult to challenge but is nevertheless keenly perceived by the child, or explicitly to the child. Equally, without the approval and practical support of contact by the resident/caregiving parent, the child will feel a conflict between his/her wishes and the need to please and retain the positive relationship with the current parent. These relationships form a triangle, within which all the relationships need to be free of tangible conflict if the child's interests are to be assured.

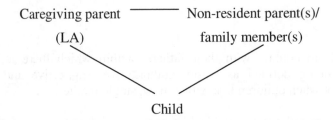

Caregiving parent ———— Non-resident parent(s)/
(LA)   family member(s)

Child

Children's wishes

The issue of a child's wishes is both central and problematic for a number of reasons. Not acceding to, or not heeding a child's wishes requires careful consideration. The age of the child is an important factor and the older the child, the greater the weight that will be attached to that view.

Most children wish for contact with parents, siblings and extended family when separated from them. Children often want more contact than is being offered. Children's wishes about contact change over time and this fact needs to be recognised, anticipated and accommodated in the decision-making process about contact, which therefore has to be an ongoing one, or one into which periodic review is incorporated.

Acceding to children's wishes?

While it is important to elicit a child's wishes about the nature of future contact, children may well wonder why they are being consulted if their wishes are then not followed. Whenever possible, children's wishes for contact should be acceded to. Reasons for not doing so need to be explained to the child honestly and in an age-appropriate way and will be likely to include those mentioned above.

It appears at times to be easier to refuse a child's wishes for contact, than to accept a child's refusal of contact. A child's reluctance or refusal of contact needs to be understood before it can be acted upon, either by agreeing or by finding a way of helping the child to change their view and wishes, if that is considered appropriate.

Children's reasons against contact

Some children continue to fear a parent or sibling with whom they no longer live. This fear is usually understandable in the light of past experiences such as abuse by that person of violence which was witnessed. The child may not be able to voice their fear spontaneously. An extreme form of such fear if post-traumatic stress disorder, in which even the thought of meeting the person again may trigger intense fear. Again, such fears may not be immediately apparent.

Following separation, a child may continue to harbour unresolved anger at a parent or sibling for abuse or violence perpetrated by them. Loyalty to a resident parent who was subjected to violence is allied to such anger and may lead to the child not wishing to have contact with the non-resident parent.

The role of the child's current caregiver in determining the child's reluctance or refusal to have contact is frequently raised. This may be an adoptive or foster parent, but is more likely to be a divorced or separated parent.

CONTACT IN SPECIFIC CONTEXTS

Despite the apparent differences between decisions in private law cases and care planning in public law cases, the principles to be considered regarding contact are, as has been outlined here, very similar. The following section examines some principles for enhancing the likelihood of establishing and maintaining contact which will be of benefit to the child, in different contexts.

Negotiating for contact

When there is a need for negotiation in order to establish contact, the process will usually be a prolonged and pains-taking one, requiring skilled, sensitive practice and human resources. It requires exploring with the child the reasons for their reluctance, which the child may not be able to articulate immediately, even when they emanate from the child. Such conversations might more fruitfully explore what the child fears or worries might happen if contact were to be established and what the effect would be on others close to the child. This introduces the possibility of contact rather than discussing reasons for avoiding it. It also opens the way for dispelling fears, finding ways of overcoming the feared circumstances. It might also shed light on reality-based and reasonable fears which need to be respected.

Work will also be required with the child's current caregivers, and the person with whom contact is being sought separately. In private law disputes, entrenched spousal positions which ignore the effect on the child and the child's interests may well amount to emotional abuse of the child, which should be named. It is important also that the non-resident parent conveys and maintains a genuine interest in child rather in the perpetuation of a battle over the child.

Contact post separation/divorce

Much has been written about this subject and principles are well recognised. Suffice it to say that some direct mode of communication is necessary between parents so that the child does not need to act as a conduit for any information exchange between the parents.

Contact post domestic violence

For contact to be established and supported following domestic violence and parental separation, there is a need for the following:

The parent responsible for the violence needs to offer some acknowledgement and accept some responsibility for the violence. The parent also needs to accept the fact that the violence has affected the other parent and the child(ren) adversely. Domestic violence is a poor model for conflict resolution and it is to the child's and the parent's benefit if the child can be helped, preferably by that parent, to develop appropriate attitudes to violence and more adaptive ways of solving disputes and conflicts.

Contact during interim placements

Following the placement of children in interim care, frequent contact is instituted in order to maintain the relationship between the child and their family in the interim. This contact is often observed for the purpose of supervision, to ensure the child's well-being and safety. However, a valuable opportunity is often lost to assess the parents' capacity for change. This can be achieved by providing the parents with regular feedback about aspects of their interactions with the children during contact which are of concern, and offering detailed guidance towards change. This might convert the interim period into what could be termed 'constructive months'.

Contact during transitions

Although children are now moved less frequently during the process of decision-making about the child's future, children rarely undergo a single move only. If contact can be maintained with previous carers during a period of settling into another placement, the adverse impact on the child of, possibly repeated, disruptions in caregiving will be reduced. This can continue also when the child is placed in a permanent alternative family, or is returned to the biological family. With such overlapping care, the effects of discontinuity are reduced. There is no evidence that maintaining initial, and diminishing, contact with a previous carer will prejudice the formation of new attachments. Rather, such an arrangement is more likely to soften the separation and loss which the child experiences when leaving the care of a parent figure.

Contact following decisions for permanent alternative care

Following a decision that a child will not return to the care of his/her parents, there is usually a period of waiting before the child is placed in an alternative permanent family. During this period, reduced contact is usually maintained until the permanent placement. Children are rightly aware of court proceedings and decisions. However, as the child will usually remain in the same placement for some time, it is important to reduce the frequency of contact immediately, in order for the child to comprehend and experience the reality of the court's decision.

Contact in permanency

Certain principles have been found important in order to ensure that direct contact between children in permanent alternative families and their biological family can take place and will be of benefit to the children.

- A named person who is preferably familiar to both the biological and the 'new' family needs to act as an intermediary.

- There needs to be some mode of communication between the 'biological' and the 'new' parents. From the child's perspective, direct meetings are preferable, but this cannot necessary be achieved. The purpose of this communication is for the child to feel comfortable in maintaining a relationship with both families.

- Contact requires preparation of the child, the permanent parents and the biological family.

     The child may become distressed either at meeting their family of origin or on leaving the contact. This distress may extend and continue upon return to their permanent family and may be expressed in a variety of ways which may be disturbing to the child and their family. Predicting this possibility and preparing the child and their (permanent) parents for this possibility reduces the discomfort and anxiety about the effects of contact and enables the parents to support the child after contact. The child's parents may have concerns about the contact, particularly if the child shows a marked reaction following contact. In order for them to remain supportive of contact, their concerns need to be heard and responded to.

The child may have unrealistic expectations of their birth family, both fearful and idealised. The child may feel anxious in anticipation of the contact, particularly if it is not frequent. It is helpful to talk about the child's anticipations before the contact.

The birth family needs to be prepared for the contact, particularly if it is infrequent. This is often a very sensitive and emotive experience for the parents and the child needs to be shielded from the intensity of the parents feelings.

- Contact in permanency should be sufficiently infrequent to allow child to settle into their new family and to be sustainable by the new parents and the biological family. It needs to be sufficiently frequent to be meaningful and not too unusual so as to become very special and possibly disruptive to the child's life. Birthdays and special occasions such as Christmas are now part of the child's life in their permanent family and are rarely appropriate times for contact.

Contact between siblings in different placements

The purpose and meaning of maintaining contact between siblings in separate placements is different from contact with parents. Sibling contact should be held separately from contact with birth parents and is often more frequent. The children's permanent carers are the most appropriate persons to organise this contact. Siblings also require honest explanations about the reasons for placing them separately.

Contact in kinship placement

When children are placed within their extended families, there is sometimes concern about the effect of contact between the child and their birth parents, or possibly siblings. It is, however, rarely realistic to prohibit contact, it may not be possible to rely on the family to supervise the direct contact, telephone contact is very likely and it is difficult to prescribe the frequency of contact. The child and the kinship carer are both very likely to carry conflictual loyalties towards the excluded biological parent.

CONCLUSIONS

Contact arrangements are complex and costly of resources if they are to be implemented with benefit to the child. They will need to be adapted for each individual child and family and arrangements may need to be adjusted over time with the child's age and changes in circumstances of the child and their birth family. Much time is spent during final hearings in discussing and planning contact arrangements. The subsequent reality does not necessarily conform to these plans, particularly if the permanent alternative parents whose views will need to be included in the implementation of contact are not yet identified.

Finally, the question needs to be asked always: For whose benefit is this contact?

REFERENCES

Argent, H (ed) *Staying connected* (BAAF, 2002)

Dunn, J 'Annotation: Children's relationships with their nonresident fathers' (2004) 45 Journal of Child Psychology and Psychiatry 659–671

Erickson, E *Childhood and society* (Penguin Books, 1977)

Macaskill, C *Safe contact?* (Russell House Publishing, 2002)

Quinton, D, Rushton A, Dance, C & Mayes, D 'Contact between children placed away form home and their birth parents: Research issues and evidence' (1977) 2 Clinical Child Psychology and Psychiatry 393–413

Quinton, D, Selwyn, J, Rushton, A & Dance, C 'Contact between children placed away form home and their birth parents: Ryburn's "Reanalysis" analysed' (1999) 4 Clinical Child Psychology and Psychiatry 519–531

Sturge, C & Glaser, D 'Contact and domestic violence – the experts' court report' (2000) 30 Family law 615–629

CONTACT WITH NON-RESIDENT PARENTS AFTER SEPARATION AND DIVORCE

Joan Hunt

Senior Research Fellow, Oxford Centre for Family Law and Policy, Department of Social Policy and Social Work, University of Oxford

A number of beliefs have come to dominate the current public debate about contact after separation and divorce (see, for example, the House of Lords debate on the Second Reading of the Children and Adoption Bill [Hansard, 29 June, 2005, col 249 on]):

- first, that contact is almost always in the interests of the child;
- second, that substantial proportions of children have too little contact with their non-resident parents, typically fathers;
- third, that the primary reason for this is unreasonable resistance to contact by the resident parent, usually the mother;
- fourth, that other jurisdictions handle these matters much better than we do.

This paper will examine the research evidence for these beliefs.

IS CONTACT ALMOST ALWAYS IN THE INTERESTS OF THE CHILD?

There are many reasons to think that contact *can* be of value to children. *Sturge and Glaser*[1] (2000) summarise the theoretical benefits as: meeting the child's needs for: warmth; approval; feeling unique and special to a parent; extending experiences; developing or maintaining meaningful relationships; information and knowledge; reparation of distorted relationships or perceptions. It can also help to preserve/establish links with the wider family and maintain children's social capital (Amato (1996)).

Moreover research indicates that most children want contact (Maccoby et al (1993); Wallerstein and Kelly (1980); *Dunn et al* (2001); *Mitchell* (1985); O'Brien and Jones (1996); *Walczak and Burns* (1984); Taylor et al (2001)) and see their non-resident parent as an important figure in their lives, who is still part of their 'family' (Furstenberg and Nord (1985); Funder (1996); *Dunn* (2001)). The loss of contact is painful for children and has even been found to be the worst aspect of parental separation (Kurdek & Siesky (1980), cited by Pryor and Rodgers (2001)). Wallerstein and Kelly (1980) write that 'the intense longing for greater contact persisted undiminished over many years, long after the divorce was accepted as an unalterable fact of life' and *Walczak and Burns* (1984) that 'some of the saddest feelings came from adults who had lost a parent for ever'. There are, of course, children who refuse contact (Johnston (1993)); and a UK study of children subject to welfare reports (*Buchanan et al* (2001)) found that about a third would be prepared to forego contact if it meant a cessation of parental conflict. However even in this study two-thirds of the children said that they usually enjoyed their contact visits, and even higher figures are reported by McDonald (1990) and Taylor et al (2001).

However research does not show that contact, in itself is demonstrably good for children. A review of 32 US studies (Amato (1993)) reported that while 15 did find contact to be positively associated with well-being; 10 found no association and seven found negative effects. A later meta-analysis which pooled the results of 63 US studies (Amato and Gilbreth (1999)) found that while positive child outcomes were linked to the payment of child support, there was no such link with frequency of contact. The study did find stronger associations between frequency of contact and child well-being in more recent studies, and suggested this might be because contact fathers were now more committed to the parental role and have better parental skills. Future

---

[1] References to UK literature are in italics.

studies, therefore, they hypothesised, might begin to produce stronger evidence that contact benefits children. However recent UK studies confound this expectation: while *Dunn* (2003), reports 'unequivocal' findings that more contact was associated with fewer adjustment problems, two others (*Smith et al* (2001) and *Iervolino et al* (forthcoming)), have found no association. On the basis of research to date, therefore, one must conclude, in the words of Pryor and Rodgers (2001) that 'the assumption that contact per se is measurably good for children does not stand up to close scrutiny'.

What research does show is that whether children benefit from contact depends on the nature of their relationship with the contact parent; the quality of parenting provided and the extent to which they are caught up in inter-parental conflict. In sum, it is the quality of contact, rather than frequency, that is important' (Hetherington, Bridges and Insabella (1998); Lamb, Sternberg and Thompson (1997); Lamb (1999); Emery (1999); Rodgers and Pryor (1998); Taylor et al (1991); *Iervolino et al* (forthcoming)). To quote again from Pryor and Rodgers:

> 'The mere presence of fathers is not enough. Children benefit from having them in their lives when the relationship is positive, supportive, and involved and this is true whether parents are together or apart. Conversely, negative, intrusive and abusive father-child relationships are not good enough for children, regardless of family structure.' (Pryor and Rodgers (2001))

The relationship between the child and the contact parent

Many recent studies report that a good relationship with their non-resident father can have a positive effect on children's well-being (*Iervolino et al (forthcoming),* Amato and Gilbreth (1999); *Dunn (2003); Dunn et al* (2004); King, Harris and Heard (2004); Manning and Lamb (2003); *Smith et al* (2002); White and Gilbreth (2001); Amato and Rivera (1999); Buchanan & Maccoby (1996); Salem et al (1998)). While the findings are not totally consistent, Amato and Gilbreth's meta-analysis of 63 studies found that 'feelings of closeness' between the child and the contact parent was positively associated with children's academic success and negatively associated with children's externalising and internalising problems. Moreover, while some research (Bray and Berger (1999)) suggests that the effects may dissipate over time, a recent UK study (*Iervolino et al* (forthcoming)) found that 'relationship quality was an important predictor of adjustment both concurrently and longitudinally'. Further, these effects were independent of children's relationships with resident mothers and stepfathers.

The quality of parenting

> 'To the extent that men remain involved in parenting after separation, or assume parenting practices they have not done before, they have a positive influence. As in intact families, the most effective way they can parent is by providing authoritative parenting. In both original and separated families it is these aspects of parenting encompassing monitoring, encouragement, love and warmth that are consistently linked with child and adolescent well-being.' (Pryor and Rodgers (2001))

Another important factor affecting whether children benefit from contact is the extent to which the non-resident parent engages in *authoritative parenting,* as distinct from being a *fun* dad who provides treats and adopts a role more akin to that of an adult friend (Buchanan and Maccoby (1996); Furstenberg & Cherlin (1991); Hetherington, Bridges and Insabella (1998); Simons et al (1994); Pryor and Rodgers (2001)). Amato and Gilbreth's meta-analysis (1999) found this to be linked to academic success and the absence of internalising and externalising problems. Indeed one study (Simons et al (1994)) found 'active parenting', providing 'emotional support, praising the child's accomplishments and discipline' to be even more important for the well-being of adolescents than how close they felt to their contact parent. It should be noted, however, that a recent UK study of secondary school children found, contrary to expectations, that even 'involved' non-resident fathers had no measurable impact on their well-being (*Welsh et al* (2004)).

The significant of exposure to inter-parental conflict

> 'The level and intensity of parental conflict is the most potent factor in children's post-divorce adjustment. High conflict between parents is the single best predictor of a poor outcome.' (Garrity and Baris' (1996))

'What was unacceptable for the children was conflict which impacted on them. Such conflict ... can lead to significant unhappiness. At the least, children wanted their parents to contain their disputes so they did not have to be involved, or used as emotional props, or turned into allies, spies of go-betweens in a parental war.' (*Smart et al* (2001))

Some of the most consistent and compelling research findings concern the impact on children of being exposed to inter-parental conflict (Amato and Rezac (1994); Amato and Sobolewski (2001); Buehler et al (1997); Davies and Cummings (1994); Doolittle and Deutsch (1999); Emery (1982, 1999); Goodman et al (2004); Grych (2005); Grych and Fincham (2001); Hetherington (1999); Kelly (2000); Lamb et al (1997); Long et al (1988); Johnston et al (1989); Wekerle and Wolfe (1999)). A recent summary by Grych (2005) reports that:

'Children are at risk for developing a range of emotional and behavioural problems, both during childhood and later in life. In addition to higher levels of anxiety, depression and disruptive behaviour, children who witness hostility and aggression are more likely to be abusive towards romantic partners in adolescence and adulthood and to have higher rates of divorce and maladjustment in adulthood.'

Johnston (1994) found that children of high conflict divorce were two to four times more likely to be clinically disturbed in emotions and behaviour. A meta-analysis of 68 US studies (Buehler et al (1997), cited Grych (2005)), found that the association between inter-parental conflict and child adjustment was nearly twice that reported for the effect of divorce on children.

Though there is scant UK evidence, one study of children subject to welfare reports (*Buchanan et al* (2001)) found that almost half showed significant levels of emotional and behavioural difficulties. Interviewed 12 months on, the proportion showing abnormal levels of distress were nearly twice the level expected in the general child population and comparable to children who had been involved in care proceedings. For children in cases where domestic violence was an issue rates were three times as high. *Cockett and Tripp* (1994) found lower levels of self-esteem in children whose parents continued to fight after separation and *Lund* (1987) that where the parental relationship was conflicted and contact was continuing children were less well-adjusted than in families where the relationship was harmonious (although better than those where there was no contact).

A degree of conflict, of course, is an inescapable part of family life and may be regarded as almost normative in the early stages of separation (Shifflett and Cummings (1999)). Nor is conflict in itself, even frequent conflict, necessarily damaging (Buehler (1997); Grych (2005); Goodman et al (2004)) and children will vary in their susceptibility (Johnston (1994)). Indeed some studies have found no, or only weak, associations between poor adjustment and conflict per se (Amato and Keith (1991), King and Heard (1999)). Rather what appears to be important is the extent to which children are exposed to/caught up in conflict which relates to them, the duration of the exposure; the level of conflict and how it is expressed; whether and how it is resolved (Buchanan et al (1991); Camara and Resnick (1989); Cummings and Davies (1994); Grych and Fincham (1993, 1999); Johnston et al (1987); Sales et al (1992)). As Grych has recently written:

'The type of conflict most closely associated with maladjustment is destructive conflict (Cummings et al (2001)) ie disagreements that are hostile, aggressive, poorly resolved and pertain to the child...What is most critical is how parents manage the disagreements: conflict is increasingly threatening to children as it increases in hostility, anger, contempt and aggressiveness. Children are unlikely to be affected by conflict that is expressed calmly, respectfully, and resolved effectively. Couples who cannot resolve arguments constructively but can keep them behind closed doors, will shield children.' (Grych (2005))

Unfortunately, it is the destructive type of conflict to which children tend to be exposed where there are prolonged disputes over contact. The children find themselves the focus of, and are likely to witness and/or be caught up in, their parent's conflict. It is the feelings of caughtness which may be particularly critical (Buchanan et al (1991)) and the words children use to describe this – 'elastic band', 'a tug of war', 'the eye of a cyclone', and 'being in the middle of World War 3' – (Taylor et al (2001)) speak volumes. Indeed Buehler's meta-analysis found that the impact of conflict which was expressed by, for example, denigrating the other parent, was almost as great as that of conflict which was more overtly aggressive, involving yelling, threatening and hitting.

Our first 'belief', then, that contact is almost always in the interests of children would seem to go well beyond the research evidence. Research does not, as is often said, show that contact is good for children. Rather it says that children benefit where they enjoy good relationships with supportive parents who are able to protect them from their own conflicts. This has major and challenging implications for the family justice system. It may be legitimate, as a general principle of family policy, to promote contact as a mechanism to sustain/develop a relationship which is important and potentially beneficial to children. The families who need to involve the courts, however, are, almost by definition, high conflict and many of the children are clearly suffering from being caught up in that conflict. In these circumstances it is hard to see how the principle that contact is almost always in the interests of the children can be sustained as a starting point.

ARE THERE SUBSTANTIAL PROPORTIONS OF CHILDREN HAVING TOO LITTLE CONTACT?

Despite, or even perhaps because of, the considerable research now available on levels of contact it is impossible to give precise figures for the proportion of children who have little or no contact with their non-resident parent. The 'facts' vary according to the source of the data. While this is likely to be the case in any research, a consistent theme in this area is that research based on information from resident parents reports lower levels of contact than that drawing on information from non-resident parents (Braver et al (1991); Seltzer (1994); Funder (1996); *Wikeley* (2001); *Blackwell and Dawe* (2003)).

There are also a number of other factors which mean that the data does not tell a straightforward story. Some studies report contact by child, others by parent. Definitions of *no contact* vary, with studies reporting variously no contact, very infrequent contact, no contact within the past 12 months, no face-to-face contact. Most studies report on contact irrespective of the gender of the non-resident parent, although this is known to make a difference, with, in general, a lower proportion of non-resident mothers losing touch (*O'Brien and Jones* (1996)). Most studies also do not differentiate between the previous marital status of the parents, although this is known to be a key factor (*Maclean and Eekelaar* (1997)). Incidence levels will also vary according to the length of time since separation, given that contact is generally reported to diminish over time (Pryor and Rodgers (2001)).

When it is claimed, therefore, that we know that 40% of non-resident fathers lose touch within two years, which seems to be the figure commonly bandied around, it needs to be remembered that this merely represents the findings of one study, whose representativeness may be compromised by a low response rate and which was also based only on information from resident mothers. It is not a consensus figure drawing on the whole of the available evidence, which suggests the proportion could be as low as 9% (*Attwood et al* (2003)) or as high as 43% (*Bradshaw and Millar* (1991)). A survey carried out by the Office for National Statistics for the Department of Constitutional Affairs (*Blackwell and Dawe* (2003)), which should provide the most accurate and up-to-date figures, found that no contact was reported by 15% of non-resident and 28% of resident parents. In line with developments observed in other countries (Kelly (2000)), this suggests that fewer non-resident parents are losing touch than was the case in the past and that the situation may not be as dramatic as is sometimes claimed.

Moreover some children are having fairly frequent contact, with UK studies reporting that, where there was any contact, between a third to almost three-quarters were seeing their non-resident parent at least weekly (*Bradshaw and Millar* (1991); *Bradshaw et al* (1999); *Dunn* (2003); *Iervolino et al* (forthcoming); *Smith* (2001); *Welsh et al, Wikely* (2001)). The ONS survey (*Blackwell and Dawe* (2004)) found that 17% of all non-resident fathers had some form of contact every day, with 8% seeing their child daily, 49% at least weekly and 69% monthly. Between half and two-thirds had overnight stays at least once a month. Again these figures suggest a somewhat less gloomy picture than is often portrayed, even if they fall well short of the demands for 50/50 parenting time.

Figures alone cannot tell us whether too many children are being deprived of contact which might be of benefit to them. Given that a sizeable proportion of separating families will have a history of domestic violence, child abuse and neglect, substance abuse or psychiatric illness, there will be some cases where contact will be damaging and should not be taking place anyway. A fairly consistent theme in research, however, is that not only do most children want contact, even when they do have contact some want more (Amato (1999); Wallerstein and Kelly (1980); Funder (1996); McDonald (1990); Parkinson et al (2004); Taylor et al (2001); *Cockett and Tripp* (1995); *Mitchell* (1985); *Dunn* (2003)). *Dunn* gives a proportion of one in four; *Cockett and Tripp* (1995) half. A study of US college students with divorced parents reported that *most* had wanted to spend more time with their fathers (Fabricius and Hall (2000)). The majority of parents interviewed in the ONS survey (*Blackwell and Dawe* (2004)) were satisfied with the contact arrangements. However among those dissatisfied insufficient contact was a key theme, with 17% of non-resident and 31% of resident parents wanting there to be more contact. Together these suggest that there is justification for trying to increase both the incidence and levels of contact.

HOW SIGNIFICANT IS MATERNAL OBSTRUCTION?

Another notable feature in the public debates on contact is the seamless slide from alleged fact to assumed cause, ie the percentage of children losing touch with their non-resident parents is equated with the proportion in which resident parents refuse or obstruct contact. The research suggests a much more complicated picture.

A number of factors have been consistently found to be associated with continuing contact (*Hunt* (2003); Pryor and Rodgers (2001)): a cooperative post-separation relationship between the parents; the child wanting contact; parents previously married rather than cohabiting or never living together; proximity; and the contact parent being employed, having a higher income and education, paying child support; not having further children. The only UK study to look in depth at why some families manage to make contact work, rather than merely happen (*Trinder et al* (2001)), provides a useful classification which illustrates the complexity of the issues. It identifies *direct determinants* (commitment to contact, role clarity, relationship quality); *challenges* (the nature of the separation, new adult partners, money, logistics, parenting style and quality, safety issues); and *mediating factors* which influenced how challenges were handled (beliefs about contact, relationship skills, the involvement of family, friends and external agencies). All these factors interacted over *time*. The researchers emphasise that: 'No single ingredient or individual was responsible for making contact work or not work. It was the attitudes, actions and interactions of all family members that shaped contact.'

Obstruction by resident mothers is certainly a major theme in research on no-contact fathers (*Hunt* (2003)). A second, however, concerns the fading away of contact because of difficulties arising from the very nature of the non-resident father's role, which as *Simpson et al* (1995) emphasise, is 'vulnerable'. 'Feelings of unfairness and anger are built into visitation even if the custodial parent never hampers it' (Loewen (1988)). The role is 'artificial' (Loewen (1988); Lamb (1999)), limiting the father's ability to play a proper parental role (*Bradshaw et al* (1999)) and emotionally distressing (*Murch* (1980); *Lund* (1987); *Richards* (1982); Arendell (1995); Radovanovic (1994)). It also requires many fathers to sustain a relationship with their children that previously was mediated by their partner (*Simpson et al* (1995); *Smart et al* (2001); *Trinder* (2001)):

> 'In most marriages – and therefore in most divorces – the role of the father is mediated by that of the mother. At divorce this dynamic is made highly explicit. Once structures which underpin and sustain the image of the father in the family are dismantled, the support which he might have expected can no longer be assumed. Indeed it may be actively withdrawn. ...Once motherhood is removed from the equation, the non-custodial father, to a greater or lesser extent, may not have the resources, in terms of knowledge, information or emotional insight, to be able to relate to children on his own terms.' (*Simpson et al* (1995))

Other factors identified in the research as contributing to fathers ceasing contact of their own volition (rather than because of prohibition or denial by the resident parent or the child) are concern about the impact of contact on the child (*Murch* (1980); *Richards* (1982); *Simpson* (1995)); practical difficulties (*Kruk* (1993); *Simpson et al* (1995); *O'Brien and Jones* (1996); Dudley (1991); Greif (1997); Smyth et al (2001)); pressure from new commitments and relationships (Wallerstein and Lewis (1998)) and the father's well-being (Wallerstein and Lewis (1998); Radovanovic (1994)). Hetherington and Kelly (2002) even mention 'lethargy and lack of attachment'.

There are, then, a whole variety of reasons why insufficient contact may be taking place, of which perceived maternal obstruction is only one. Indeed several studies record mothers' complaints that fathers do not do enough to keep in touch with their children and want them to have more, not less, contact (Arendell (1986); *Gingerbread/Families Need Fathers* (1982); *Blackwell and Dawe* (2004); *Simpson et al* (1995); *Murch et al* (1999); Perry et al (1992); Richardson (1988); *Smart et al* (2005); *Stark et al* (2001)). (This point seems to be generally ignored or, if acknowledged, dismissed on the basis that forcing unwilling fathers into contact would not benefit children. However since research is indicating that fathers do not typically drop out because of lack of interest (*Bradshaw et al* (1999); *Simpson et al* (1995)), there would seem to be scope for initiatives to try to help them to remain involved).

The picture presented in research, therefore, is somewhat different from the one currently dominating public perceptions – of children deprived of contact principally because of unreasonably obstructive mothers. This does not mean, however, that such mothers do not exist. As resident parents, mothers have 'situational power' (*Neale and Smart* (1999)) and it is likely that some will use that for reasons which have nothing to do with concern for the well-being of the child.

What we do not know is how widespread a phenomenon this is. All the reports and consultative documents leading up to the new Children Bill (Advisory Board on Family Law 2002; DCA 2004; DCA 2005; House of Commons 2003 and 2005a and b) seem to accept that resistance to contact is a significant problem and that therefore something needs to be done. What is striking is that none of them were able to draw on any substantial empirical evidence on either the incidence or the aetiology of the phenomenon on which to base an assessment of the severity of the problem or the appropriateness of the proposed measures. Indeed it was only with the publication of the Green Paper (DCA 2004) that figures were given for the proportion of contact applications which involved alleged breaches of orders[2] and no data is available on what proportion were substantiated.[3]

Research in different jurisdictions, undertaken at different periods of time, consistently reports a substantial proportion of fathers citing obstruction by resident mothers as a reason for lack of contact (*Mitchell* (1980); *Lund* (1987); *Kruk* (1993); *Simpson et al* (1995); *Bradshaw et al* (1999); *Wikeley* (2001); Dudley (1991); Greif (1997); Hetherington and Kelly (2002); Radovanovic et al (1994); Smyth et al (2001)). Bradshaw for instance (*Bradshaw et al* (1999)) found that obstruction was the most common reason fathers gave for having lost contact (47% of those with no contact). Similarly *Simpson et al* (1995) report that 60% of fathers who rarely or never saw their children were in dispute with their ex-partners about this:

> 'Nearly all of those who had no contact with their children claimed they had made considerable efforts to maintain positive relationships, and that they had only given up contact because of serious frustrations and wrangles. Many non-resident fathers identified their ex-wives as the principal impediment to contact. Words like "vindictive" and "manipulative" were common as was the allegation that ex-wives had deliberately turned children against them or sought to 'poison' the relationship.'

11% of the calls (by parents) to the Children's Legal Centre Contactline are reported to be about obstruction of contact (*French and Hamilton* (2002)).

---

[2]   In the Green Paper (DCA et al 2004) the DCA stated its own survey of 300 files indicated that one in six applications and 34% of repeat applications involved breaches. The study has not been published and no further details are given.

[3]   Research in Australia on applications to enforce contact orders would suggest that the majority would not be substantiated (Rhoades 2002).

Resident parents, not unexpectedly, are much less likely to acknowledge obstruction (Ahrons (1983); Braver et al (1991); Wallerstein and Kelly (1980) (all US)). Nonetheless it seems clear that it does occur. In the UK *Pearce et al* (1999) and *Smart and Neale* (1999), refer to 'some' instances while *Mitchell* (1980) reported that 'one-fifth of the resident parents had not wanted their children to have any access and most had successfully discouraged any continuing contact'. A quarter of resident parents in one US study (Braver et al (1991)) admitted undermining or denying contact at least once and two earlier (US) studies put the proportion at 40% and 50% respectively (Fulton (1979); Kressel (1985)). 39% of resident parents in a Canadian study reported denying access at one time or another (Perry et al (1992)). What is not usually clear, however, is what is meant by obstruction/denial, in particular whether these figures refer to occasional or short-term denial, after which contact resumes, or to entrenched resistance. *Buchanan et al* (2001), for instance, found that while contact had been stopped in two-thirds of cases subject to a welfare report, this was typically a temporary disruption and permanent cessation of contact was rarely sought.

Even less is known about the range of circumstances which give rise to contact denial and the extent to which it might be deemed warranted. There is evidence that some mothers do not subscribe to current thinking about the importance of fathers to children (Wallerstein and Kelly (1980); Pearson and Thoennes (1998); *Mitchell* (1980)); act out of revenge (Kressel (1985)) or in retaliation for non-payment of child support. Some commentators suggest that extreme resistance reflects a form of mental disturbance, perhaps even the controversial Parental Alienation or Divorce-Related Malicious Mother 'Syndromes' (Turkat (1997)). Conversely mothers may be seen to be acting rationally in the interests of their particular children (*Day Sclater and Kaganas* (2003)). Sometimes contact is refused in circumstances any reasonable person would consider to be justified, such as the contact parent being under the influence of drink or drugs (Perry et al (1992)). There may be a history of or current concerns about domestic violence or child abuse: an Australian study which investigated enforcement proceedings reported that 'the one-sided unreasonableness of the hostile mother stories was noticeably absent'; 65% of applications involved major concerns about the care provided by the non-resident parent (Rhoades (2002)). Contact denial may also be a response to chronic conflict (*Trinder et al* (2001); Strategic Partners (1998)).

HAVE OTHER JURISDICTIONS GOT IT SORTED?

The short answer is 'No'. Claims that they do *X* in *Y* country/state and it *works* should usually be taken with a large pinch of salt. Contact is an active social policy issue in many other jurisdictions which are similarly struggling to come up with some creative responses. Most other European states are no further forward than the UK (with the possible exception of Germany, where there are some interesting recent developments) and, apart from Denmark, where contact cannot be litigated, have fairly similar approaches. There are some promising approaches in the US, Canada, Australia and New Zealand. However the research which would enable one to say that they work is usually very limited and not very robust. In general, therefore, we are talking about interesting ideas rather than validated interventions (Hunt (2005)).

The gap between innovation and validation is particularly marked in the US, which has been something of a powerhouse for the development of new services. Those involved in their development are typically enthusiastic; word spreads and the idea takes off. However usually conviction is not matched with robust evaluation, or even with the collection of monitoring data which would provide objective measures of impact. So a particular form of intervention spreads before its effectiveness has been demonstrated. This can be seen in the development of court-related education classes for divorcing parents which are now commonplace across the US and much of Canada. Yet a recent systematic review of research available in peer-reviewed journals concluded that: 'the almost wholesale endorsement of these programmes has occurred prior to the conducting of ongoing serious systematic research into their effectiveness' (Whitworth et al (2002)).

This does not mean, of course, that there is nothing we can learn from other countries, nor that service development has to await incontrovertible research evidence. It does require, however, greater clarity about the evidential basis on which new ideas are being promulgated and the criteria which are used to assess effectiveness. Is the only evidence the views of practitioners who introduced a new service or system and are convinced that it works – as appears to be the case with the much heralded 'Florida model'? If there is data indicating improved settlement rates, for example, is there any to indicate that agreements last? If litigation rates can be shown to be reduced, is there evidence that this is for 'acceptable' reasons and in the interests of children? If service recipients express high levels of satisfaction is there any evidence that this translates into behavioural change? Have participating parents been compared with parents not invited to participate? Without such a comparison group any change, eg in reported conflict levels, may only reflect the passage of time.

The Government's commitment to the development of services to meet the needs of all separating families, not just the high conflict families who preoccupy the family justice system, (DCA (2005)) is to be welcomed. The UK has lagged behind some other countries in this respect and therefore there is a pool of ideas which can be drawn on, but more as a stimulus to the formulation of our own rather than as off-the peg 'solutions' to be adopted uncritically. The contact debate to date has not been distinguished by its reliance on objective evidence. If real progress is to be made this needs to change.

REFERENCES

Advisory Board on Family Law: Children Act Sub-Committee *Making Contact Work. A Report to the Lord Chancellor on the Facilitation of Arrangements for Contact between children and their non-resident parents and the enforcement of court orders for contact* (LCD, 2002)

Ahrons CR 'Predictors of paternal involvement post-divorce: Mothers and fathers perceptions'. (1983) 6 Journal of Divorce 55–69

Amato PR 'Children's adjustment to divorce: theories, hypotheses and empirical support'. (1993) 55 Journal of Marriage and the Family 23–8

Amato, PR 'Fathers' contributions to their children's lives: human, financial and social capital'. (paper presented at the Australian Institute of Family Studies Family Research Conference, 1996): cited in Taylor et al, 1991

Amato, PR 'Children of divorced parents as young adults' in Hetherington, EM (ed) *Coping with Divorce, single parenting and Remarriage: a risk and resiliency perspective* (Mahwah, NJ, Lawrence Erlbaum Associates, 1999)

Amato, G and Gilbreth, JG 'Non-resident fathers and children's well-being: A Meta-analysis'. (1999) 61(3) Journal of Marriage and the Family 557

Amato, PR and Keith, B 'Parental divorce and the well-being of children: A meta-analysis'. (1991) 110 Psychological Bulletin 26–46

Amato PR and Rezac, S 'Contact with non-resident parents, inter-parental conflict and children's behaviour' (1994) 15 Journal of Family Issues 191–207

Amato, G and Rivera 'Paternal involvement and children's behaviour problems' (1999) 61 Journal of Marriage and the Family 375–84

Amato, PR and Sobolewski, JM 'The effects of divorce and marital discord on adult children's psychological well-being' (2001) 66(6) American Sociological Review 900–921

Arendell, T *Mothers and Divorce: Legal, Economic and Social Dilemmas* (Berkeley, CA, University of California Press, 1986)

Arendell, T *Fathers and Divorce* (Thousand Oaks, CA, Sage, 1995)

Attwood, C, Singh, G, Prime, D, Creasey, R and others *2001 Home Office Citizenship Survey: people, families and communities* (London, Home Office, 2003)

Blackwell, A and Dawe, F *Non-resident parental contact* (London, ONS, 2003)

Bradshaw, J & Millar, J *Lone Parent Families in the UK* (DSS Report 6 HMSO, 1991)

Bradshaw, J, Stimson, C Skinner, C and Williams, J *Absent Fathers?* (Routledge, London, 1999)

Braver, SH, Wolchik, SA, Sandler, IN, Fogas, BS, Zvetina, D 'Frequency of visitation by divorced fathers – differences in reports by fathers and mothers' (1991) 61(3) American Journal of Orthopsychiatry 448–454

Buchanan, A, Hunt, J Bretherton, H and Bream, V *Families in Conflict: perspectives of children and parents on the Family Court Welfare Service* (Bristol, Policy Press, 2001)

Buchanan, CM & Maccoby, EE *Adolescents after Divorce* (Harvard University Press, Cambridge, Mass, 1996)

Bray, JH and Berger, SH 'The developing stepfamily' (1990) 6 The Family Psychologist 31–32

Buehler, C, Anthony, C, Krishnamkmar, A, Stone, G, Gerard, J and Pemberton, S 'Interparental and youth conflict and youth problem behaviours: a meta-analysis' (1997) 6 Journal of Child and Family Studies 233–247

Camara, K and Resnick, G 'Styles of conflict resolution and cooperation between divorced parents: Effects on Children's Behaviour and Adjustment' (1989) 59 American Journal of Orthopsychiatry 560

Cockett, M & Tripp, J *The Exeter Family Study: Family Breakdown and its impact on children* (University of Exeter Press, 1994)

Cummings, EM & Davies, P *Children and Marital Conflict: the impact of family dispute and resolution* (NY, Guildford Press, 1994)

Cummings, EM, Goeke-Morey, MC and Papp, LM 'Couple conflict: It's not just you and me babe' in Booth, A; Crouter, AC, and Clements, M (eds) *Couples in Conflict* (Mahwah, NJ: Erlbaum, 2001) 117–148

Davies, PT and Cummings, EM 'Marital conflict and child adjustment: an emotional security hypothesis' (1994) 116 Psychological Bulletin 387–411

Day Schlater, S and Kaganas, F 'Mothers, Welfare and Rights' in Bainham, A et al (eds) *Children and their Families, Contact, Rights and Welfare* (Oxford, Hart Publishing, 2003)

Department for Constitutional Affairs, Department for Education and Skills and Department for Trade and Industry *Parental Separation: Children's Needs and Parents' Responsibility* Cm6273 (Norwich, the Stationery Office, 2004)

Department for Constitutional Affairs, Department for Education and Skills and Department for Trade and Industry *Parental Separation: Children's Needs and Parents' Responsibility: Next Steps* Cm 6452 (Norwich, the Stationery Office, 2005)

Doolittle, DB and Deutsch, R 'Children in high conflict divorce: Theory, research and intervention' in Galatzer-Levy & Kraus, L (eds) *The scientific basis of child custody decisions* (Wiley, 1999) 425–433

Dudley JR 'Increasing our understanding of divorced fathers who have infrequent contact with their children' (1991) 40 Family Relations 279–285

Dunn, J & Deater-Deckard, K *Children's views of their changing families* (York, York Publishing Services, 2001)

Dunn, J 'Contact and children's perspectives on parental relationships' in A Bainham et al (eds) *Children and their Families: contact, rights and welfare* (Hart Publishing, 2003)

Dunn, J, Cheng, H, O'Connor, TG and Bridges, L 'Children's perspectives on their relationships with their non-resident fathers: influences, outcomes and implications' (2004) 45 Journal of Child Psychology and Psychiatry 553–566

Emery, RE 'Interparental conflict and the children of discord and divorce' (1982) 92(2) Psychological Bulletin 310–330

Emery RE *Marriage, divorce and children's adjustment* (Newbury Park, CA Sage, 2nd edn, 1999)

Fabricius, WV and Hall, J 'Young Adults' perspectives on Divorce Living arrangements' (2000) 38(4) Family and Conciliation Courts Review 446–461

Funder K *Remaking families: Adaptation of parents and children to divorce* (Melbourne, Australia, Australian Institute of Family Studies, 1996)

Fulton, JA 'Children's Post-Divorce Adjustment' (1979) 35(40) Journal of Social Issues 126–39

Furstenberg, FF Jnr & Cherlin, AJ *Divided Families: What happens to children when parents part* (Cambridge, Harvard UP, 1991)

Furstenberg, FF, Jr. and Nord, CW 'Parenting Apart: patterns in childrearing after marital disruption' (1985) 47 Journal of Marriage and the Family 893–904

Garrity CB and Baris *Caught in the Middle, Protecting the Children of High-Conflict Divorce* (NY, Lexington, 1994)

Gingerbread and Families Need Fathers *Divided Children: A Survey of Access to Children after Divorce* (London, Gingerbread, 1982)

Goodman, M, Bonds, D, Sandler, I and Braver, S 'Parent Psychoeducational Programs and reducing the negative effects of interparental conflict following divorce' (2004) 42(2) Family Court Review 263–279

Greif, GL *Out of Touch: When parents and children lose contact after divorce* (New York, OUP, 1997)

Grych, JH 'Inter-parental conflict as a risk factor for child maladjustment: implications for the development of prevention programs' (2005) 43,1 Family Court Review 97–108

Grych, JH and Fincham, FD 'Children's appraisals of marital conflict: initial investigations of the cognitive-contextual framework'(1993) 108 Psychological Bulletin 267–290

Grych, JH & Fincham, FD 'The Adjustment of Children from Divorced Families: Implications of Empirical research for clinical intervention' in Galatzer-Levy, RM and Kraus, L (eds) *The Scientific Basis of Child Custody Decisions* (New York, Chichester, Wiley, 1999)

Grych, JH and Fincham, FD *Interparental conflict and child development: theory, research and applications* (New York, Cambridge University Press, 2001)

Hetherington, EM, Bridges, M and Insabella, GM 'What matters? What does not? Five perspectives on the association between marital transitions and children's adjustment' (1998) 53, 2 American Psychologist 167–184

Hetherington EM and Kelly, J *For Better or For Worse: Divorce reconsidered* (WW Norton and Company, 2002)

House of Commons Committee on the Lord Chancellor's Department *Children and Family Court Advisory and Support Service* HC614–II (London, The Stationery Office, 2003)

House of Commons Constitutional Affairs Committee *Family Justice: the operation of the family courts* HC 116–II (London, he Stationery Office, 2005a)

House of Commons, House of Lords *Report of the Joint Committee on the Draft Children (Contact) and Adoption Bill* HC 400–I, HL Paper 100–I (London, The Stationery Office, 2005b)

Hunt, J *Researching Contact* (London, One Parent Families, 2003)

Hunt, J *Managing Litigated Contact: ideas from other jurisdictions* (Department of Social Policy and Social Work, University of Oxford, 2005)

Iervolino, AC, O'Connor, T and Dunn, J 'Stability of non-resident father-child contact and relationship quality: social and demographic predictors' (forthcoming, 2005)

Johnston, JR 'Children of Divorce who refuse visitation' in Depner CE and Bray, JH (eds) *Non-residential parenting: new vistas for family living* (Sage, 1993)

Johnston, J 'High Conflict Divorce' (1994) 4(1) The Future of Children 167–181

Johnston, J, Kline, M and Tschann, JM 'On-going post-divorce conflict: effects on children of joint custody and frequent access' (1989) 59 American Journal of Orthopsychiatry 576

Johnston, J, Gonzalez, R, and Campbell, L 'On-going post-divorce conflict and child disturbance' (1987) 15(4) Journal of Abnormal Child Psychology 493–509

Kelly, JB 'Children's Adjustment in conflicted marriage and divorce: a decade review of research' (2000) 39 Journal of the American Academy of Child and Adolescent Psychiatry 963–973

King, V, Harris, KM, and Heard, HE 'Racial and ethnic diversity in nonresident father involvement' (2004) 66 Journal of Marriage and the Family 1–21

King, V and Heard, HE 'Non-resident father visitation, parental conflict and mother's satisfaction: What's best for child-well being?' (1999) 61 Journal of Marriage and the Family 385–396

Kressel, K *The Process of Divorce* (New York, Basic Books, 1985)

Kruk, E *Divorce and Disengagement* (Halifax, Fernwood, 1993)

Kurdek, LA and Siesky, AE 'Children's Perceptions of their Parents' Divorce' (1980) 3 Journal of Divorce 339–78

Lamb, M 'Non-custodial fathers and their impact on the children of divorce' in RA Thomson and PR Amato (eds) *The Postdivorce Family: children, parenting and society* (Sage, 1999)

Lamb, ME, Sternberg, KJ and Thompson, RA 'The effects of divorce and custody arrangements on children's behaviour, development and adjustment' (1997) 35(4) Family and Conciliation Courts Review 393–404

Loewen, JW 'Visitation fatherhood' in P Bronstein & CP Cowan (eds) *Fatherhood Today: men's changing role in the family* (NY, Wiley, 1988) 195–213

Long, N, Slater, E, Forehand, R and Fauber, R 'Continued High and Reduced Parental Conflict following Divorce in Relation to Young Adolescent Adjustment' (1988) 56 Journal of Consulting and Clinical Psychology 467

Lund, ME 'The non-custodial father: common challenges in parenting after divorce' in C Lewis & M O'Brien (eds) *Reassessing Fatherhood* (Lexington, Lexington, 1987)

Maclean, M & Eekelaar, J *The Parental Obligation: a study of parenthood across households* (Hart Publishing, Oxford, 1997)

Maccoby, EE; Buchanan, CM, Mnookin, RH. & Dornbusch, SM 'Postdivorce Roles of Mothers and Fathers in the Lives of their Children' (1993) 7(1) Journal of Family Psychology 24–38

Manning, WD and Lamb, K 'Adolescent well-being in cohabiting, married, and single parent families' (2003) 65 Journal of Marriage and the Family 876–893

McDonald, M *Children's perceptions of access and their adjustment in the post-separation period* Research Report No 9 (Family Court of Australia, 1990)

Mitchell, A *Children in the Middle: Living through Divorce* (London, Tavistock Publications, 1985)

Murch, M *Justice and Welfare in Divorce* (London, Sweet and Maxwell, 1980)

Murch, M, Douglas, G, Scanlan, L, Perry, A, Lisles, C, Bader, K & Borkowski, M *Safeguarding children's welfare in uncontentious divorce, a study of s41 of the Matrimonial Causes Act 1973* (LCD, 1999)

Neale, B and Smart, C 'In whose Best Interests? Theorising Family Life Following Parental Separation and Divorce' in *Undercurrents of Divorce* (1999)

O'Brien M and Jones D 'Young People's Attitudes to fatherhood' in Moss, P (ed) *Father Figures: Fathers in the families of the 1990's Children in Scotland* (HMSO, 1996)

Parkinson, P 'Satisfaction and dissatisfaction with father-child contact arrangements in Australia' (2004) Child and Family Law Quarterly (Nov)

Pearce, J, Davis, G and Barron, J 'Love in a Cold Climate – Section 8 applications under the Children Act 1989' (1999) Family Law 22

Pearson, J and Thoennes, N 'The Denial of Visitation Rights: A preliminary look at its incidence, correlates, antecedents and consequences' (1988) 10(4) Law and Policy 363–380

Perry, D et al *Access to children following parental relationship breakdown in Alberta* (Calgary, Canadian Research Institute for Law and the Family, 1992)

Pryor, J and Rodgers, B *Children in Changing Families: Life after Parental Separation* (Oxford, Blackwell Publishers Ltd, 2001)

Radovanovic, H, Bartha, C, Magnatta, M, Hood, E, Sagar, A and McDonough, H 'A Follow-up of families disputing child-custody/Access – Assessment, settlement, and family relationship outcomes' (1994) 12(4) Behavioural Sciences and the Law 427–435

Richards, M 'Post-divorce arrangements for children: A Psychological Perspective' (1982) 133 Journal of Social Welfare Law 1551

Richardson, CJ *Court-based Divorce Mediation in four Canadian Cities: overview of research results* (Ottawa, Ministry of Justice, 1988)

Rhoades, H 'The no contact mother' (2002) 16 International Journal of Law, Policy and the Family 87

Rodgers, B and Pryor, J *Divorce and Separation: the outcomes for children* (York, Joseph Rowntree Foundation, 1998)

Salem DA, Zimmerman, MA and Notaro, PC 'Effects of family structure, family process, and father involvement in psychosocial outcomes among African-American adolescents' (1998) 47 Family Relations 331–41

Sales, B, Manber, R & Rohman, L 'Social science research and child-custody decision making' (1992) Applied and Preventive Psychology, 1, 23–40

Seltzer, J 'Consequences of marital dissolution for children' (1994) 24 Annual Review of Sociology 235–66

Simons RL, Whitbeck, LB, Beaman, J & Conger, RD 'The impact of mother's parenting, involvement by non-resident fathers and parental conflict on the adjustment of adolescent children' (1994) 56 Journal of Marriage and the Family 356–374

Simpson, B, McCarthy, P & Walker, J *Being There: Fathers after Divorce* (Newcastle, Relate Centre for Family Studies, 1995)

Shifflett, K, Cummings EM 'A program for educating parents about the effects of divorce and conflict in children: an initial evaluation' (1999) 48 Family Relations 79–89

Smart, C. & Neale, B *Family Fragments?* (Polity Press, 1999)

Smart, C, Neale, B and Wade, A *Changing Childhoods, Changing Families* (Cambridge, Polity Press, 2001)

Smart, C, May, V, Wade, A, and Furness, C *Residence and Contact Disputes in Court* Vol 2 (London, DCA (2005))

Smith M, Robertson, J, Dixon, J, Quigley, M and Whitehead, Z *A Study of Stepchildren and Step-parenting. Report to the Department of Health* (London, Thomas Coram Research Unit, 2001)

Smyth, B, Sheehan, G & Fehlberg, B 'Patterns of parenting after divorce: A pre-Reform Act benchmark study' (2001) Australian Journal of Family Law 114

Stark, C, Laing, K and McCarthy, P 'Giving information to parents' in J Walker (ed) *Information Meetings and Associated Provisions within the Family Law Act 1996: Final Report* Vol 2 (London, Lord Chancellor's Department, 2001)

Strategic Partners Ltd *Contact Services in Australia Research and Evaluation Project* (Legal Aid and Family Services, Attorney-General's Department, 1998)

Sturge, C and Glaser, D 'Contact and Domestic Violence – the experts court report' (2000) Family Law 615

Taylor, N, Smith, A and Gollop, M *Child-parent contact following separation and divorce: the implications for family law of New Zealand and International research* (Otago, Children's Issues Centre, 2001)

Trinder, L, Beek, M and Connolly, J *Making Contact* (Joseph Rowntree Foundation, 2001)

Turkat, ID 'Management of visitation interference' (1997) 36 Judges Journal (Spring)

Walczak, Y and Burns, S *Divorce: the child's point of view* (London, Harper and Row, 1984)

Wallerstein JS and Kelly, JB *Surviving the Breakup: how children and parents cope with divorce* (New York, Basic Books, 1980)

Wallerstein, J and Lewis, J 'The long-term impact of divorce on children. A first report from a 25-year study' (1998) Family and Conciliation Courts Review 368–383

Welsh, E, Buchanan, A, Flouri, E and Lewis, J *Involved fathering and child well-being: fathers' involvement with secondary school age children* (National Children's Bureau, 2004)

Wekerle, C and Wolfe, DA 'Dating violence in mid-adolescence: theory, significance and emerging prevention initiatives' (1999) 19 Clinical Psychology Review 435–456

White, L & Gilbreth, JG 'When Children Have Two Fathers: Effects of relationships with stepfathers and noncustodial fathers on adolescent outcomes' (2001) 63 Journal of Marriage and the Family 155–167

Whitworth, J, Capshew, TF and Abell, N 'Children Caught in the conflict: are court-endorsed divorce parenting education programs effective?' (2002) 37 Journal of Divorce and Remarriage 3–4, 1–18

Wikeley, N *National Survey of Child Support Agency Clients* (DWP, 2001)

CONTACT WITH NON-RESIDENT FATHERS: CHILDREN'S AND PARENTS' VIEWS

Professor Judy Dunn
Social, Genetics and Developmental Psychiatric Research Centre,
Institute of Psychiatry, King's College London

SUMMARY OF PAPER

Professor Dunn's material comes from two studies. The first is the ALSPAC study of approximately 8,000 families comprising of 90% of women in the Avon health district who were recruited when they were pregnant. The children are now 13. This is a large study in which Professor Dunn became involved when the children were five. The second study comprises 50 families in four situations. This study has been following these families for nine years and enables the researchers to look at durable solutions.

Jaffe proposed that non-resident father behaviour is crucial to as to whether it is good for the child to have contact. The question arises as to direction of effects and whether the arrow goes from child to parent or parent to child, the reality is probably both.

The studies have been able to explore the reality for children living in two houses and the children's experience of contact. Researchers asked what worried children and what they enjoyed: responses included repeated concerns as to unreliability of the non-resident parent and feeling their loyalty split.

The more elaborately one looks at non-resident father-child relationships, the more a complex network is apparent, not simply a relationship between the child and one of the parents. Positive relationships can exist between a step-father and a non-resident father. Both these roles are linked to children's well-being, but independent of one another. Negative relationships in these situations have many similar features.

The ALSPAC study shows the importance of the relationship between the child and the non-resident parent in terms of child adjustment. This relationship was able to predict adjustment over time independent of the relationships of the resident parent and any new partner.

The Avon study explored relationships between brothers and sisters and was a positive story to the extent that children's concerns and problems appeared to decrease over time.

These studies leave some questions unanswered. In approximately one-third of cases the researchers were not permitted to contact the non-resident father and researchers had to rely on the children.

The perspective of the children was a key focus of the study, and methods were developed to capture children's views on their relationships and families. These included the use of concentric circle diagrams, and drawings as well as interviews. The researches found the use of concentric circle diagrams useful in their work with children. Whereabouts the children placed their father and step-father on these diagrams allowed the researchers to predict child adjustment beyond the factors already known to be influential. The children enjoyed this exercise and it provided useful and valid information.

This study demonstrated the importance of communication between resident and non-resident parents as a child's involvement in conflict between mother and non-resident father is a key to adjustment problems.

INTRODUCTION

When parents separate, few fathers end up being the parent with whom children live. With the rapid rise in frequency of parental separation and divorce over the last two decades, this means that increasing numbers of children have fathers who live in different households from mother-and-child. Over 20% of all dependent children in the UK live away from their fathers, it's recently been estimated (National Statistics (2003)). How significant for children's outcome and well-being is the frequency of contact and the quality of the relationship between children and their fathers who live 'in the other house'? It is a question with major implications for policy makers, lawyers, and practitioners (see the recent Government consultation paper) – one which is currently hotly debated, with fathers' rights groups arguing with increasing militancy for increased contact and custody.

What has been learned about the links between children's relationships with their non-resident fathers, and their adjustment – and what are the lessons of this research? Does the picture from recent UK research parallel what's been reported elsewhere in the world, in particular in the US, where the bulk of research has been conducted? Given the theme of this meeting, what evidence do we have on the longitudinal patterns linking child–non-resident father relationships and their outcome? We look first at father–child contact and economic support (the focus of most research attention and of legal wrangles) and then at the growing and consistent evidence for the significance of the quality of non-resident father–child relationships.

CONTACT AND ECONOMIC SUPPORT

On economic support, recent meta-analyses (Amato & Gilbreth (1999)) show that payment of child support is closely linked to children's adjustment, good health and academic success; it's plausibly argued that these effects are probably mediated through the quality of the father–child relationship and contact (Pryor & Rodgers (2001)). Demographics are important here: large-scale studies in the US, New Zealand and the UK have shown that young, non-resident fathers may have special difficulty providing economic support for their children, and that there are links between low income, unemployment and low father–child contact (eg, Simpson, Jessop, & McCarthy (2003)).

Evidence that the frequency of father–child contact is important for children's adjustment is more mixed than the evidence on payment of support. First, note that patterns of contact may well be changing over time – children may now be seeing their non-resident fathers more frequently than in they were in the 70s and 80s, reviews of research suggest (Amato & Gilbreth (1999); Pryor & Rodgers (2001)). And the links between contact and children's adjustment and academic success have increased in effect in size over time: Amato & Gilbreth suggest that non-resident fathers in recent years may be more committed to involvement with their children. In the UK, the evidence for the importance of frequency of contact per se for children's adjustment is mixed – and it is not clear what explains these inconsistencies – differences in samples, in methods, in measurement? The issue of direction of effects is also important: where a link is found, it could be that fathers enjoy and encourage more frequent contact as a *consequence* of their children's well-being and lack of problems, or that the father–child contact *contributed* to their well-being. Both effects are likely to be involved.

Whether contact between father and child is associated with children's well-being depends in part on the personality and adjustment of the father. For instance, in a large-scale study of five-year-old twins in the UK, a focus on fathers' anti-social behaviour showed that when the fathers engaged in high levels of anti-social behaviour, children had more conduct problems when their fathers lived with them (16% with conduct problems) than children whose anti-social fathers were not living with them, than children whose fathers engaged in little anti-social behaviour *and were not resident with them* (Jaffee, Moffitt, Caspi, & Taylor (2003)). There was a genetic contribution to the risk of child anti-social behaviour, but the anti-social behaviour of resident fathers contributed to the children's behaviour problems independently of this genetic risk.

What do children say about contact? Most studies report that children want contact with their fathers: In the London study of Smith and colleagues, only 4% had negative feelings about contact (Smith, Robertson, Dixon, Quigley, & Whitehead (2001)). Losing contact with their fathers was seen by the children in one US study as the worst aspect of their parents' separation (Kurdek & Siesky (1980)). And frequent themes in children's concerns about contact include: fathers' unreliability about arrangements, feeling 'caught in the middle' between their parents, concern about witnessing their fathers' distress, as well as being unhappy about their father's new partner, babies, or stepsiblings.

Quality of children's relationships with their non-resident father: what matters for adjustment?

Unlike the mixed evidence on the significance of frequency of contact there is a much more consistent story on the significance of the quality of child–father relationships for children's adjustment. Here, the dimensions of the relationship that are highlighted are warmth and emotional closeness, support, authoritative parenting (involving affection, support and limit-setting), and involvement (see however (Welsh, Buchanan, Flouri, & Lewis (2004)) for conflicting findings). For example, when children were asked about their own relationships with their non-resident fathers in two recent UK studies in (Dunn, Cheng, O'Connor, & Bridges (2004); Smith et al (2001)) these positive aspects of the relationship were linked to low levels of the children's adjustment problems. The links between warm affectionate father–child relations and children's adjustment are especially strong for children growing up in single-mother families. But father–child relationships differ markedly in quality (more so than mother–child relationships: see White & Gilbreth (2001)), so the question of what accounts for this variability is an important one. What stands out in the recent research? Most importantly, the links with other family relationships.

Connections with other family relationships

How children get along with their non-resident fathers is particularly clearly linked to the various other relationships in their family worlds – especially the relationships between father and ex-partner, and between child and mother. For example, cooperation, support and communication between non-resident fathers and their former partners – the children's mothers – are consistently found to be positively associated with warmth and affection in the child–father relationship. In their meta-analysis of studies involving children whose parents separated before they were five years old, for instance, Whiteside and Becker (2000) showed that there were indirect effects of cooperation between parents on both child–father relationships and children's developmental outcome. Conflict between non-resident fathers and their ex-partners is associated with poor child outcome, though some studies suggest this effect is mediated by the relationship between child-and-mother. The impact of parental conflict on children's adjustment has been repeatedly shown in observational, experimental and interview studies (Grych & Fincham (2001)), and children's own reports highlight how sensitive children are to such conflict.

Are children who get on well with their mothers likely also to be close to their fathers? If so, are the links between child–father relations and children's adjustment to be explained by the children's relationships with their *mothers*? Evidence from research is mixed here. In one study of adolescents in stepfamilies, for instance, a good relationship between non-resident father and child was associated with good adjustment outcome *independently* of the mother–child relationship (more so than was the child–stepfather relationship: White & Gilbreth (2001)). Studies of younger children are not consistent on this point – suggesting that for younger children the relationship with the mother may be of key importance.

What about the situation of children whose mothers have formed new partnerships – those who have both a non-custodial father and a stepfather? Having a good relationship with a non-resident father is associated with well-being, and so too is a good relationship between child and stepfather; these links with adjustment outcome appear to be independent. While the positive warm aspects of the two father–child relationships are not linked, conflict in the relationship between child and non-resident father is reported to be correlated with conflict in both child–mother and child–stepfather relationships. The direction of effects in these patterns is not clear, but the notion that difficult children contribute to conflicted relations with all three parents is plausible.

PATTERNS OVER TIME

Here we face the issue of durable solutions directly. The little evidence from longitudinal research in the US comes from a study of children growing up in stepfamilies (Bray & Berger (1990); Bray & Berger (1993a); Bray (1999)), and a longitudinal study of children growing up in single mother families (Simons et al, (1994)). These studies show that while children's relationships with their non-resident fathers are important *concurrent* predictors of adjustment, their impact decreases over time. In Bray's study whereas more frequent contact and a more positive relationships between fathers and children predicted better child outcome in the first six months of stepfamily formation, non-resident fathers' involvement was unrelated to the children's adjustment 4–5 years later. Similar conclusions were reached in a study of 207 divorced women and their children (Simons et al (1994)). Relations with non-resident fathers become less closely linked to adjustment as the time since separation increases. Parental conflict tends to decrease with time which is likely to affect the father–child relationship.

Children's age at the time of separation is likely to affect the *way* that they respond to separation: conflict between parents is a less powerful predictor of adjustment for younger children than for those older at the time of separation, while younger children are more likely to blame themselves for the family change. But the large-scale meta-analyses found that links between father–child relations and adjustment did not differ with children's age. These are largely cross-sectional studies.

We next briefly summarise key points from two longitudinal studies in the UK concerning child–non-resident father contact and relationships.

The first study is based on the families in the Avon Longitudinal Study of Parents and Children, followed over a three-year period; we examined patterns of stability and change in contact and child–father relationship quality (Iervolino et al (2005)). First, concurrent data showed that children had more frequent contact with their non-resident fathers if they lived in a single-mother family, if their mother had given birth to them at a later age, if their mothers and fathers had a more positive relationship and more frequent contact, and if their fathers had a positive relationship with them. Relationship quality showed similar patterns to those of contact frequency: however the negative aspects of their relationship was related only to the negative aspects of the mother and ex-partners' relationships, and the negativity in the mother-child relationship.

The longitudinal analyses over a three-year time period showed:

(1) Contact: there was a significant average decrease in the frequency with which the children saw their fathers, similar for both boys and girls, but more marked for children in single-mother than stepfather families.

(2) Despite this mean decrease in contact, individual differences in contact were highly stable over the three years; this high correlation reflected chiefly the stability of the 'no contact' group of children, who were therefore excluded from the remaining analyses.

(3) Quality of relationship: There was a significant mean decrease in father–child positivity over time, however individual differences in both positivity and negativity were highly stable.

PREDICTING PATTERNS OVER TIME

Regression analyses were used to examine changes over time. These showed children who had a more positive relationship with fathers at the second time point had had more frequent contact at time point 1, and also that more frequent contact at time 3 was related to a more positive relationship three years earlier. When the children's adjustment was added into the analyses, results showed negativity in the father–child relationship was associated with more behaviour problems, and lower levels of positivity and higher levels of negativity in children's relationships were linked to greater indices of behaviour problems. Stepwise regressions showed that the impact of negativity in child–father relationships was independent of the impact of children's relationships with their mothers and stepfathers. A more positive relationship with the non-resident father was related to lower levels of behaviour problems at the later time point.

Changes over time since family transition points are evident in children's own accounts of their lives since parental separation, which were studied in detail in an intensive subsample of around 200 families (Dunn et al 2004). On the whole, children's accounts of problems in their 'divided lives' decreased over time (eg, their negative feelings about having two household, their reports of 'feeling caught' between resident parents, acting as a go-between between parents, and feeling that the difficulties in the family were caused by them), while child reports of depressive symptomatology also decreased with time since their parents separated. In general, these problems were linked to problems in communication between children and their parents, which for the majority of children decreased over time (Bridges et al 2005).

Fathers' perspectives

Research that examines in depth the views of fathers has highlighted two centrally important issues (eg, Simpson et al (2003)). The first is the difficulties faced by fathers in maintaining their relationships with their children after separation. Unemployment and financial problems are key, with the limited housing circumstances that follow. Unemployed fathers and those in manual occupations are more likely to lose contact with their children. Fathers who only see their children intermittently, and are distanced from the every-day events in children's lives not only miss the intimacy of daily routines, but also find discipline and control issues harder to deal with. It is much harder for them to be the 'authoritative' fathers whose children are on average less troubled.

The second issue is that fathers' accounts further underline the significance of the relationship between father and ex-partner. Around 60% of the fathers in one study who rarely or never saw their children said they wished to se their children but were in dispute about contact (Simpson et al (2003)). The frequency of disputes about contact, and blaming the ex-partner for obstructing access to the children demonstrate yet again how the relationship between father and child depends importantly on that between father and ex-partner.

Controversies and new directions

The gaps and the problems in research that attempts to understand what will support the relationship between non-resident fathers and their children and provide durable solutions are clear. Sampling and selection effects are real problems: studies are likely to include only those fathers who are still in contact with their children (and that leaves out a substantial proportion – estimates vary between 11 and 40% of separated fathers), and are unlikely to be representative. Informants are likely to be mothers rather than fathers, observational methods are rarely used. A variety of techniques for getting children's perspectives on family transitions have been developed and provide predictive power in terms of later adjustment (eg, Sturgess, Dunn, & Davies (2001)); these accounts highlight family issues that adult accounts have missed – such as the importance of closeness to grandparents and friends.

Controversies abound. To what extent do mothers exercise 'gate-keeping' and influence their children's feelings towards their fathers? What about the protection of children who have witnessed domestic violence? The emotional history of father–child relationships before separation is rarely studied or included in research, and yet is likely to be central in the relationship with adjustment outcome. Findings on gender are mixed and inconsistent. New ideas on the significance of father absence for girls' sexual activity and adolescent pregnancy have been raised, framed within evolutionary models, and need further investigation.

There's clearly a great deal to be learned about how the family changes that so many children experience affect their relationships with their fathers; a general message is that this research needs to be framed within the network of family relationships, and that the impact of custody arrangements on the quality of children's relationships with all their parents deserves attention. Collaboration between psychologists and those involved in the law is proving fruitful and generative (see Bainham et al (2003)). Exciting new directions in this research include the use of multi-level modelling strategies that enable us to investigate differences *within* families in children's relationships and outcome, a focus on children's interpretation of events as mediating the effects on their adjustment, a recognition of the particular vulnerability of children in single-mother families to difficulties in their relations with their fathers, and of the difficulties faced by non-resident fathers in developing close relations with their children. The message that the quality of the father–child relationship predicts children's well-being deserves attention from psychologists (clinical, developmental, social) and from those concerned with the law and family policies.

REFERENCES

Amato, P, & Gilbreth, JG 'non-resident fathers and children's well-being: a meta-analysis' (1999) 61 Journal of Marriage and the Family 557–73

Bainham, A, Lindley, B, Richards, M & Trinder, L *Children and their families: Contact, rights, and welfare* (Oxford, Hart Publications, 2003)

Dunn, J, Cheng, H, O'Connor, TG & Bridges, L 'Children's perspectives on their relationships with their non-resident fathers: influences, outcomes and implications' (2004) 45 Journal of Child Psychology and Psychiatry 553–566

Grych, JH, & Fincham, FD (eds) *Child Development and Inter-parental Conflict* (Cambridge University Press, 2001)

Iervolino, A, Dunn, J et al *Stability of non-resident father–child relationship quality and contact: social and demographic predictor* (2005)

Jaffee, SR, Moffitt, TE, Caspi, A, & Taylor 'A Life with (or without) father: The benefits of living with two biological parents depend on the father's anti-social behavior' (2003) 74 Child Development 109–126

Kurdek, LA & Siesky, AE 'Children's perception of their parents' divorce' (1980) 3 Journal of Divorce 339–378

National Statistics CENSUS 2001: National Report for England and Wales (2003)

Pryor, J & Rodgers, B *Children in changing families: Life after parental separation* (Oxford, Blackwell Publishers, 2001)

Simpson, B, Jessop, JA & McCarthy, P 'Fathers after divorce' in A Bainham, B Lindley, M Richards & L Trinder (eds) *Children and their families: Contact, rights, and welfare* (Oxford, Hart Publications, 2003)

Smith, M, Robertson, J, Dixon, J, Quigley, M & Whitehead, E *A study of stepchildren and stepparenting* (unpublished report to the Department of Health, 2001)

Sturgess, W, Dunn, J & Davies, L 'Young children's perceptions of their relationships with family and friends: Links with family setting and adjustment' (2001) 25 International Journal of Behavioural Development 521–529

Welsh, E, Buchanan, A, Flouri, E, & Lewis, J '"Involved" fathering and child well-being: Fathers' involvement with secondary school age children' (London, National Children's Bureau, 2004)

White, L & Gilbreth, JG 'When children have two fathers: Effects of relationships with stepfathers and noncustodial fathers on adolescent outcomes' (2001) 63 Journal of Marriage and Family 155–167

Whiteside, MF & Becker, BJ 'Parental factors and the young child's postdivorce adjustment: A meta-analysis with implications for parenting arrangements' (2000) 14 Journal of Family Psychology 5–26

MAKING DECISIONS ABOUT CONTACT IN FOSTER CARE AND ADOPTION: PROMOTING SECURITY AND MANAGING RISK

Dr Gillian Schofield

Co-director of the Centre for Research on the Child and Family,
University of East Anglia

Contact for children separated from their birth family, whether temporarily or permanently, in foster care or adoption, is one of the most significant and yet contentious areas in planning for and achieving durable solutions for children. Managing two families, practically and psychologically, is a major task both for the child and for those parents, carers and professionals who wish to promote the child's well-being into adult life. But there are no easy answers, no rules of thumb (Sinclair (2005)) that can provide a shortcut to making decisions about the 'right' type and frequency of contact for each child. The professional judgements that need to be made (and then revised as necessary over time) must be supported by well-thought-through arguments that rely as much on knowledge of child development and accurate assessment of the particular child, their caregivers and their birth relatives as they rely on outcome research. In individual cases the plan for contact needs always to ensure that arrangements promote the particular child's sense of security and that risks, whether of significant harm or emotional stress and confusion, are successfully managed.

This paper will begin by looking at some of the issues that underpin contact decisions and then explore contact in relation to each age group, paying attention to issues in short-term, task-centred placements (for assessment or bridging to a new family) and planned permanent placements in foster care and adoption. The plan will affect the frequency of contact but it is not an automatic fit. There will be some permanent placements where birth family contact is more frequent than in some short-term or bridge placements, depending on the age and circumstances of the child, the characteristics of the foster or adoptive parents and the role of the birth family. This paper is designed to provoke some discussion about these controversial areas.

MANAGING TWO FAMILIES

Fostered and adopted children, in particular those who are late placed, commonly have divided loyalties between their foster carers or adopters, who are their current sources of care and protection, and their birth families, for whom they may have strong but often ambivalent feelings of love and anxiety (Beek and Schofield (2004a) and (2004b), Schofield and Beek in press, Thomas and Beckford et al (1999)). Children must find ways to think through and accept the membership of two families (Fahlberg (1994), Thoburn (1996)), whether temporarily or permanently, while also managing their personal histories in ways that do not involve excessive anxiety or blame. Contact is the point at which the two families overlap in the child's life and mind and is therefore a delicate and complex area. It holds the potential to assist children in managing their dual identities and to develop or sustain positive relationships with their relatives, built on realistic understandings and appreciation of their strengths and difficulties, while also building relationships in the foster or adoptive family. However, contact can involve difficult transitions, the arousal of painful memories and feelings, and the exploration of relationships that have been destructive in the past. The *quality* of contact can therefore have a positive or negative impact on the child's capacity to return to the birth family or the child's sense of permanence in the foster or adoptive family. What is absolutely critical to this issue is that children cannot be expected to manage the contact experience and these two families in their minds without help from sensitive and committed adults, carers and social workers. Situations where children are ferried to contact in neutral venues and where foster carers and birth relatives do not meet too often leave children to manage these tensions alone, creating extra barriers to a sense of coherence in their already troubled minds.

THE DEVELOPMENTAL IMPACT OF CONTACT

The premiss on which this paper is based is that contact plans should be defensible in each case on the grounds that they are developmentally beneficial for the particular child – not that contact is deemed to be an automatically required feature of any family placement. This developmental focus should not mean that contact is less likely to happen, but that in each case there should be a careful assessment of its benefits for the specific child. The presumption of reasonable contact in the Children Act 1989 operates within the overall paramountcy principle of the welfare of the child. Within the Adoption and Children Act 2002 there is no presumption of contact and so a case will always need to be made and that case must be put in terms of the overall plan for the child's development and welfare throughout childhood and into adult life.

Within a family placement context, the welfare and development of the child is broadly defined and will include the security associated with attachment alongside safety, health, education, emotional and behavioural development, roots and identity. The impact of contact on the *developing mind of the child* needs to be assessed when decisions are made (see Figure 1), with contact arrangements designed or assessed, for example in terms of their ability to promote self-esteem or to help children make sense of their histories. Contact can promote or be detrimental in all such areas.

Contact and the developing mind of the child (Figure 1)

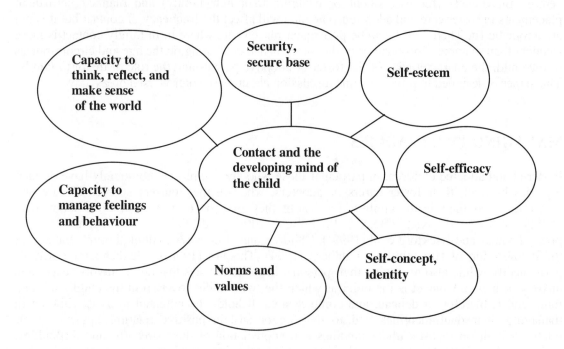

Alongside these developmental questions about the impact of contact on the inner world of the child, there are also questions about its impact on the outer world of the child. So contact arrangements should also be tested in terms of the role they play in enhancing the *developing social world* of the child (see Figure 2), eg the quality of relationships within the foster, adoptive and birth family – and the child's ability to engage with activities, school and friends.

Thus contact arrangements that are too rigid to allow the growing child to play for the school football team or go to a friend's birthday party or attend a birth family wedding where this is appropriate need to be thought about very carefully.

Contact and the developing social world of the child (Figure 2)

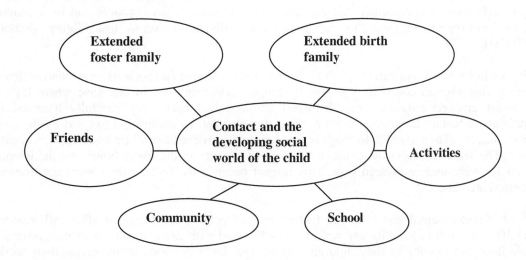

The quality of contact therefore can be seen as relying on an interaction between factors in the child, the foster carers or adopters, the birth family and the professional network that plans and supports contact and the placement. (see Figure 3, adapted from Beek and Schofield (2004b))

An interactive, dynamic model of contact (Figure 3)

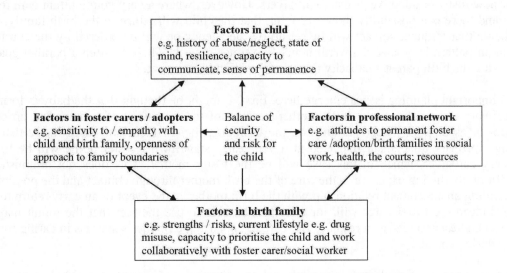

Contact can be involved in both upward and downward developmental spirals and will be affecting children differently depending on the range of such factors that contribute to the balance between security and risk. Research on contact in foster care and adoption suggests that contact can be a very constructive part of foster and adoptive placements (Beek and Schofield (2004a), Fratter et al (1991), Neil (2004a), (2004b), Logan and Smith (2004), Sellick et al

(2004), Thoburn et al (2000), Thoburn (2004)), but this will only be the case where contact is safely and sensitively managed (whether by social workers, foster carers or adopters in collaboration with birth relatives) and promotes the general welfare of the child. Contact can be distressing (57% of fostered children in the study by Sinclair et al (2005)) or even harmful, when contact leaves already traumatised children feeling unsafe or dysregulated (Howe and Steele (2005)) or when emotionally entangled children find themselves taking responsibility for birth relatives (Beek and Schofield (2004b)). On the other hand the absence of contact where there is the potential for constructive relationships between children and birth relatives is a seriously missed opportunity that can also affect children's development and be a source of anger and resentment through to adulthood, especially in relation to 'lost' siblings (Schofield (2003)).

It should be noted that careful analysis of risk and protective factors is as important while cases are going through courts as it is for the longer term solutions. In one case where high risk contact arrangements for very disturbed children had been very carefully assessed in a permanent foster placement and set at three times a year, an application to court by the mother for contact led to a plan for fortnightly contact during proceedings while assessment was carried out. The significance of the children's source of security in the foster home and the impact of contact were underestimated – perhaps in part because the foster carers were not present or represented at court.

Such developmental and systemic factors around contact are likely to affect all aspects of children's sense of security and need to be addressed with care, since contact may promote or diminish the possibility that children will recover from previous harm, revise their working models of the world, become less defensive, more open, more resilient and be more likely to become stable in permanent placements in birth, foster or adoptive families.

INFANCY 0–18 MONTHS

Infants who come to a foster or adoptive home straight from hospital or in the early weeks will not have formed an attachment to their birth parents and will build their first attachment with their new foster or adoptive primary caregivers. However, where a very young infant is in foster care and there is a possibility, however faint, that the child will return to the birth family, it is probable that frequent contact will be set up by the agency or will be ordered by the court – a common pattern is blocks of several hours five times a week. There is often a parallel goal of assessing the birth parent's capacity to parent the infant via contact.

Two important planning issues emerge here. First, it might be thought that the baby is forming its primary attachment to the birth mother because of the frequency of contact and an often unspoken assumption about building on the biological tie. In fact, it is more likely that the infant's primary attachment if placed at a very early stage in the foster home will be to the primary caregiver, which in this case will be the foster mother. This does not diminish the benefit of continuing exposure to the care of the birth mother through contact and the possibility of building an attachment relationship with the birth mother in the event of an early return to her care. Indeed the foster carer will, for example, be able to use the fact that the infant may be relaxed and easy to feed as a result of her care to enhance the mother's success in caring for the child during contact.

However, the role of the foster carer as the primary attachment figure for the infant must not be overlooked or undervalued, nor should the contact plan mean that the foster mother should pull back from immersing herself in the *maternal preoccupation* that Winnicott (1965) described and is so critical to the healthy development of the infant through these early weeks and months. As Neil and Howe (2004b: 226) put it: 'It is within the child–parent relationship that young minds form.' A misreading of attachment theory might suggest that the foster mother should in some way stand back emotionally and cognitively from the infant – either to facilitate the attachment to the birth mother or to avoid the pain of loss when the child moves, or to facilitate the new attachment in an adoptive family. In fact the primary gift of sensitive caregiving is *not* in the fact that the relationship will last, although this is to be valued when it happens, but to reduce anxiety, shape the baby's developing mind (and brain, Shore (2001)) and awaken the baby's potential for play and exploration. Even where the birth mother is offering good care during contact and the foster carer wishes to support this, there should be no sense that the baby is simply being looked after physically by the carer with the birth mother providing the emotional input through contact. For the foster carer, loving and fully engaging with the mind and whole person, as well as the physical needs, of a baby can only be beneficial to the baby – grief can be managed better by a very young mind than the prolonged absence of loving care in the sensitive early months of life.

Promoting security will mean managing the framework of the contact experience to ensure that the infant has a meaningful, positive and undisruptive experience, which includes providing calming and reassuring non-verbal messages to the infant but also calming and encouraging messages to the contact relative. This will be true both for young infants and for infants who already have formed an attachment to their birth parent. Continuity will be important as part of a message to the infant that the world is a predictable place which it is safe to relax in and this may need to be negotiated with birth relatives and taken into account by courts when contact arrangements are agreed. Very often the disruptive contact programmes that are set out for infants are potentially very damaging.

One of the more challenging aspects of planning contact in infancy, therefore, is determining the *amount of time* that might be deemed necessary to preserve or build or make more secure the attachment to a birth parent. There is no evidence that any particular amount of time is more or less likely to be associated with preserving an existing or building a new attachment relationship in the context of contact. More does not mean better. It is helpful for the young infant to continue to be familiar with the sight, voice, smell, touch and presence of the birth parent and for the older infant to be able to experience play and games with the birth parent so that this can provide a platform for the relationship if the infant returns home. But the appropriate amount of contact time will depend on age, on what is reasonable AND what will not disturb the infant establishing natural rhythms. For very young infants the likelihood is that of four hours contact time, two–three hours will be when the infant is asleep. If birth parents are sitting in the foster home during this time it is likely to be a major problem for them, but also for the foster carer. Contact needs to be planned around the role that the parent can reasonably play in the child's life, but it should not be done arithmetically by weight of hours. As with a placement for adoption, contact prior to placement can be stepped up prior to return home.

Even more challenging in terms of providing predictable, sensitive and available care in the foster home and building security in the mind of the infant is the contact plan that means the infant is taken to *a neutral venue*, such as a family centre, for frequent and extended periods of supervised or unsupervised contact. This arrangement gets round the problem of possible intrusion into the foster home and may appear to promote the freedom of the birth parent to parent the child in a more relaxed manner, away from possible competition or criticism by the foster carer. However, the key premiss of attachment theory is that when anxious, as when separated from the current caregiver or when confronted with birth relatives who may now be unfamiliar or have been rejecting or frightening, the infant will seek proximity to an attachment figure who offers care and protection. Since this role is likely to be filled by the foster carer, the infant is in a dilemma that is akin to that which promotes disorganisation (Main and Solomon (1986)). The infant may only have access to a caregiver who is a source of anxiety. Even infants who may be thought too young to remember can have memories which can make contact distressing and disturbing. (Even a new-born baby will respond to a familiar nursery rhyme told to them during pregnancy, so infants should never be thought too young to remember.) It is not unusual to hear of infants under six months old who become very distressed when taken to contact but not when taken to see other places and people. But primarily the problem is one of disrupting the infant's predictable and continuous care in a relationship.

Where there is to be contact away from the home for whatever reason it is still desirable for the foster mother to be present if at all possible, so that there is availability in times of stress, but also so that messages of availability are reinforced in the child's internal working model. If this is not possible then the length of time away from the foster mother should be limited and other sources of security and continuity should be built in, such as using the same supervisor each time (someone who comes into the foster home to greet the baby and returns the baby with a debrief for the foster carer), and the use of transitional objects such as teddies from the foster home. This may appear to be reinforcing the child's ties with the foster home, but in fact if the infant's anxiety is reduced, the infant is more likely to relax and accept care or play with the birth parent and the parent is more likely to find the child rewarding. Whatever the arrangements, where the infant shows distressed, disoriented, disorganised behaviours in the presence of the birth relative that are not evident at other times, then there should be concerns, as mentioned above, about the dysregulating effect of contact for the child.

In planning contact the primary task of caregivers and supervising social workers, in all their talk, behaviour, non-verbal messages and practical arrangements around contact is to reassure the infant, reduce anxiety, make it a positive and security promoting experience – and avoid experiences that unsettle and frighten the infant and actually decrease the likelihood of a successful permanent move, whether back home or to a new family.

TODDLERS AND PRE-SCHOOL CHILDREN

This age group presents particular challenges and opportunities for contact, whether contact is aimed at facilitating a return to the birth family or is in the context of a plan for permanence in foster care or adoption. Young children will be seeking to find meanings that give a shape to and make sense of their experience. However, they have both a very limited capacity to make sense of the complex circumstances of loss and separation and a limited capacity to handle their emotions and their behaviour. Such difficulties are exacerbated for young children who are insecure and for whom the world is full of uncertainties and dangers. Although pre-school children have gained some skills in language and, to a certain extent, perspective taking (Dunn (1988)), it is not surprising that they find it difficult to make sense of why their mum and siblings arrive at the strange house, smile at them, but then go away leaving them behind. They struggle to understand why they go in a car to a strange place to see the parents, brothers and sisters, whom they used to get up with every morning.

Although over time some toddlers and pre-school children may accept the routine of these events, because they have no power to influence them, other children will continue to struggle with their feelings each time. These feelings may of course be mixed and change. Given that realistically it is going to be very difficult to help a three year old understand that they are in foster care because, they are, for example, at risk of physical or sexual abuse or neglect, the focus must be on building the child's developmental health and defining a role for contact in that process. The plan then must be about how contact can promote and not put further at risk the child's sense of security. Seeing birth relatives can potentially give some helpful messages to children about who they are, about the fact that they are still valued and that people they know do not disappear into thin air just because they do not live with them anymore.

As with infants, *assessment* through observation and interpretation of toddlers' and pre-school children's (and parents') behaviour at contact is rarely straight forward and developmental theory can usefully be applied. By the latter half of the second year, children have learned how to pretend to feel what they do not feel and, in cases of abuse and neglect, to suppress expressions of negative feelings (Crittenden and Di Lalla (1988)). At contact this is an age when children may be struggling to manage feelings of longing, anger and/or anxiety. Feelings will sometimes be suppressed (a still face or a fixed smile) and sometimes spill out (persistent crying/chaotic behaviour). Children at this age are unlikely to be able to explain their views or experience of contact and it is only in their often ambiguous behaviour that they will express their feelings. This is not to suggest that older children in this age group should not be consulted about their wishes and feelings about seeing birth family members, but it does mean that recording and making sense of children's *behaviour* at times when they are not having contact and then before, during and after contact are very important pieces of assessment work.

With this age group, non-verbal *scaffolding* or shaping of the experience of contact can be used alongside language and explanation to give messages that relationships in the foster or adoptive home are offering security and that contact with birth family members will enhance security and contribute to the child's trust in the environment. In order for this to be the case, contact needs to be predictable, both in terms of the timing, the presence of the birth relative, the comfortableness of the venue and, where relevant, the presence of the foster carer, adopter or supervisor. It is also important that where birth parents have drug or alcohol problems that they are not intoxicated, even though this may mean that the contact meeting is postponed or curtailed. Parents' failure to attend contact can perhaps be dealt with by planning another activity which can take its place if necessary – although actively engaging the social worker or an assistant to bring the parent to contact is preferable to serial disappointments. Less frequent but reliable contact is preferable.

For young children, as for infants, the presence of the foster carers or at the very least a familiar social worker is likely to be helpful. If there is to be a point during contact when the foster carer or adopter is not in the room then it will be important for the child to have clear communications and even evidence that they will be returning to the foster carer after the meeting – such as the foster carer holding the child's coat or the child having a small cushion from the foster home (Schofield and Beek (2006)).

Although *face-to-face contact for young children in adoption* is less common than in foster care, evidence suggests that it can work well in some cases and does not appear to negatively affect the new attachment relationship with the adoptive parents (Neil (2004a), (2004b)). Indeed, as Neil's research has found, contact can be helpful and reassuring to adoptive parents as well as children, and birth relatives value the opportunity to retain their sense of themselves as a mother or father or grandparent and to know their child is doing well (Young and Neil (2004)). This kind of post-adoption contact is often in a context where children have been removed from the birth family in infancy and do not have established relationships with birth relatives. What appears to be most helpful is the unambiguous fact that in adoption the child is permanently a member of the adoptive family and so contact is facilitated by the adoptive parents. This includes controlling the timing and the venue as well as being present as the child's parents, but empathy towards the birth relatives is a key part of this success (Neil (2004a)).

Although in long-term foster care the social worker is often playing a more active role in planning contact, unlike post-adoption, it is also the case that contact works best where foster carers feel themselves to be key players in the decision making about contact and are also able to be sensitive or empathic to the child and the birth family (Beek and Schofield (2004a), Neil et al (2002)). A belief system that supports the notion that children can be members of more than one family is also valuable in enabling adoptive parents and foster carers to work comfortably but actively to ensure that contact is a success.

There are clearly many cases in which contact is a constructive force in young children's lives, facilitating a sense of security in the foster family through reducing anxiety, guilt and split loyalties, while also ensuring positive experiences with birth relatives which in short-term foster care may lead to returning to them. But there are contact arrangements in both temporary and permanent foster placements in which traumatised children are retraumatised through their contact with birth relatives (Howe and Steele (2004)). In the presence of a disturbed or frightening caregiver, children of three or four will slip back into their previous defensive strategies, for example controlling and being contemptuous of the parent or freezing – and then back in the foster home they may go berserk with rage and anxiety, attacking family pets or younger children, smearing faeces and so on.

Where young children have contact with relatives who have previously maltreated them, they may be particularly at risk for a number of reasons. First, toddlers and preschool children have fewer strategies for communicating their distress directly and behaviours that arise from anxiety before, during or after contact are not always easy to interpret as linked to contact, when children may generally be showing difficult behaviours, such as tantrums and bed-wetting. Secondly, limited understanding of language and the world around them makes it difficult to understand the explanation that 'Daddy is talking like that because he has a mental illness'. Thirdly, because of their age and size they are more likely at contact to be picked up, experience a nappy change or a feed, sit on a lap or be held close. Thus the child will experience a great deal of physical proximity that should be a positive part of contact, but if there is a history of maltreatment this may be experienced as distressing and intrusive, even when children show little reaction.

Of course, young children can also be distressed by cutting off contact. It is still sometimes said that children should not have contact with birth family members for a period when they first come into care or should not have contact with bridge foster carers for a period when they move into adoption, so that they have time to 'settle' or to form a new attachment. Each case must be looked at carefully, but unless birth relatives or former foster carers are likely to create a significant problem at contact, then the benefit to be gained from reassuring the child that they have not just been abandoned and that they are wished well in their new home must outweigh the possible upset. Children are more likely to turn to their new caregivers for comfort if they feel that the world still makes sense and if they are not so overwhelmed with anxiety about loss that they shut down on their feelings.

SCHOOL AGE 5–11

For this age group, contact in foster care and adoption can be a significant part of helping children to make sense of who they are and where they fit in society and within the range of their relationships but needs careful support (Schofield et al (2000), Logan and Smith (2004), Selwyn (2004)). At an age when identity, self-concept and self-esteem are important aspects of development, contact should be playing a part in clarifying the 'facts', reinforcing positives and enabling children to work through more troubling and worrying questions about their histories and themselves. As Owusu-Bempah and Howitt ((1997): 201 cited in Howe and Neil (2005)) put it: 'Socio-genealogical knowledge is fundamental to our psychological integrity. It is essential to our sense of who we are, what we want to be, where we come from and where we belong in the order of things.'

But the narratives of fostered and adopted children are complex and do not fit culturally available frameworks. There are many truths and a number of realities to which children may have been exposed, both in relation to why they are not with their birth parents and their care or adopted status. Discontinuities may have occurred not only in family environments, but also in relation to ethnicity, religion, language and community. Contact can be useful in helping to makes sense of the narrative, but most children will need active help from caregivers to process this information into a coherent story that allows them to get on with their lives.

As the developmental model suggests, if contact arrangements in all types of placements are working well they should be contributing to all aspects of the child's welfare in this age range, as well as 'roots and identity'. Contact should help build children's self-esteem, for example, which is so important at this age, so that messages such as, 'Well done for your school work' or 'What a lovely new haircut' accompany the family membership messages, 'We still value you as our son/grandson/brother'. One difficulty is that in living apart children's lives move on and birth families may not know what matters to the child. Foster carers and adoptive parents may be keeping birth families up to date at varying intervals and where close working relationships can be established between caregivers and birth families, birth parents will receive school reports or be involved in school parents' evenings. But social workers may need to be active in facilitating information exchange.

Important to note here is that research on *indirect contact* in adoption suggests that this is far less straightforward and successful in ensuring exchange of information than may have been thought, given that it is almost universal in adoption arrangements (Neil (2004), Young and Neil (2004), Selwyn (2004)). The letterbox system can work well, but appears to have many potential problems, with birth relatives and adopters being unsure what to write, administrative delays between letters and responses, variable censorship of letters and the children often being entirely left out of the loop. Indirect contact in the absence of face-to-face contact and without adequate support to aid the communication process can in fact lead to increased anxiety and resentment, with neither party getting the information they want and need and frequent misinterpretations of what the other thinks and feels. In particular, adopters may feel if letters stop that birth relatives have lost interest in the child, when they may actually have fears of being intrusive or simply have given up struggling to keep such a difficult communication going. Primary age children will be looking for signals about their birth family and it would be unfortunate if, due to problems in the system, even when birth relatives may have genuinely wanted to offer their support the message that comes to the child is rather negative.

This issue alone highlights the range of possible information exchange and 'overlap' between families and how this will define and be defined by how contact works. In bridge placements, in this age group and younger, where foster and birth families are working closely together to achieve the child's return home, foster carers may be making regular visits to the birth family's house to get the child accustomed to seeing it as home again, and the foster carer may be able to offer help and support to the birth family in parenting the child more effectively. Even in some long-term foster placements there can be a significant degree of overlap. In long-term foster families which previously provided respite care for children with disabilities who are now placed permanently with them, contact may be frequent, medical appointments can be shared and birth families may provide the respite care (Schofield et al (2000)). In a few cases where long-term foster carers have confidence in the permanence plan, are able to establish a good relationship with the birth mother or father and there is no risk to the child, contact in this age group may be as often as fortnightly. Some spontaneity also becomes possible where there are good relationships between carers and birth relatives. A spur of the moment decision to drive her three foster daughters round to their different mothers on Mother's Day to drop off cards and presents was one foster carer's way of setting up brief but informal 'contact' outside normal arrangements, but in a form that helped children and birth mothers feel special (Beek and Schofield (2004a)).

More commonly in permanent placements for foster care or adoption, contact is more limited, but can still demonstrate to the child some good will between their two families (Beek and Schofield (2004a), Neil et al (2003)). Infrequent but regular contact, as in ordinary extended families, becomes an opportunity to catch up on news and, if made a special occasion such as a trip to the zoo or to the seaside, it can offer a chance to enjoy time together and provide memories of the kind that the child can process and revisit. One adopted child, Sue (10), commented on her time with her birth mother at the park.

> 'We go for a walk around the park and we've bought some crisps and go out to the ducks and give them cheese-and-onion flavoured crisps or something. Then mum starts to tell jokes and I, I can't tell any jokes and we'd all be drunk, feel as though we were drunk by the end of it.' (Thomas and Beckford et al (1999):93)

More formal arrangements in more risky situations can be said to be 'safe enough' through special care being taken to ensure that supervision is appropriate, birth parents are on time and so on. Almost invariably this works best when foster carers, like adopters, are actively involved. Where children have a secure relationship with carers and a sense of permanence they can use the explanations their carers provide to help them feel secure and reflect on their contact with birth parents, even where birth relatives talk of wanting the child back (Schofield (2003)).

What works less well is where, as in infancy and early childhood, the arrangements for contact are perceived as out of the foster carers' or adopters' hands. Too often bridge and permanent foster children in this age group are taken by different escorts to social services venues, where supervisors may not know the child and the foster carer then gets poor or no feedback on how the contact visit went. In some cases disturbed children who have experienced extreme neglect and sexual abuse in their birth family are involved in contact of this kind (Beek and Schofield (2004a)). One long-term foster carer reported that because of the low priority given to this arrangement, the new supervisor had not checked who was allowed to have contact with her ten year old foster daughter and a family member who had sexually abused the child was allowed to attend the contact. It is unrealistic to expect the child to speak out against the presence of a family member, even when she is frightened or possibly when he has brought presents. But more generally, as stressed at the beginning of this paper, for children to be left to resolve the tensions created by relating to separate families on their own can leave them completely split and unable to reconcile their lives into something that is coherent and makes sense. They do not know how to feel safe.

Sometimes children do communicate their feelings.

> Donna (5) had been physically and sexually abused and neglected up till the age of three. Her father was a frightening figure who dominated and attacked her learning disabled mother. In foster care she was hard to get close to. Like a little doll, she was well-behaved at home and school, but had little facial expression, showed no variation in her mood and was fixed in her behaviour, which at times included sitting in a trance like state for up to 20 minutes at a time. She was taken to contact by a social work assistant, who over time discovered that she needed to take a plastic bag each time, since Donna was invariably physically sick on her way to and from contact with her birth parents.

In this case Donna's view – that she wanted to return to her mother's care – was being taken very seriously by the court, but this account of contact, which was consistent with what was known of her history, suggested that her relationship with her parents was still dominated by fear and confusion.

Planning for contact in this age group needs awareness of the entire range, from the most enjoyable and secure to the most risky and insecure – frequency is only part of the picture in relation to the overall plan and the impact on the child must be ascertained and reviewed through observation and consultation with the child and the carers whatever the frequency or the plan.

ADOLESCENCE

Although in adolescence contact may well be more flexible and, with the advent of mobile phones, out of the control of carers and adopters, teenagers often still need support to make the most of contact. In fact, mobile phones can be useful in keeping the secure base in reach. Amanda (a 15-year-old in long-term foster care) had only had sporadic contact with her parents since the age of three, partly because of their prison sentences for drug-related offences. When contact was reinstated, she went to meet her birth mother in the local shopping centre, but her mother did not appear. Immediately, Amanda telephoned her foster father as arranged and he was instantly available to pick her up (Beek and Schofield (2004a)).

In some situations, the physical presence of the carer during the contact meetings may still be needed as an explicit reminder of the availability of the secure base and could be of great reassurance even to the older child. Samantha (a 14-year-old with learning difficulties) had become highly stressed by her birth mother's erratic attendance at contact meetings hosted and supervised by Social Services. Her foster mother decided to change the arrangements so that she could supervise them herself and the birth mother could chose a venue in which she felt comfortable. When Samantha had easy access to her secure base in this way, she no longer wet the bed the night before and was able to relax and enjoy her contact and also to manage her loyalties to both families.

Special gestures outside of normal contact arrangements and orchestrated by the foster mother can also enrich the contact relationship for this age group and enhance the role of birth relatives. In one long-term foster case, two sisters (aged 14 and 10) were helped by the foster carer to wrap up 30 small birthday presents for their birth mother's 30th birthday. The carer felt so confident of her relationship with the children that she was not threatened by frequent contact and enjoyed the pleasure the children and the mother had in their relationship.

In contrast, one adoptive mother accepted the contact plan ordered at court for her 11-year-old son (Philips (2004)) even though she had some misgivings. She knew that it was important for him to have contact with both his drug-using parents, but during his teenage years she was at times very uncomfortable at leaving him in households for several hours when drug taking was likely to be going on. She felt unable to challenge the plan as it had been agreed at court and as an adopter was unable to access the support she needed. A request for supervision of contact by social services was met by a discussion about whether she could pay the charge.

Of course, being mature enough as an adolescent to have a choice about contact may not make it easier to 'choose'. Joshua (15), for instance, was in a long-term foster family but had very frequent contact, spending part of most weekends with his birth father. The arrangement was flexible, and could be altered by agreement if the foster family had a commitment or the birth father had to work longer hours. However, this comfortable arrangement did not mean that there were no complications. Joshua's loyalties could feel torn, but his carers accepted this and encouraged him to talk through his complex feelings. Using his secure base in this way, Joshua was able to reach a compromise regarding Christmas arrangements so that he could spend Christmas Day with his foster family and Boxing Day with his birth father.

For some adolescents, painful memories of the birth family mean that contact is something that they would not welcome. This adopted boy, aged 12, put it this way: 'They just signed the form that we could be given to anybody else and that was it then. We never saw them again. And thank God we didn't.' (Thomas and Beckford et al (1999))

In some extreme cases, though, fostered teenagers are exposed through contact to fearful relationships that have persisted from early childhood. Patrick (13) had been physically abused by his father as a younger child and continued to be exposed to his father's violent temper towards his partner during contact. Earlier in this foster placement, Patrick's carers were extremely anxious about this and noted that he was often in a 'trance-like state' when they collected him from his father's home. It seemed that the traumatising and disorganising effect of the fear and dread that he had experienced in his father's care was repeated during contact. As an accommodated child (Children Act 1989, s 20), the local authority felt that there was little they could do. In spite of exceptionally committed, loving and sensitive carers, Patrick's anti-social and violent behaviour escalated and the local authority moved him into a residential facility, where his behaviour was continuing to deteriorate. It seemed that Patrick had, in his foster family, a window of opportunity to heal some of his early damage, but his carers had no way of protecting him from his father through contact arrangements that were out of their control.

In adolescence contact needs to be managed in co-operation with the young person, but ensuring that the overall plan must be to ensure stability and security into adult life. Thus building constructive connections to birth family members through contact is very appropriate, but so also is managing the risk of young people spiralling out of control and out of placements.

CONCLUSION

The picture of contact presented in this paper is one of diversity; children and young people who have birth family contact that enhances their sense of self, children for whom contact has represented a serious risk, and much variation in between. Given this range and complexity, decisions about contact in foster care and adoption must always be thought about both in the context of the plan and in the context of the child's secure development if it is to contribute to durable solutions. It is what is going on in the child's mind that needs to be thought about most carefully and this will require an understanding of the differences between the minds of the three-month-old baby, the toddler, the school age child and the later adolescent. Then we need to place that knowledge about this specific child's perceptions, experience and needs in the context of the interacting factors that are likely to promote the healthy development of the child's mind and social world through well-planned and supported contact – which may range from the empathic qualities of the foster or adoptive parent through to the departmental policy on bus fares for parents attending contact to the attitude of courts to permanence in foster care.

Contact has so much potential to benefit children and so much potential for putting their security at risk, that sensitive professional practice in planning, monitoring and supporting contact must be seen as an essential contribution, not only to stability of placements, but also to the long-term psychosocial health of fostered and adopted children.

REFERENCES

Beek, M and Schofield, G *Providing a secure base in long-term foster care* (London, BAAF, 2004a)

Beek, M and Schofield, G 'Promoting security and managing risk: contact in long-term foster care' in Neil, E and Howe, D (eds) *Contact in adoption and permanent foster care: Research, theory and practice* (London, BAAF, 2004b)

Crittenden, PM and DiLalla, D 'Compulsive compliance: The development of an inhibitory coping strategy in infancy' (1988) 16 Journal of Abnormal Child Psychology 585–599

Dunn, J *The Beginnings of Social Understanding* (Oxford, Blackwell, 1988)

Fahlberg, V *A Child's Journey through Placement* (London, BAAF, 2nd edn, 1994)

Fratter, J, Rowe, J, Sapsford, D and Thoburn, J *Permanent Placement- a decade of experience* (London, BAAF, 1991)

Howe, D and Steele, M 'Contact in cases in which children have been traumatically abused or neglected by their parents' in Neil, E and Howe, D (eds) *Contact in Adoption and Permanent Foster Care: Research, theory and practice* (London, BAAF, 2004)

Logan, J and Smith, C 'Direct post-adoption contact: experiences of birth and adoptive families' in Neil, E and Howe, D (eds) *Contact in Adoption and Permanent Foster Care: Research, theory and practice* (London, BAAF, 2004)

Main and Solomon, J 'Discovery of an insecure disorganised/disoriented attachment pattern' in Brazelton, TB and Yogman, MW (eds) *Affective Development in Infancy* (Norwood, NJ, Ablex, 1986) 95–124

Neil, E 'The 'Contact after adoption' study: indirect contact and adoptive parents' communication about adoption' in Neil, E and Howe, D (eds) *Contact in Adoption and Permanent Foster Care: Research, theory and practice* (London, BAAF, 2004a)

Neil, E 'The 'Contact after Adoption' study: face-to-face contact' in Neil, E and Howe, D (eds) *Contact in Adoption and Permanent Foster Care: Research, theory and practice* (London, BAAF, 2004b)

Neil, E, Beek, M and Schofield, G 'Thinking about and managing contact in permanent placements: the differences and similarities between adoptive parents and foster carers' (2003) 8(3) Journal of Clinical Child Psychology and Psychiatry 401–418

Neil, E and Howe, D 'Conclusions: A transactional model for thinking about contact' in Neil, E and Howe, D (eds) *Contact in Adoption and Permanent Foster Care: Research, theory and practice* (London, BAAF, 2004)

Owusu-Bempah, J and Howitt, D 'Socio-genealogical connectedness, attachment theory and childcare practice' (1997) 2(4) Child and Family Social Work 199–208

Philips, R (ed) 'Children exposed to parental substance misuse' in *Adoption with contact – the impact of drug use* (London, BAAF, 2004)

Schore, A 'The effects of a secure attachment relationship on right brain development, affect regulation and infant mental health' (2001) 22(1–2) Infant Mental Health Journal 201–269

Schofield, G *Part of the Family: Pathways through Foster Care* (London, BAAF, 2003)

Schofield, G, Beek, M, Sargent, K with Thoburn, J *Growing up in Foster Care* (London, BAAF, 2000)

Schofield, G and Beek, M *Attachment Handbook for Foster Care and Adoption* (London, BAAF, 2005)

Sellick, C, Thoburn, J and Philpot, T *What works in Adoption and Foster Care?* (Ilford, Barnardos, 2004)

Selwyn, J 'Placing older children in new families: changing patterns of contact' in Neil, E and Howe, D (eds) *Contact in Adoption and Permanent Foster Care: Research, theory and practice* (London, BAAF, 2004)

Sinclair, I *Fostering Now: Messages from Research* (London, Jessica Kingsley, 2005)

Sinclair, I, Wilson, K and Gibbs, I *Foster placements: Why some succeed and some fail* (London, Jessica Kingsley, 2005)

Thoburn, J 'Psychological parenting and child placement' in Howe, D (ed) *Attachment and Loss in Child and Family Social Work* (Aldershot, Avebury, 1996)

Thoburn, J 'Post-placement contact between birth parents and older children: the evidence from a longitudinal study of minority ethnic children' in Neil E and Howe D (eds) *Contact in Adoption and Permanent Foster Care: Research, theory and practice* (London, BAAF, 2004)

Thoburn, J, Norford, L and Rashid, SP *Permanent Family Placement for Children of Minority Ethnic Origin* (London, Jessica Kingsley, 2000)

Thomas, C and Beckford, V with Lowe, N and Murch, M *Adopted Children Speaking* (London, BAAF, 1999)

Winnicott, D *The Family and Individual Development* (London, Tavistock, 1965)

Young, J and Neil, E 'The Contact after Adoption Study: the perspective of birth relatives after non-voluntary adoption' in Neil, E and Howe, D (eds) *Contact in Adoption and Permanent Foster Care: Research, theory and practice* (London, BAAF, 2004)

THINKING THE UNTHINKABLE:
THE IMPLICATIONS OF RESEARCH ON WOMEN AND CHILDREN IN RELATION TO DOMESTIC VIOLENCE

Dr Cathy Humphreys

School of Health and Social Studies, University of Warwick

PREAMBLE

This chapter argues that the central issue identified in the Report to the Lord Chancellor on the Question of Parental Contact in Cases where there is Domestic Violence (1999) – namely that safety was being compromised at the expense of contact – is a problem which still needs to be addressed. While a number of initiatives have been taken (guidelines for judges and magistrates, developments in case law, C1A forms), the evidence provided by research studies and the official statistics indicate that there has been little or no change. In fact, some of the data suggests that the situation is worsening.

The official statistics indicate that in fewer than 1% of contact applications is a 'no contact order' given. The serious incongruity between this figure and the data on domestic violence homicide and serious assaults raises major issues of concern. These data show that on average two women a week are killed by a partner or ex-partner; that 54% of rape is carried out by a partner or ex-partner; and that of the domestic violence murders which were reviewed in London during a 14-month period, 76% involved separation and almost 50% involved arguments about child contact (Richards and Baker, 2003).

Similarly, research studies are consistent in showing that there are serious negative impacts on the physical, cognitive and emotional well-being of children living with domestic violence, including high rates of direct child abuse. Up to two-thirds of children on the child protection register are children living with domestic violence. It is also a consistent theme in child death reviews.

The lack of responsiveness to the issues of serious domestic violence within the decision-making about child contact, and the current lack of any clause within the Children (Contact and Adoption) Bill which specifically ensures children's safety or that of their primary carer (usually mother), suggests that the child contact arena has failed to take on the mounting evidence from the criminal justice and child protection systems about the damaging and sometimes lethal impact of serious domestic violence. This chapter calls for a shift in attitude, policy and practice to address the serious shortcomings which are raised by the research evidence in this area.

BACKGROUND

In 2003, 67,000 applications were made for contact under s 8 of the Children Act 1989 (Department of Constitutional Affairs (2004)). Only 601 cases were refused – a figure of fewer than 1% of all applications and one can only assume the lowest figure of any country where there is a well-developed system of family courts. This paper will argue that such a figure, when taken alongside what is known about domestic violence and other forms of child abuse, represents a very significant 'institutional failure to protect'.

The paper will begin with a discussion of the backdrop against which issues of domestic violence and child abuse are raised within family court proceedings, including the polarised debates between father's rights groups and women's and children's advocates. It will look briefly at the attempts which have been made so far to address the issue of domestic violence and child abuse before looking more closely at the salient data on post-separation violence. The implications for child-contact decisions are then explored, including the 'unthinkable' notion that while in some cases of domestic violence and child abuse accommodations in relation to supported and supervised contact can be made, for another group protection and recovery from the terrifying effects of severe domestic violence can only be made through indirect contact or no contact orders.

HIGH LEVELS OF AGREED CONTACT

Any discussion of the debates currently raging in the family court context needs to have some perspective on the extent of the problem. Data is dependent upon how contact is measured, who is being asked (resident, non-resident parents or children), and the extent of the study (Hunt and Roberts (2004)). A study by the Office of National Statistics of 661 parents (649 resident parents and 312 non-resident parents) reporting on the contact arrangements for 1,506 children showed the following results:

- At least half of all children had direct or indirect contact with their non-resident parent at least once a week.

- 43% of children in the resident parent sample and 59% of children in the non-resident parent sample had *direct* contact at least once a week.

- Slightly fewer than one in five (18% of both samples) saw their non-resident parent at least once a month. A further one-twentieth saw their non-resident parent only in the school holidays or once every three months.

- 24% of children in the resident parent sample and 10% of children in the non-resident parent sample have no direct or indirect contact with their non-resident parent (Blackwell and Dawe (2003)).

Another study of children in Bristol (Dunn (2003)) found that for the 82% where any form of contact was taking place, one-third had weekly contact and 90% had direct contact at least once a month. This Bristol cohort, in common with the Home Office Citizenship Survey (Attwood et al (2003)), show only a very small number of children with no contact with their resident parent – 10% and 9% respectively. In each study, the level of contact is reported to be higher in the immediate post-divorce period than after three or four years.

An overview of studies in this area (Hunt (2003)) showed that resident parents generally want their partners to see their children more often, not less. In the large ONS study (Blackwell and Dawe (2003)) more resident (31%) compared with non-resident parents (17%) felt that contact was insufficient and that children could benefit from seeing their fathers more often.

In short, there are very high levels of contact informally agreed between parents in the community. There are also groups of resident and non-resident parents who would like more contact. Only a minority of parents use the law to make decisions about child contact. The ONS study (Blackwell and Dawe (2003)) showed this occurred for an estimated 10% of parents. There is also a group of parents who do not take their cases through the family courts but who are also unhappy with contact arrangements.

WHO IS IN THE 10%?

It is difficult to ascertain the constituency of those who comprise the 10% of parents making applications as detailed aggregated data from the different courts is not kept, or at least is not publicly available. Hunt and Roberts (2003) in their overview estimate that between 75% and 86% of applicants will be fathers and 9% to 16% will be mothers. Eight out of 10 applications are about contact. Residency is less contested. Within this 10% are approximately 15% of 'intractable cases' which continue for many years and take up substantial amounts of court time (Buchanan et al (2001)).

'The 10%' are a diverse group who will include non-resident fathers who want more contact with their children and where there are no issues of abuse, child neglect or violence. There will also be resident mothers who are unhappy with child contact arrangements and where there are also no issues of abuse, child neglect of violence from the non-resident father.

Also within the 10% are also a group of men and women where domestic violence and child abuse have been major issues. It is this group who provide the focus of the rest of the article. The probation service estimates that there are 16,000 cases (24% of total applications) where there is domestic violence (Association of Chief Officers of Probation (1999)). The study by Buchanan et al (2001) of 'intractable cases' suggested that domestic violence featured in the majority of these cases. In three out of four of the intractable cases (78%) at least one parent reported fear as some point and over half (56%) reported physical violence. The violence reported by women in their study was generally at the severe end of the continuum of domestic violence, with two thirds reporting chronic violence with injuries ranging from severe bruising to broken bones, internal injuries as well as sustained harassment, emotional abuse and intimidation. This level of violence is also where issues of significant harm to children are at the forefront of concerns.

This scene-setting exercise emphasises that when discussing situations of domestic violence and child abuse that reference is being made to a significant but minority group and that there is no suggestion that the issues raised for this group are applicable across the spectrum of child contact. They apply quite specifically to this group of parents and their children.

CLARIFYING THE CONCEPT OF DOMESTIC VIOLENCE

Unfortunately there is little agreement within the family court arena about the concept of domestic violence. The definition used by CAFCASS is as follows and indicates that issues beyond physical violence need to be considered:

> 'Patterns of behaviour characterised by the misuse of power and control by one person over another who are or have been in an intimate relationship. It can occur in mixed gender relationships and same gender relationships and has profound consequences for the lives of children, individuals, families and communities. It may be physical, sexual, emotional and/or psychological. The latter may include intimidation, harassment, damage to property, threats and financial abuse.' (CAFCASS *Domestic Violence Assessment Policy* (2005))

Research in the late 1990s also highlighted unequivocally the close links between domestic violence and child abuse, through both direct abuse as well as the harmful effects of living with and often witnessing domestic violence (Mullender and Morely (1994); NCH Action for Children (1994)).

There is little shared agreement between groups advocating fathers' rights and women and children's advocates about the nature of domestic violence. Within this contested arena both groups argue strongly that they have the best interests of children at the heart of their dispute. The issues are helpfully summarised by Jaffe et al (2003, p 12).

Issue	Father's rights	Domestic violence advocates
Post separation parenting arrangements	Shared parenting is best	Shared parenting endangers abused women
Prevalence of domestic violence	Domestic violence is exaggerated	Domestic violence is under reported
Nature of domestic violence	Women are as violent as men	Male violence is more severe, injurious and greater risk to life
Allegations of domestic violence	Allegations are used to bolster custody (access) claims	Mothers are punished for raising any allegations and counter accused of being alienators.

The evidence base will be looked at in relation to a number of these issues.

Firstly, in relation to the under-reporting of domestic violence there is certainly a significant amount of evidence in all studies of domestic violence which show that there is under-reporting to formal agencies such as the police (Hester and Westmarland (2005)), though the level of reporting from confidential surveys such as the latest British Crime Survey suggest that both men and women report significant levels of physical and emotional abuse within their domestic relationships (Walby and Allen (2004)).

13% of women and 9% of men report being subjected to domestic violence in the past year. However, when the most heavily abused are considered, based on the frequency of attacks, the range of forms of violence and the severity of injury, women are overwhelmingly the most victimised. Among people subjected to four or more incidents of domestic violence, 89% were women. Moreover 81% of all incidents were attacks on women (Walby and Allen (2004)). Women are twice as likely to be injured, and three times as likely to report living in fear than men (Mirrelees-Black (1999)). When homicide is considered, 37% of women homicides were committed by a partner or former partner, as against 8% of male homicides. At least 54% of rape and serious sexual assault are perpetrated by a male partner or former partner (Walby and Allen (2004)). Domestic violence incidents and recorded crime again show overwhelmingly gendered patterns, with 90% of incidents involving a female victim and a male perpetrator (Scottish Executive (2003)). This is therefore not to deny the levels of violence which about 10% of male victims of domestic violence experience which is severe and chronic, though some of this occurs within gay relationships.

The research on domestic violence therefore suggests that it is not a homogenous concept, but one which covers a wide range of abusive behaviours. This raises very real issues for the family courts in assessing what is meant by 'domestic violence'. Risk and safety assessments are required when there are allegations of domestic violence as the 'story of the violence' is significant in determining the incidence and severity of the emotional and physical abuse which also has a profound a damaging effect on children. Different levels of protection and safety will need to address the complex issues of safe contact.

IS DOMESTIC VIOLENCE TAKEN SERIOUSLY?

There is no doubt that there have been steps by those with responsibility for policy and practice in relation to family court decision-making to take domestic violence more seriously than has been evident in the past. Steps include:

- A widespread Government consultation on domestic violence and child contact which led to the publication of a *Report to the Lord Chancellor on the Question of Parental Contact in Cases Where There is Domestic Violence* (1999). This report acknowledged that 'the issue is not currently being fully or appropriately addressed by the courts' and that there was a widespread view across most stakeholders in the sector that the courts had swung too far towards an assumption that 'all contact was in the best interests of the child' with too little consideration of the issues of safety and risk of harm.

- Prior to four judgements in the Court of Appeal where domestic violence was a feature, an expert's report was called for to review the evidence on domestic violence and its effects on children. This report (Sturge and Glaser (2000)) recommended that there should be no presumption that contact was in the best interests of the child where there had been domestic violence; in fact the evidence all pointed in the opposite direction.

- The judgements in the Court of Appeal did not order direct contact in any of the four cases before them (*Re L; Re V; Re M; Re H* [2000] 2 FLR 334; or in the earlier judgement *Re M (Contact; Violent Parent)* [1999] 2 FLR 321).

- An outcome of this work was the publication by the Lord Chancellor's Department of *Guidelines for Good Practice on Parental Contact in Cases Where There Is Domestic Violence* (2001)) which recommended that an early finding of fact needed to be established where there were allegations, that contact should only be ordered where it could be guaranteed to be safe before, during and after contact, and helpful guidelines were given which raised the wide range of concerns that needed to be addressed when considering the appropriate orders when there were allegations of domestic violence.

- Development of supervised and supported child contact centres and standards has created places which provide different levels of supervision for contact. These developments have been double edged for women and children where there is serious domestic violence. However, they do provide contact provision which is beyond unsupervised contact, though often the pressures to 'move on' mean that even the protection provided by low-level observation may be short-lived (Aris et al (2001)). High-level, supervised contact is expensive and in relatively short supply with many areas having no access to this provision.

- Changes to the definition of harm through the Adoption and Children Act 2002 which now includes 'impairment suffered from seeing or hearing the ill treatment of another', means that domestic violence is now named as a potential form of harm to children which needs to be considered.

- The C1A or 'Gateway Forms' which attach to applications for contact and the response by the resident parent have recently been introduced and should allow for early reporting of abuse allegations. However, they have yet to be evaluated and it is unclear how they will be used by both resident and non-resident parents.

- A *Risk Assessment and Guidance for CAFCASS on Domestic Violence* (2005) has been developed, though is yet to be implemented.

While the list suggests that action is being taken to ensure safe contact, there have been other processes which have undermined progress which on the surface suggests that contact is safer. Such actions have included:

- A very successful campaign by father's rights groups that have consistently argued that men are disadvantaged in child contact cases. The public perception as a result of this publicity is that this is a majority rather than a minority of non-resident fathers and that widespread reform is needed in the court system.

- Very strong presumptions in favour of contact created by case law including: Latey J in *M v M (Child: Access)* [1973] 2 All ER 81 at 88 which emphasises the long-term advantages to the child of keeping in touch with the non-resident parent which outweigh any initially minor and superficial upset; *Re H (Minors) (Access)* [1992] 1 FLR 148 per Balcombe LJ which provides the accepted test for child contact –'are there any cogent reasons why this father should be denied access to his children?'; *Re P (Contact: Supervision)* [1996] 2 FLR 314 and *Re O (A Minor) (Contact: imposition of conditions)* [1995] 2 FLR 124 in which it is stated that 'it is almost always in the interests of a child whose parents are separated that he or she should have contact with the parent with whom the child is not living' (*The Report to the Lord Chancellor on the Question of Parental Contact in Cases Where There Is Domestic Violence* (1999)). Research suggests that the presumption is such that few judges are able to countenance anything other than direct and preferably unsupervised contact in their decision-making even where there was evidence of severe abuse of either women or children (Bailey-Harris et al (1999)).

- *Making Contact Work* (2002) was a consultation which followed on from the Children Act Sub-Committee Report on Domestic Violence. The Report highlighted that there were high levels of dissatisfaction expressed particularly by non-resident fathers, but that enforcement should nevertheless only be used as a last resort. Women's groups were particularly concerned about enforcement being used when there had been inadequate assessments about why either resident mothers or their children may be resisting contact. In many cases this was due to domestic violence or child abuse. Almost all of the recommendations have been accepted by the Government.

- At this stage, it is unclear whether and how 'The Gateway forms' will be used and whether the number of non-resident fathers reporting low level domestic violence will override their usefulness as a mechanism for exploring issues of severity and frequency of abuse for seriously abused men, women and children. This issue is planned to be the subject of evaluation by the Department of Constitutional Affairs in the future.

- The draft Children (Contact and Adoption) Bill has now been the subject of consultation and has also received attention from the Scrutiny Committee which oversees all draft legislation. In spite of 'safe contact' being mentioned in several places there was initially no mechanisms, sections or clauses about how safety will be ensured and under what circumstances. At the time of writing it is unclear whether a redrafted amendment to include risk and safety assessments will be included. The Bill has been written as though none of the prior policy backdrop on domestic violence has occurred (Masson and Humphreys (2005)).

  'Both the Constitutional Affair's Committee and the Scrutiny Committee have raised serious concerns about the proposed legislation. It asserts that "the interests of children should be paramount" in disputes between adults over children and that the Bill in its current form did "little to challenge the 'adult to adult' character of this litigation." In the Committee's opinion, the Bill "reflected one particular view of the nature of problems over contact...that these reflect the intransigence...of the resident parent." It suspected that contact disputes which reached the courts were "considerably more complex...and not easily resolved by ... one-off enforcement measures."' (para 35) (Masson and Humphreys (2005))

In summary, a range of measures have been taken to both address safety and enforcement of contact. Ideally, these should deal with different cases. However, grave concerns have been expressed by both children's charities and women's advocates that unless nuanced risk and safety assessments are undertaken and recommendations acted on by the courts, contact will be enforced where there is a history of violence and abuse either towards resident mothers or the child or both.

WHAT IS THE EVIDENCE OF CHANGING PRACTICES ABOUT DOMESTIC VIOLENCE?

At this stage, there is little evidence of substantial change towards taking domestic violence seriously.

- Clearly the statistics quoted at the beginning of the article suggest that the chances of gaining an order for no contact are virtually nil, no matter what the severity of abuse (Department of Constitutional Affairs (2004)). From a very low baseline, the figure of less than 1% represents a continuous trend towards fewer and fewer orders refused from 3% in 1998, 2.7% in 2000, while in 2001 there were 55,030 contact orders granted by the courts and only 713 (1.3%) were refused (Lord Chancellor's Department Judicial Statistics).

- Further evidence from a case file analysis of 300 cases of applications before the courts shows that in 61% of cases there were allegations of domestic violence. In one third of cases the allegation was proved, though the researcher suggests this was an under-estimate due to under-reporting and difficulty in adducing evidence. In the vast majority of cases, fathers were granted contact with their children regardless of their violent and abusive behaviour. While 58% of men had some contact when they came into the court arena, this had risen to 94% by the end of the legal proceedings, though 5% was indirect contact (National Association of Probation Officers (2002)).

- A case file analysis based on a random selection of 430 cases found that 22% of cases involved allegations of domestic violence. Direct contact was granted in half these cases. In only four cases during the proceedings was there an order for no contact. In one of these cases the father then withdrew the application, while in the other three cases contact was eventually granted (Smart et al (2003)).

- A survey of 178 Women's Aid refuges in 2003 undertaken to gather views from the domestic violence sector about whether practice had developed which was more sensitive to the needs of women and children leaving situations of domestic violence since the introduction of the *Good Practice Guidelines* (Lord Chancellor's Department (2001)) makes depressing reading (Saunders and Barron (2003)). Workers cited cases of 21 children since the new guidelines were introduced where unsupervised contact has been ordered with a Schedule 1 offender or with a parent whose behaviour caused the child to be on the child protection register. 20% of respondents knew of cases where residence had been granted to a domestic violence offender, totalling 101 children. Threats by CAFCASS officers or judges that there would be a change to the residence order if mothers did not allow contact were the most common way of coercing women survivors of domestic violence and their children into agreeing to contact. This was cited in cases concerning 64 women.

- The British Crime Survey of domestic violence showed that in 19% of cases where there was child contact it had been court ordered (Walby and Allen (2004)).

In summary, there is little in this evidence which suggests that domestic violence is being taken seriously. More supervised and supported contact is being ordered, but many of these centres are not set up to manage the safety issues involved in domestic violence and child abuse, and they are not established to deal with contact in either the medium or long term (Aris et al (2002)). The worst fears in relation to the enforcement of contact where there is domestic violence are not allayed by any of these studies of court practice. In fact, the opposite is true.

AN INSTITUTIONAL FAILURE TO PROTECT

The unprecedented levels of contact which are being ordered in cases where there are substantial issues of child abuse and severe domestic violence suggest that some of the evidence base in relation to these issues has not been understood by the family courts.

Strong evidence exists from several different sources which highlight the seriousness of the harm to children and the parent (usually mother) living with the fear of domestic violence.

- Within the criminal justice system and police response to domestic violence the dangerousness of separation where there has been a history of domestic violence is now highlighted. At the top of the risk assessment factors which London police take into account when attending an incident of domestic violence is whether there has been a separation following a history of violence. The London murder reviews and serious physical and sexual abuse on which the London risk assessment tool was developed (Richards (2003)) showed that there were 56 murders in a 14-month period. Of the 30 cases analysed, in 76% of cases separation had occurred and in 47% of these murders arguments about jealousy, separation and child contact featured. In 30% of cases children witnessed the murder of their mother.

- Other studies indicate that the most serious domestic violence offenders in the relationship (those which have resulted in hospitalisation, use of weapons, attempted strangulation, sexual assault, obsessively controlling and jealous, threats to kill) are also the ones who are most dangerous following separation. This includes both physical violence (Morrison (2001); Burgess et al (1997))[1] and serious psychological abuse (Davis and Andra (2000); Mechanic et al (2000)).

- While the immediate post-separation period may be extremely dangerous, a significant amount of early violence and threat may subside. In a study of women using domestic violence outreach services it was found that in about one-third of cases post-separation violence continued and these were often the most persistent and dangerous offenders (Humphreys and Thiara (2003)). This finding is supported by US research which showed that the length of time since separation was the strongest predictor of increased stalking (Mechanic et al (2000)). These persistent and long-term stalkers are dangerous and survivors (usually women) and their children are in need of protection from these offenders.

- Child contact is continually cited as an arena through which domestic violence offenders continue their violence and abuse of both women and children (Walby and Allen (2004); Humphreys and Thiara (2003)).

Looking at this research based within the *criminal justice arena*, it can be seen that the dangerous consequences of domestic and post-separation violence are now being taken more seriously in this arena. Risk assessment tools (Richards (2003)) have been developed as a means through which high-risk offenders can be targeted and apprehended and victims and their families better protected.

Emerging from within the *child protection arena* are also studies which are highlighting the connections between significant harm to children and domestic violence. In understanding these connections, it needs to be recognised that generally only the most serious cases of child abuse come into the statutory child-protection system with most cases being referred out to voluntary sector agencies or 'no further action'.

- An audit of the Cheshire Social Services database of 3,321 case files open to statutory children and families' workers during a one-week period showed that in 41% of cases domestic violence was a feature of the case. The significance of domestic violence increased with the seriousness of concerns, with 66% of cases on the child protection register featuring domestic violence (Sloan (2003)).

- Studies such as that by Ross (1996) of 3,500 cases of marital conflict and child abuse found that the men who were most violent towards women were also physically or sexually abusing their children in virtually 100% of cases. Ross (1996) suggests that this finding has important implications for child contact.

---

[1] Care needs to be taken about over-stating this relationship. Statistics Canada (1994) in the most comprehensive prevalence study of domestic violence found 8% of women reported violence commenced at separation – a similar finding to Walby and Allen (2004).

- A systematic overview of the relationship between child abuse and domestic violence shows that between 30–66% of children who suffer physical abuse are living with domestic violence (Edleson (1999)).

Within the child contact research arena there are also numerous research studies which consistently show that children are continuing to suffer harm when they are subjected to post-separation violence and high levels of conflict.

- At the extreme end children are being killed. At least 29 child homicides have occurred at child contact or handover since 1994 of which 10 occurred in the past two years. In five of these families, contact was ordered by the court (Saunders (2004)). While the death of Victoria Climbie galvanised changes to the child protection system, these children's deaths appear to have no impact on court practice.

- The study by Buchanan et al (2001) of intractable child contact cases found that children living with high levels of post-separation conflict were as emotionally distressed as children in care proceedings. In the backgrounds of at least 56% of these children were issues of domestic violence, much of which was at the severe end of the continuum. When domestic violence was an issue in the proceedings the children scored on tests three times more than would be expected within the general population (Buchanan et al (2001), p 78).

- Increasingly, a body of research is developing which indicates that child contact may be of little benefit to children if it occurs under highly conflictual circumstances including where there is post-separation violence (Kelly (2000)).

In short, the over-arching principle that 'all contact is in the best interests of the child' needs to be reassessed in the light of the harm to children created through post-separation violence.

CONCLUDING COMMENTS

Within the arena of statutory child protection, many women are now being urged to leave violent partners as a means of protecting their children (Humphreys (2000)). This strategy is useless if these same women who are criticised for their 'failure to protect' are then railroaded into child contact proceedings in which protective action on their part and a reluctance to engage with child contact is construed within the family proceedings courts as 'implacable hostility'. Hester (2004) has referred to the chasms between the criminal, public and private law sectors as 'child care on different planets'. Such incongruities between these different sectors are intolerable for the children and domestic violence survivors (usually women) involved.

This paper does not argue that all situations of domestic violence should be resolved with no-contact orders. Sensitive risk and safety assessments using agreed protocols need to be utilised to assess the level of risk and harm (Radford et al (2006)). No contact and indirect contact should not be unthinkable given the knowledge we now have about the serious risk of harm to children and survivors of domestic violence. The father's rights to contact and the child's need to know their father should not be allowed to over-ride issues of trauma, fear, depression, poor cognitive development, the valorisation of attitudes of violence and abuse of women and at the most severe end, the fear of (or actual) homicide of survivors and their children. A group of these women and children come before the family proceedings courts seeking protection from on-going violence and abuse, they should not be met by 'an institutional failure to protect'.

REFERENCES

Aris, R, Harrison, C and Humphreys, C Safety and Child Contact: an analysis of the role of child contact centres in the context of domestic violence and child welfare concerns (London, Lord Chancellor's Department, 2002)

Association of Chief Probation Officers *Response to the consultation on contact between children and violent parents* (London, 1999)

Attwood, C, Singh, G, Prime, D, Creasey, R *Home Office Citizenship Survey: People, Families and Communities* (London, Home Office, 2003)

Bailey-Harris, R, Barron, J and Pearce, J 'From utility to rights? The presumption of contact in practice' (1999) 13 International Journal of Law, Policy and the Family 111–131

Blackwell, A and Dawe, F *Non-resident parent contact* based on data from the *National Statistics Omnibus Survey for the Department of Constitutional Affairs* (London, 2003)

Buchanan, A, Hunt, J, Bretherton, H and Bream, V *Families in Conflict* (Bristol, Policy Press, 2001)

Burgess, A, Baker, T, Greening, D, Hartman, C, Burgess, A, Douglas, J and Halloran, R 'Stalking behaviours within domestic violence' (1997) 12 Journal of Family Violence 389–403

Department of Constitutional Affairs *Judicial Statistics* (London, Stationary Office, 2004)

Davis, K and Andra, M 'Stalking perpetrators and psychological maltreatment of partners: anger-jealousy, attachment insecurity, need of control and break-up context' (2000) 15 Violence and Victims 407–25

Dunn, J 'Contact and children's perspectives on parental relationships' in Bainham, A, Lindley, B Richards, M and Trinder, L (eds) *Children and Their Families: Contact, Rights and Welfare* (Oxford, Hart Publishing, 2003)

Edleson, J 'Children witnessing of adult domestic violence' (1999) 14 Journal of Interpersonal Violence 839–870

Hester, M 'Future Trends and Developments – Violence Against Women in Europe and East Asia' (2004) 10 Violence Against Women 12

Hester, M and Westmarland, N 'Tackling Domestic Violence: Effective Interventions and Approaches' at www.homeoffice.gov.uk/rds/pubsintro1.html (Home Office Research Study 290, 2005)

Humphreys, C *Challenging Practice: Social Work, Domestic Violence and Child Protection* (Bristol, Policy Press, 2000) 47

Humphreys, C and Thiara, RK 'Neither justice nor protection: Women's Experiences of Post-separation Violence' (2003) 25(4) Journal of Social Welfare and Family Law195–214

Hunt, J *Researching Contact* (London, Council for One Parent Families, 2003)

Hunt, J and Roberts, C 'Child contact with non-resident parents' (2003) Family Policy Briefing 3 (Oxford Centre for Family Law and Policy, Barnett House, Oxford)

Jaffe, P, Lemon, N, and Poisson, S *Child Custody and Domestic Violence: A Call for Safety and Accountability* (London, Sage, 2003)

Kelly, J 'Children's Adjustment in Conflicted Marriage and Divorce: A Decade Review of Research' (2000) 39 Journal of the American Academy of Child and Adolescent Psychiatry 963–974

Masson, J and Humphreys, C 'Responding to the 10%: the proposals for facilitating and enforcing contact' (2005) Family Law (July)

Mechanic, M, Weaver, T and Resick, P 'Intimate partner violence and stalking behavior: exploration of patterns and correlates in a sample of acutely battered women' (2000) 15 Violence and Victims 55–72

Mirrlees-Black, C *Domestic Violence: Findings from a New British Crime Survey Self-Completion Questionnaire* (London, HMSO, 1999)

Morrison, K 'Predicting violent behaviour in stalkers: a preliminary investigation of Canadian cases in criminal harassment' (2001) 46 Journal of Forensic Science 1403–10.

Mullender and Morley (eds) *Children Living with Domestic Violence* (London, Whiting and Birch)

National Association of Probation Officers *Contact, Separation and the Work of Family Court Staff* (London, NAPO, 2002)

NCH Action for Children *Hidden Victims: Children and Domestic Violence* (London, NCH Action for Children, 1994)

Radford, L, Blacklock, N and Iwi, K 'Domestic violence risk assessment and safety planning in child protection – Assessing perpetrators' in C Humphreys and N Stanley (eds) *Domestic Violence and Child Protection: Directions for Good Practice* (London, Jessica Kingsley Publications, 2006)

Richards, L *Findings form the multi-agency domestic violence murder reviews in London* (London Metropolitan Police, 2003)

Ross, S 'Risk of physical abuse to children of spouse abusing parents' (1996) 20 Child Abuse and Neglect 589–598

Saunders, H *Twenty-nine child homicides* (Bristol, Women's Aid, 2004)

Saunders, H and Barron, J *Failure to Protect? Domestic Violence and the Experiences of Abused Women and Children in the Family Courts* (Bristol, Women's Aid, 2003)

Scottish Executive Justice Department *Recorded Crime in Scotland, 2002* (Edinburgh, Scottish Executive, 2003)

Sloan, D *Children in Need Census 2003* (Social Factors Survey, Domestic Violence Analysis. www.cheshire.gov, 2003)

Smart, C, May, V, Wade, A and Furniss, C *Residence and contact disputes in court* (London, Department of Constitutional Affairs, Research Series 6/03, 2003)

Sturge, B and Glaser, D 'Contact and domestic violence – the experts' court report' (2000) Family Law (September) 615–629

Walby, S and Allen, J *Domestic violence, sexual assault and stalking: Findings from the British Crime Survey, Home Office Research Study 276* (London, Home Office Research, Development and Statistics Directorate, 2004)

PERMANENCE FOR LOOKED-AFTER CHILDREN

USING INTERNATIONAL COMPARISONS TO REFLECT ON PERMANENCE OPTIONS FOR CHILDREN IN OUT-OF-HOME CARE IN THE UK

Professor June Thoburn CBE
School of Social Work and Psychosocial Studies, University of East Anglia

SUMMARY OF PAPER

Professor Thoburn highlighted three key themes from her paper: the continuity across national boundaries of placement stability as a key goal for children in out-of-home care; the difficulty of achieving it as shown up in evaluations; and the potential as well as the pitfalls of transferability across national boundaries and judicial systems of child welfare initiatives.

Looking internationally, Professor Thoburn referred the conference to the first table in her paper. This table illustrates the difference between children already in care which is an historic cost and those coming into care which we are still able to do something about. In England the number of children coming into care is going down but the number of children in care is going up which means that the children must be spending longer in care.

It is fascinating to explore inter-country differences in care rates and practices. This is affected by attitudes to family. For example, continental Europe on the whole is very pro family, particularly the extended family. In England, care is often seen (contrary to the philosophy in the Children Act 1989) as a system for rescuing children from failing families rather than for helping families experiencing difficulties. She also commented on differences towards providing care for teenagers illustrated by the third table in the paper. In Sweden, for example, almost all young offenders in out-of-home public care are in the child welfare system rather than in custody provided by the justice system.

Professor Thoburn turned to look at the second table in her paper and noted big differences, especially in the use of residential care and placement with kin as placement options. She noted that the table illustrates that only in Canada, the US and the UK is adoption used to any extent as a route out of care. She moved on to say that, despite different placement patterns, when outcomes for English children looked after are compared with those for similar children in care in other developed countries, the results are seen to be broadly similar. Looking just at those who cannot return home and are placed with adoptive or permanent foster families, around one in five placements breaks down. However the average is not useful: we need to break the statistics down further to look at outcomes for 10-year-olds, outcomes for babies etc. Statistics for those entering care as infants (from countries where young children remain in foster care rather than being adopted), and for those entering care past infancy in all countries, show that those who remain in care for longer (and especially those who grow up in the same foster family) tend to have the best outcomes. She commented that the research data do not support the media commentators and politicians who often misquote the research as indicating that the majority of children entering care have poor outcomes. In part this is because they often look retrospectively at the earlier lives of, for example, young people in prison (the 'failures' of the system) rather than looking prospectively at the outcomes for all the children who enter care at a particular time. Thus, these commentators tend to ignore the successes of the system - those who return safely home or go out of care to live with relatives or are successfully adopted. Also, many of those children who successfully put down roots in foster families are not included in 'leaving care' studies, which tend to focus on those who come into care late and who are both troubling and troublesome even before they enter care.

She concluded by saying that the statistics indicate that when compared with other countries we are doing well in placing children for adoption. Given the age and needs profile of children starting to be looked after, there is not much scope for increasing this and focusing too heavily on percentages is not helpful. The majority of children starting to be looked after have good outcomes when the child's circumstances before care are considered, and better outcomes than if they had remained at home. However, in England as in all countries, an important minority are failed by the care system and some are significantly harmed, especially those for whom the system fails to provide stability and the benefits of family membership. To focus too heavily on percentages and targets for one placement type and legal status rather than another may be to miss the opportunity to improve the service to the full spectrum of children and young people who need to be looked after away from home. In order to do this, there is value in a careful consideration of programmes and initiatives in other countries.

INTRODUCTION

This paper draws on a research project on children in out-of-home care[1] in around 15 countries or states with child welfare policies and problems similar to those in the UK to provide a broader perspective on 'permanence'[2] policies in the UK. It is a particularly good time to do this as we increase the available options with the introduction of the special guardianship order, and as placement with relatives as a preferred choice gathers pace. Globalisation is (appropriately) having an impact on child welfare policies (as well as on related policy areas such as anti-poverty strategies) in order to improve outcomes for vulnerable children. But there are also potential pitfalls associated with incorporating research findings and practice interventions from one country into the practice of another. Alongside peer-reviewed research, routinely-collected administrative data (see for example National Statistics and DfES (2005)) can provide necessary context for these cross-national debates and initiatives. But even with these large data sets, inappropriate comparisons between apparently 'successful' outcomes in different countries can result in misleading conclusions and inappropriate changes to policy and practice. In this chapter data and information on permanence policies from two European countries – Italy and Sweden as well as Australia, New Zealand and US are used alongside data from England.[3]

A BRIEF HISTORY OF PERMANENCE POLICIES IN THE UK

Providing stability and the benefits of family membership throughout childhood and into adult life are goals for all countries. All the countries on whose policies and outcomes I have information are aware that, in this respect, they fail to achieve their aim for too many of the children in their care. There are, however, important historical and cultural differences which influence the approach taken to achieving these objectives. Most European states and Australia and New Zealand emphasise the family of origin as the main route to permanence, whether through providing support within the family, family reunification policies or maintaining family links so that adult relatives and siblings remain part of the child's network during the stay in care and when the young person eventually leaves care. While UK policy, practice and legislation also emphasise the parents or relatives as the first permanence options, along with the US, the four UK nations have been more willing than other countries to sever legal links and allow birth family relationships to wither, and therefore have given a greater role to substitute families in achieving stability and family life for children who are assessed as unable to go safely home. These cultural differences go some way to explain the differences between countries in the emphasis placed on achieving permanence, and especially on the use of 'legal permanence' through adoption against parental wishes, for children in care. It comes as no

---

1   The term's 'out-of-home care' and 'in care' are used in this paper alongside the Children Act 1989 term 'looked after' as they are more widely used in other countries.

2   I have placed 'permanence' in quotes to indicate that it is a complex concept which will be understood differently by different readers. For some, it is synonymous with 'adoption'. For others, it has come to mean any family placement outside the home, whilst for others it includes all routes to achieving stable family membership, with primacy given to permanence in the family of origin. See especially Maluccio et al (1986).

3   With devolution, although permanence policies in the four UK nations are broadly similar, legislation, especially in Scotland, is different and statistics are collected separately. Scotland, Northern Ireland and Wales are included in the research but data reported in this paper are from England.

surprise, therefore that the US and UK have a longer history of using adoption as a route out of care, and make greater use of it than other countries. Indeed, the term 'permanence' is in some countries never used, other than to refer to US and UK policies, and in other countries has only come into policy discussions in the past five to ten years.

In the US, permanence policies have provided the underpinning rationale for child placement since the early1970s. They crossed the Atlantic to the UK in the mid 1970s and had an influence on the Children Act 1975. This legislation strengthened the power of the courts to limit or terminate parental rights, and strengthened the ability of foster carers to ensure that children settled with them could not be removed by parents without court agreement. As developed in the US, permanence policies emphasised the birth family as the major permanence option, but demonstrated that adoption, if necessary without parental consent and usually after the termination of birth family contact, could be successful for children in care of all ages and with a wide range of difficulties. In the UK, however, the influential research of Rowe and Lambert (1973) published as *Children Who Wait,* which also argued for a range of permanence options including strengthening reunification policies and increasing stability in foster care, was widely (mis)interpreted as arguing for adoption as the major permanence option. This had the positive result of encouraging some local authorities and adoption agencies to learn from the successes in the US and develop policies and practices for placing children from care with specially recruited adoptive families, including older children and those with disabilities and challenging behaviour. The down-side – a loss of interest in (and resources provided for) family reunification and long-term foster care as 'permanence' options – was recognised by the Short Report (DHSS 1984). This parliamentary select committee commented that permanence in a placement 'should not have become a synonym for adoption. The search for permanence in our view could be accomplished in many ways'. The Short report paved the way for the Children Act 1989 which reasserted the importance of family support and reunification. While clarifying the legislation that could lead to adoption in appropriate circumstances, the Adoption and Children Act 2002 brings adoption more fully into line with the 1989 Act and again seeks to achieve the balance between children's assessed needs, children's wishes, and the human rights of children, birth relatives and others, including current carers, who are important to the child. It builds on the lessons learned by the failure of 'custodianship' introduced in the 1975 Act, and introduces the new permanence option of 'special guardianship' for children and their carers who need legal security to underpin the stability of their family life, but for whom adoption is not appropriate. Depending on how the contact provisions are interpreted by practitioners and the courts, the new legislation has the potential to increase the extent of meaningful post-adoption contact so that, in appropriate cases, and especially if that is what they want, more children will have the benefit of legal stability through adoption without losing the benefits of continuing (to variable extents and with different family members) 'social' membership of the birth family.

In bringing adoption legislation into line with children legislation, and with the s 1 requirement to look at all available alternatives, the Adoption and Children Act 2002 has posed again the question, raised by the Short Report in 1984, but given very little attention since, about the place of 'long-term' and 'permanent' foster care in securing the benefits of stability and family life for larger numbers of looked-after children. The Department of Health (now Department for Education and Skills – DFES) *Choice Protects* programme has provided both impetus and some funding for developments to improve the outcomes of foster care, whether it provides respite as part of a family support service, therapy in order to return children safely home, or as a stable alternative for those whose families cannot provide long-term safe care.

The crucial importance of improving the success of long-term foster care as a permanence option is underlined by the data on placement for children in care, since they clearly point to the limitations of adoption as the main vehicle for providing permanence. If one takes from the 61,100 children looked after in 2004 those for whom a permanent placement will not be appropriate (the 25% already placed with parents or relatives, teenagers in independent living arrangements and the approximately 12% (around 7000) who are likely to be placed for adoption) there remain around 30,000 needing the benefits of high quality stable care, preferably in a family environment and with the opportunity of making lasting relationships (DfES, 2005). Most of these will already be in foster placements and most will be hoping (against the odds) that they will be able to go home, or that they will be able to stay with their current foster families. Sinclair (2005), the author of the recently published DfES overview *Fostering Now: Messages from Research* and co-author of a major study of foster care (Sinclair et al, 2004), found that, despite the fact that the majority of those responding to a questionnaire said they wanted to stay with their current foster carers, only a quarter were still there three years later. Two recent studies throw more light on which children are in the minority who will leave care through adoption and the larger number who, if they are to achieve a 'sense of permanence',[4] will do so via a 'stranger' or 'kinship' foster placement. (Although it is likely that some in both of these placement types will leave care when their carers apply for a residence or a special guardianship order.) Lowe and Murch (2002) studied permanence plans for looked-after children who could not go safely home and found that foster care was more likely than adoption to be the eventual outcome for children who were: over the age of four; of minority ethnicity; had emotional or behavioural problems; had been physically and/or sexually abused; had experienced a failed attempt at return to the birth parents and were attached to their current foster carers. Selwyn et al (2003) found that only 80 (61%) of 130 children who were aged between 3 and 11 when a 'best interest is adoption' plan was agreed were living with adoptive families at the follow up time (on average seven years after the 'best interest' decision). A further 10 had been matched but not placed or the placement had disrupted. 34 had found stability in long-term foster care and 16 (12%) were in unstable care situations. Kemp and Bodonyi, 2002, demonstrate that an even larger proportion of children with an adoption plan in US are not placed for adoption and Courtney et al, 2005, show that a large proportion of young people who 'age out' of care between 18 and 20 had an unfulfilled adoption plan. As with the Lowe and Murch study, Selwyn et al found that the adopted children were younger at the time of coming into care. When compared with children placed for adoption and permanent foster care in the early 1980s, the children placed now, especially for adoption, are on average considerably younger, suggesting that priority is being given to finding permanent families for the youngest (easiest to place) children, possibly at the expense of older children. Of 1,165 children placed from care for adoption or permanent foster care in the early 1980s, only 28% were aged 0–4 when they joined their new families and 54% were aged 12 or over (Fratter at al (1991)). In contrast, 92% of those adopted from care in England in 2004 were under the age of five when they started to be looked after and the average age on joining the adoptive family was three years (National Statistics and DfES 2005). Since only 34% of children who started to be looked after in England in 2004 were under the age of five, there is a danger that the emphasis on meeting adoption targets may be giving a message that works against the *Choice Protects* message that the full range of permanence options should be sought out and then supported for the full range of children needing long-term family placements.

In summary, the concentration on adoption as the preferred permanence adoption came about in the 1970s because prevention and reunification policies were under-resourced or unsuccessful (and almost certainly both), resulting in too many children exposed to the damaging impact of unstable and unplanned placements. The current increase in interest in long-term foster care as a permanence option comes about for exactly the same reason. Numbers of children looked after are going up, even though the numbers coming into care each year are going down. In other words, once in care, they are staying longer. Efforts to increase the numbers adopted have been successful, but the heavy emphasis on adoption has done little to meet the needs of children entering care when past infancy. It may have had unintended consequences, such as an increase in separating siblings as the numbers of families coming forward to adopt sibling groups does not meet the need (*Adoption Register for England and Wales* (2003)). So can we learn anything from other countries?

---

4   Lahti et al (1982) in one of the earlier large scale research studies of US permanence policies found that it was the 'sense of permanence' rather than 'legal permanence' that was associated with better outcomes.

SOME INTERNATIONAL COMPARISONS OF LONG-TERM FAMILY PLACEMENT

The first point of comparison to be looked at when considering if the context of care work in a particular country has similarities with that in the UK are the rates of children in out-of-home care at a particular date each year, and the rates of children entering care during a 12-month period. Absolute numbers within the care system may also have an important bearing on what may of may not be possible in a particular country, as will national income and the resources available to universalist and family support services as well as for children in care. The extent to which young offenders are included within child welfare populations or are mainly within separate youth justice systems also impacts on rates and characteristics of the 'in-care' population. (In Sweden the vast majority of young offenders are within the child welfare system and included in child welfare statistics.) Table 1 shows that the range was between 45 per 10,000 children under 18 in Australia and 72 in US. It also shows that there can be big differences within countries as demonstrated by the high rate for aboriginal children in Australia.

Table 1 Rates entering care and rates in care in four countries

Rates	England	Australia (estimate)	Sweden	USA (estimate)
Rate in care per 10,000 0–17 years	55 per 10,000 (n=60,800)	45 per 10,000 (but 237 for indigenous chn) (n=21,795)	63 per 10,000 (n=14,911)	72 per 10,000 (n= 532,000)
Rates entering care per 10,000 0–17	21 per 10,000 (n= 24,100)	19 per 10,000 (n= 12,819)	30 per 10,000 (n=6855)	41 per 10,000 (n=303,000)

• Federal data for Australia and US are compiled from data supplied by States in aggregated form

As indicated earlier, lessons from the US were learned in the 1970s and 80s. In 2002–3 only a slightly lower proportion of UK children was placed from care for adoption (6%) than was the case in the US (9%). However, in terms of placing children for adoption with families not previously known to them, the UK is now outperforming the US since the US figures include many more adoptions by kin and by their current short-term foster parents than is the case for the UK. The international comparisons undertaken for the Prime Minister's review of adoption (Performance and Innovations Unit, 2000) showed that within Europe only Portugal and France placed between 1% and 2% of children in care for adoption and the other eight countries surveyed placed fewer than 1%. When adoptions from care do occur in these countries, this is usually by the foster carers with whom a child has lived for some years, and with parental consent. Perhaps as a consequence of the success in finding adoptive families for older children and the need for many of them to retain links with their birth families, the model of adoption with which we have become familiar in the UK is very different from the model that is called to mind when the word 'adoption' is used in Australasia and continental Europe. In those countries adoption is still seen as a service for babies and childless couples, and most often involves children from other countries. Thus, in these countries, if children who cannot return safely home are to achieve the benefits of stability and family membership, it has to be through foster family membership. Even where, as in some Australian states and in Sweden, legislation now allows for dispensation with parental consent so that children can be adopted by their foster parents, this provision is rarely used. The now familiar attributes of UK adoption, including the placement of children past infancy, post-placement financial and social work support, and (in around 80% of cases) direct or indirect contact with the birth family, do not fit with public perceptions of adoption in most countries.

Table 2 Placement patterns for children in public out-of-home care

Placement	England	Australia	Sweden	Italy	US
'Stranger' foster carers	47%	40%	Approx 60%	24%	46%
Kinship foster carers	18%	54%	Approx 12%	26%	23%
Prospective adopters	5%	-	-	-	5%
Residential/ other	13%	4%	25%	50%	19%
Birth parent/s	10%	-	1%	-	4%

- Data in Tables 2 and 3 adapted from AFCARS (2002); Australian Institute for Health and Welfare (2005) DfES (2002); Instituto degli Innocenti (2002); Socialstyrelsen (2004)

Given these differences in culture and child placement philosophy and practice, it is not surprising that placement policies aimed at achieving permanence and family membership differ in different countries. However it is important to note that there are differences between countries in the characteristics of children who come into public out-of-home care, and these also have an impact on the range of 'permanence' options and on 'success' rates in achieving stability and family membership.

In the light of the Lowe and Murch (2002) conclusions on which children are most likely to be adopted, a comparison of the children coming into care points up some possible explanations for differences. Table 3 shows that in England 16% of children coming into care in 2003–4 were under the age of 12 months, a larger proportion than in most other countries. In contract, 48% of those coming into care in Sweden were aged 15 or older. While some Swedish children enter care as infants or toddlers, and remain in foster family care until they reach adulthood (Andersson (2005)), the major task for Swedish child placement workers is to provide stability and family life for troubled and disaffected young people entering care when aged 10 or older, most of whom would not be willing to be adopted even if the service were available. Ethnicity is also relevant. As noted in Table 2, aboriginal children are greatly over-represented amongst those coming into care in Australia. Given the evidence of the impact of earlier attempts to 'rescue' these children from their families and culture ('the stolen generation') it comes as no surprise that adoption is little used as a permanence option, and that kinship foster care is the most frequently used placement option (Table 2). There are some similarities with the position in England, where it is more likely that African-Caribbean children will be placed as long-term foster children, and with substitute parents who wish to keep siblings together and facilitate continuing contact with birth parents (Thoburn et al (2000)).

THE OUTCOMES OF THE DIFFERENT PERMANENCE OPTIONS

When considering outcomes, it is important to differentiate between outcomes for the children (for example levels of self esteem, well-being as young adults, ability to make satisfactory relationships as an adult, providing 'good enough' parenting to their own children) and 'service outcomes' or 'outputs' such as: was the child adopted? did the child experience multiple placements? Achieving permanence, defined as being securely part of a family at the age of 18 and beyond, is a desirable 'service outcome' because it is associated with improved well-being and provides support for the continuing growth and development of the young adults. It is therefore a reliable 'proxy' for well-being as an outcome. The outcome/output measure used in most large-scale studies is whether the placement lasted or disrupted, but few large-scale studies follow cohorts of adopted and foster children up into adult life. (Exceptions are Courtney and Dworsky (2005); Thoburn et al (2000), and the new DfES (2005), series providing data on care leavers when they reach the age of 19.) Well-being measures (using a range of standardised and 'softer' measures) and expressed satisfaction of the young people and substitute parents are often used alongside disruption rates for small-scale qualitative studies and some postal surveys (see Sellick et al (2004); Thoburn (2000); Wilson et al (2004), for overviews of this growing body of research). Very rarely are data on wellbeing or satisfaction of birth parents or relatives collected (but see Logan (1999); Monck et al (2003), Neil (2003); Schofield et al (2000); Sinclair et al (2004)).

Table 3 Children entering public out-of home care by age at entry

Age at entry	England	Australia*(est imate)	Sweden	US* (estimate)
0–4 [of whom <12 mths]	34% [16%]	37% [12%]	(0–3) 11%	(0–5) 40% [14%]
5–9	18%	28%	(4–9) 15%	(6–10) 20%
10–15/10–14	42%	27%	25%	29%
16–17/15–17	4%	7%	(15–20) 48%	11%

- Federal data for Australia and US are compiled from aggregated data provided by the states and methods of collection and children included in the statistics as 'in care' may differ from state to state.

Using disruption rates as a measure, studies that have followed up large enough cohorts of children placed from care when past infancy for adoption or with permanent foster families not previously known to them, conclude that around one in five will experience placement breakdown before they reach adulthood (Barth and Berry (1988); Fratter et al (1991)). However, care must be exercised when using this statistic since outcomes will differ for different groups of children.

VARIABLES ASSOCIATED WITH MORE OR LESS SUCCESSFUL OUTCOMES

Characteristics of the child, the birth family, the substitute family and the legal, placement and support processes all have a bearing on success. This complexity, and the very many aspects of intervention over, in some cases, 18 years, make it impossible to say with any certainty what leads to 'success' of permanent placements in general, although the research can be helpful in predicting likely success in individual cases.

A key variable is the age of the child at placement and this can be used as a 'proxy' variable for many other characteristics that are found in more or less successful placements with adopters or long-term foster parents. The disruption rate (in terms of a permanent breakdown in relationships with the adoptive or foster family at some time before the 18th birthday) for infants placed under six months is around 5%; while, for children placed when 10 or older it is somewhere between 40 and 50% (Howe (1997); Fratter et al (1991)). Satisfaction rates for adopters and adopted adults show less variation with age at placement, with around 80% of adopters and adopted young people being generally satisfied with the experience and 20% expressing at least some level of dissatisfaction (Howe (1997); Howe and Feast (2000)).

Despite the increased risks of disruption with older age at placement, it is also important to note that some early placed children experience difficulties, most often around issues of identity, and some older children do well. In Sweden, young people can come into care until the age of 20 and, despite a disruption rate of 41% in non-kinship foster placements of teenagers, there are successes in helping some late-placed young people to establish lasting relationships with their foster carers (Sallnas et al (2003)). Schofield (2000) and Thoburn et al (2000) describe some heartening UK success stories of young people placed late with foster carers or adopters who became 'part of the family', while often retaining links with birth relatives and previous foster carers. Being emotionally or behaviourally disturbed at the time of placement and having a history of maltreatment prior to placement are associated with poor wellbeing and placement breakdown (Gibbons et al (1995); Fratter et al (1991)). In summary, the children we might most want to 'rescue' from traumatic and neglectful birth families are the ones we have most difficulty in placing successfully with permanent substitute families. A 'softer' variable emerging from some studies (Sinclair (2005); Thoburn et al (2000)) is that children and young people who are not reconciled to the need for a substitute family, or do not want to change their legal status to that of adoption, are more likely to experience placement breakdown (the 'willing to cut your losses' factor, although it is important to make a distinction between being willing to find a place in a new family and being willing to end meaningful relationships with birth family members – a distinction which I find, from expert witness work, is not always clearly made).

There is even less 'hard evidence' about the attributes of adoptive and foster families that are associated with successful permanent placements. Research throws up different results with respect to easily measurable characteristics such as age, marital status, ethnicity or 'home grown' children in the family. Those looking to increase the supply of adopters and foster carers can be encouraged by the finding that a very wide range of parents can be successful substitute parents. Successful families also describe a wide range of motivations, usually combining self-directed motives – such as wanting to have, or to increase, a family – with altruistic motives, often linked with positive (and sometimes negative) experiences in their own early lives, or, as with some minority ethnic families, their own experience of discrimination and disadvantage. Other, less easily quantifiable characteristics identified by researchers as important are: enjoying spending time with children and being family-centred; being highly sensitive towards the emotional life of the child; accepting the child for who he or she is; being sensitive and proactive around birth family issues; and providing active parenting in respect of education, activities and life skills. Enjoying a challenge also often comes up when successful adoptive or foster parents are interviewed.

Turning to the placement process and legal options, the care plan requires a consideration of whether a kinship or 'stranger' placement will be the preferred choice, and the preferred legal status, together with contingency plans if the first option proves not to be achievable within a timescale appropriate to the child. The Adoption and Children Act 2002 requires a placement order to be sought if the agency has concluded that a placement for adoption is in the child's interest. This, of course, gives leave to place for adoption, but is not a mandate to place for adoption, and does not preclude the pursuit of other options concurrently with looking for an adoptive placement. The care plan also requires details of the contact arrangements that fit with the child's needs and wishes. Unless contrary to the child's welfare, and in consideration of human rights legislation and the UN Convention on the Rights of the Child, due consideration must given in all these respects to the expressed or otherwise ascertained wishes of the child and the wishes of siblings, parents and other adult birth relatives who are important to the child (or may be important throughout the child's lifetime as stressed by s 1 of the Adoption and Children Act 2002).

In the latest DfES research review *Foster Care Now: Messages from Research,* Sinclair (2005) summarises the research on the placement options. Return home after more than a few weeks in care is the least stable option, and Sinclair calls for strenuous efforts to improve the quality of practice in supporting vulnerable families and decision making about which children come into care and return home. The research (including interview and surveys responses of children looked after) indicates that questions should be asked as to whether, unless far more resources are devoted to family support and reunification, the goal of reducing the numbers looked after is only achievable at the expense of some children remaining at home when their welfare might be better served by them being looked after (Dickens et al, (2005); Sinclair et al (2004); Timms and Thoburn (2004)). That the numbers coming into care are going down, but the numbers looked after at any one time are going up, is an indication that the diminishing availability of short-term accommodation may be resulting in those entering care staying longer and being more difficult to establish in permanent substitute families (DH (2002); Packman and Hall (1998).

The research on disruption rates for kinship care as a permanence option generally points to lower disruption rates than for 'stranger' foster care, although more recent studies in US and UK are less clear cut. However, the 'satisfaction' studies indicate that this form of permanent placement is the first choice for the majority of children who cannot live safely with their birth parents. Qualitative studies point to the need for much more, and more flexible, emotional and financial support. The next most 'successful' permanence option is the confirming of a short-term foster family placement as a permanent placement, whether through affirmative practice if the child remains in care (Beek and Schofield (2004); Thoburn (1991)) or through adoption by the foster carers. Most research studies of permanence options look at placement with families not previously known to the child. Because few of the youngest children are placed for permanence in foster care, it is not possible to compare disruption rates for young children placed in permanent foster care in the UK with those placed for adoption. Some comparisons can be made with countries such as Sweden where adoption without parental consent is very rarely used and therefore more young children grow up in foster care. However, comparison is difficult as very rarely are these placements made with the intention of 'permanence' from the start. (Even though most children in her sample of long-term foster children were in voluntary care, Andersson (2005)) found that most identified with their foster families and developed a sense of permanence.) The broad conclusion across countries (Sinclair (2005); Wilson et al (2004)) is that, irrespective of the age at placement, the longer a child remains with a foster family, the better the outcome on a range of welfare indicators. Courtney and Dworsky (2005) found that young people who remained in care until the age of 20 did better on a range of measures than those who left care between the ages of 16 and 18. UK and US longitudinal studies with large enough numbers conclude that, when like children are compared with like, there is no significant difference in breakdown rates between those placed for adoption and those placed in foster families with the intention that they will become a long-term members of the foster family (Fratter et al (1991); Moffatt and Thoburn (2001)). When young people, adopters and foster parents are interviewed by researchers, it is clear that adoption tends to be preferred by those who are adopted, and foster care by those who become established as full members of their foster families. Sinclair ((2005), p 30) concludes on this point:

> 'The core studies leave no doubt that:
>
> - foster care can provide long-term stable care in which children remain in contact with their foster families in adulthood. This is particularly so when the placement is intended to be permanent from the start;
> - for most children the care system did not provide this long-term stable alternative to care at home.'

He makes clear that for many children adoption is not an alternative, often because they do not want it. There are many messages in the research studies he reviewed that point the way to improving the record of courts and family placement agencies in securing a greater sense of permanence for foster children and their foster families.

As a route to permanence adoption has much to offer for all age groups, but the research already cited indicates that it is not without risks. The matching decision is of crucial importance since there is much evidence in the qualitative research that, although post-adoption support and appropriate and appropriately timed therapy can make a difference when adoptive families are under stress, the wrong placement can rarely be 'mended'. At best it can be patched up. Finding the placement that has most chance of meeting important identified needs is therefore the major joint task of the courts and adoption agencies. In looking at the rewards of adoption I have commented elsewhere (Thoburn (2003) p 400) that successful matching involves finding a family with

> 'the ability to empathise with the child, and having the skills and competence to meet any special needs associated with physical or learning disability or emotional or behavioural problems. Finding a family that can keep a sibling group together if that is considered to be in their interests, and finding a family of a similar ethnic background and culture are also important aspects of securing the best possible fit between new family and child. It will also mean finding a family that is comfortable with the legal status that is most appropriate to the child's wishes and circumstances and new parents who are able to facilitate appropriate continuing contact with birth parents, adult relatives, siblings and previous carers to whom the child has become attached.'

Returning to the agreed way forward for meeting the child's needs as spelled out in the care plan, there is some evidence in research (and I am aware of this from my work as an expert witness) that there are cases when 'pragmatics' take over and the agreed care plan is departed from in important respects, especially around the placement of siblings together and contact with adult birth relatives and siblings. Most studies of permanent or long-term foster care and of adoption have concluded that continuing birth parent and sibling contact are 'protective factors' (associated with more successful placements) or have, on average, no impact on placement stability. It is rare for contact, in itself, to prevent attachments from being formed, although this may be a contributory factor if the contact needs of the child have not been matched with the wishes and skills of the adopters with respect to facilitating contact. What is clear is that, whether adopted or fostered, most children who have had a relationship, albeit ambivalent, with members of their birth family before placement want more frequent contact than is actually arranged for them; that they sometimes want it with some family members but not others; and that it is often stressful to children, birth relatives and substitute family members and needs skilled and empathic foster or adoptive parents and social workers to manage the stress (Cleaver (2000); Neil and Howe (2004); Sinclair (2005); Thomas and Beckford (1999)). There are occasions when a change in care plan will be appropriate. However, when changes do occur, much will rest on the judgement of the Independent Reviewing Officer (IRO) as to whether the proposed changes accord with the child's wishes and welfare, and whether the court, through the CAFCASS children's guardian, should be alerted. That will be especially the case in the period after an adoption placement order has been made and before the case comes back to the court's attention when adoption proceedings are started.

To conclude this section on choice of legal status, a range of studies indicates that for some children needing a permanent substitute family placement, only adoption or only foster care (possibly proceeding to special guardianship) will be appropriate. Also, some substitute families will only feel comfortable with the legal status of adoption or of foster care. However, for some children (probably the majority of those past infancy, and including some under fives for whom it is important to be placed with their siblings) the legal status is less important than finding a family with the skills and empathy to meet any special needs and where they can put down roots knowing that they are not going to be moved on. 'Parallel planning' in the sense of looking at the same time for either an adoptive or a permanent foster family, or carefully checking out whether the short-term foster family should be confirmed as their 'permanent' family, is likely to lead to more children being placed more quickly in placements that are less likely to break down. Where children are past infancy, are members of sibling groups and/or have complex needs, including the need for continuing birth family contact, the sequential approach followed by many agencies of looking for perhaps 12 months for an adoptive family, and only then starting to look for a foster family, increases delay. In some cases it leads to placement in an adoptive family not able to meet important identified needs, thus increasing the risk of disruption or the child's unhappiness. Also, if an adoption plan is eventually dropped in favour of a plan for foster care, the child will often feel let down and their self-esteem will be diminished if what they have been told is the 'best option', adoption, does not materialise.

CONCLUSION

Judges, solicitors, medical practitioners and social workers have much to be proud of in their record of ensuring that many children in care who can not live safely with their birth parents or relatives have the benefits of stability and family membership through permanent placement with a substitute family, often without totally losing their links with their first family. Other countries can learn from the emphasis we place in this country on reducing placement instability and making placements intended to last into adult life. However, too many children have too many placements before they move in with their new families and too many children are cut off from birth relatives and previous carers who are important to them. Too many adoptive and foster placements end in disruption, or perhaps worse still are unhappy or even unsafe places for the children who 'walk with their feet' when still immature and vulnerable or are pushed out of the family circle they thought they belonged to. There are lessons to be learned from research in this country and overseas to improve both the planning and placement processes and the ways in which children, birth parents and substitute parents are supported.

I end with stressing the importance of making, and then achieving, care plans that are based on the needs and wishes of the child and not being diverted by pragmatics or performance targets. The Adoption and Children Act 2002 is an opportunity to use all the options now available, and to devise support plans based around the needs of the 'adoptive kinship network' (Wrobel et al (2003) p 61) of child, birth family and substitute family to increase the proportion of children for whom we secure the benefits of permanence.

REFERENCES

Adoption Register for England and Wales *Annual Report* (London, 2003)

DHSS *Report of the House of Commons Social Services Committee* (London, HMSO, 1984) 75–8

Adoption and Foster Care Analysis and Reporting System (AFCARS) *The AFCARS Report for 2003* (Washington, US Dept for Health and Human Services, 2005)

Andersson, G 'Family relations, adjustment and well-being in a longitudinal study of children in care' (2005) 10.1 Child and Family Social Work 43–56

Australian Institute for Health and Welfare *Child Protection Australia 2003–4* (www.aihw.gov.au/publications/cws/cpa03-04/cpa03-04-c04.pdf) (2005)

Barth, R and Berry, M *Adoption and Disruption: rates, risk and responses* (New York, Aldine de Gruyter, 1988)

Beek, M and Schofield, G *Providing a Secure Base in Long-term Foster* Care (London, BAAF, 2004)

Cleaver, H *Fostering Family Contact, Studies in Evaluating the Children Act 1989* (London, The Stationery Office, 2000)

Courtney, M and Dworsky, A *Midwest Evaluation of the Adult Functioning of Former Foster Youth: outcomes at 19* (Chicago, Chapin Hall, 2005) (and personal communication with the author re later follow up)

Department of Health *The Children Act Now: Messages from Research* (London, The Stationery Office, 2002)

Dickens, J, Howell, D, Thoburn, J and Schofield, G 'Children starting to be looked after by local authorities in England' (2005) British Journal of Social Work (pre-release electronic version)

Fratter, J, Rowe, J, Sapsford, D and Thoburn, J *Permanent Family Placement: a Decade of Experience* (London, British Agencies for Adoption and Fostering, 1991)

Gibbons, J, Gallagher, B, Bell, C and Gordon, D *Development after Physical Abuse in Early Childhood* (London, HMSO, 1995)

Howe, D 'Parent-reported problems in 211 adopted children' (1997) 38(4) Journal of Child Psychology and Psychiatry 401–411

Howe, D and Feast, J *Adoption, Search and Reunion The long-term experiences of adopted adults* (London, The Children's Society, 2000)

Instituto degli Innocenti *I bambini gli adolscenti in affidamento familiare: Rassegna tematica e riscontri empirici* (Firenze, 2002)

Kemp, SP and Bodonyi JM 'Infants who stay in foster care: child characteristics and permanency outcomes of legally free children first placed as infants.' (2000) 5(2) Child and Family Social Work 95–106

Lahti, J A follow-up study of foster children in permanent placements, Social Services Review (Chicago: University of Chicago, 1982)

Logan, J 'Exchanging information post-adoption: views of adoptive parents and birth parents' (1999) 23(3) Adoption and Fostering 27–37

Lowe, M and Murch, M *The plan for the child: Adoption or long-term fostering* (London, BAAF, 2002)

Maluccio, AN, Fein, E and Olmstead, KA *Permanency Planning for Children: Concepts and Methods* (London, Tavistock, 1986)

Monck, E, Reynolds, J and Wigfall, V *Permanent placement of young children: the role of concurrent planning* (London, BAAF, 2003)

Moffatt, PG and Thoburn, J 'Outcomes of permanent family placement for children of minority ethnic origin' in (2001) 6 Child and Family Social Work 13–21

National Statistics and DfES *Children Looked After by Local Authorities year ending 31 March 2004* (London, DfES)

Neil, E 'Accepting the reality of adoption: birth relatives' experiences of face-to-face contact.' (2003) 27(2) Adoption and Fostering 32–43

Neil, E and Howe, D (2004) *Contact in adoption and permanent foster care. Research, theory and practice* (London: BAAF)

Packman, J and Hall, C *From Care to Accommodation* (London, The Stationery Office, 1998)

Performance and Innovations Unit *Prime Minister's Review: Adoption* (London, The Cabinet Office, 2000)

Rowe, J and Lambert, L *Children Who Wait* (London, ABAFA, 1973)

Sallnas, M, Vinnerljung, B and Kyhle Westermark, P 'Breakdown of teenage placements in Swedish foster and residential care' (2004) 9(2) Child and Family Social Work 141–152

Schofield, G *Part of the family: Pathways through foster care* (London, BAAF, 2002)

Schofield, G, Beek, M, Sargent, K, with Thoburn, J *Growing Up in Foster Care* (London, British Agencies for Adoption and Fostering, 2000)

Sellick, C, Thoburn, J and Philpot, T *What works in adoption and foster care* (Barkingside, Barnardos, 2004)

Selwyn, J, Sturgess, W, Quinton, D and Baxter, C *Costs and Outcomes* of Non-Infant Adoptions: Report to the Department for Education and Skills (London, DfES, 2003)

Sinclair, I *Foster Care Now: Messages from research* (London, Jessica Kingsley, 2005)

Sinclair, I, Baker, C, Wilson, K and Gibbs, I *Foster Children: Where they go and how they get on* (London: Jessica Kingsley, 2004)

Socialstyrelsen *Barn och unga- isatser ar 2003* (Stockholm, 2004)

Thoburn, J 'Permanent family placements and the Children Act 1989: Implications for foster carers and social workers' (1994) 15(3) Adoption and Fostering 15–20

Thoburn, J 'The effects on child mental health of adoption and foster care' in Gedler, M et als (eds) *New Oxford Textbook of Psychiatry* (OUP, 2000)

Thoburn, J 'The risks and rewards of adoption for children in the public care' (2003) 15 Child and Family Law`Quarterly 4

Thoburn, J, Murdoch, A and O'Brien, A *Permanence in Child Care* (Oxford, Blackwell, 1986)

Thomas, C, Beckford, V, with Murch, M and Lowe, N *Adopted Children Speaking* (London, British Agencies for Adoption and Fostering, 1999)

Wilson, K, Sinclair, I, Taylor, C, Pithouse, A and Sellick, C *Fostering Success: An exploration of the research literature in foster care* (London, Social Care Institute for Excellence, 2004)

Wrobel, G, Grotevant, H, Berge, J, Mendenhall, T and McRoy, R 'Contact in adoption: the experience of adoptive families in the US', 27(1) Adoption and Fostering 57–67

WHOSE CARE PLAN IS IT ANYWAY?

David Spicer
Assistant Head of Legal Services, Nottinghamshire County Council

SUMMARY OF PAPER

Mr Spicer began with the comment that the problem with care plans is not a lack of supervising jurisdiction and independent officer; the problem is why such supervision and review are needed? This is because local authorities are not sufficiently familiar with the legislation and detail. The route through which this is created is set out in the first diagram in Mr Spicer's paper.

The Home Secretary has sought to address some concerns. For example it became clear that there was a desire for amendments under s 47 and welfare became a key issue. Under s 47, local authorities are required specifically to address whether there should be a child safety order, but this is often not done despite Home Office guidance.

When public authority work is undertaken, this is carrying out a statutory function and it is key that good skills are applied to do this. This is not asking simply for a social worker to be a good social worker but rather to use good social work skills to carry out the statutory functions. There are two sets of relevant regulations which should be reviewed regularly and copies of the relevant parts of the plan should be given to other professionals.

The schedule to the regulations deals with the formation of a care plan and what the local authority has to provide. By way of example, this does not include a report from a doctor as to the current state of health of the child but a health history and information as to a child's educational history. The aim is to place a bureaucratic parent in the same information position as a caring parent would have been. This information is not regularly kept on the file despite the fact it is a statutory duty to do so. Mr Spicer commented that the only time he routinely sees this information is when a child has died.

The duty to ascertain a child's wishes and feelings is not qualified by any duty relating to age and understanding. The only qualifying statement is what is reasonably practical. When a decision is made the local authority must go on to consider age and understanding including any reason for not understanding. Children's wishes and feelings must be taken into account before conducting a review of the child's case.

It is a criminal offence for parents not to keep the local authority informed of a change of address when the child is looked after. The parents have a positive duty to keep us informed and therefore the number of cases in which we lose track of a parent should be very small.

Mr Spicer expressed some concern over the new arrangements. The court can review a matter and refer this to CAFCASS where necessary, thereby putting resources into a new case.

He concluded that local authorities must be more familiar with and consistently practising the regulations as they stand.

The concern over the extent to which children committed to care have influence over the plans made for their future is longstanding. It is however important to recognise that this is simply a symptom of the overarching failure of managers and practitioners within local authorities to understand and apply legal obligations or demonstrate the levels of skill necessary for the management of services for vulnerable children, including but not exclusively related to the planning and reviewing children's cases.

It is also important to acknowledge that this failure impacts on vulnerable children generally and not only those whose welfare is considered by the courts. It would indeed be unusual if the only case in which staff involved failed to carry legal duties were the one that happened to attract judicial scrutiny. Reforms intended to address court concerns in individual cases need to be considered in the context of the need to improve the life chances for all vulnerable children.

The policy intentions of government that lie behind legislation may be clear but the implementation is often uncertain, dependent as it is on a bureaucracy delivering sensitive services. The route from policy to practice is familiar:

Government Formulates Policy

▼

Legislation to Implement Policy

▼

Guidance to Assist Implementation of Legislation

▼

Local Procedures/Protocols

▼

Practice

If there is any dislocation in this process, the policy will not be delivered. In particular, it must be understood by those devising protocols, those managing services and those in practice that guidance assists the implementation of legislation but does not replace it. A thorough knowledge of the legislation and its interpretation is essential in order to appreciate the context of the guidance, protocols and procedures. As Lord Laming drawing on the evidence given during Phase II of his Inquiry noted:

> '.... the legislative framework for protecting children is basically sound. I conclude that the gap is not a matter of law but in its implementation .... it is not just 'structures' that are the problem, but the skills of the staff that work in them.' (Report of the Victoria Climbié Inquiry, para 1.30)

Lord Laming also appreciated the impact on services where other pressures distract managers from properly carrying out legal obligations:

> 'Sadly, many of those from social services who gave evidence seemed to spend a lot of time and energy devising ways of limiting access to services, and adopting mechanisms designed to reduce service demand.' (para 1.52)

> 'The use of eligibility criteria to restrict access to services is not found either in legislation or in guidance, and its ill-founded application is not something I support.' (para 1.53)

However, as Lord Nicholls of Birkenhead noted in *Re S; Re W* [2005] UKHL 10: 'But the problems are more deep-seated than shortage of resources.'

PRE CHILDREN ACT 1989

In the much weaker statutory framework, before the implementation of the Children Act 1989 in late 1991, children committed to the care of local authorities through the wardship jurisdiction and High Court matrimonial proceedings were subject to a regime of continued judicial oversight and direction relating to the arrangements for their care. Anxieties concerning delays or failures to carry out stated expectations could be referred to the court and anxious judges (who often took a personal interest in 'their ward') routinely required reports to be produced concerning progress.

Children committed to care through the jurisdiction of the county court and juvenile courts which exercised statutory jurisdictions did not attract the same measure of oversight although individual circuit judges often devised mechanisms locally by which they did assume to themselves a power to play a continuing role in reviewing the arrangements.

The extent to which in a formal way children were involved in decisions about their future was then very limited.

Developments that may have been encouraged by judicial supervision were halted when the House of Lords emphasised in *A v Liverpool City Council* [1981] 2 All ER 385 that:

> 'Because Parliament had by statute entrusted to local authorities the power and duty to make decisions as to the welfare of children without reserving to the courts any right of review on the merits (subject to certain limited rights of appeal in relation to care orders), the courts had no jurisdiction to review a local authority's discretionary powers under a care order except under the supervisory jurisdiction to review the legality of administrative decisions.'

The division of responsibilities between local authorities and the courts received consideration and debate during the period preceding the comprehensive revision of the law brought in by the Children Act. Although articulated in different ways, the arguments in favour of judicial reviewing functions relied on the concern that local authorities could not be trusted to ensure that the expectations spelt out at the time an order was made would in fact be met or that if unable to be delivered the basis of the original proposals would be revisited.

In September 1985, the Government published as a consultation document the report of an interdepartmental working party that prepared a report to ministers of their 'Review of Child Care Law'. The Report states that:

> 'There are clearly difficulties inherent in any large organisation attempting to act as a parent, and we are anxious to provide a legal framework which will enforce the parental responsibilities of local authorities rather than fragment them' (p 217)

and

> 'One of our guiding principles has been that the court should be able to determine major issues such as the transfer of parental rights and duties where there is or may be a dispute between parents and local authorities, while the management of the case should be the responsibility of the local authority.'

In this they followed a principle recommended by the House of Commons Social Services Committee that:

> ' … the courts should make long term decisions impinging directly on the rights and duties of children or their parents, and that the local authority or other welfare agency should make decisions on matters which, although they may be of equal or greater importance, are not susceptible to clear and unambiguous resolution.'

After considering alternative arrangements suggested to it, the Working Party concluded that:

> 'We therefore support the emphasis currently placed by the government on improving the working of the system of reviews by local authorities of all children in their care at fixed intervals under the existing legislation.'

It was accepted that 'some machinery for the resolution of disagreements relating to children in care should be provided' but that courts had significant disadvantages in these circumstances because of:

- their formality;
- time taken to prepare for and hear and resolve disputes;

- limited number that could realistically be referred to courts.

The 'better way forward' was to place: '… responsibility to decide the dispute on those with responsibility for implementation'.

The Children Act, statutory regulations and comprehensive guidance addressed to local authorities provided the framework for the delivery of this approach – detailed arrangements for planning and reviewing children's cases, and statutory representations and complaints procedures, including requirements for the involvement of children.

This of course depended on the detailed provisions being read and understood by the staff with responsibility to implement them.

POST-CHILDREN ACT 1989 – PLANNING AND REVIEWING CASES

The Children Act 1989 has 38 enabling provisions. Exercising these functions in 1991 the Secretary of State made regulations imposing further statutory functions on local social services authorities that detailed the manner in which the substantive Children Act functions should be carried out.

In addition 10 volumes of guidance on the practice to be followed in performance of the functions were published. These were issued under s 7 of the Local Authority Social Services Act 1970 which empowers the Secretary of State to give guidance to authorities on how they shall exercise their social services functions, including the exercise of any discretion. Some of the guidance has since been amended to reflect changes in legislation. As a matter of law the guidance must be followed unless there are exceptional circumstances justifying departure.

So far as planning and reviewing children's cases are concerned, the relevant provisions include the Arrangements for the Placement of Children (General) Regulations 1991 (SI 1991/890), the Review of Children's Cases Regulations 1991 (SI 1991/895) and Volume 3 'Family Placement's and Volume 4 'Residential Care of the Children Act 1989 Guidance and Regulations'.

Copies of these volumes cannot easily be found in social services offices and are said to be no longer in print.

Regulation 3 (1) of the Placement Regulations provides that:

> 'Before they place a child the responsible authority shall, so far as it is reasonably practicable, make immediate and long term arrangements for that placement and for promoting the welfare of the child who is to be placed.'

Paragraph 2.9 of Volume 3 explains that:

> 'In these Regulations the expression "arrangements" is used … This is referred to in the guidance by the social work term "*plan*"'

and requires that

> 'the plan should reviewed on an ongoing basis.'

It also provides that:

> 'There is no statutory requirement to plan, review and monitor the case of a child who is provided with a service other than accommodation. However, good practice requires that in cases when the local authority is providing a significant level of services to a child …. to extend the same philosophy and principles … to the management of those cases.'

The Review Regulations require the plan to be reviewed on a regular basis. Paragraph 2.17 of the Guidance summarises these requirements:

'The .. Regulations place a statutory duty on responsible authorities to draw up a plan in writing for a child ... in consultation with the child, his parents and other important individuals and agencies in the child's life. Planning ... should begin prior to placement. After placement, the plan should be scrutinised and adjusted (if necessary) at the first review four weeks after the date the child was first looked after and at subsequent reviews.'

The Guidance provides detail about the making of the plan, the purpose, addressing the welfare of the child so far as health, education and race, culture, religion and linguistic background are concerned, the planning process, and at para 2.62 'The Contents of the Plan for the Child.'

The importance of the document for inter-agency working to address a child's needs is stressed. Copies of relevant parts, including those aspects with which the child agrees or otherwise, should be made available to relevant professionals. The Foster Placement (Children) Regulations 1991 require a statement to be provided:

'... containing all the information ... necessary to enable the foster parents to care for the child, in particular, information as to –

(a)   the authority's arrangements (ie the plan) for the child and the objectives of the placement ...'

Similar requirements apply to children placed in residential care.

What is clear from these provisions is that a written plan should be drawn up at the time a significant level of services is delivered. That plan should evolve in response to developments. If a court application is made, the plan should already be in existence – it may require adjustment and refinement but should not be written purely because the court requires a document.

JUDICIAL EXPERIENCE

Despite the extent and clarity of the legal obligations, in the years following the implementation of the Children Act, concerns regarding the absence of carefully considered proposals for the future care arrangements for children who were the subject of public law proceedings and the failure to fulfil expectations regarding services following the making of orders continued.

In *Manchester City Council v F, Note* [1993] 1 FLR 419 Eastham J focused on the law and guidance and stated that the care plan should, so far as reasonably possible, accord with the Children Act Guidance and Regulations, referring specifically to Volume 3, para 2.62.

In *Re J (Minors) (Care: Care Plan)* [1994] 1 FLR 253 Wall J was urged to make a series of interim care orders until the care plan was clearer. He emphasised that the power of the High Court to monitor and review care orders had been specifically excluded by the Children Act. The court was required to scrutinise the care plan and if not satisfied the plan was in the best interests of the child could refuse to make a care order. However the making of interim care orders should be 'approached with great caution'. There was a need for balance between the need to satisfy the court and 'an over-zealous investigation into matters that were within the administrative discretion of the local authority'.

The regulations and guidance, and in particular para 2.62 of Volume 3, were considered by Wall J:

'In the hope, therefore, that the criteria therein referred to will become better known in the profession, I propose to read out the matters listed in para 2.62 in their entirety into this judgment.'

Advocates and judges sought to devise means by which the local authority could be required to alter their proposals according to the court's view of what best would meet the child's needs and continue to be accountable to the court for the performance of responsibilities after the making of a care order.

In *Re S and D* [1995] 2 FLR 456 the circuit judge disagreed with proposals to rehabilitate children and refused to make a care order. Instead he made a supervision order and by an injunction prohibited the mother from removing the children from foster parents. Allowing the appeal and making a care order, Balcombe LJ made nevertheless commented:

> 'It is regrettable that under the Children Act 1989 a situation may arise where a judge has no alternative but to choose between two evils, and either make a care order with the knowledge that the care plan is one of which he does not approve, or make an order with the consequence of leaving the children in the care of an inappropriate parent.'

Research, studies, and representations made to the Department of Health from various sources, and consideration of the issues at the President's Inter-disciplinary Conference in 1997 led in August 1999, to the issuing under s 7 of the 1970 Act LAC 1999/29 which was 'approved by the President'. Local authorities were referred specifically to the Children Act Guidance and Regulations and given further guidance on the structure and content of care plans within the court process.

The circular did not address the issue of supervision of care plans and quality of service and decision-making once an order had been made.

There were clear indications from many sources that the outcomes for children in public care were not as would be expected if services were being delivered in accordance with the statutory framework.

The National Children's Bureau report published in 1995 included the following assessment of performance by public authorities:

- 10,000 leave care each year
- 75% have no qualification against 11% nationally
- 3% with five GCSEs against 64% nationally
- 0.4% attend college against 44.7% nationally
- 80% at 18–24 jobless against 16% nationally
- 55% single homeless been in care
- 60% suffer serious health problems
- 80% experience destitution
- 38% young prisoners been in care
- 22% say been abused while in care.

In November 1997 Sir William Utting's review of safeguards for children living away from home was published. A letter subsequently sent by the Secretary of State to elected members of social services authorities emphasised their responsibility for the quality of the services highlighting:

> 'Many children were harmed rather than helped. The review reveals that these failings were not just the fault of individuals – though individuals were at fault. It reveals the failure of a whole system.'

In autumn 1998, the Government launched the Quality Protects Programme intended to rectify a situation in which, had clear statutory duties been performed, many could not have arisen.

Intensive measurement of local authority performance by setting targets and performance indicators was introduced.

Unfortunately meeting many of the targets indicates little about the quality of the service provided. For example targets are routinely met for the holding of meetings on appropriate dates that form part of the reviews of children's cases – they may be met because staff are instructed not to cancel or postpone meetings under any circumstances. However, the meeting of that target indicates nothing about whether the appropriate professionals were present or the relevant issues addressed or the quality of the decisions made or the child appropriately involved and so can be misleadingly reassuring.

If the target is that a percentage of looked-after children should attain one GCSE, it will be met because of the consequences for failing to achieve the target – but this informs nothing about whether an individual child with proper support could have attained five or more GCSEs or even gone on to a higher education.

The NCH Report, 'Close the Gap', published in September 2005 highlighted that although there was some improvement in educational attainment of children looked after, the gap between them and the general child population was growing – this suggests that the extent of disadvantage is worse now than before the various initiatives.

Lobbying led to MPs considering the Children Bill in Committee adding a clause which became s 52 Children Act 2004 in force with effect from 1 July 2005. Section 22(3A) was inserted into the section of the Children Act 1989 providing for the general duties relating to children looked after:

> 'The duty of a local authority under subsection (3)(a) to safeguard and promote the welfare of a child looked after by them includes in particular a duty to promote the child's educational achievement.'

This is described on the DFES website 'Every Child Matters' as a 'new duty', although clearly the duty to safeguard and promote welfare must have included this obligation, much of the guidance issued has addressed educational needs, and the Quality Protects Programme focused particularly on this area.

At the Michael Sieff Conference in 2001, Sir David Ramsbottom, former Chief Inspector of Prisons, presented the results of research commissioned by him into the welfare needs of young people who had been received custodial sentences. The material included the following:

	Male	Female
Victims of sexual abuse		33%
Previous suicide attempt	16%	32%
Mental age less than 12 years	34%	32%
History of local authority care	36%	32%
Hazardous drinker	62%	51%
Death of close relative or friend	63%	72%
Mental disorder under Mental Health Act	95%	95%
Drug user	72%	62%

Sir David's point was that these young people were children in need before and after the commission of the offence that led to custody but had not and were not receiving services consistent with statutory obligations.

Should the Howard League in 2002 have found it necessary pursue judicial review to the High Court to establish that remit of the Children Act duties extend into custodial institutions?

Amendments to s 47 of the Children Act 1989 introduced by the Crime and Disorder Act 1998 required from 2000 all child protection inquiries concerning children under 10 years to be directed towards considering whether an application should be made for a child safety order in addition to Children Act functions.

Home Office guidance published in the same year explained that:

> 'This order supplements the existing welfare provisions under the Children Act 1989 and should be seen in that context. Local Authority social services departments will need to decide which power within its widened range it should make use of to deal with the problems of a particular child.'

The benefits of this order include the naming of the responsible officer within the order, and the ability to attach any requirement to the order concerned with providing for the welfare of the child. A parenting order may also be made.

Consideration of this response however is absent from child protection practice and the preparation of care plans since, those in practice and their managers are not sufficiently familiar with the amendments or the substantive legislation.

This problem has been recognised by government. Mr Jack Straw, then Home Secretary, commented in a speech to magistrates to explain the policy intentions behind the 1998 Act:

> 'One of the great errors which Ministers and Departments can make is in thinking that once a Bill is an Act then the work is over. We, however, recognise that implementation is the most important aspect.'

SIGNIFICANT LEGAL IMPERATIVES UNDERPINNING PLANNING AND REVIEWING CHILDREN'S CASES

The following examples illustrate how important it is to have regard to and understand the detail of the legal imperatives.

The Placement Regulations (reg 4) require local authorities to have regard to the considerations listed in the four schedules to the Regulations when formulating a plan for a child. Among the considerations in Schs 2 and 3 are current health and educational circumstances and:

- the child's health history;
- the child's educational history.

These considerations are intended to place the bureaucratic parent in the same position as a caring natural parent with access to the child's history. They should also inform decisions at each review of the child's case. The mechanism by which the necessary information is obtained should be by the local authority exercising powers under s 27 of the Children Act 1989 to require assistance from health and education agencies to provide these histories.

Despite the clarity of the legal duty, this information is not routinely secured and does not appear on child care files. The exception to this is when serious case reviews are held under Part 8 'Working Together' following a child's death or serious injury and all this information is then routinely collected.

The Review Regulations set out the detail of how reviews are to be prepared and carried out, and what information must be considered. A common error is to fail to recognise that reviews are processes that themselves require careful planning and not simply meetings. This is compounded by the fact that it is the holding of a meeting within the review that satisfies the performance indicator requirements.

Schedule 1, para 2 requires the local authority at each review to keep ' ... informed of the name and address of any person whose views should be taken into account in the course of the review'.

Those persons are the child, his parents, those with parental responsibility and any other person whose views are considered relevant (reg 7).

If met, this requirement should reduce significantly the circumstances arising where the local authority are unaware of the whereabouts of parents since there must be a pro-active responsibility to take reasonable steps to ensure they have informed themselves.

This is the other side of the coin from the duty in para 15(5) of Sch 2 of the Children Act 1989 under which it is a criminal offence for parents not to keep the local authority informed of their address when their child is looked after.

Unfortunately, these provisions are not well known to practitioners. Parents remain uniformed of their duty and steps are not taken to secure the whereabouts of parents if contact is lost. One consequence is that absent parents continue to cause delay by appearing in the late stages of adoption processes requiring assessment of their capacity to care or the appropriateness of contact.

Regulation 7 requires specifically that

> '(1) Before conducting any review the responsible authority shall, unless it is not reasonably practicable to do so, seek and take into account the views of –
>
> (a)   the child. ...'

The Plan and the need for any change must be considered (Sch 2, para 5) so the views must at the very least concern consideration of the plan.

The involvement of the child is not satisfied by inviting him/her to any meeting held within the review, since this work must be carried out 'before' conducting any review. In 2003, the NSPCC funded and published a study undertaken by Timms and Thoburn, 'Your Shout: A Survey of the Views of young People in the Public Care'. They involved 725 children looked after by local authorities. 45% were unable to name their care authority and 29% did not know what their care plan was. The authors reasonably commented: 'They should have been involved in writing it.'

The obligation to obtain the 'views' of the child complements but does not replace the duty in s 22 of the Children Act 1989:

> '(4) Before making any decision with respect to a child whom they are looking after, or proposing to look after, a local authority shall, so far as is reasonably practicable, ascertain the wishes and feelings of –
>
> (a)   the child...'

This goes beyond simply asking a child's opinion and applies whether or not a child can express 'views'. Ascertaining wishes and feelings is a more complex and skilled piece of work. The duty is qualified only by reasonable practicability, not by age or understanding in themselves. Wishes and feelings of children who by reason of age or understanding cannot articulate views may nevertheless be ascertained.

Subsection (5) makes clear that age and understanding are factors relevant to assessing what consideration should be given to ascertained wishes and feelings but not to whether they are ascertained:

> 'In making any such decision a local authority shall give due consideration –
>
> (a)   having regard to his age or understanding, to such wishes and feelings of the child as they have been able to ascertain.'

RESPONSES TO THE PROBLEM

Various approaches have continued to explore means by which the restrictions on interfering with local authority areas of discretion can be overcome.

Disagreement on the form of a care plan was considered in *R (on the application of CD) v Isle of Anglesey County Council* (2004) 3 FCR 171. A disabled child aged 15 years with learning difficulties applied for judicial review. The care plan involved moving her from foster parents whom the authority deregistered because the home was unsuitable for caring for disability. Wilson J commented on the need to refer to her wishes:

> 'This claim has been heard over one and a half days; and ... C has been present in court almost throughout. The argument has been a fairly dry forensic exercise ... One could not have expected C. to pay close attention to all of it; but apart from when a reference to a particular feature of the ... plan distressed her ... she sat quietly in court almost throughout.'

He considered the detail of the authority's statutory duties under the Children Act and found that the care plan represented an unlawful decision on the part of the authority because it would:

> '(a)   fail to promote her welfare by providing a range and level of services appropriate to her needs (s17 (1));
> (b)   fail to provide services designed to minimise the affect upon her of her disabilities (s 17(2) and para 6 Sch 2);
> (c)   fail in relation to the accommodation to give due consideration to her wishes, having regard to her age and understanding (s 20(5)); and
> (d)   fail to secure the accommodation is not unsuitable to her needs (s 23(8)).
>
> The bona fides of the local authority are not in doubt. Like a computer virus, some demon has, in my judgment, come to infect the local authority's decision making ...'

He also found the deregistration decision sound but the timing unsound and unlawful and therefore set it aside.

The failure to properly administer a care plan and review the cases of two boys was considered in *F v Fulham London Borough Council* (2001) 3 FCR 738 on the application under s 34 of the Children Act 1989 by parents for unsupervised contact. There had been no effective planning and the boys had drifted 'lost in care'.

Munby J found that the authority was in breach of statutory duties under the Children Act 1989, in breach of duties under s 7 of the Local Authority Social Services Act 1970 to act under relevant guidance, and had failed to properly exercise powers under s 27 of the Children Act 1989 to ensure services were provided by other agencies.

'The bargain between the state and the children had been dishonoured' and the failure of duties to children and parents constituted infringements of Art 8 of the European Convention on Human Rights.

Is it likely that the practitioner staff and managers involved with this case over a period of five years were fully aware of the duties of the local authority and the implications of the European Convention on their obligations, and chose to disregard those obligations?

The European Convention provided the foundation for the assault by the Court of Appeal on the established position of judicial involvement in local authority affairs, reviewed by the House of Lords in *Re S, Re W* [2002] UKHL 10.

There had been a 'striking and fundamental' failure to implement the care plan for two children. In considering the jurisdiction of the court to influence local authority conduct after the making of a care order, the Court of Appeal made two major adjustments and innovations in the construction and application of the Children Act 1989.

The 'Starred Milestones' approach echoed the arrangements within the wardship jurisdiction, when progress reports were often required and the court intervened to correct matters which may have gone wrong. The encouragement to provide supervision through interim care orders in contradiction of the clear meaning of the relevant section of the Children Act 1989 reintroduced a previously criticised approach.

While declining to support the innovations or accept that human rights failures by local authorities established that the Act itself was not compliant with the Convention, Lord Nicholls of Birkenhead stressed the need for urgent government action:

> 'I cannot stress too strongly that the rejection of this innovation on legal grounds must not obscure the pressing need for the government to attend to the serious practical and legal problems identified
> .... One of the questions needing urgent consideration is whether some degree of court supervision of local authorities' discharge of their parental responsibilities would bring about an overall improvement in the quality of child care provided by local authorities.
>
> ... I would strongly urge that the Government and Parliament give urgent attention to the problems ... so that we do not continue to fail some of our most vulnerable children.'

The Government's response to this through the Adoption and Children Act 2002, amendment of the Review Regulations, and the Independent Reviewing Officers Guidance (2004), was to increase the robustness of the approach recommended in 1985 by the Interdepartmental Working Party with an independent element in the review of children's cases and by introducing 'a last resort' element of referral to CAFCASS and progress to the courts in the event of failures.

Referral to CAFCASS and involvement of the courts applies to all cases of children looked after and not only those in which the court has committed a child to care. The legal proceedings may be further family proceedings, a free-standing application under the Human Rights Act 1998 or an application for judicial review.

The Advocacy Services and Representations Procedure (Children)(Amendment) Regulations 2004 reinforced the requirements for advocacy services for those requiring assistance with pursuing a complaint, that might also be promoted by the Independent Reviewing Officer or CAFCASS.

WHAT IS THE PROBLEM?

The problem is clearly not a lack of care or clarity in the drafting of legislation or the comprehensiveness guidance and regulations.

Has the problem been a lack of independent reviewing of children's cases and court supervision, or has it been a serious knowledge and skills deficit in the workforce employed to carry out clearly and carefully drafted statutory provisions and guidance?

The difficulty is not wilful refusal to perform statutory duties or lack of good faith or intention. Judicial concerns and those cases that proceed through the complaints procedures and published Ombudsman's Reports highlight an unawareness of statutory duties and a lack of skills in any event to carry them out.

Addressing the problem of failure to sufficiently understand and carry out legal obligations has in effect been to add to and reinforce those legal obligations. Unless the underlying problem is addressed, circumstances for vulnerable children are unlikely to improve but resources will be applied to process and enforcement.

In the education and training of local authority staff there is no longer an emphasis on appreciation that the responsibility of local authorities and their employees is to carry out statutory functions. The social work 'job' within a local authority is not to be a good social worker – it is to apply good social work and managerial skills to the task of carrying out statutory functions. Without a sound knowledge of the legal obligations the services will not be delivered to the quality that the careful drafting requires and skills are unlikely to be developed that are essential to good practice in their delivery.

Since few staff have had the training necessary to ensure that an understanding of human rights principles is embedded in practice, it is not surprising that when practice is examined against Convention principles, it is often found lacking.

One of the performance indicators sets a target for the percentage of children looked after who should directly communicate their views to a statutory review, by attendance or by written or electronic communication or via an advocate.

However, unskilled involvement of children may be damaging to their interests. High quality skills in communication with disadvantaged and damaged children, required throughout engagement and not just at times of the formal review of cases are in short supply. In particular good knowledge about the cognitive development of children is important.

Communicating with vulnerable children: a guide for practitioners by Consultant Child Psychiatrist, Dr David Jones and published by the Department of Health, was written with the involvement of a widely representative Department of Health Advisory Group and the President's Interdisciplinary Committee, Advisory Group. Unfortunately, it is not extensively in use as a practice tool.

In this environment, messages from government intended to improve the quality of services can easily be misinterpreted and the intended improvement fail to materialise. Researchers at York University in 2003 interviewed staff at a number of local authorities. They found that the majority interpreted the encouragement to increase preventive work as a requirement to reduce the immediate need for a service rather than assessing needs with a view to reducing medium- and long-term impairment.

There is a danger that the welcome current focus on involvement of children, if not accompanied by an appropriate increase in skills, may lead inappropriately to a delegation of the responsibility for decision-making to children themselves.

After the initial period of looked-after status, children's cases are reviewed at six-month intervals, sufficient time (particularly for younger and significantly impaired children) for a failure to follow statutory duties and apply high quality skills to impact significantly on the prospects for a child. Furthermore, the amended Review Regulations now provide at para 2A:

> 'The independent reviewing officer must be registered as a social worker in a register maintained by the General Social Care Council ...'

Is this the background necessary to review and monitor the performance of legal duties? The Council has emphasised that registration will depend on possessing one of the recognised social work qualifications. However, none of those qualifications equip graduates with knowledge of the legal provisions or training in the practice skills necessary to work in this field.

The Regulations also now include:

> (3) 'The independent reviewing officer must, in the opinion of the responsible authority, have sufficient relevant social work experience to undertake the functions in paragraph (1) ...'

However, what is required is experience and knowledge of the law, the legal principles of decision-making, human rights and the guidance related to the whole field of child welfare. It is this that an authority should be required to be satisfied about before appointment.

In addition, circumstances identified during the review of a case, giving rise to concerns sufficient to involve a court application, are likely to be indicative of a wider problem within that authority potentially affecting all vulnerable children entitled to services. Lord Nicholls in *Re S; Re W* was concerned that the debate about introducing a court supervisory role should involve considering whether this would lead to an 'overall improvement in the quality of child care provided by local authorities'.

Lord Laming emphasised the need for accountability in this field – a theme echoed in *Every Child Matters*. The requirement for children's services authorities to appoint a Director of Children's Services and a Lead Member for Children introduced under the Children Act 2004 is designed to encourage accountability for the quality of services.

Courts might consider requiring Directors of Children's Services and Lead Members to appear before them to give an account of the arrangements within their authority including training and selection that has allowed the circumstances involving an individual child to occur that require the exercise of the court's supervisory jurisdiction.

THE ROLE OF THE INDEPENDENT REVIEWING OFFICER – A PRACTITIONER'S VIEW

Amanda Checkley
Independent Reviewing Officer

SUMMARY OF PAPER

Mrs Checkley introduced her paper by explaining that she believed that by working with tenacity and determination she was achieving what the new Review of Children's Cases Regulations intended and that she was excited by these achievements. However, her paper was based only on her own experience and other reviewing officers might hold different views.

She began by outlining her professional background, as she believes that this has had a significant influence on the way she operates as an independent reviewing officer and her understanding of the role. Mrs Checkley began her professional life as a social worker in an area team, working mostly with children and families. Following a career break she became a magistrate and has sat and chaired for the last 12 years in family proceedings courts. She extended her social work by training as a family mediator, a family group conference co-ordinator and as a complaints' investigator and chair of complaints' appeal panels for social service departments. In carrying out this combination of tasks it became increasingly clear to her that there was a role for someone independent to monitor care plans and work to resolve issues. In this way, first and foremost, the needs of the children would met in a robust and appropriate way and, secondly, the complaints procedure would cease to be the main, but inappropriate and slow, way to resolve issues around the implementation of a suitable care plan. She was pleased therefore to have the opportunity to work as an independent reviewing officer under the new regulations.

The new regulations cover all looked-after children, both those accommodated under s 31 and s 20 of the Children Act 1989. In relation to those accommodated under s 31 there has been at least been one opportunity, in court, for the care plan to be independently scrutinised. However, even if this care plan is implemented in the early months, as a child grows and develops the care plan needs to change to meet the new needs. It is her role to secure permanency, prevent drift and ensure that the child's needs are met on an ongoing basis. In relation to children who are accommodated under s 20, a care plan has never been independently scrutinised. The older children are unlikely to return home but again it is about ensuring that they are receiving appropriate education and health care and that plans are being made for them to move towards independence. Asylum-seeking children and children with a disability receiving respite care or residential care are also accommodated under s 20. Asylum-seeking children are often completely alone in the country, with limited English and no knowledge or understanding of support systems.

Mrs Checkley went on to explain that the independent reviewing officer has the authority and power to identify and help resolve issues that the social worker has failed or struggled to manage. It is often difficult for social workers to access an appropriate response from another agency, usually health or education, or in some cases from a different team within their own department.

Mrs Checkley continued by addressing a number of concerns in relation to whether working as an independent reviewing officer she can be truly independent, if the authority for whom she work funds her. Firstly she may not be perceived as truly impartial; secondly, if she is too critical, there is a danger that her employment may be terminated; and, finally, because she is paid by the authority on a fixed fee basis. Although there are opportunities to negotiate payment for extra time, this may impede her ability to undertake as thorough a job as she would wish. It was her view that she would prefer to be paid by a third party, possibly CAFCASS.

Finally, Mrs Checkley questioned how those with whom she worked viewed her. Her perception is that, for the most part, parents, relatives and foster carers see her presence and intervention as positive. She is able to ensure that their voices are heard. Children are pleased to see the same face at each review, even if the social workers are constantly changing. In relation to social workers and the department, she believes that she is often seen as challenging and over demanding. She had been concerned that this view might ultimately compromise her position. However, she had learnt recently that the assistant director of the service had stated that if he were a child in care he would wish her to be his independent reviewing officer. She believes that this confirms the department's acceptance and appreciation of the new role of the independent reviewing officer.

INTRODUCTION

In September 2004 the Review of Children's Cases (Amendment) (England) Regulations came into force. These regulations amend the Review of Children's Cases Regulations 1991 by introducing the role of the Independent Reviewing Officer (IRO). Local authorities must now have IROs in place to chair the statutory review meetings of all looked-after children.

The IROs must, as a minimum requirement, be independent of the line management of the cases they are reviewing and the decision-making process about the allocation of financial resources to those cases. An IRO must be registered as a social worker with the General Social Care Council and should be an experienced, skilled and authoritative professional with at least equivalent status within their host organisation to an experienced team manager.

It is now one year on and in this paper I intend to look at the background to the introduction of these regulations and at the new role of the IRO. I will also give my views on some of the strengths and weaknesses of this role, based on my experience undertaking reviews for one local authority during this period of time.

In this local authority, a team of reviewing officers employed specifically to undertake this work, chair the first three reviews of all looked-after children. A pool of around 12 self-employed IROs, of which I am one, undertakes all subsequent reviews. The cases are allocated to us on an availability and interest basis and, once allocated, we become the named IRO for all future reviews for that young person. We report to and consult with the Manager of the Child Care Reviewing Service. We are responsible for our own administration, including the typing up of each review.

BACKGROUND

The Children Act 1989 Guidance and Regulations and the Review of Children's Cases Arrangements 1991 set out detailed arrangements in relation to care planning and the review of care planning for children looked after by local authorities. The guidance identified the concept of a review as 'a continuous process of planning and reconsideration of the plan for the child'. It recommended that the review of the child's case should be chaired by an officer of the local authority at a more senior level than the case social worker.

In relation to the implementation of review decisions, the guidance stated that 'as part of the review system each responsible authority will need to set in place arrangements for implementing decisions made in the course of a review of a child's case'. In addition 'responsible authorities are required to set in place a system for monitoring the process of the review system'.

Under the old guidance and regulations, reviewing officers were able to monitor the activity of the local authority as a corporate parent, work to prevent drift and ensure that plans were meeting the needs of the children. However, as an independent social worker, working for more than one authority as a reviewing officer and undertaking other social work tasks for a number of local authorities, I was constantly aware of both the gaps in the implementation of review decisions and the potential for the local authority not to take a sufficiently robust approach to care planning for a child. Many reviewing officers had at least some line management for a case and were therefore less than independent. Even if the reviewing officer was external, as I was, the role carried no actual authority and there was no final redress if all attempts at resolution failed.

The old guidance acknowledged that there might be disagreements between the child and the parents, the child and the responsible authority or the parents and the responsible authority. In such cases, when an agreement could not be reached, the authority had a duty to advise the parties of the complaints procedure. At no point did the guidance acknowledge that there might be a disagreement between the reviewing officer and the local authority and, if there was such a disagreement, how it was to be resolved.

In March 2002, the House of Lords in its judgement on two conjoined appeals, *Re S* and *Re W*, in effect confirmed the frustration experienced by practitioners (*Re S (Minors) (Care Order: Implementation of Care Plan)*; *Re W (Minors) (Care Order: Adequacy of Care Plan)* [2002] UKHL 10, [2002] 1 FLR 815). These cases concerned the powers of the court to monitor the discharge of the local authorities' obligations, including the implementation of the care plan, once a care order had been made. The judgement concluded that the courts had no general power to monitor the discharge of the local authority's function but that a local authority that failed in it duties to a child could be challenged under the Human Rights Act 1998. The most likely challenge would be under Art 8, relating to the right to family life. The judgement also expressed concerns that some children would have no adult to act on their behalf and would therefore have no means to initiate such a challenge.

The provision for making the IRO a legal requirement is intended to remedy this problem. If it is the view of the IRO that the local authority is failing in its duty to the child to such an extent that the child's human rights are being breached, the IRO can refer the case to CAFCASS to make an application to court for a judgement as to whether the child's human rights have been breached.

The Adoption and Children Act 2002 amends parts of Children Act 1989 so that local authorities are now required to appoint IROs to:

- participate in the review of children's cases;
- monitor the authority's function in respect of the review;
- refer a child's case to CAFCASS, if the failure to implement aspects of a care plan might be considered to be a breach of the child's human rights.

These regulations apply to all looked-after children. This includes children who are subject to a care order (under s 31 of the Children Act 1989) or who are provided with accommodation on a voluntary basis for more than 24 hours (under s 20 of the Children Act 1989). The latter includes children with a disability receiving residential care and respite care and unaccompanied asylum seekers.

THE ROLE OF THE IRO

Purpose of the review

Under the new regulations, the purpose of the review remains unchanged. This is to consider the plan for the welfare of the child and then to monitor the progress of the plan and make decisions to amend the plan as necessary, in light of changed knowledge and circumstances.

Content of the review

In relation to the content, the checklist of matters to be considered at each review remains as set down in the previous regulations. These include:

- a consideration of the local authority's plans for the child in relation both to the wishes and feelings of the child and its parents;

202 Durable Solutions

- a consideration of whether the plans for the child will safeguard and promote the child's welfare. This includes consideration of:
  - whether or not the order can be discharged or varied to a lesser order
  - whether the placement continues to be appropriate
  - the views of the child's carer
  - whether the plan meets the religious, racial, cultural and linguistic needs of the child
  - arrangements made for the child's health and education
  - arrangements for contact with the child's family
  - reunification of the child with his/her parents and family
  - arrangements for aftercare.

In addition, under the new regulations the IRO must ensure that children are aware of the local authority's responsibility to provide them with an independent advocate and their right to make complaints to the local authority.

Functions of the IRO

The role of the IRO is now divided into three clear functions:

1. Participate in the review of the case in question

It is the responsibility of the IRO to chair the review meetings of all looked-after children. This allows the chair to monitor the appropriateness of the care plan, its implementation and to establish that the milestones set out in the plan are being achieved in a timely way. A crucial role is to ensure that there is no undue delay in implementing actions within the plan.

As chair, the IRO must ensure that all those involved in the meeting are able to make a meaningful contribution to the review. A key task is to ensure that review meetings remain child centred. More than one meeting may be required to ensure that the views of all the relevant people inform the review, without the meeting becoming too large.

The regulations state that the IRO may wish to meet the child before and/or after the meeting to hear the child's view and clarify anything that the child does not understand. I always make myself available to meet with a child before and after the review.

The IRO should be satisfied that contributions are obtained from disabled children and effectively presented at the review, even if the child is not able to be present or has impaired communication skills.

Where the first language of the child and/or the parents is not English the IRO should ensure that they are all able to participate fully in the review. This might involve the appointment of two independent interpreters.

The IRO should ensure that the views of the birth parents are heard at the review even if they are unable to attend or if their attendance is not appropriate. Wider family members may also wish to contribute to the review and the IRO should ensure that the views of significant adults in the child's life are heard. The IRO should also take into account the views of the foster carers and residential care workers caring for the child.

It is the responsibility of the IRO to check that information from all the relevant professionals in the child's life is made available to the review. Professionals should not swamp the meeting and it may be more appropriate for them to make a contribution in writing or in some other way.

At the end of the review it is the responsibility of the IRO to set the date for the next review. The regulations stipulate the maximum period of time between reviews but it may be the view of the IRO or of the child or of anyone else attending the review that there is a good reason for bringing the next review forward.

The IRO records the discussion and decisions made during the review and is then responsible for producing a typed-up copy for distribution in a time framework set out by the regulations. Under the new regulations the review record should:

- monitor the child's developmental progress over time and identify unmet or partially unmet needs;
- update key information on the child's progress;
- consider the impact of services on a child and identify where planned services have not been provided;
- consider whether the care plan and placement continue to meet the needs of a looked-after child;
- identify and recommend any changes to the plan for the child.

The record identifies the name of the person responsible for implementing a decision and the timescale within which this must be done.

2. Monitor the authority's function in relation to the review

The IRO must as far as is reasonably practicable take steps to ensure the review is conducted in accordance with the regulations and in particular ensure that:

- the child's views are understood and taken into account;
- the person responsible for implementing any decision taken in consequence of the review are identified;
- any failure to review the case in accordance with the regulations or to take steps to make arrangements in accordance with them is brought to the attention of the persons at an appropriate level of seniority within the responsible authority.

One of the key roles now of the IRO is that of problem resolution. Where there is evidence that suggests poor practice, the IRO will need to consider what action is necessary to bring this to the attention of the local authority. Wherever possible the IRO will attempt to resolve a problem by negotiation, initially with the social worker and team manager. If this is unsuccessful the IRO will take the matter to senior management, the Assistant Director, the Director and ultimately to the Chief Executive. Whenever a problem is identified it is essential to advise staff at each stage of the timescale in which the problem must be solved

The regulations are clear that decisions in the review should be taken in response to the identified needs of the child, rather than any particular interagency relationship. In practice, this may leave the IRO with a more complex problem to solve, if it appears that another agency, for example health or education, has failed to respond or complete a task, as identified in the review. In such circumstance the IRO may need to work with and through senior management in order to resolve the issue with the relevant staff in another agency.

3. Refer the case to CAFCASS

If the IRO exhausts all avenues of negotiation within the local authority, and a satisfactory resolution has not been obtained, the IRO may refer the case to CAFCASS, who will consider legal proceedings. The regulations emphasise that this should be a last resort, in extreme cases where all other attempts to resolve a problem within the local authority have failed, as legal proceedings create delay which is not in the interests of the child. Referral to CAFCASS can only be taken if:

- the IRO has made every attempt to resolve the problem within the local authority, including to the level of Chief Executive;
- there is no other person able and willing to take the case on the child's behalf.

Key outcomes

If the IRO is managing the task successfully the following goals should be achieved:

- care planning and decision making will improve;
- review meetings will be efficiently chaired with the full involvement of the child and other key adults;
- review meetings will take place in accordance with the required timescales;
- care plans will be effectively implemented;
- the developmental needs of the child will be met;
- a timely and appropriate route to permanence arrangements will be secured.

THE ROLE OF THE IRO IN PRACTICE

The expanded role and authority of the IRO has and is creating a culture shock for many local authorities. It seems from anecdotal evidence that some local authorities have responded more quickly and fully than others. The new IRO may be perceived as a challenge from outside, with whom the authority does not wish to engage. The more open-minded have welcomed the new role, albeit with some nervousness.

Working with the local authority

In the local authority where I work as an IRO, the manager of the Child Care Reviewing Service responds to all emails from IROs within 24 hours and is most supportive in taking action to help resolve difficulties. I have attended three meetings with the Assistant Director, a meeting with the legal department, meetings with service managers, team managers and social workers. I have met with and/or talked with teachers and health professionals. This would have been unlikely to happen before the new regulations came into force and all these meetings have helped resolve issues. I have also talked informally to CAFCASS about one case. However, colleagues working in some other authorities report a less co-operative response.

In some cases, I believe that my intervention has had a long overdue impact on a child's care plan, in others that early intervention has prevented issues escalating or creating difficulties in the future. The first six months saw less significant improvements and seemed to involve endless complaints and demands to team managers and service managers. The second six months has seen a greater number of improvements in the care planning and some of these have been achieved more quickly.

Successful intervention

The 10-year-old boy, who has been in care since he was two years old, with no long-term placement, has finally begun introductory visits to a long-term foster family. His therapy is now being increased from once a week to twice a week and he is so excited by the improvements in his learning, as a result of after-school private tuition that he has requested that this too be increased. He knows that his mother is no longer alive and some of the details about her death.

I chaired the first truly independent review of his case in March 2004. A team manager had chaired all previous reviews. At this review it emerged that he had not been told that his mother had died three months earlier, that he could barely read or write, and that he was receiving no therapeutic support, despite the fact that he had been sexually abused and soiled both day and night. His current placement was one of a long string of short-term placements.

He remains a deeply troubled child but he will not be moving to the 52 weeks a year residential placement that the local authority, supported by health and education, was proposing in October 2004. I was not willing to endorse this as a care plan and believed that it was only being proposed because, through my intervention, all three departments had finally become aware of the length of time this child's needs had been overlooked. They had become immobilised by the apparent enormity of the task of meeting his need for a family, supported by both appropriate education and therapy. A residential placement would in theory cater for all his needs under one roof and they were, I believed, choosing the easy option. It was my belief, supported by research, that a child of his age was more likely to flourish in a family setting. At the time he was showing some signs of progress in a short-term foster placement and he and his aunt were clear that he wanted to live with a family.

The proposal for a residential placement seemed to me to be in breach of his right to family life and therefore had the potential for challenge under the Human Rights Act. I brought this case to the attention of the Assistant Director. He convened meetings with health and education and invited me to attend. I was not satisfied that the matter was being resolved and, with the support of the manager of the service, sought independent legal advice. This case was already under judicial review and it was therefore not clear as to the best way forward. I spoke on an informal basis with an officer from CAFCASS. After extended negotiations, an appropriate care plan was formulated and executed without further legal intervention.

It is my firm belief that without my role, he would not now be moving to a long-term foster placement. I also believe that my ability to access independent legal advice increased my negotiating powers. However, it has been a long, slow process involving constant pressure and intervention on my behalf. It is of course the agencies themselves who have identified and commissioned the resources, but I do not believe they would have put the same effort into the search without my intervention.

Initial resistance

Initially there was significant resistance by some staff members to my involvement in the cases in any way, outside the review meeting itself. I was considered to be interfering and involving myself in areas that were not my responsibility. I was concerned that I might be seen as so critical that this would impede my ability to work in collaboration with social work staff and management. It became increasingly important therefore to recognise and report on good practice, at the same time as the poor practice.

A legal issue

A five-year-old boy was being looked-after by his child minder, following the mental breakdown and subsequent death of his mother. He would talk of going to the airport so that he could take a plane to join his mother in heaven and of wanting to die. The child minder was failing to meet his emotional needs. However, she was the one constant person in his life. The school was finding him uncontrollable.

His legal status was uncertain. His mother had agreed to him being accommodated at some time before she died but it was not clear whether subsequently he had returned to her care. The team and the legal department were insistent that the department did not need to initiate care proceedings. The education department had refused to statement the child but there was no-one with parental responsibility who could appeal this decision. I was adamant that the authority should take further expert legal advice. The advice of counsel was that, in this case, the department should initiate care proceedings.

Positive feedback

At the same time that I was working to resolve this child's legal status, the social worker, supported by the family finding team, was sourcing an alternative placement for him. She was working very closely with the child to support him in the move that the department believed was necessary. The child minder and her partner were ambivalent about the move and the headteacher was against it. The child was quite clear that he did not want to move. On one occasion when the social worker visited him, he had painted himself all over with white household paint. He frequently talked of not being alive in the future.

The move was achieved and the child settled much more easily and positively than had been anticipated due, without any doubt, to the endeavours of the social worker. I ensured that my views of her competence and hard work were shared with her and her manager. They in turn were positive about my involvement.

Unaccompanied young people

The regulations make it clear that all looked-after children will have an IRO and this therefore includes unaccompanied young people and disabled children in receipt of residential or respite care, accommodated under s 20 of the 1989 Children Act. In my experience the role of the IRO is already proving very important for both groups of children.

In the case of one unaccompanied young man, the department had commenced the age assessment process formally, 18 months after he had first entered the county. He was troubled by the ongoing uncertainty of his situation and the effect that this was having on planning for his future. I ensured that he received support from an advocate to challenge the delay. Six months later, when the issue still remained unresolved, the department finally agreed not to pursue the matter any further.

Another unaccompanied young person was looking to be adopted by his carer. They had approached a local solicitor together and had made an application at the local magistrates court. It seemed to me that the young man's hopes were being raised unrealistically and I sought a meeting with the service manager and the legal department to consider the legal status of this application and the likelihood of it succeeding. Unaccompanied young people have no adult to support them if the care plan is not meeting their needs nor, in many cases, any knowledge that improvements or changes should be made to the care plan.

Children with a disability

In the case of disabled children or young people in receipt of respite care or residential care, parents are constantly being told that resources are limited. They may be frightened to challenge a care plan, lest the package of services for their child becomes reduced. A severely autistic child was making significant progress in the educational unit of her residential placement and was taking part in an increasing number of outings. However, the care unit in the placement was refusing to take her on holiday for the second year running, had only told the social worker of this shortly before the forthcoming trip and had failed to advise the family at all. The mother explained at the review that she would have been willing to accompany her daughter on the trip. As the newly-appointed IRO, I had significant concerns about whether the care unit part of this placement was meeting the child's needs and, in addition, about why there was no interpreter present. The first language of the family was Turkish and the mother was not able to participate fully in the review.

Timescales and CAFCASS

Timescales in problem solving are essential. I have learnt to shorten the timescale within which I will accept a resolution of an issue so that, if it becomes necessary to progress the matter to a more senior level, as little time as possible is lost. Nonetheless, one of the flaws of the regulations is the number of different levels of management that must be approached before the matter can be referred to CAFCASS, and the time that this takes. Finally, even if all avenues of negotiation have failed, it is only possible to refer a case to CAFCASS if there is no other person able or willing to pursue the matter on behalf of the child. My 10-year-old, without a long-term placement, had a close relative who had instigated judicial review proceedings on his behalf. This was not achieving a resolution to his situation but hampered my ability to refer the matter to CAFCASS.

Interagency communication

I have become increasingly aware of the fact that delay and drift are often the result of the department's failure to engage appropriately with the health or education departments. The social worker may contact one of these departments with a request and is then uncertain how to proceed when he/she receives no response. The young person who has been excluded from school or who has moved into a different borough remains without education. Another child may be failing to access psychiatric support or appropriate medication. I am learning how best to support the department to resolve these interagency issues. However, the lack of accountability across the agencies provides the potential for issues to remain unresolved or to result in substantial delay. It is to be hoped that the creation of children's trusts and of the new post of Director of Children Services will address and resolve these issues.

Pay structure

The position of the IRO is insecure. We are employed on a fixed fee basis for each review. This covers preparation for the review, including contact with the allocated social worker, which starts one month before each review, the conduct of the review, including a meeting with the child before and/or after the review and the recording of the review and completion of other quality assurance documentation. Additional payment can only be requested for specific extra meetings or tasks. The IRO may be inclined to limit intervention or take a less than robust approach to a case so as not to be out of pocket. In addition, the local authority for whom we are carrying out the review pays us. This must appear, at the very least, to compromise our independence.

A vulnerable position

My line manager works within the local authority and I believe that this is the practice elsewhere. This must again raise questions about the integrity of the service that I provide. I am dependent on her to access the management structure and this may place her in conflict with colleagues. She might choose therefore to be less than supportive. Furthermore, if I create too many challenges, the local authority could choose to terminate my work. A staff member who feels criticised could make a complaint against me that would be difficult to disprove. The structure of the service could therefore leave me weak and vulnerable. This is in no way my experience at present, but these thoughts do lead me to wonder whether the role and management of the IRO would be better placed outside the local authority.

Expert advice

The local authority did initially agree to provide me with independent legal advice in the case of the 10-year-old boy, to which I referred earlier. However, this was subsequently withdrawn, when the legal department realised that I could progress the matter to CAFCASS for advice. The local authority is in a position to seek legal advice from its own department and counsel and this may leave IROs in a weak position, as there is no structure under which they can source their own independent legal advice. Likewise, the IRO is unable to seek a second or expert opinion in areas such as health or education.

CONCLUSION

The success of the implementation of the regulations, in relation to the role of the IRO, depends on the support of a good manager, the willingness of the department to accept the new role and the determination and tenacity of the reviewing officer. The process remains slow and is partially dependent on the IRO having an understanding of roles and responsibilities within the education and health departments and of interagency relationships. The IRO may feel vulnerable and insecure and lack access to expert support and advice. As I write this article, CAFCASS has not yet taken on a case. This must leave some unanswered questions.

KEY OUTCOME

At any one time, I have chosen to act as IRO for about 20 children. I believe that, with this number, I can maintain a consistent overview and the necessary energy levels to ensure a high level of both monitoring and problem resolution. Many of the children in the care system are amongst the most troubled and damaged in their peer groups. Nonetheless, as the corporate parent, the local authority has a duty to provide them with help and support to achieve the goal all parents seek for their children: the opportunity for them to achieve their potential and to be happy and healthy. Through careful monitoring of the care plan, I believe that the Independent Reviewing Officer can make a significant contribution to this goal.

REFERENCES

The Children Act 1989 Guidance and Regulations Volume 3 Family Placements
The Review of Children's Cases Arrangements 1991
The Review of Children's Cases (Amendment) (England) Regulations 2004
Independent Reviewing Officers Guidance Adoption and Children Act 2002

PERMANENCE FOR LOOKED-AFTER CHILDREN

Paul Clark

Director of Children's Services, Harrow

This paper considers the

– issues

– tensions

– dilemmas

associated with delivering 'permanence and stability' for looked-after children in the context of care plans placed before the courts. The paper outlines the professional tensions and uncertainties that play a part in the devising of the plan, its presentation to court and its delivery in practice. Having set out some of the issues that influence care plans delivery to and acceptance in court, it comments on the wide range of variables that impact on the 'simple' task of managing the future for vulnerable children to deliver stability and permanence.

BACKGROUND AND THE ISSUE

Ever since the introduction of the Children Act 1989 and its 13 associated volumes of guidance, a great number of professionals – such as social workers, lawyers, the court, commentators, academics and the media – have attempted to find the perfect solution to planning the future lives of children following a break-up or crisis in the birth family. This has resulted in a range of different solutions, proposed by all of the interested commentators and parties.

In essence, all of this effort is an attempt to manage the future of a child.

Any parent knows that, even on a good day and with most of the world in their favour, the various tasks involved in managing, supporting, ensuring, allowing, developing and delivering any aspect of their children's future are at best uncertain and at worst problematic, worrying and unnerving.

With absolutely the right motives, social workers, families, courts, lawyers and academics strive, in an adversarial system, to establish the best plan to deliver the best outcomes for children.

CURRENT SITUATION

All those engaged in the family justice system are seeking positive outcomes for the child. They strive to deliver the following:

• the key facts of a case;

• clear, cogent and concise opinions based on research, evidence and professional skill;

• an option appraisal (risk assessment) of what is likely to happen to the child for the coming (18) years considering the impact of the crisis, and any problems and issues in the child's life to date;

- carers sufficiently skilled and resilient enough to ameliorate those difficulties and deliver a happy and wholesome future for the child – with any support and special assistance needed to get there.

Alongside these simple (!) expectations there is also the need to deliver a multi-track set of plans, so that an unachievable first plan can immediately be replaced with the second or indeed the third or fourth plan. In this way, progress for the child and family is clear and speedy, planning is well established and set out clearly based on facts, good evidence and skilled risk-assessed judgments, and the administration of the process can proceed at speed.

There are a range of bureaucratic and necessary processes within this set of expectations, which are not always in tune with each other.

The courts have a clear process that they need to go through in order to manage the outcomes without delay.

The lawyers, families and participants in the case have their own processes to go through to present their views in line with the court's requirements and timescales. Alongside this, there are requirements of the management of local authority social work to deliver the very best outcomes for children from the most challenging backgrounds and circumstances – within a restricted budget. Currently there seems to be an imperative to offer more instructions and tighter targets, and in effect greater 'punishment' to workers and authorities for any slippage or failure.

Looking at this situation from within the world of local authority social work, there are some interesting and perplexing dilemmas.

For example, a qualified social worker with two or more years post-qualification experience, working in a well-managed local authority with a moderate but reasonable budget available, will have the following people expressing strong views as to how they should conduct themselves, come to an opinion and ensure it is delivered:

- lawyers, both supporting the social worker and those acting on behalf of the child,

- other adult parties and the guardian,

- the parents or members of the family, sometimes not in agreement,

- the local authority manager, attempting to keep within local authority procedures and budgets and manage competing demands,

- CAFCASS and the guardian ad litum, coming from the standpoint of supporting the best interests of the child (as all involved) but without the constraints of managing within local authority budgets and resources.

Supporting this system is the existing law – sometimes very clear, sometimes subject to change through case law – the 13 volumes of guidance in the Children Act (plus the many other volumes of guidance based on research), current expectations, changing expectations and pressures from different groups within society.

Alongside this, there may well be a local authority panel that seeks to balance the very best available placements against the realistic expectations that can be delivered within a restricted budget, difficult staffing situations and demands on workers. There will be media – local, national, and maybe even international – suggesting that the social worker should not intervene, should intervene immediately, should have taken a certain point of view or should not have taken a/b/c or anybody else's point of view. Within many of the cases, there will be so-called experts giving detailed forensic analysis of the situation, commentary based on their clinical and medical experience and asserting the rightness of their cause. Following this, there will be the expectation of government that all parties hit targets on efficiency savings, reducing expenditure, speeding up work, reducing delay, minimising process and maximising engagement.

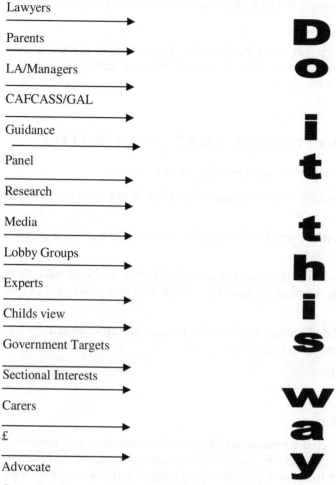

Overall, of course, there will be the issue of how much time and money can be expended on this case in the context of all the other demands upon the service. Lastly and most importantly there are the children themselves, who will have a view wanting resolution and whose voice must be heard strong and loud throughout the proceedings – and yet, because of their background, stress and difficulties may be ill equipped to understand the process.

In this situation, the development of the local authority care plan – to time and to a high degree of quality, consistency and clarity – has many different voices urgently pressing to take a particular view and course of action. The question that the local authority social worker, manager and colleagues face is how, in this context of so much advice, strong opinion, urgency and restricted finances, can I deliver a high quality assessment, multi-layered care plan and deliver to the court the 'expert' and clear view as to the best interest and the options to evaluate the court to make its decision?

One example of the tensions in the work that leads up to the design of the care plan and its presentation at court is set out in Jonathan Dickens' analysis of the relationship between social workers and lawyers in care cases.[1] In summary, the main complaint from the lawyers was that they were getting dragged too far into giving social work advice, rather than pure legal advice, and that they were often being asked to make decisions (or substantially rewrite statements). On the other hand, from the social services' point of view, there was resentment that the lawyers were stepping too far into social work areas; and when social services did make attempts to

---

[1] J Dickens 'Risks and responsibilities – the role of the local authority lawyer in child care cases' in (2004) 16(1) Child and Family Law Quarterly 25.

restrict their role, these were often met with unhappiness from lawyers, who spoke of the risks that would go unattended as a result.

This is just one illustration of the various tensions and uncertainties involved in the drawing up and presenting of a care plan to court.

During the court process, the plan is often subject to modifications in an effort to reach a speedy and effective decision. The 21-stage process that starts from a referral and ends up with a care plan in court can be summarised as follows:

THE SOCIAL CARE PRE-COURT PLANNING PROCESS – AN OUTLINE

(1) **Contact** with Children's Services leads to a **referral** being made to either:

- **referral and assessment** (front door of the Service) if the child is not known or already allocated

- **children in need and looked-after service** (long-term service) if the child is already known and allocated.

(2) In accordance with the **Framework for the Assessment of Children in Need and their Families** (DoH, 2000) – make a decision about how to respond within a maximum of one day.

(3) Undertake an **assessment** of need and circumstance – this assessment process gathers and analyses information across three domains including:

- the child's developmental needs

- the parenting capacity

- the family and environmental factors.

(4) An **initial assessment** (to be completed within seven days) – this assessment will determine whether the child is in need. The assessment process will gather and analyse information across the three domains in order to form a judgement and make a decision about what services will be required in order to reach the desired outcomes.

(5) A **core assessment** (to be completed within 35 days) – this assessment will be undertaken whenever a s 47 child protection investigation is initiated and when the complexity of the child's needs and circumstances dictates that a more in-depth and comprehensive assessment is required.

(6) Have a **child protection strategy discussion/meeting** with **police child abuse investigation team** and relevant others:

- to decide whether to undertake a **s 47 child protection investigation**

- and, if so, to agree **a co-ordinated strategy** for how this will be done

- including any **emergency protective action** that may be required to safeguard and protect the child(ren).

(7) Consult with **legal services** and seek advice about any emergency protection action that may be required involving court.

(8) Complete the **assessment and planning** process for children in need;

- to implement a **support plan** to support and strengthen families to enable children to remain at home in their local communities

- to proceed to an initial child protection conference to decide whether to place a child's name on the child protection register and implement a **protection plan**

- to move to look after a child and implement a **care plan**.

(9) The on-going assessment, planning, monitoring and review process will help to determine whether the necessary action is being taken and that **positive changes** are being made to **improve the child's life experience and opportunity.**

(10) SW's are required to undertake **regular statutory visits** to see and speak with all LAC and those on the CPR. SW's are required to work **in partnership** with parents and often develop **written agreements** to clarify the parental role, responsibility and expectations to ensure that the aims of the support, care or protection plans are realised.

(11) SW's are also expected to **work together** with professionals from a wide range of partner agencies and disciplines sharing relevant information to co-ordinate and deliver services for the child\and family.

(12) In respect of children on the **child protection register**:

- **core groups** will be held to monitor and develop the protection plan

- **review child protection conferences** are independently chaired to determine whether the registration criteria continues to be met

- if so the child's name will remain on the CPR.

(13) In respect of looked-after children:

- regular **LAC reviews** are convened and independently chaired (within the first month, three months thereafter and at six-monthly intervals thereafter) to consult, discuss and agree the child's care plan;

- a **permanence plan** is required by the second LAC review;

- LAC are expected to have an annual **health assessments**, a developmental check and immunisations, dental and optician check ups;

- meetings to set and review **personal education plans** are also undertaken at regular intervals.

(14) In respect of children in need:

- regular **network planning meetings** are convened to discuss the Support Plans and agree whether and what on-going support and intervention is required.

(15) **Family network meetings** are convened to facilitate and support the child's family to explore and recommend its own plans and proposals to decide key arrangements for the child including care, contact and support.

(16) **Parent assessment planning meetings** are convened to review existing parenting assessments and determine whether and what additional parenting assessments may be required.

(17) **Childcare panel/complex needs panel** – to agree single/joint/tripartite funding arrangements and plans for placements and provisions, particularly the use of private and voluntary out of borough resources.

(18) **Legal planning meetings** are convened to consider the evidence relating to children are suffering/likely to suffer significant harm and plan any agreed proceedings in accordance with the judicial protocol (2003):

- review the available assessments and identify any gaps requiring further/specialist input

- determine whether and in what way the threshold criteria is met

- detail all efforts to engage and work in partnership with parents/carers

- outline the primary and parallel care plan and contact arrangements

- outline application process and timescale.

(19) SW and manager to advise the professional network and inform the child and his/her parents/carers of the decision to initiate care proceedings.

(20) SW to prepare and managers to authorise the:

    (a) application

    (b) statement

    (c) chronology

    (d) care plan.

(21) Serve papers and appear at court.

Thus a care plan developed in a system of variable skill levels, differing views as to role and responsibility, restricted resources, tight timescales and a changing evidence and research base is adapted by the court process – and then given back to the local authority to deliver.

As a context to all of this, it is worth noting that just over 70% of local authorities are predicting an overspend on their children's services budget this current year, and around half are having difficulties in recruiting and retaining suitably qualified, experienced and skilled children's social workers. In some authorities, this means a vacancy rate of 40–50% and workers having to carry larger caseloads. In others, 50% of workers are agency staff who may not stay long and will therefore add to the turnover of significant adults in the child's life, as well as potentially changing of views and opinions in the conduct of care planning.

OPTIONS, ISSUES AND OUTCOMES

Having set what could be perceived as a rather gloomy background and description of current practice, let us now consider the options for the system as a whole to work together and support the delivery of best outcomes, best plans and best engagement for the benefits of children and young people.

In response to the problems with this area of work, there has been a pressure to give more instruction, more monitoring and more calling over of practice by those in authority. One example of this came in 2001, when the Court of Appeal made a landmark decision that seemed set to give the courts much more power over the local authority care plan. Although the House of Lords rejected this judgement in 2002, *Re S* and *Re W* were indicative of a broader attempt to solve the tricky problem of authority in care plan decisions.[2] One option presented in the original judgement looked at 'starring' care plans but, as Harwin and Owen reported in 2003, this presented its own problems:

> 'The term "implementation" has not been formally defined in relation to care plans and lack of clarity over the meaning and expectations of implementation was one reason why the Court of Appeal's proposal to introduce starred elements in care plans was likely to prove unworkable. As the authors have discussed elsewhere, it would have been difficult to say categorically which part of the plan in these disputed cases was most important and, therefore, required starring. Was it implementation of the placement arrangements, contact, services, long term commitments to reunification or all of these?'[3]

This is a difficult issue, and seems to be at the centre of debates around care planning. What can be considered the 'key' elements of a plan? In their study of the implementation of 100 care plans, Harwin and Owen reported the following:

> 'Four items in the court plan each had above average rates of success (60% or more) provided that they were recorded in detail. They were:
> - type and details of the proposed placement;
> - arrangements for contact and reunification;

---

[2]   http://www.parliament.the-stationery-office.co.uk/pa/ld200102/ldjudgmt/jd020314/inres-1.htm

[3]   J Harwin and M Owen. 'The implementation of care plans and its relationship to children's welfare' in (2003) 15(1) Child and Family Law Quarterly 72.

- how the children's needs might be met; and
- services to be provided by the local authority.

It is not difficult to see why these particular headings were linked to placement plans fulfilment. Detailed completion demanded positive forward thinking and action to ensure that the necessary arrangements were in place. In the best plans, social workers went beyond a simple description of need (which was the core of some less satisfactory plans) to a clear analysis of how children's needs should be met, and there was also recognition of the interrelationship between the placement, contact and services. When plans are being scrutinised by courts and social services, the four items mentioned above seem to deserve special attention in order to maximise the chances of the plan being fulfilled.'[4]

So, having examined the evidence of 100 care plans, four factors are highlighted as the most important for local authorities to consider. This is highly instructive for social work practice, but there are three other key elements to consider when making up a plan:

(1) **Children evolve and their needs change.** The care plan needs to be responsive to those changing needs. It is interesting to note, for example, that Harwin and Owen also found 16 cases (almost a fifth of the sample) where good welfare outcomes were achieved when the plan was unfulfilled.[5] Adaptability is important – perhaps even more so than getting the plan right in the first place. The care plan presented in court, for instance, may identify the need for the child to be placed with a particular carer. If the placement does not work out, the 'needs' of the child will remain – and even if the placement appears to be successful, there is no guarantee that the child's needs will not later change.

We need to accept that not all placements and care plans fail because the plan is not right. Circumstances may contrive to undermine a perfectly good care plan, and resilience and flexibility are required to learn the lessons and check what this means for the child.

Processes need to be in place to learn the lessons quickly:

- disruption meetings – by an independent person

- inter-agency consultation and ownership.

Care planning is a continuum, and its durability will be tested by new events and circumstances. People will come and go, as will the child him/herself. The different disciplines need to have processes in place to ensure the continuity of care planning and co-working.

(2) **A sustainable, durable care plan needs to be based on accurate and reflective knowledge of the child and, wherever possible, on their own wishes and feelings.** The four factors identified by Harwin and Owen (type and details of the proposed placement; arrangements for contact and reunification; how the children's needs might be met; and services to be provided by the local authority)[6] will all need to be composed with reference to the child's individual characteristics.

How will the plan for the child represent all the facets of the child's views (eg, where he/she would like to live / the type of carers / what they will be able to provide / allay child's fears / issues of identity and developing a strong sense of self)? Mechanisms need to be established by which we can gain insight of the child's world, as they may express their views in different ways. We need to encourage this through:

- advocacy

- independent visiting

- mentoring

- voluntary groups

- key working.

---

[4]   Ibid, p 81.
[5]   Ibid, p 78.
[6]   Ibid, p 81.

We also need to be mindful of the influence and role of the extended family and network. Care planning needs to incorporate their views and what they can offer.

(3) **Joint working and co-operation between different professionals is essential for a care plan to prove successful.** There has to be agreed understanding about inter-agency collaboration in the assessment, planning and implementation of the care plan:

- identify needs

- joint working

- child focused

- promoting ownership.

The inter-agency work needs to identify who will be able to monitor specific areas of the child's life and measure outcomes. The question of which professional does this is less important than the need to ensure that it is done, and linked to this is the issue of who will be able to assess the progress of the child in the wake of the 'expert' opinions during the court process. We need to be clear about how we measure outcomes and how interpret successes for the child as well as room for improvement and change. Furthermore, do the various review processes (ie, child case review, PEPs, health plans) have the ability to evaluate the progress a child makes? This is especially pertinent when the importance of adaptability is considered – changing progress may warrant a changing care plan.

As Harwin and Owen conclude: 'The question of agency accountability runs through and beyond these debates. It is a question with which courts are heavily and inevitably involved; but it is only by courts and social services working in partnership that the balance between plan fulfilment and children's welfare can be achieved.'[7]

In addition, the care plan has to consider how the identified services and resources will promote the life chances of the child, and what will need to take place if the expected outcomes do not come about.

There is so much to do around the care planning process that we can end up being 'curtailed' and driven solely by the process itself. We need to think out of the box and the immediate needs of the care planning process to look at different ways by which we can engage children, parents, and other professionals. Finally, care planning needs to have the some elements that we ask of children themselves:

- resilience

- understanding

- flexibility

- honesty

- open (and to change)

- patience

- aspiration.

It is I think unhelpful to continue to add to the wealth of guidance instructions and critical analysis of the individual performance and practice. The family justice system focussing on some of the most vulnerable children in our society needs to reflect on how it may work more co-operatively and thoughtfully together to deliver the best outcomes. It needs to develop the analysis and learning approach rather than investigation to apportion blame so that the system works together as much as possible to deliver the best outcomes for children.

---

[7] Ibid, p 83.

THE SOLUTION

The system is complex and the task – managing the future welfare of a disadvantaged child – is demanding and not open to 'mechanistic' solutions.

The latest attempt to raise standards in the system came with the Adoption Act 2002, which gave Independent Reviewing Officers a key role and set considerable expectations on them:

> 'The IRO will improve care planning and decision making and make an important contribution to the consistency of the local authority's approach. Review meetings will be efficiently chaired by the IRO with the full involvement of the child and key adults in decision making process. The IRO will help provide effective care planning for looked-after children by ensuring that review meetings take place in accordance with the required timescales and care plans are implemented effectively.

> The IRO will ensure that the developmental needs of the child are identified and met through the care planning and review process. The IRO will have a crucial role in ensuring that looked-after children are properly safeguarded wherever they live and in securing a timely and appropriate route to permanence arrangements.'[8]

This extract from the guidance of IROs, whilst at one level reasonable – at another expects 'super' powers in one voice in a multi-layered system. The key to this, of course, is that this is a post-hoc arrangement – the IROs' powers only come into play once the care plan has failed. Whilst this is a useful check, it is important to remember that, if the previous steps have been carried out correctly, their intervention will be unnecessary.

WHERE TO NOW?

The system has the right focus – the welfare of the child – and provides ample opportunity for challenge. The areas of most uncertainty are those associated with the four key areas noted by Harwin and Owen:

- child's needs
- placement
- contact
- services

All are changing and based on human growth/development (or lack of it) and need money and skill to ensure success.

The competing demands of best plan/placement must be set on the reality of available placements, funds to support them and the difficulty of recruiting, retaining and training social work staff.

The system is by and large 'good enough'; but the focus (on these four issues) is sometimes masked by progress, personality, adversarial issues. As a result, the future for the child suffers.

The remedy (if there is just one) is to get agreement on the key questions within the four issues throughout the system, at the earliest stage' to work as a team system, not separate and competing individuals, from the first point of the 21-stage process that leads to court and from then on to ensure the IRO is equipped to do the tasks necessary to deliver key outcomes.

If anything, we need less of a system, more discussion, less pointing and blame, and a clearer focus on a day in the life of a child.

---

[8] DfES *Independent reviewing officers guidance (the Review of Children's Cases (Amendment) (England) Regulations 2004)* (DfES, 2004), p 22.

This paper merely makes the point that this is a difficult business: the system is fit for purpose, the task extraordinarily complex.

Managing the future for a child – the people in the system are under pressure, and the focus is sometimes wide of the mark (being on system rather than outcome).

The answer:

- we are better together
- focus on a few (four) key issues
- set out the key questions
- work on answers together
- don't just tell people 'they have got it wrong'
- don't add more blame and checking
- do improve communication during and after court
- inform parties of the success of the child.

SMALL GROUP DISCUSSIONS: PLENARIES 2–6

SMALL GROUP A

PLENARY 3: MODELS FOR ACHIEVING SUCCESSFUL AGREED AND ORDERED OUTCOMES IN PRIVATE LAW CASES.

- Praise was given for the early Intervention scheme piloted by District Judge Crichton. What had been achieved within the scheme was beyond the group's expectations. It was disappointing that there was a lack of support for this scheme because the court could not make participation in the scheme compulsory.

- Principles can be taken from this pilot scheme and others like it; children should be involved. There should not be a rule of thumb as to what age a child should be to be engaged in the process.

- A facility which allowed children and young people to speak to each other about their experience of the court process would be useful to them. Such a service should not be restricted to parents. This type of service could be arranged through Local Family Justice Councils.

- The question was raised as to where both children and adults get mental health support and how to make this support mainstream. In working with couples where mental health problems are an issue, a solicitor should not be the first port of call for the couple. The roles of a doctor and a lawyer cannot be intertwined and medical help should be in place before the case reaches court. There needs to be intervention in the process of breakdown. Discussions should centre on mental health, not simply mental illness.

- The group noted that simply establishing contact is not necessarily in itself beneficial for the child. The limitations of court mediation in controlling the child's experience of contact need to be recognised.

PLENARY 4: GENDER, PARENTING AND THE COURTS

- Every member of a family will see the same situation differently from their own perspective. There is a danger in moving from rules of principle to brief rules of thumb.

- There is a key connection between being child focused and future focused.

- It is not always clear who a child can look to for support in the case of family breakdown. Children are sometimes tempted to take the side of one parent to gain this support. Solicitors provide partisan support for the parents and there is no equivalent for children. Some, but not all, schools have mentoring facilities for children in these situations.

PLENARY 5: CONTACT IN PRIVATE AND PUBLIC LAW CASES: MANAGING TWO OR MORE FAMILIES.

- The balance between flexibility for contact and protection of children needs to be found.

- It is very important to maintain continuity of foster carers for children.

- The family group conference is a useful model which should be utilised in private law proceedings as well as public law proceedings.

- Using concentric circle diagrams to depict a family is of assistance in determining levels of contact for extended family members. The diagram will be different for every child. Children do learn to manage complex relationships but these must be controlled and planned.

- There is a tendency to take some assumptions for granted. These must be challenged and their validity considered.

PLENARY 6: PERMANENCE FOR LOOKED AFTER CHILDREN

- There is a distinction between types of targets some of which are useful, for example targets for levels of adoption are less useful but a target that every child is allocated a social worker is positive. There is a danger of social work by numbers and targets distressing social workers rather than motivating them.

- A system is needed for reporting back the outcome of a case to those involved. This need is two-fold. Firstly and most simply, this means informing experts who are not present for judgment of the outcome. Secondly, this envisages reporting back to judges what happened to a particular child or family, one year and five years after the judgment was given.

SMALL GROUP B

PLENARY 3: MODELS FOR ACHIEVING SUCCESSFUL AGREED AND ORDERED OUTCOMES IN PRIVATE LAW CASES.

- We would like to encourage the development of services to follow up the families who have reached agreement at conciliation appointment, to address the 'lower level of satisfaction' in the conciliation process described by those in Liz Trinder's study.

- Services for families in breakdown are not sufficiently cohesive. Individual services for individual issues do not meet the needs of ordinary family breakdown.

- We see an opportunity to point up the deficits in the current Children (Contact) and Adoption Bill; we would like to highlight the value of family assistance orders which, we believe, should be capable of being made without requiring the consent of the parties. (By comparison, 'parenting orders' have been successful.)

- We would also wish to underline the importance of sustained core funding for voluntary services to advise, assist and befriend.

- As a long-term objective, there should be greater focus given to consideration of cases according to the categorisation of:

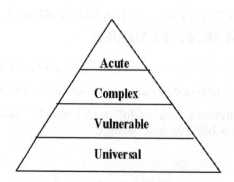

Within this categorisation, there is a need to re-distribute the resources – training and services – down the pyramid. At present, too much is dedicated to the 'acute' cases.

- We consider that there needs to be a 'triage' service to evaluate at an early stage the category into which each family falls, and what services would best meet the needs for each family.

- Generally, there needs to be a shift of money from litigation services to support services, and into training to create services.

- The researchers need to inform us what support services would be most likely to work for each type of case.

- We recognise that there is a 'ritual' to family breakdown, though we believe that it does not need to be a court-based 'ritual'; there is a clear argument for removing the 'ritual' from the court and reserving the court for the resolution of family disputes only. We recognise that in order to achieve this, the change would have to be fundamental/legislative.

- There is nonetheless a value for some families in the court determining factual issues; it was agreed that it was an important part of the process for some couples to assist them to put to rest the past.

- Judges should be empowered to refer families to the mental health services.

PLENARY 4: GENDER, PARENTING AND THE COURTS

- The important question of *safety* within contact needs to be addressed before the court considers making contact orders and making orders enforcing contact.

- Particular care needs to be paid at the enforcement stage to orders which have been made by consent (ie where there has been no judicial enquiry at the point at which the contact order was made). We believe that this should be explicitly addressed in the Children (Contact) and Adoption Bill and/or by amendment to the Children Act 1989.

- It is important to make an explicit link in the statute between the promotion of contact and the protection of victims of domestic violence, and children exposed to it.

- There is a strong case for promoting the practice which is already operational in Manchester by which police records, and 'call-out' records of all parties involved in Children Act 1989 (private law) proceedings are routinely available to the court within each application, within a short time of the application being made. This is usually facilitated by CAFCASS. Further, CAFCASS makes an automatic referral to social services where the material revealed by the police records gives cause for concern.

- Many of the issues of danger and safety arising from domestic violence span the fields of criminal justice, child protection, family justice and children in need. In the circumstances, there should be wider access by the family justice system to 'perpetrator' programmes available to the criminal courts – including those run by the probation service. It would, we believe, be more cost-efficient to 'join up' the contexts in which the system is dealing with dangerous men. There is a concern that the issue of domestic violence has been to an extent subordinated to the lobby of fathers seeking contact.

- Area Family Justice Councils should be encouraged at an early stage to invite police domestic violence units and child protection units to speak to them – so that local practitioners are aware of local police practices. Area Family Justice Councils should be encouraged to develop protocols with the police to improve the faster and more efficient flow of information from the police to the family courts.

- There is a role for the DfES to initiate long-term education programmes for children and young people, teaching them about attitudes to violence.

PLENARY 5: CONTACT IN PRIVATE AND PUBLIC LAW CASES: MANAGING TWO OR MORE FAMILIES.

- When the court is considering a private law contact application, there needs to be an early understanding and resolution of the degree of conflict within a family, so that an early decision can be made about whether any, and if so what, efforts should be made to promote contact with the non-resident parent.

- In this respect, we need to encourage those in the family justice community to review current attitudes and assumptions about contact disputes – in the interim and long term. We see the value of the preparation of a jointly-prepared paper on this issue from the researchers who have prepared papers for this Dartington conference; this paper should be formally validated by the conference, and introduced to the courts through the JSB and by other routes. This paper should particularly focus on, and question, the assumption that contact is necessarily beneficial.

- In the public law cases, there should be greater consultation with foster carers about the quantum and timing of contact between children and the natural families.

- It would be valuable for the social services and the courts explicitly to distinguish between different types of 'supervised' contact to be arranged between parent and child; for example, contact should be expressed to be 'facilitated'/'accompanied'/'assessed' – so that the purpose of the contact (particularly in the public law context) is more clearly understood by all.

- There should be a more widely accepted acceptance of flexibility in contact arrangements in private and public law cases; it is important that contact should be adjusted to meet the changing needs of the child.

PLENARY 6: PERMANENCE FOR LOOKED AFTER CHILDREN

- In order to reduce delay in the process, to promote consistent planning for children and to achieve better and more durable outcomes for children, we need to have better paid, well-trained, and appropriately resourced social workers. Then the expertise of social workers will be more generally recognised and accepted.

SMALL GROUP C

PLENARY 3: MODELS FOR ACHIEVING SUCCESSFUL AGREED AND ORDERED OUTCOMES IN PRIVATE CASES

There was general agreement that some of the children and families in the private law process are in severe emotional distress.

It is recognised that there is a group of vulnerable children caught up in parental separation and conflict, within which group only a relatively small percentage were before the court.

There is a need to provide a range of support services and a debate as to whether this should be through CAFCASS or otherwise. Families of vulnerable children could be referred to:

- CAHMS
- Home Start

- extended social services
- counselling
- and all this within the 'Every Child Matters' programme.

If that support network could be developed we could prevent a number of cases entering the family court system.

PLENARY 4: GENDER, PARENTING AND THE COURTS

The group focussed discussion on domestic violence.

There should be more robust use of family assistance orders to get cases out of the immediate court arena, especially where an agreement in principle may not necessarily represent consent.

We would recommend the removal of the requirement for consent in family assistance orders.

The extension of family assistance orders to 12 months would allow for constructive work to be undertaken consistently over a period of time by a single worker or by commissioning support packages which could, if necessary, continue post-order.

Gender issues

Despite efforts to address issues raised by both gender groups, there is still an apparent divide in that neither gender group believe that the family justice system is currently adequately addressing their concerns or serving their interests.

Some professionals fail to recognise the significance of gender issues in their own preconceptions about them.

In all section 8 applications, the court should be provided with safeguarding checks including:

- the previous convictions, if any, of the applicant and respondent;
- any FWIN computer records which might be relevant;
- any risk assessment, including OASIS and MAPPA assessments which are available to the police.

This list is not intended to be exclusive.

Where documentation, including the above material and the application forms, reveal a significant child protection issue, CAFCASS should make a referral to the relevant social services department.

The importance of providing support for those families who have 'lost' a child to adoption or long-term care must be remembered. It should be more fully recognised that many of these are themselves vulnerable because of disability or mental health problems and some should be provided with protective support services in their own right since they are under the age of 18.

PLENARY 5: CONTACT IN PRIVATE AND PUBLIC LAW CASES: MANAGING TWO OR MORE FAMILIES

The group expressed concern that despite considerable information over the last five years regarding domestic violence, this was not being paid sufficient attention. There was a question as to whether legislation was needed if judges were not following the existing guidelines. Further research was needed to explore how the current system was working and this should include improved statistics provided by the court service.

PLENARY 6: PERMANENCE FOR LOOKED AFTER CHILDREN

There is an urgent need for a well-funded longitudinal study of all the children coming into care during a given year. For such a study to give a balanced picture of outcomes and 'what works' in providing durable solutions for the full range of children entering out-of-home care, those who leave care through reunification, placement with kin and adoption should remain within the research sample followed up at regular intervals until their mid 20s. If, as has often happened with previous outcome studies, only those who leave care post-16 are 'counted', outcomes can seem worse than they in fact are, since most of the children included in the samples entered care when 10 plus. These older entrants tend to have worse outcomes than those who enter when younger. A performance target to keep down the numbers of children coming into care may mean in practice that the children come in later in their lives but stay longer. The group questioned the benefit of performance targets, how targets were measured and questioned whether this was compatible with primary consideration being given to a child's welfare. The group suggested that financial rewards or penalties for local authorities who do not meet their adoption targets should be abolished.

The group clarified that they were not against any performance measurements as such but there was a need to set some proportionality about what should be measured and ensure this was a qualitative as well as quantitative measurement. Siblings should not be split up simply to meet such targets. Performance targets should be for the proportion of children provided with a long-term permanent family, and not just those who are adopted. There is a need to reduce the competitive blame culture and replace this with the cohesiveness of being in the situation together. We also need to celebrate success.

There was discussion as to whether independent reviewing officers should be employed outside the local authority, for example by the National Care Standards Board, although there were arguments both ways on this point. At present, if an independent reviewing officer refers a case to CAFCASS, there is no mechanism for CAFCASS to return this to court. We need to look closely at providing a way for CAFCASS to do so where necessary.

[*A summary of the discussions and conclusions of Small Groups D and E are to be found in Plenary 9.*]

SMALL GROUP F

PLENARY 3: MODELS FOR ACHIEVING SUCCESSFUL AGREED AND ORDERED OUTCOMES IN PRIVATE LAW CASES, PLENARY 4: GENDER, PARENTING AND THE COURTS, PLENARY 5: CONTACT IN PRIVATE AND PUBLIC LAW CASES: MANAGING TWO OR MORE FAMILIES, PLENARY 6: PERMANENCE FOR LOOKED AFTER CHILDREN

The group drew from Liz Trinder's research the finding that conciliation has a function, but that conciliation is not enough on its own to improve relations between parents. Further, contact of itself will not improve a child's well-being. A child's well-being was improved where parental well-being was improved, so it was important that parents manage their conflict so as not to affect the child. It needed to be understood that children who were *not* having contact did not necessarily do worse than those that did have contact. It was the *quality* of the contact that mattered.

It was also important to recognise that other family members could undermine contact agreements, once the agreement was reported back to the wider family circle. Thought needed to be given to bringing the wider family into the equation. There were moves in Wales to have 'family group conferences' in these cases.

There needed to be much more education about conflict to inform other professionals about the damaging effects of family/parental conflict. Education should be extended to public health, schools and outlets in a much more imaginative way. The education would be on avoiding conflict, managing conflict and the impact of conflict on children. There is a need to make greater connections between private and public law in terms of dealing with those involved in both arenas. It was also important that professionals in the family justice system understood these issues, especially as the system was encouraging and relying on the greater use of pre-court settlement.

There was no understanding/basis of knowledge of what children needed and how to produce durable solutions. There was a lack of understanding of child development and communication issues.

It was disappointing that more cases had not come to the Family Proceedings Resolution Pilot, but the evaluation of this pilot should be studied carefully to see what elements might be taken forward to build a future initiative. The experience from the United States was that many parenting/education programmes did not work entirely as envisaged but this could mean that they should be developed rather than abandoned.

It was important not to have unrealistic expectations of the court. The court's jurisdiction was exercised at the behest of the parties. The court's function was to resolve disputes. The vast majority of separated couples did not bring issues about arrangements for children to the court. This was highly desirable and should not change.

However, while more cases should not come into the court, those that did needed different services. Liz Trinder had made the point that conciliation went so far but there needed to be services to work with families both alongside and after the court process in order to provide durable solutions. The court provided an important framework to hold families while their problems were addressed. But cases were not in the hands of the court for long (overall) and research showed that some children remained adversely affected by conflict around contact arrangements long after the case had left the court. Additional services were needed to work with these cases.

Katherine Gieve's paper raised the issue of fathers being forced post separation into a role they had not previously had for the child prior to separation. Children understood that there were different roles for parents but the system was not good at dealing with children's distress at the dislocation of parenting following separation. It was debatable how far the adjudication system could determine that there was a change in the systems of parenting and how far it could continue the parenting roles prior the split.

Simplistic solutions had been proposed on contact – 'move on', 'let's have 50/50' etc. Durable solutions were likely to be complex but they needed to match the complexity of the case. This meant a lot more skilled listening and management of the complexity.

It was recognised that services were unlikely to be significantly increased. Some aspects of the court system, however, needed addressing. Listing too many cases at one time could force unsatisfactory settlements. Different judges dealing with a series of interim matters was not desirable. There should be judicial continuity in all matters, though this posed challenges in the way responsibilities were divided between judges in some courts.

Some families responded well to the authority of the court. A substitute earlier authority might be usefully explored.

Things could stick or be resolved because the judge had said them, but there could be resistance if the judge was considered too hard. It was important to look at how to involve children more creatively in the process and to ensure there was flexibility for the future.

Finally the group returned to its theme of the previous day – the state's role in private law cases – in discussing domestic violence. It was important that there was screening before cases entered the system. The group discussed whether there should be a 'triage' system, how robust the CAFCASS process was, whether there should be early hearings on domestic violence and the responsibility of the court in investigating where there were allegations of violence but a later application for a consent order; and where there were not allegations.

HELPING TO ENSURE SOLUTIONS WORK FOR CHILDREN IN THE LONGER TERM

ADOPTIVE PARENTS AND CHILDREN – SUPPORT FROM PLACEMENT TO ADULTHOOD

John Simmonds
Director, Policy Research & Development,
British Association for Adoption and Fostering

There is a significant amount of evidence to demonstrate that as a piece of social policy, adoption has been an extraordinarily successful intervention in establishing the conditions that promote the health and development of children. In a recent study (Trisilioltis (2005)) of 126 adults who had been adopted before 1975, 80% reported that they were happy about being adopted, felt loved by their adoptive parents and had developed a sense of belonging. On the Goldberg General Health Questionnaire, 74% of these adults were assessed as having good emotional health, 12% moderate emotional health and 14% severe emotional health problems. This distribution compares favourably to the general population. In a study (Gilleard (2005)) of 1,500 adults who had consulted their general practitioners in Wandsworth, it was estimated that 30% had some form of mental health problem with 12% showing symptoms of mental illness. Generalising this to the population of Wandsworth as a whole, the study estimates the prevalence rate for mental health problems to be 18%. Setting this against whole population studies in the UK, mental health problems are estimated to affect about one-quarter of adults in one study (NHS Centre for Reviews and Dissemination (2001)) and in another (Singleton (2002)) just over 20% are estimated to have a clinically significant problem.

While mental health status and emotional well-being is only one factor among many that might be used to assess the success of adoption as an intervention in the 1960s and early 1970s, these kinds of figures replicated in any other kind of radical measure to tackle a social problem would be impressive. It is therefore not surprising that adoption has been the focus of a programme of modernisation and legislative reform since the late 1990s, taking shape with the Prime Minister's Review of Adoption (2000), the Adoption White Paper (2000) and the Adoption and Children Act 2002 and raft of associated developments. The focus of this programme is to increase the number of children adopted from care and to reduce delay in placing them. The background to this is undoubtedly the concern about the life chances of principally younger children in the public care system. The prediction that a child who has been in care for more than six months has a 60% of remaining in care for four years or more which then increases to 80% at 12 months has been significant. When combined with other figures such as the number of placements children might have, their overall level of need and what is known about the outcome for young people leaving care in terms of homelessness, employment, offending, mental and physical health and early pregnancy, the need to find radical solutions is blindingly obvious. However, some of these statistics do need to be carefully unpacked as they have generated some messages that are unhelpful – in particular a view that the care system always fails or is dangerous. A number of studies (Ward (2005), Wilson (2004), Sinclair (2005)) have demonstrated that for many children being in care has made a real difference to them which staying at home would not have given them. When it works well, the looked-after children system is capable of meeting children's needs in a helpful and important way.

Building on what works well in the care system is important although the challenges cannot be underestimated even after 50 years. However, there continues to be a serious problem about designing appropriate interventions that maximise the life chances of children where their birth families cannot do so even at a basic level. It is here that the lessons from the past and the success of adoption inevitably influence policy especially when combined with what people instinctively know and experience – that a loving home where a child belongs and feels secure is fundamental to healthy development. Even where individuals have not experienced this as children, it is probably something they long for and wish to create in their own adult lives with partners and children of their own.

The combination of the past success of adoption, an understanding of the central importance of family life in the development of children and the problems of designing alternative interventions and 'durable solutions' for families that 'fail' do then drive current policy in relation to adoption. But this policy, at its best, cannot be built on the naïve assumption that if we do what we did in the past, then we will reproduce its successes in the present. It is widely acknowledged that most children available for adoption are not babies, that most are not 'relinquished' but subject to care proceedings and the dispensation of parental consent in relation to the adoption application, that they have complex special needs as a result of abuse and neglect and an uncertain developmental future, may be one of a sibling group with many having a minority cultural, religious and ethnic heritage. Adoption in its current form may therefore share little with what adoption was in the past apart from the legal termination of the rights of the birth parents in favour of the adoptive parents.

Does therefore the past success of adoption reported in the Trisiliotis (2005) study have anything to tell us about the issues currently posed by adoption practice? This is a matter of some interest to me as I am the adoptive father of two children who, while they were adopted in the 1980s, nonetheless fall into the earlier era of adoption. They were both placed as babies by their mothers and in one case the father as well who had decided that they could not provide them with the kinds of lives they wished for them. Both my children are now young adults who are establishing themselves as happy and successful people in the way that any parent would hope for their children. Having read the Trisiliotis study, I can identify with much of what it says in terms of the hopes, aspirations, fears and anxieties of living in an adoption triangle and the way this weaves its way in many different ways into family life. At the same time as my own 'lived experience' has played itself out, I have been heavily professionally involved in the development and implementation of the Adoption and Children Act 2002 and its associated policy, regulatory and practice developments. The personal and the professional exist side by side but not in any straightforward way. While it is true that one informs the other and indeed has developed the other, it is also true that there is much that these two realms of experience do not share and are separate.

For example, I feel exasperated and do despair at the length of time some children now wait for placement even if national figures indicate they are reducing. Sometimes this is due to attempts to return children too many times to circumstances that have little chance of meeting the child's needs. At other times this seems to be due to extraordinary delay in the social services, health and court systems. The window of developmental opportunity for young children is narrow. We have known this for a long time and indeed it fuelled my own personal determination to try to ensure that any child placed with me should not have to wait needlessly for placement. But at that time, in the early 80s, the agency that had approved us had a policy of placing babies directly from hospital and, even then, had a small number of 'relinquished' babies, so it was possible. Now this is almost impossible except for the small number of concurrency projects (Monck (2003)) although even with these, the circumstances are very different. The advantages this brought to us and to our children I believe are incalculable. We were rightly warned of the risks that the birth parents may change their minds or of discovering some serious developmental abnormality but they were outweighed by the advantages of a good and early start. I see my own children in the faces of every child featured in BAAF's family-finding newspaper *Be My Parent* – waiting, waiting, waiting, and while in the last year 277 of them were successfully linked with prospective adopters, sadly a large number were not. Even with all the advances in developmental psychology that have taken place in recent years, the methods and technologies we have developed to enable developmental catch up following early adversity are remarkably crude. Children are not reprogrammable and cannot return to default mode when we have significantly damaged them. At best, we can enable children to stabilise and then progress. But this is often through super-human effort on the part of adoptive parents or foster carers supported by therapists and others (Cairns (2002), Hirst (2005), Bond (2005), Cairns (2004), Beek (2004)). Many 'late-placed' children (Rushton (2003)) may develop close and satisfying relationships with their adoptive parents and make good developmental progress, but this should not blind us to the fact that this is by no means true for all late-placed children and does not take into account what a child's developmental potential might have been whatever catch up or progress has taken place. Early placement at the youngest possible age is still the most reliable predictor of the best developmental progress for the child. (Rutter (1998),(1997); Hodges (2003))

The past, however, was not a golden age. Adoption has for a significant part of its history been a solution to the problem of infertility for which it seems largely well suited. It has also been a solution to the problem of children conceived out of wedlock and to the preservation of marriage and the family as a social and religious institution. In some instances it has also been an explicit mechanism to manage 'problematic' aspects of social class and ethnic purity. It has therefore had a social control function. Birth parents talking now in the Trisiliotis study as mature adults demonstrate the deeply compromised position many of them found themselves in at the time of the birth or the long-term impact of this. It changes how one might understand the actual exercise of choice for birth parent/s underpinning the term 'relinquished'. Indeed the framing of the wording of the form of consent where the birth parent 'freely, and with full understanding of what is involved, agrees unconditionally to the making of the adoption order'[1] seems rather problematic set in the context of these social control imperatives. It may be that adoption was the only solution at that time in history and its associated circumstances given the lack of available alternatives for the birth parent/s – no practical, emotional or social support plus the likelihood of social stigma and shame being brought on the individual or their family. The social coercion involved in the decision to place for adoption cannot be lightly dismissed and the consequences of this for all those involved.

There were also issues for adopters over this period. It was a procedure that was reserved for the 'perfect' – white, Christian, home loving, morally sound, married couple, man at work, woman in the kitchen or the nursery. The process of selecting and approving such couples depended on the capacity of adoption agencies to identify such 'ideal couples'. Adoption agencies exerted and continue to exert considerable power in the mysterious process of uncovering those attributes that make the perfect adopter despite significant efforts to make the process more realistic and positive. The experience of this legal/bureaucratic process is discussed by Howe (2003) where he reports:

> 'Because it was such an anxious time for many, with so much resting on the outcome, various psychological strategies were adopted in the face of the investigation. These ranged from being allegedly relaxed and indifferent to feeling anxious and well guarded against close and personal scrutiny. If the couple had already been subject to the indignities, intrusions and ultimate disappointment of infertility investigations, they reacted in one of two ways. Either they felt well prepared for the further invasions of a psychological assessment, or they felt even more exposed and vulnerable at the prospect of yet another procedure which had to be endured on the long, uncertain road to parenthood.' (p 27)

Babies had to be perfect too – white, no flaws either inherited or developed.

Taking all this together, this image of 'perfection' now appears oppressive especially when it was accompanied by the veil of secrecy that was supposed to descend on all three parties. But in circumstances where there are underlying emotional and social forces connected with infertility and sexuality, social stigma and personal shame, envy and guilt, powerful defences (Menzies Lyth (1988)) will come into effect to protect individuals and the social system against anxiety. One of the most powerful defences of all is denial so it is not surprising that secrecy surrounded and dominated the process for fear of revealing not only the 'guilt, anxiety and shame' of the individuals but of the social system that generated it.

Within a social system driven by such powerful societal and institutional defences, the placement of the child was regarded as a new beginning and to be treated as if nothing that went

---

[1]   Children Act 1975, s 12(1)(b).

before had happened or was of any significance. If a significant psychological issue did emerge that needed to be addressed, it was largely confined to the problem of 'telling' – to tell or not to tell about the facts or circumstances of the child's adoption status – and the associated problem of the child's curiosity about origins – 'where did I come from and why was I given up?' Views about this were variable. Wieder (1978) gave a stark warning that in his experience children's behaviour, thoughts and relationships changed once 'told', so the issue should not primarily be one of 'telling' but creating a sense of 'belonging'. Ansfield (1971) takes the most extreme stance when he advocates constructing an elaborate deception, including involving older siblings, as long as the secret is maintained. On the other hand, Kornitzer (1976) suggests using the term adoption as 'term of endearment … as a rhythm, as a sound, with loving overtones with the child eventually coming to associate adoption with both his own experience and a profound sense of love. Concern over the impact of telling on the security of the placement and the development of the child has continued to be expressed in a number of different ways' (Kraft (1985a), (1985b), Byrd (1988)). This has also had a significant impact on the development of the 'closed' status of adoption records and the information they contain. The Houghton Committee's Report in 1972 recommended the continuation of 'closed records' and therefore the continuation of secrecy, fearing interference by birth or adoptive parents or support for a belief that the birth link was still in existence.[2] It was only Triseliotis (1973) research on the positive impact of the opening of Scottish adoption records that turned this around and extended the provision to England and Wales.

Apart from this contentious issue, the placement of the child in an adoptive family was the solution to meeting the child's needs. The consequence of this was that bringing up an adopted child was thought to require nothing very different from bringing up a 'born to' child. The psychology of adoptive family life was the psychology of 'born to' family life with the added dimension of 'telling'. If anxiety, guilt and shame or even curiosity were experienced then the overriding impression was that they were better not talked about. The psychology of adoption was largely therefore a psychology of young children but living with an uncomfortable family secret.

We know from the Triseliotis (2005) study that 86% of their sample of adopters actually told their child before they were four and that 97% felt comfortable about talking about adoption although this did not mean that they actually did talk about it. This undoubtedly reflects the difficulty of knowing whether to introduce the subject for discussion, wait for the child to raise it or try to weave it into other topics of conversation. Is it a routine part of family life or a special issue? Is it associated with the kinds of feelings Kornitzer is advocating or are there painful, upsetting and disturbing elements to it which make treating it as a routine issue unhelpful? And of course, it is not just a matter for the child and the adoptive parents as grandparents, uncles, aunts and other family members will become involved and eventually a very wide range of formal and informal social institutions (Kirk (1964), Simmonds (2000)).

The focus so far on this period of adoption practice should not blunt the fact that the question of secrecy has disappeared to be replaced by a more widely shared conviction supported by research that openness in adoption has distinct advantages to the child, the adoptive parents and the birth parents. There are numerous aspects to this including pre-adoption meetings between prospective adopters and birth parent/s/families, the exchange of detailed information about the child's needs, development, heritage and history and contact arrangements either direct or indirect with potentially a wide range of birth family members. Each of these issues needs to be underpinned by preparation, consultation and on-going support to the parties involved. In itself, the concept of openness (Gritter (1997)) has developed from the idea of 'structured openness' to that of 'communicative openness' (Grotevant (1998), (2000)). In the former, the adoption arrangement might be designated as open. However, as lived family experience while there may have been pre-placement meetings, sharing of information and some form of contact all of this is suffused with anxiety or discomfort. On the other hand, arrangements may be designated as closed with no meetings, little information and no contact but the openness of the family to the

---

[2]   Paragraph 29.

significance of the adoption in their life makes information exchange between them and recognition of the complex feelings that might be stirred up manageable. This form of openness is called by Brodzinsky (2002) 'communicative openness'. The emphasis then is not on the structure of the arrangement but the family processes and dynamics that facilitate it. Brodzinsky (2004) reports in a study of 63 adopted children adopted under 18 months that both structural and communicative openness was positively correlated with children's rating of their self-esteem as well as age at placement. A poor level of communicative openness was the only variable that independently predicted behavioural problems. The concept is enormously valuable in explaining the need that all human beings have to create coherent meaning about events in their lives especially where this is challenging or disturbing. It strongly suggests why secrecy is so damaging and why coherent narratives of even very painful events might be so important. It is of course the basis for much counselling and psychotherapy practice (McClusky (2005)).

There are a number of related strands of research that support this. The 'Contact After Adoption' study (Neil (2000), (2002), (2003), (2004a), (2004b)) has indicated the complexity of contact arrangements and the extent to which they depend on the capacity of various parties to understand its purpose, manage it 'thoughtfully' and sustain this over time. Neil (2003) says 'the most successful contact arrangements were those in which the parents or carers demonstrated high levels of empathy or sensitivity towards the child and the birth parent.'[3] They continue:

> 'sensitive adopters and foster carers could understand the child's experience and were constantly trying to make sense of the past and present for the child. Most could calmly anticipate that the child would have further issues to address regarding birth family relationships through adolescence and adulthood.'[4]

The psychological foundation of these issues is well articulated in attachment theory – particularly those developments that elaborate the process by which secure attachment relationships lay the foundation for mind mindedness and reflective function – the capacity to understand that other people have thoughts, emotions and behave in ways that may be similar or different to one's own. (Fonagy (2002)) In particular these become coherent narrative expectations of internal representations of the self in relationships. (Bowlby (1969); Heard (1997)) This can be summarised in the general rule:

> 'If I am upset, then A will understand this and know how to comfort me in a way that makes me feel better.'

This process involves the combined sensory modes of communication – sight, touch, hearing, smell and probably taste – formed into a rhythmic and patterned form of interaction. The obverse of this narrative expectation is:

> 'If B is upset, then I can understand this and know how to comfort B in a way that makes them feel better.'

This is a simple idea but a powerful one when human beings strive to create and build relationships and establish meaningful forms of cooperative endeavour in families, with friends, at school, work or at play.

The Thomas Coram Adoption study (Hodges (2003), (2004)) has explored the nature of these narrative representations of helpful interactions with two groups of children placed for adoption – those placed under one year and a group of older children (mean = 6 years 1 month) who had various experiences of maltreatment. These two groups of children were asked to complete an unfinished story about animals or other children in routinely stressful circumstances. The way the child engaged with the task and completed the story indicates their typical ways of understanding the above script – are people likely to be helpful and can they be approached if

---

there are problems? The maltreated, late-placed group showed more avoidance of the task itself, the dilemmas in the stories and could show extreme aggression by or towards the characters and catastrophic endings to the stories than the infant-placed group. Follow up after a year demonstrated some positive change in the maltreated group of children. They conclude:

> 'internal working models of attachment relationships were far from transformed …. On the whole, positive adult characteristics increased, but negative ones did not significantly decrease…. It appears that aspects of new and more positive relationships develop but they do not automatically transform the already established representations.'[5]

After two years in placement, progress had continued for most of the later-placed children with an increase in their capacity to find credible solutions to dilemmas (in the story stems), and in children seeking help.'[6] Similar issues are discussed in the Rushton (2003) study. They report that 73% of the parents of 61 children placed between five and nine years of age had developed an attachment relationship by the end of the first year of placements. In the remaining 27%, most of the non-attached relationships were reciprocated by both the child and the parents. As with Steele's sample, these children were reported as showing non-compliant behaviour, anger and rage as well as puzzling behaviours. There was an absence of warmth towards the parents, or false affection, superficiality and distancing – all indicative of defences against intimacy.

The implications of this kind of research confirm the view that the later the placement is made combined with the nature, intensity and length of the child's adverse pre-placement experiences, the more challenges the adoptive parents will face in creating a family life that is satisfying for them and satisfactory for the child. It is almost too simple to say, but a combination of 'helpfulness', 'concern' and 'cooperation' expressed in a thoughtful way is the key to resolving most of the 'story stems' of daily living in family life –getting up in the morning, going to bed, eating, washing, dressing, going to school, homework, playing, going on holiday. However, when these fundamental expectations about the positive resolution of daily living have become thwarted in the early experiences of the child – a belief in and knowledge about the dynamics of how to be helpful, how to express concern and how to be cooperative is in serious danger of deteriorating into a disturbing relationship. A parent's greater belief in and understanding of these critical issues is important in engaging the child in more cooperative relationships. But it is by no means always the case that adults/parents do evidence this greater belief or understanding – indeed it is likely to have played a significant part in the reason why the child was placed for adoption. In relation to adoptive parents, these factors have been demonstrated in the Coram study to be significant in the measurement of adopters' 'attachment status'. 70% of their adopters were rated as 'secure' or 'earned secure' in the adult attachment interview, a rating which is consistent with an approach to problem-solving which is informed by helpfulness, concern and cooperation. However, 11 adoptive mothers were rated as 'unresolved' in their attachment status where their own unhappy childhoods still preoccupied them in an unhelpful way which in turn interfered with their capacity to understand or develop any insight or empathy for their child's hostile or rejecting behaviour. In both children and adults if beliefs and expectations about helpfulness, concern or cooperation become dominated by the anticipation that something bad will happen or by a memory that the expectation will be frustrated, ignored and responded to in some bizarre, dangerous or threatening way, it can make family life very difficult indeed.

The current picture of adoptive family life is a complex one. There is not a single study which questions from a child development perspective the advantage and importance of early placement wherever possible. The Rushton studies indicate that a large enough proportion of late-placed children make satisfactorily and satisfying relationships for those concerned. However, a significant number do not or at least have not. It is then that the resilience of adoptive parents becomes critical. Steele (1999) quotes some of their views: 'She's an angel and a devil.' Another says that she is a 'gorgeous pain in the neck, fun to have around'. Another said 'some days you love him to bits other days you want to send him to the other part of the world.'

---

5   P 360.

6   P 64.

One parent clearly experienced a range of emotions: 'she's done things with my emotions no one else has, she brings me from complete and utter happiness to the depths of despair in half an hour.'[7]

There are complex messages from these adopters. They represent on the one hand a reflective appreciation of the very different sides to these children's characters – something these parents know and have found a way of thinking and talking about. On the other, there is nothing 'cute' about the discovery of a 'devil at the table' or wanting to send a child to the other side of the world. They are experiences that can have real consequences for adopters and their physical and mental health. The consequence of living with these powerful splits in the characters of children over time needs to be carefully evaluated.

It is clear from many studies that the evolution of openness in adoption practice has been very important even if there are many aspects of it that are not fully understood. The recent development of the concept of communicative openness is helpful in emphasising the importance of adoptive families allowing themselves to think about, talk about and understand adoption-related matters even if they are painful and upsetting. But having moved into this new phase and in the process dismantled the earlier social and individual defence of the 'perfection' of both adopters and children considerable care needs to exercised. We know, whatever the defensive images in the past, that adopters were never perfect and even with the advantage of early placement and the absence of significant developmental adversity associated with abuse and neglect, family life was still family life – complex. The anxiety of dealing with adoption-related information and adoption-related family dynamics was never easy. In the current context, openness means being open to a wide range of issues:

- acknowledgment that adoptive family life is different to born to family life

- the child has a 'born-to' heritage that will be different to the heritage they acquire through adoption – ethnicity, class, culture, language, materially, religion, location, aspiration

- discontinuity brought about through transfer from one family to another whenever it occurred will be significant and may evoke strong feelings of loss, rejection, longing and disapproval

- where there are discontinuities of experience in a child's life, these do not readily translate from one setting or 'language' into another

- the child who is loved and cherished in their adoptive home may have been caused considerable pain or been damaged by their pre-adoption experience and still remain loyal to those people involved

- the child may develop along a developmental pathway distinct from that that might be expected from a born-to child

- the 'born-to' family and the adoptive family may influence one another in a series of interlocking spirals

- the child's personal adoption identity may easily come subject to public scrutiny in school, in sporting, artistic and recreation activity and in health provision

- any of this will change in the course of time in unexpected ways

- feelings of belonging and family membership may exist alongside feelings of longing for another family and betrayal.

These are profound emotional and social discontinuities and they can make themselves felt at any time. They are discontinuities that add to those already experienced in non-adoptive family life. Family life by its very nature involves numerous dimensions of developmental transition – the parental relationship and the way it changes, sibling relationships, extended family, and the arrivals and loss of members over time. There are also the accidents and mishaps of life.

---

[7]   P 35.

Growth, loss, change, loyalty, betrayal, jealousy, rivalry and many other feelings arise from and fuel these transitions. How these disjunctions, discontinuities and their effects work themselves into family life over time is very difficult to predict. How families manage disjunction and discontinuity in an open way without being overwhelmed by the threats or risks they pose is also important.

In the kinds of placements currently made, these are serious questions. Openness to the past may well mean being open to the trauma of the past in the present. (Howe (2004), MacAskill (2002)) The adoptive family may well inherent the birth parent/s difficulties – their pain and trauma – through the medium of the child's fearfulness and anxiety and the defences they use to protect themselves. Not thinking or not being able to think about what has been left behind or what has been carried forward may be characteristic of these defences. These may be overlaid by confusing and distracting emotional and behavioural strategies. For many adoptive families their resilience, empathy and support networks will carry them through. For a significant number of others, the impact of the secondary trauma on the family (Cairns (2002)) that results from importing the child's original trauma will be such that they may be in danger of being overwhelmed. They may then present themselves to health and particularly mental health, education and social services for help. It is to be hoped that the new duties on local authorities to assess for adoption support services under the Adoption and Children Act 2002 will respond. The dynamics of helpfulness, concern and cooperation identified above must drive both assessment and service provision. The risk is that the traumatised nature of some social service, education and health provision may make this difficult. (Hornby (1993)) This is not just a question of resources but of the dynamics of help-seeking and help-giving in traumatised circumstances. Communicative openness is not just a matter for adoptive families but for adoption services as well whether they are generalist or specialist. Professionals coming into contact with traumatised families can easily become the recipients of powerful and disturbing feelings and indeed it may be important for them to do so to be effective. It is difficult for professionals to empathise with a family's predicament if they are not open to the feelings they are struggling with. These feelings are infectious in their quality and dynamics and can make helpful thinking particularly difficult. Bureaucratic approaches to assessment of adoption support needs may be important in creating fair and equitable systems of resource distribution and public accountability but they can be experienced as defensive and become easy objects for the transmission of infectious emotion.

In conclusion, adoption can be a durable solution for children in the most difficult of circumstances. It is by no means a straightforward solution and, apart from Portugal, is not available as an option for children in the public care system in the rest of Europe. The present system has evolved out of a relatively long period of practice involving many thousands of children where the evidence of its success is excellent. However, it is not easy to import the lessons from that period because both social circumstances and the characteristics of the children needing placement are so different. The one lesson that has been learnt has been the importance of openness and particularly the more recent concept of communicative openness. It is a concept that is well supported by what we know about the conditions and dynamics which promote the healthy development of children and family life generally. However, for many adoptive families this means being open to the impact of significant discontinuity as well as the potential for importing experiences of traumatic origin. The fright, panic and confusion this can cause and its presentation by family members in various symptoms and problem constellations to different professional groups must be taken seriously. Adoptive family life is a privatised solution to a public health issue. Responding to and supporting these families throughout the life cycle in an open, communicative and non traumatising way will be a serious challenge.

REFERENCES

Ansfield, J *The Adopted Child* (Springfield, Il, Thomas, 1971)

Beek, M, Schofield, G *Providing a Secure Base in Long-Term foster Care* (London, BAAF, 2004)

Bond, H *If you don't stick with me, who will? The challenges and rewards of foster care* (London, BAAF, 2005)

Bowlby, J *Attachment and Loss* vol 1 (London, Hogarth Press, 1969)

Brodzinsky, D, Pinderhughes E 'Parenting and child development in adoptive families' in Bornstein, M *Handbook of parenting*: *Children and parenting* (Hillsdale, NJ, Lawrence Erlbaum Associates, 2nd edn, 2002)

Byrd, AD 'The case for confidential adoption' (1988) 46 Public Welfare 20–23

Cairns, B *Fostering Attachments: Long-term outcomes in family group care* (London, BAAF, 2004)

Cairns, K *Attachment, trauma and resilience: therapeutic caring for children* (London, BAAF, 2002)

Catherine MacAskill *Safe Contact: Children in Permanent Placement and Their Birth Relatives* (Lyme Regis, Russell House Publishing, 2002)

Cm 5017 (London, HMSO)

Fonagy, P, Gergely, G, Jurist, E, Target, M *Affect Regulation, Mentalization, and the Development of the Self* (New York, NY, Other Press, 2002)

Gilleard, C, Pond, C, Scammell, A, Lobo, R, Simporis, K, Rawaf, S *Well-Being in Wandsworth: A Public Mental Health Audit* (London, Wandsworth Primary Care Trust & South West London and St. George's Mental Health NHS Trust, 2005)

Gritter, J *The Spirit of Open Adoption* (Washington DC, Child Welfare League of America, 1997)

Grotevant, H, McRoy, R *Openness in Adoption: Exploring family connections* (Thousand Oaks, CA, Sage Publications, 1998)

Grotevant, H, Dunbar, N, Kohler, J, Esau, A 'Adoptive Identity : How contexts within and beyond the family shape developmental pathways' (2000) 49 Family Relations 379–387

Heard, D, Lake B *The Challenge of Attachment for Caregiving* (London, Routledge, 1997)

Hirst, M *Loving & Living with Traumatised Children* (London, BAAF, 2005)

Hodges, J, Steele, M, Hillman, S, Henderson, K, Kaniuk, J, 'Changes in the Attachment Representations Over the First Year of Adoptive Placement: Narratives of Maltreated Children' (2003) 8–3 Clinical Child Psychology and Psychiatry 351–367

Hornby, S *Collaborative Care: Interprofessional, Interagency and Interpersonal* (London, Blackwell, 1993)

Houghton Committee Report *Report of the Departmental Committee on the Adoption of Children* (London, Home Office and Scottish Education Department, 1972)

Howe, D *Adopters on Adoption* (London, BAAF, 2003)

Howe, D, Steele, M 'Contact in cases in which children have been traumatically abused or neglected by their birth parents' in Neil, E, Howe, D *Contact in Adoption and Permanent Foster Care* (London, BAAF, 2004)

Kaniuk J, Steele M, Hodges J 'Report on a longitudinal research project, exploring the development of attachments between older, hard-to-place children and their adopters over the first two years of placement' (2004) 28–2 Adoption and Fostering 61–67

Kirk, H *Shared Fate* (New York, Free Books, 1964)

Kornitzer, M *Adoption* (London, Putnam, 1976)

Kraft, A, Palumbo, J, Mitchell, D, Woods, P, Schmidt, A 'Some theoretical considerations on confidential adoptions, part 2' (1985a) 2 The Adoptive Parent, Child and Adolescent Social Work 69–82

Kraft, A, Palumbo, J, Woods, P, Schmidt, A, Tucker, N 'Some theoretical considerations on confidential adoptions, part 3' (1985b) 2 The Adopted Child, Child and Adolescent Social Work 139–153

MacAskill, C *Safe Contact: Children in Permanent Placement and Their Birth Relatives* (Lyme Regis, Russell House Publishing, 2002)

McClusky, U *To Be Met as a Person: The dynamics of attachment in professional encounters* (London, Karnac, 2005)

Menzies Lyth, I *Containing Anxiety in Institutions* (London, Free Association Books, 1988)

Monck, E, Reynolds, J, Wigfall, V *The Role of Concurrency Planning: Making Placements for Young Children* (London, BAAF, 2003)

Neil, E 'The reason why young children are placed for adoption: Findings from a recently placed sample and implications for future identity issues' (2000) 5 (4) Child and Family Social Work 303–316

Neil, E 'Contact after adoption: The role of agencies in making and supporting contact plans' (2002) 26(1) Adoption and Fostering 25–38

Neil, E, Beek, M, Schofield, G 'Thinking about and managing contact in Permanent Placements: The Differences and Similarities between Adoptive Parents and Foster Carers' (2003) 8(3) Clinical Child Psychology and Psychiatry 401–418

Neil, E, Howe *Contact in Adoption and Permanent Foster Care* (London, BAAF, 2004b)

Neil, N 'The 'Contact after Adoption' study: indirect contact and adoptive parents' communication about adoption' in Neil and Howe *Performance and Innovation Unit (2000) Prime Minister's Review of Adoption* (Cabinet Office, 2004a)

Rushton A, Mayes, D, Dance, C, Quinton, D 'Parenting Late-Placed Children' (2003) 8–3 Clinical Child Psychology and Psychiatry 389–400

Rutter, M 'Clinical implications of attachment concepts: Retrospect and prospect' in L Atkinson & K Zucker (eds) *Attachment and Psychopathology* (London, Guilford Press, 1997)

Rutter, M 'Developmental catch up, and deficit, following adoption after severe global early deprivation. English and Romanian adoptees (ERA) study team' (1998) 39 Journal of Child Psychology and Psychiatry 465–476

Secretary of State for Health *Adoption: a new approach* (2000)

Simmonds, J 'The Adoption Narrative: Stories that We Tell and Those that We Can't' in Treacher, A, Katz I *The Dynamics of Adoption* (London, Jessica Kingsley, 2000)

Sinclair, I *Fostering Now: Messages from Research* (London, Jessica Kingsley, 2005)

Singleton et al *Psychiatric Morbidity among Adults living in Private Households* (The Office of National Statistics, 2001)

Steele, M, Kaniuk, J, Hodges, J, Haworth, C, Huss S 'The Use of the Adult Attachment Interview: Implications for Assessment in Adoption and Foster Care' in *Assessment, Preparation and Support: Implications from Research* (London, BAAF, 1999)

Triseliotis, J *In Search of Origins* (London, Routledge and Kegan Paul, 1973)

Triseliotis, J, Feast, J, Kyle F *The Adoption Triangle Revisited* (London, BAAF, 2005)

Ward, H, Skuse, T, Munro, E 'The Best of Times, the worst of times: Young people's views of care and accommodation' (2005) 29–1 Adoption and Fostering 8–17

Wieder, H 'On when and whether to disclose about adoption' (1978) 26(4) Journal of the American Psychoanalytic Association 793–811

Wilson, K, Sinclair, I, Taylor, C, Pithouse, Sellick C *Fostering Success: An Exploration of the Research Literature in Foster Care* (London, Social Care Institute for Excellence, 2004)

THE DRAFT CHILDREN AND ADOPTION BILL

Lord Justice Wall
Court of Appeal

SUMMARY OF PAPER

Lord Justice Wall welcomed the draft Children and Adoption Bill but made reference to the article produced in the July edition of 'Family Law' by Judith Masson and Cathy Humphreys. Nicholls LJ thought an alternative version of the Sermon on the Mount might be appropriate – 'blessed are those who expect nothing'! Now the Bill is published we can see it does more than was expected. The Bill is due to go before the Grand Committee very shortly. The debate on the Bill in the House of Lords was disappointing and of rather poor quality. The amendments made were rather silly and it is hoped this will be rectified when the Bill is properly debated.

It is clear that parents need to be empowered and able to make proper decisions. The court is not the right place to debate these decisions and thus the court should have facilities to point the parties in other direction. When the work began to consider the difficulties with contact it was a project to consider enforcement. It was then realised that the problem was broader than that, and what judges need now are measures both for facilitation and enforcement. Statutes are designed to be expansive and no doubt the advocates will try to achieve this in the Court of Appeal!

There has been one amendment to which Wall LJ made particular reference and that was Family Assistance Orders. Originally these were not in the Bill at all but it has now been agreed that these should be put in. Use of the orders has been limited because to date the orders only lasted for six months. The Government has now taken on board the point as to 12 months but still thinks all the parties must agree to a Family Assistance Order being put in place. Wall LJ failed to see the logic of that. He wished to propose to Thorpe LJ a resolution from the conference which urged the Government to consider that the final Bill should remove the need for the consent of all those who are to be named in a Family Assistance Order. Although these types of order would be something of a different animal, there was a need for both.

Lastly, Wall LJ turned to the question of resources. The Bill would be a burden on CAFCASS but was seen as an opportunity to create fully integrated services for the family. The changes were supposed to be cash neutral. Wall LJ commented that he was disappointed that new initiatives cannot be expansive but always need to come at the expense of something else. He was concerned to read that there were no additional resources although the Scrutiny Committee were clear in their recommendations. The scheme was to be properly funded if it is to have potential for judicial and professional innovative thinking. The Bill does not address domestic violence which is a key factor to consider in making contact work. This is a mistake which has been made previously and should not be repeated.

As if in expiation for having added the eponymous Family Law Act 1996 to the list of family law statutes abandoned or repealed before implementation, the Government seems recently to have gone into healthy, if not altogether co-ordinated, legislative overdrive in the family justice field. Europe, of course, is never far away. Apart from legislation emerging directly from the European Commission, such as Brussels II and Brussels IIA, s 19(1)(a) of the Human Rights Act 1998 requires the relevant minister in charge of a Bill in either House of Parliament to make a statement of compatibility with ECHR. And in the case of the Gender Recognition Act 2004 for example (which will permit a transsexual person who has obtained a full gender recognition certificate to marry a person of the gender opposite to the transsexual person's acquired gender)[1] there can be no doubt that the Act derives its existence from decisions by the Grand Chamber of the European Court of Human Rights and the decision of the House of Lords in *Bellinger v Bellinger* .[2]

We also have the creation of an English Children's Commissioner in the Children Act 2004, although his general function is vague ('promoting awareness of the views and interests of children in England')[3] and his powers extremely limited. It remains to be seen what the first incumbent does with the post.

In passing, s 62 of the Children Act 2004 causes a wry smile to cross the faces of those who deal regularly with government, and should, perhaps cause others to raise a glass to Munby J who, in a judgment handed down on 19 March 2004[4], told Members of Parliament that they were in contempt of court every time their constituents attended a surgery to consult them about litigation involving their children – especially if, in the process, the constituent disclosed confidential documents about the proceedings to the unwitting MP. Nothing arouses the legislative instincts of MPs more than a suggestion they may be doing something unlawful and the result, before you could say, 'Parliamentary draughtsman' was s 62 of the Children Act 2004 which effectively – and, it has to be said, sensibly – decriminalises contempt in a number of situations, notably, of course, where the litigant seeks advice from his MP, the CAB or a McKenzie friend.[5]

In addition, apart from the long overdue Adoption and Children Act 2002, we have the recognition of the rights of same sex couples in the Civil Partnership Act 2004. We still do not, however, have statutory recognition of the rights of cohabiting heterosexual couples – a reform long overdue (and fortunately on the agenda of the Law Commission). Also missing, of course, are proposals for the reform of the current, highly unsatisfactory, law of divorce.

Some legislation plainly has its origins in the fact that the issues it addresses remain high on the political agenda. Thus the Domestic Violence, Crime and Victims Act 2004 seeks to address a mixed bag of issues, perhaps the most relevant of which for family practitioners is the provision which makes breach of a non-molestation order a criminal offence. Quite how this will operate in practice, and quite how much it will exacerbate delays in the system – particularly if alleged contemnors opt for jury trial in the Crown Court – remain to be seen.

The piece of prospective legislation which I have been asked to address falls into the same generic mould, although against some of the major pieces of social legislation I have identified so far, it may seem curious that I should be addressing a paper and speaking to something which is not even yet an Act, and may never become so, namely the Children and Adoption Bill (hereinafter 'the Bill'), a measure being introduced in the House of Lords in the very week when, behind schedule, I began to write this paper.[6]

For me, the Bill was a welcome surprise when the Government produced it prior to the General Election. It remains no less of a surprise that it has resurfaced after 6 May 2005, and now begins its interrupted progress through Parliament. Unfortunately, the main committee stages of the Bill will not begin until October, and the Bill, if enacted, is unlikely to be on the statute book before the spring of next year at the earliest. I will not, accordingly, be able to update the conference in September about the Bill's progress. On the other hand, the timetable does allow for comment and attempts to persuade the Government to amend parts of it.

---

[1]   Gender Recognition Act 2004, ss 1, 9 and 11.

[2]   [2003] UKHL 21, [2003] 2 All ER 593.

[3]   Children Act 2004, s 2(1).

[4]   *Re B (A Child) (Disclosure)* [2004] EWHC 411 (Fam), [2004] 2 FLR 142 at 190 (para 136).

[5]   As to the latter, see also the decision of the Court of Appeal in the cases of the children of Messrs O'Connell, Watson and Whelan [2005] 2 FCR 563.

[6]   The Bill was printed on 13 June 2005: the first opposition amendments are dated 30 June 2005.

Part I of the Bill[7] has its origins in the proposals contained in the report, entitled *Making Contact Work*, published in March 2002 by the Children Act Sub-Committee (CASC) of the Lord Chancellor's Advisory Board on Family Law (ABFL).[8] I propose, therefore, to examine it by reference to those recommendations.[9] Space does not permit an analysis of the Government's eventual green paper in response,[10] but the report of the House of Commons Constitutional Affair Select Committee[11] is significant, as is the pre-legislative scrutiny the Bill received from a joint Commons/House of Lords committee[12] (hereinafter called 'the Scrutiny Committee'), and the Government's reply.[13] I am also grateful to Judith Masson and Cathy Humphreys for their article 'Facilitating and Enforcing Contact: The Bill and the Ten Per Cent'.[14]

I have attached the entirety of CASC's recommendations as an Appendix to this paper, partly because it is instructive to compare original recommendations with statutory proposals, but also because I think it important to note that CASC was not simply addressing the enforcement of contact orders. It saw the approach to contact between separated parents and their children as multi-faceted, and as requiring a wide variety of responses. I remain convinced that if we are to provide a durable framework for such contact, it must be part of a coherent, much broader post-separation parenting strategy which will, in turn, provide a much greater variety of options for parents and children, one of which will be access to the courts, albeit that such an option will be low on the list, save perhaps where it is required to protect parents and children from abuse.

The context in which CASC gave its advice is clear from the Report, and it is, I think worth reproducing from the body of the text CASC's statement of the themes which emerged from its consultation. These were:

(1) a general dissatisfaction with the legal process as a mechanism for resolving and enforcing contact disputes;

(2) the need at an early stage to provide information for separating parents and their children about the likely effects of the separation, the difficulties they are likely to encounter, and the means whereby those difficulties can be addressed;

(3) the need to address the problem by a wide range of different mechanisms which are not based on court proceedings; and

(4) the need to ensure that those alternative mechanisms to court proceedings are in place and are accessible to those who need them.

As to the provision of information for separating couples and their children – a matter which CASC saw as being of critical importance – it identified the following broad areas as being of particular importance:

---

[7] This paper addresses only Part I of the Bill, which relates to contact and Family Assistance Orders. Part II relates to adoptions with a foreign element.

[8] ABFL was set up to advise the Government on the implementation of the Family Law Act 1996. The creation of ABFL broadly coincided with the Government's much criticised disbandment of the Children Act Advisory Committee (CAAC). In part as a result of the protests at the disbandment of CAAC, a sub-committee of ABFL was created to address issues of policy arising under the Children Act 1989. This took the title of the Children Act Sub-Committee (CASC). The members of CASC were Wall J, Sir Thomas Boyd-Carpenter (Chair of ABFL), two solicitors (Naomi Angel and Jane Simpson), a psychiatrist (Dr Carole Kaplan), an Assistant Chief Probation Officer (David Skidmore), Anthony Wells, former Director of the National Council for Family Proceedings, and Arran Poyser, senior inspector with HM Magistrates' Courts Service Inspectorate. As the Government decided not to implement the Family Law Act 1996, ABFL became defunct, and CASC fell with it. Fortunately, due largely to the efforts of Thorpe LJ and the President's Inter-disciplinary Committee, the struggle to create a Family Justice Council was finally successful in 2004.

[9] CASC's recommendations were set out in Chapter 16 of its report which, for ease of reference, is attached to this paper as Appendix 1.

[10] *Parental Separation: Children's Needs and Parents' Responsibilities* (Cm 6273, July 2004 (available at www.dfes.gov.uk/childrensneeds)).

[11] *Family Justice: the operation of the family courts: House of Commons Constitutional Affairs Committee*: fourth report of Session 2004–5 published 2 March 2005: HC 116–1.

[12] Joint Committee on the Draft Children (Contact) and Adoption Bill: First Report HL Paper 100–1/HC 400–1.

[13] Cm 6583, June 2005.

[14] [2005] Fam Law 548.

- the importance to children of maintaining contact wherever possible with the parent with whom they are not living;

- the very substantial difficulties involved in successful post-separation parenting for both parents;

- the serious harm caused to children by continuing acrimony between their parents; and

- the services which are available to assist in the resolution of difficulties over contact.

THE BILL

So what does Part I of the Bill do? In essence, it does two things. The first is to add a series of sections (11A to 11P) to s 11 of the Children Act 1989 (the Act) which, as originally drafted, is headed 'General principles and supplementary provisions'. The second is to amend s 16 of the Act, which deals with Family Assistance Orders. I will deal with each of these in turn.

Section 11(7) of the Act already provides that an order under s 8 of the Act (which, of course, includes a contact order) '(a) may contain directions about how it is to be carried into effect' and '(b) impose conditions which must be complied with' by the person in whose favour the order is made (sub-s (7)(b)(i)), the child's parents (sub-s (7)(b)(ii)), any non-parent with parental responsibility (sub-s (7)(b)(iii)) or with whom the child is living (sub-s (7)(b)(iv). These conditions may be time-limited (sub-s (7)(c)). Finally, a s 8 order may 'make such incidental, supplemental or consequential provision as the court thinks fit' (sub-s (7)(d)).

Widely as those provisions were drawn, there is a limit both to judicial inventiveness, and to the extent to which the broad discretionary power given by s 11(7)(d) can be used to impose enforceable conditions. For example, a condition imposed under s 11(7) that a man found to have been violent to his partner will not have contact with his child unless and until he has successfully completed a course for the perpetrators of domestic violence could not require the man to go on the course. Equally, it is difficult to see how s 11(7)(d) could be used to address the problems posed by the recalcitrant resident parent who is obstructing contact. Section 11(7)(d) would not empower the court, in my view, to require her to attend an information meeting or a parenting programme. It is, therefore, in my view, perfectly logical both to add and to spell out specific facilitative and coercive provisions to the court's powers at this point in the Act.

Clause 1 of the Bill (the proposed s 11A of the Act) seems to me reasonably clear. When the court is considering whether to make a contact order or an order varying or discharging a contact order, the court is empowered to make a 'contact activity direction' (henceforth 'the / a direction') (s 11A(1) and (2)). The direction is defined in s 11A(3) as a direction 'requiring an individual who is a party to the proceedings to take part in an activity that promotes contact with the child concerned'.

The direction has to specify the activity and the person providing the activity (s 11A(4)), and the activities in which the individual may be required to take part include (s 11A(5)):

(a) programmes, classes and counselling or guidance sessions of a kind that may assist a person as regards establishing, maintaining or improving contact with a child;

(b) session in which information or advice is given as regards making or operating arrangements for contact with a child, including making arrangements by means of mediation.

The direction does not, however, permit the court to require a party to undergo medical or psychiatric examination, assessment or treatment (s 11A(6)(a)); nor can an individual be required to take part in mediation (s 11A(6)(b)). A direction cannot be given on the same occasion as the court disposes finally of the proceedings as they relate to contact with the child concerned, but in considering whether to make a direction, s 1(1) of the Act applies, and the welfare of the child is the court paramount consideration.

So far, the position is clear, albeit open to some criticism. The proposed s 11B is headed, ominously, 'Contact activity directions: further provisions', and s 11B(1) is a bad start:

> 'A court may not make a contact activity direction in any proceedings unless there is a dispute as regards the provision about contact that the court is considering whether to make in the proceedings.'

In the Bill as first drafted, a contact activity direction could only have been made where the making of an order for contact was opposed. This formulation was criticised by the Family Law Bar Association, and its criticism was endorsed by the Scrutiny Committee. This appears to be the Government's response. In my view, the object of the exercise is to give the courts the maximum flexibility to deal with the wide variety of cases presented to it. Section 11A(1) provides an appropriate gateway. The court should have the powers in any case in which it is considering to make, vary or discharge a contact order. Section 11B(1) as drafted seems to me inconsistent with the objectives of the Bill.

Section 11B(2) excludes children from being the subject of directions (unless the child is one of the parents of the child who is the subject of the application). Section 11B(3)–(5) exclude directions being made in contact applications in adoption proceedings. Section 11B(6) appears to identify the circumstances in which a direction may come to an end and s 11(7) limits directions to individuals habitually resident in England and Wales.

Section 11C moves on to 'contact activity conditions' (hereinafter 'conditions'). It applies if in any family proceedings the court makes a contact order or an order varying contact. In these circumstances, the court may impose a condition 'requiring an individual to take part in an activity that promotes contact with the child' (s 11C(2)). The condition must specify the activity and the person providing the activity (s 11C(3)) and s 11A(5) and 11A(6) apply to conditions as they apply to directions.

Section 11D provides that a condition may not be made if the court is finally disposing of a contact application and providing for the adult and the child to have no contact. The person subject to the condition must be a party to the proceedings, and it can only apply to a child if the child is a parent of the child concerned in the proceedings. Similar conditions apply to orders made in the context of adoption proceedings and to the need for the recipient to be resident in England and Wales.

Section 11E identifies the criteria for making directions and conditions. The proposed activity must be appropriate to the circumstances of the case (s 11E(2)). The provider of the activity must be suitable to provide it (s 11E(3)). The activity must be available in a place to which it is reasonable to expect the person in question to travel (s 11E(4)). The court must obtain and consider information about the individual and the likely effect of a direction, or condition, on them (s 11E(5)). That information includes any conflict with an individual's religious beliefs and any interference with his or her working hours or attendance at an educational establishment (s 11E(6)). The court can ask an officer of CAFCASS (or its Welsh counterpart) to obtain the information.

Section 11F is an enabling provision for the Secretary of State to make regulations authorising payment to assist prescribed individuals in paying charges or fees imposed by those providing specified activities.

Section 11G provides that the court may asked a CAFCASS officer to monitor compliance with a contact activity direction or condition, and to report to the court on any failure by an individual to comply. This is, I think, an important provision.

Section 11H, which is entitled 'Monitoring Contact', is also important. The court may ask a CAFCASS officer to monitor compliance with a contact order, and to report to the court on such matters relating to compliance as the court may specify (s 11H(2)). The monitoring period is not to exceed 12 months (s 11H(5)). Once again, this seems to me an important provision, with (potentially) substantial resource implications.

Section 11I creates a 'warning notice'. Every contact order must have attached to it a notice warning of the consequences of failing to comply with the contact order.

Section 11J deals with enforcement. If the court is satisfied beyond reasonable doubt that a person has failed without reasonable excuse to comply with a contact order, it may make an 'enforcement order' imposing on the person an unpaid work requirement. The burden of establishing the 'reasonable excuse' is on the person claiming it, and here the burden of proof is the balance of probabilities. The only people who can apply for enforcement orders are: (1) the person required by the order to afford contact; (2) the person in whose favour the contact order has been made; and (3) the child concerned (only with permission and if the court is satisfied that he or she has sufficient understanding to make the application. The order once made can be suspended and more than one order can be made at a time. Provision as regards an unpaid work requirement, revocation and amendment and the consequences of failure to comply are set out in a new Sch A1 to the Act.

Section 11K is largely procedural. Section 11L seeks to relate the enforcement order to the contact order. Before making the former the court must be satisfied that making the order proposed is necessary to secure the person's compliant with the contact order and that the likely effect of the order proposed is proportionate to the seriousness of the breach of the contact order (s 11L(1)). The unpaid work must be local, and information must be obtained about the effect of the order on the individual. CAFCASS may be asked to obtain it. In making an enforcement order, the welfare of the child is not paramount: the court must, however, take it into account (s 11L(7)).

Section 11M provides that on making an enforcement order 'the court is to ask' an officer of CAFCASS or its Welsh equivalent to monitor compliance and to report to the court. Section 11N provides for a notice to be attached to the enforcement order warning of the consequences of failing to comply with it.

Section 11O deals with compensation for financial loss. If the court is satisfied that an individual has failed to comply with a contact order and 'a relevant party to the proceedings' has suffered financial loss by reason of the breach, the court is empowered to make an order requiring the individual in breach to pay compensation in respect of the financial loss (s 11O(2)). There is a defence of 'reasonable excuse' for which the burden is on the person claim to have a reasonable excuse (s 11O(3) and (4)). The child who is the subject of the proceedings may claim, with the court's permission and if the court is satisfied he or she has sufficient understanding to make the application. An amount ordered to be paid as compensation may be recovered as a 'civil debt' (s 11O(11)). Once again, the child's welfare is to be taken into account, but is not paramount (s 11O(13)). Section 11P is largely procedural.

Finally, Part I of the Bill deals with amendments to Family Assistance Orders (FAO) under s 16 of the Act. These were omitted from the Bill as originally drafted, and appear to have be reinserted not least as a consequence of a protest from the Scrutiny Committee. However, although the requirement for 'exceptional circumstances' is removed, and although the period of the operation of the order is extended from 6 months to 12, and although there is a new provision empowering the court to direct the officer of CAFCASS 'to give advice and assistance as regards establishing, improving and maintaining contact to such of the persons named in the order', the Government stubbornly refuses to accept the recommendation of both the Scrutiny Committee and CASC (among many others) to remove the provision that an FAO cannot be made unless the court 'has obtained the consent of every person to be named in the order other than the child'.

DISCUSSION

It seems to me that, broadly speaking, the Bill delivers on CASC's recommendations 26–29 (see Appendix 1). The power to refer to a parent to a psychiatrist or psychologist has been omitted. I understand that, There is a difficulty about the court compelling an unwilling individual to see a doctor, although a condition that such a person must do so could be a condition of contact under s 11(7)(d) of the Act. In reality, however, the difficulty of obtaining out-patient access to psychiatric advice on the NHS, it means, I think, that there will be no adult psychiatric input into contact proceedings.

The power to refer to specified contact activity directions is, however, in the proposed new s 11A of the Act, and I am reasonably confident that (provided the relevant facilities are available) the judiciary will be able to operate the statute effectively. Any initial difficulties of interpretation or practice should be capable of being resolved by one or two test cases being decided in the High Court or the Court of Appeal.

What concerns me much more is the perennial problem of resources, both in terms of available programmes and the funding to ensure that they can be utilised. This is a matter which also concerned the Scrutiny Committee, particularly in relation to CAFCASS. It pointed out that the Regulatory Impact Assessment (RIA) which accompanied the Green Paper claimed that the proposals would be resource neutral overall, and that this assertion had been repeated in the RIA which accompanied the Bill. The reasoning was that the cost of the new provisions would be met from the reduced expenditure on the repeated contact cases which would otherwise take place. The Minister told the Committee that CAFCASS had assured her that the change of direction away from detailed report writing and earlier intervention work would mean that fewer cases would end up in court, and would thus release the resources needed for the new duties proposed under the Bill.

The Committee was not convinced, nor am I. The Committee made six recommendations. They were that:

(1) the Government reconsider their assertion that the package of proposals contained in the Green Paper will lead to a reduction in caseload. The resource implications of an increase in caseload should be calculated and presented in the final RIA;

(2) the full RIA should include a detailed explanation of how both CAFCASS and the Court Service can expect to meet their increased remits within existing costs;

(3) the Government make clear what action it would take if extra resources were requested by CAFCASS or the Court Service following implementation of the legislation;

(4) the Government carry out a review of local service provision of contact activities. Ready access to these services is essential to the successful implementation of the Bill. Where gaps are found, the Government should be prepared to invest additional money to improve service provision and therefore, it is hoped, secure the anticipated future savings;

(5) in presenting the final RIA, the Government makes clear the basis of its assumed input values, makes explicit the connection between assumptions and associated estimates, and indicates the probability of costs and savings leaning towards the low- or high-end of the estimates. We also recommend that a summary of the estimated costs and savings associated with the two options is presented, so as to allow comparison of the relative merits of each proposal;

(6) prior to the introduction of the full Bill, the Government improve their knowledge of current child contact activity in the courts, either through direct collection of statistics or through further sampling. Doing so will allow the Government to either rely less on assumed inputs or improve its confidence in its assumptions, and so narrow its costs and savings estimate ranges.

The Government's response was, it must be said, somewhat complacent. It repeated its thesis that helping people avoid the court process would reduce the number of lengthy, contested hearings and repeated applications. However, 'for purely illustrative purposes' it would include in the RIA as published alongside the Bill an assessment of the cost to Government were caseload to rise.[15] It also said:

> 'CAFCASS is already adequately resourced, but we recognise that the Bill has resource implications for CAFCASS, and there will need to be a reduction in the number and length of reports commissioned from CAFCASS by the courts in order to allow it to focus more on its new problem solving role.'

I am always troubled by the proposition that sensible reform is never seen as expansive, and that the necessary reforms being implemented has always to be at the expense of something else. Thus the pivotal – and expansive – role which CAFCASS ought to be playing in the family justice system is never seen as such. I hope very much that the proposed changes will result in there being fewer cases in which an investigation by the CAFCASS Officer followed by a singe report and evidence in court will be required, but such cases will not go away, nor should the reporting ethos simply be abandoned. We are adding roles for CAFCASS, and it is frankly simplistic to think that a saving in report writing will free up time and resources to enable CAFCASS officers to play the wider, more proactive role the Bill and the judiciary both envisage.

So the old cry has to be repeated: CAFCASS must be properly funded to encompass all the various roles which those working in the family justice system envisage for it. The Government's expressed aim is 'to refocus the existing resources spent across government on protracted disputes about arrangements for children'. As I have already said, I hope very much that the reforms proposed reduce the numbers of such cases. But they will not go away, and if they are to be properly addressed, the whole range of facilities and remedies must be available. The government in its response to the Scrutiny Committee stated its belief that it had 'an adequate evidence base for the proposals' it had developed including quantitative data. I hope they are right.

OTHER ISSUES

An issue which threatens to hijack the Bill is the suggestion, which originated with the Constitutional Affairs Committee (CAC), that the Act should be amended to make a specific reference to the importance of sustaining the relationship between children and their non-resident parents. The Scrutiny Committee supported this proposal. The Government's response was cautious, and it did not commit itself. The prospect of a debate on the point was, however, clearly signalled in the first group of amendments proposed by the opposition, which included an amendment to the Act to the effect that in applying the welfare test, under s 1(1) the court should work on the rebuttable presumption that separated parents should be as fully and equally involved in the child's parenting as possible. The opposition also proposed a rebuttable presumption in favour of 'frequent and continuing contact', and a further rebuttable presumption that a non-resident parent be allowed contact 'for at least one-third of the child's time'. Other amendments proposed placing on the President the burden of keeping a register of mediators, with compulsory attendance at a meeting with a mediator before any s 8 order was made. A further clause proposed 'Parenting time plans' and a pilot scheme on early intervention.

I am not making a political point when I say that I find it difficult to separate out the sensible from the simply inappropriate and impracticable in the first batch of amendments put down by the Opposition. Certainly, when family lawyers hear the word 'presumption' they reach for their

---

15   At the time of writing, I have not been able to gain access to this document.

red pens/blue pencils. I shall be interested at the conference to hear views on whether the Act needs to spell out the need for the importance of maintaining the child's relationship with both parents. My personal view is that it is not necessary, and that the case law on the point is crystal clear. Any amendment would, accordingly, be for public perception purposes. That, it seems to me, is a political issue. I could certainly live with an amendment, provided it did not include any presumptions, which simply generate satellite litigation. However, since provisos are clearly required (see domestic violence) I suspect that any amendment would have to be so broad and qualified as to have little meaning.

A far more interesting question is whether or not the court should have the power to compel an unwilling parent to have contact with a child. This was an idea which the Scrutiny Committee embraced, and which the Government dismissed, in reasoning which, I have to say, is less than convincing:

> 'We would be concerned about the implications that would arise if contact orders were to be used to force someone, against their wishes, to have contact with a child. The child's welfare must be the paramount consideration in making decisions about their upbringing and there are serious issues raised about the potential distress, or even harm, such contact could cause to the child or children involved.
>
> Having said that, it is open to the court, under section 11(7) of the Act to impose conditions upon a contact order which must be complied with, including by any person in whose favour the contact order is made. That could include, for example, making it a condition of the order that the non-resident parent attends the ordered contact at a specified time and place. If a court does this, then a breach of that condition by not attending contact would constitute a breach of the order.
>
> Further, if a resident parent believes that the non-resident parent is not fulfilling his or her responsibilities, for instance by failing to attend contact provided for by the court order, he or she is of course free to seek a variation of the contact order.'

It does not seem to me that the last two paragraphs of this citation address the issue. The whole point is that this sort of absent parent does not make an application for contact. I can envisage cases where it would plainly be in the interests of a particular child to have contact with an unwilling absent parent. Why should the court in these circumstances not be able to make a contact order – perhaps on the application of the child? And why would a contact activity direction designed to educate the absent parent into exercising parental responsibility properly not be appropriate?

FAMILY ASSISTANCE ORDERS

As I have already indicate, it has to be said that the Government's reasoning on FAOs is singularly unimpressive. Both *Making Contact Work* and the Scrutiny Committee recommended: (1) increase to 12 months; (2) remove 'exceptional' circumstances; (3) address to CAFCASS; and (4) remove the proposition that everyone named in the order apart from the child must consent.

In its published response to the Scrutiny Committee's report, the Government agreed with (1)–(3) although it left in the reference to local authorities. In regard to (4), however, it stated:

> '28. We do not agree, though, that the requirement to obtain consent should be removed. While we appreciate the committee's intention that FAOs should be made in as many cases as would benefit from them, we do not believe that it would be constructive to make an order to "advise, assist and befriend" an unwilling, or even hostile party. It is, of course, only those adult parties named in the FAO who need give consent, rather than all parties to the case, meaning that where an FAO is made in respect of one parent but not the other, the other could not withhold consent and thereby prevent the FAO being made.
>
> 29. Our intention is that the Bill should cover two distinct concepts: a reformed FAO which will

remain a facilitative measure which can only be used with the consent of those parties named in the order; and, separately, provision for court to require CAFCASS to carry out monitoring of compliance with a contact order (in specified cases), a contact activity or an enforcement order. This monitoring role will not require any consent by parties, and will be used if the court considers it appropriate in the circumstances. In determining what is appropriate, we would expect that courts would wish to consult CAFCASS prior to making the order, and to take into account the availability of local CAFCASS resources.'

I am not persuaded by this reasoning. It is, I think, disingenuous to suggest that an FAO can be effective if it simply does not name one of the parents. I never made an FAO unless I had the consent of all the relevant parties (in practice both parent). I envisage the reformed FAO as being operated, through CAFCASS, on an identified and structured piece of work with the family concerned. The monitoring role seems to me quite different and more limited (s 11H(2)). I see no reason why parental consent should be required for an identified piece of work which the court thinks necessary and which CAFCASS can implement. A parent can be required to comply with a direction and a condition: why not an FAO?

CONCLUSION

I welcome the Bill. I am glad that some of the inappropriate concepts (eg curfews and electronic tagging) have been dropped. I think it important that the Bill should not be hijacked for political purposes, and that it retains its limited objectives, namely as part of the strategy to facilitate and enforce contact. I am sure it can be improved. It would be helpful, I think, if at the conference we could identify and agree aspects of the Bill which we wish to see altered, so that a direct message to this effect can be conveyed to the Government.

APPENDIX 1

AN EXTRACT FROM THE CASC REPORT: MAKING CONTACT WORK

CHAPTER 16: RECOMMENDATIONS

16.1 In of this chapter, we set out our recommendations. We have not, however, repeated all the conclusions on which they are based and which are set out in the text of each of the chapters in the report.

16.2 In making our recommendations, we are conscious that some of the actions we propose cannot be implemented immediately, either because they require primary legislation or because they require the allocation of additional resources not currently included in Departmental plans. Indeed, in some areas our recommendation is for further study, because we do not consider that there is sufficient evidence on which to base a definitive recommendation. In the case of other recommendations, however, we believe that immediate action could be taken.

16.3 Our recommendations in the first part of this chapter are listed under headings which follow the order in which they arise in the text of the Report. However, following the thinking in paragraph 16.2 we have identified in each case the category into which each recommendation falls, and the agency to which it is addressed.

16.4 In part 2 of this chapter we group the recommendations under the different headings to provide a cross-check.

16.5 The recommendations fall into the following four categories:

1   Those which can be implemented immediately;

2   Those which can be implemented by Government or its agents, but which require significant additional funding;

3   Those which require legislation;

4   Those which require further study before a specific recommendation can be made.

CHAPTER 3: THE PROVISION AND DISTRIBUTION OF INFORMATION TO SEPARATING AND DIVORCING PARENTS

1. We recommend that the Lord Chancellor's Department either prepares or commissions a leaflet setting out the approach of the courts to issues of contact. This should summarise the Sturge / Glaser report. It should also contain references to the decision of the Court of Appeal in *Re L, V, M and H (Contact: domestic violence)* and the approach of the court to cases where domestic violence is an issue. It should be designed to be made available to couples with children who have separated or who are contemplating separation.

2. We recommend that the Lord Chancellor's Department enters into immediate discussions with NFPI, CAFCASS and other interested parties in a co-ordinated approach aimed at providing comprehensive information of the kind identified by this consultation on a national

basis. That information should be available at the widest possible number of outlets possible, including on video and the internet.

In relation specifically to divorce proceedings, we recommend a review of the procedure under section 41 of the Matrimonial Causes Act with the particular aim of requiring information to be made available to divorcing couples with children.

(The recommendations in this Chapter are all within Category 1, and are addressed to the Lord Chancellor's Department)

CHAPTER 4: THE PROVISION OF INFORMATION TO CHILDREN

4. The Lord Chancellor's Department should conduct a survey of the information and advice currently available to children whose parents are having relationship difficulties or who have separated in order to ascertain its scope and quality.

5. As with our recommendation numbered 2, and subject to the nature and quality of the information currently available, the Department should enter into immediate discussions with the NFPI, CAFCASS and other interested parties in a co-ordinated approach aimed at providing age-appropriate information for children on the effects of parental separation and on contact.

The Department should take specific steps to ensure that access to all age appropriate information is available to children through CAFCASS in both paper and electronic form and that wherever possible children should have access to officers of CAFCASS by telephone.

(The recommendations in this Chapter are also all within Category 1, and are addressed to the Lord Chancellor's Department)

CHAPTER 6: CAFCASS

7. In recognition of the importance of *CAFCASS* and of the vital role which it has to play in the Family Justice System, the Lord Chancellor's Department should ensure that *CAFCASS* is properly funded to undertake both the role of reporting to the court in children's cases and the important functions it has to perform in its advisory and support service. These include the provision of information to parents and children involved in relationship breakdown.

(Category 2: Agency – the Lord Chancellor's Department)

CHAPTER 7: MEDIATION

8. We recommend that judges and magistrates should be given the power to refer parties to mediation, although the involvement of children in the mediation process must be a matter for the individual mediator and the family concerned.

(Category 3: Agency – the Lord Chancellor's Department)

CHAPTER 8: CONTACT CENTRES

9. If and in so far as Contact Centres supplying 'supported' contact need or seek outside funding, it should be made available through *CAFCASS* on a regional basis or by means of an annual grant to NACCC which would then distribute the money according to need.

(Category 2: Agency – the Lord Chancellor's Department)

10. In so far as Contact Centres provide specialist facilities such as supervised contact, core funding should be provided by Government, with *CAFCASS* and others purchasing the use of these facilities as necessary.

(Category 2: Agency – the Lord Chancellor's Department)

11. Apart from supervision of contact, the Lord Chancellor's Department and CAFCASS should encourage Contact Centres to develop additional facilities such as accompanying children and parents on contact outside the centre, facilitating indirect contact and providing an information service to parents.

(Category 2: Agencies – the Lord Chancellor's Department, the National Association of Child Contact Centres and CAFCASS)

12. The Lord Chancellor's Department should fund more specialist Contact Centres like Coram Family and the Accord Centre.

(Category 2: Agency – the Lord Chancellor's Department)

CHAPTER 9: LAWYER NEGOTIATED CONTRACT

13. All lawyers undertaking children cases which are publicly funded should be accredited as competent to do so by the Law Society, the Solicitors Family Law Association or the Family Law Bar Association.

(Category 1: Agency – the Legal Services Commission)

CHAPTER 10: THE COURT PROCESS

14. The Lord Chancellor's Department should fund additional facilities for resolving contact disputes by negotiation, conciliation and mediation. Whilst there is plainly a role for the court in resolving contact disputes, there is a widespread perception that such disputes are better addressed outside the court system. There is a wide-spread feeling that an application to the court should be the last resort.

(Category 2: Agency – the Lord Chancellor's Department)

15. The Judiciary and the Court Service need to promote a culture of judicial continuity, avoiding time-wasting and inconsistency, by a more proactive management of judges' calendars and itineraries.

(Categories 1: Agencies – the Judiciary *and the Court Service)*

16. We welcome the widespread support for an in court conciliation system to be operated by CAFCASS at the first appointment in contact cases. Such a system should be operated throughout the country and at every level of court.

(Category 2: Agencies – the Court Service and CAFCASS)

17. There may be a role for family conferencing, but this is a matter for *CAFCASS* to explore in due course

(Category 4: Agency – CAFCASS)

CHAPTER 11: FAMILY ASSISTANCE ORDERS

18. The Government should legislate to make the changes required in order to make Family Assistance Orders effective. We support Family Assistance Order as potentially a very useful facility, if operated by *CAFCASS* and as part of a planned and specific programme of court led intervention. They should cease to be directed to Local Authorities, but should be directed to *CAFCASS*. The time limit of 6 months should be removed. The phrase 'exceptional circumstances', which has little meaning, should be repealed, as should the ability to refuse to consent to the making of an order.

(Category 3: Agency – the Lord Chancellor's Department)

19. We also recommend that *CAFCASS* be asked to prepare proposals in relation to specific programmes which could be operated under an Family Assistance Order, including 'educational' programmes for parents, packages of support in monitoring the implementation of contact agreements, support for indirect contact, and direct assistance to children.

(Category 1: Agency – CAFCASS)

CHAPTER 12: THE INVOLVEMENT OF CHILDREN IN THE COURT PROCESS

20. In the light of the advent of *CAFCASS*, the Lord Chancellor's Department, in consultation with the President, should review the restrictive view of children making applications to the court, which currently require the permission of a High Court Judge.

(Categories 1: Agencies – the Lord Chancellor's Department and the President)

21. Steps need to be taken to make use of the much greater degree of flexibility which the creation of *CAFCASS* offers the court when considering the question of a child's representation. The provisions now contained in the Family Proceedings Rules seem to us to be sufficiently flexible to ensure that the child's interests can be protected by appropriate representation wherever necessary. Specific consideration should therefore be given to the question of how the child's interests can be best represented in every case.

(Category 2: Agencies - CAFCASS and the Judiciary)

22. *CAFCASS* and the Judiciary should make use of the changes in the Family Proceedings Rules also give a much greater scope for *CAFCASS* officers to be more closely involved with the children on whom they are reporting, and a greater opportunity for children to be represented in court by *CAFCASS* officers with, if necessary, legal support. This is not, of course, to suggest that in every case the children should be represented: what we think it should

mean is that in cases where a straightforward investigation followed by a report is not sufficient to meet the interests of the children, the framework for the continuing involvement of *CAFCASS* exists and should be used. This prospect would be further strengthened if our proposals for the reform of Family Assistance Orders are implemented

(Category 2: Agencies – CAFCASS and the Judiciary)

CHAPTER 13. PARTICULAR FORMS OF COURT ORDERS

23. It is sensible in our view to include in a court order where appropriate a clause which enables the parties to agree further or different contact from that ordered. This frees the parties to make further agreements and can avoid an unnecessary return to court.

(Category 1: Agency – the Judiciary)

24. We also recommend imaginative and creative use of orders for indirect contact where that is appropriate.

(Category 1: Agency – the Judiciary)

CHAPTER 14: ENFORCEMENT

Wider powers for the courts

25. The courts should be given much wider powers to ensure that its orders are obeyed, or otherwise to facilitate their implementation. This means in turn that there must be legislation widening the powers to the courts to enable them, in addition to imposing fines or ordering imprisonment, to make a whole range of orders designed to address the problem posed by circumstances of the individual case. Numerous ideas emerged during the course of the consultation. We are particularly attracted by the suggestion put forward by *CAFCASS* that what is required is an approach which gives practitioners more time to work with parents and children within a framework of services.

Orders designed to engage available services

26. The courts need to be given the powers to make orders to engage a number of those services identified by *CAFCASS*, not all of which relate directly to the enforcement of an existing order, such as 'supervised Contact Centres, child counselling, perpetrator programmes, information giving meetings, conciliation meetings prior to initial directions and psychological assessments'. We strongly support and recommend the court being given the powers to make orders which enable these resources to be engaged.

27. In our view what is required is a range of options to be available to the court on the application of one of the parties (or CAFCASS, or the court of its own motion) designed to assist the implementation of an order which is not being obeyed. The range of options needs to be sufficiently flexible to address the problem, and that options themselves need to be available. There is no point, for example, directing a parent to attend a parenting class if the facility is not available.

The non-punitive approach

28. Legislation needs to provide powers that allow for two different approaches. There should, in our view, be two different options, or two stages. The first will be essentially non-punitive. The resident parent will, for example, be directed to attend an information meeting, or a parenting programme designed to address intractable contact disputes; or required to seek psychiatric advice. If that does not work, and the contact order has still not been obeyed, the court would reconsider and could impose an order with a penal sanction, such as community service or probation with conditions of treatment or regular attendance at parenting classes. Any question of fines or imprisonment would then genuinely be an issue of last resort.

The powers which the courts need

29. Legislation must provide the powers which the courts need. These are, we think, essentially the following:

(1) the power to refer a parent a parent who disobeys an order for contact to a variety of resources including information meetings, meetings with a counsellor, parenting programmes / classes designed to deal with contact disputes;

(2) the power to refer to a psychiatrist or psychologist, (publicly funded in the first instance);

(3) the power to refer a non-resident parent who was violent or in breach of an order to an education programme or a perpetrator programme;

(4) the power to place on probation with a condition of treatment or attendance at a given class or programme;

(5) the power to impose a community service order, with programmes specifically designed to address the default in contact;

(6) the power to award financial compensation from one parent to another (for example where the cost of a holiday has been lost).

(These recommendations under Chapter 14 all require legislation (category 3) and are directed to the Lord Chancellor's Department)

CHAPTER 15: RESEARCH AND FURTHER STUDY

30. For the reasons discussed in Chapter 15 of this report we recommend that the Lord Chancellor commissions research to address the issues identified in paragraph 15.3 together with the issues identified by Dr Clare Sturge and set out at paragraph 15.13. As stated in paragraphs we recommend research into the enforcement of contact, including the piloting of parental education programmes both for parents engaged in contact disputes or finding it difficult to make contact work.

31. The role of family conferences is a matter for CAFCASS to explore in due course (see paragraph 10.30).

32. Whilst, as we made clear in paragraph 14.23, we are attracted to the Australian model for the enforcement of court orders, it is, as yet, in its infancy; we do not know how it will work in practice, and we do not think it appropriate to recommend following it exactly. In any event, whilst a clear structure is required, the essence of the approach, in our judgment, is to provide the court with a substantial degree of flexibility, which our proposals would do.

33. We discuss in Appendix 3 the concept of joint parenting orders and the greater use of joint residence orders. We make no recommendation on this subject, but if the Government thinks the concept of shared parenting or the greater use of shared residence orders worth pursuing, it

might consider setting up a pilot scheme based on a small number of courts to test the effect of such orders in practice.

34. For the reasons discussed in paragraphs 14.39 to 14.42 we invite the Government in any further assessment of maintenance and the Child Support Agency to consider the desirability and practicability of legislating for an inter-relationship between child maintenance and contact.

35. We also very much agree with the Australian approach that at each stage in the process the obligations of the resident parent are carefully spelled out and the consequences which are to follow if the order is not obeyed.

36. We also suggest that the Rules committee may wish to look at the proposal found which found favour with a number of respondents and is canvassed in paragraph 14.29, namely that committal proceedings in relation to breaches of contact orders should only be permitted after a hearing without notice to the respondent in which the court considers the application and decides whether or not it should proceed to a full hearing.

(The items under this heading all fall within category 4. Some emerge from other parts of the consultation, but are conveniently addressed at this point.)

THE POLICY CONTEXT

Bruce Clark

Head of Looked After Children Division, Department for Education and Skills

I am grateful for the opportunity to attempt to set the conference discussions in the contemporary policy context. I am going to do not so much a tour of the horizon in relation to the whole of public and private law policy. Rather, it will necessarily be more like a 15-minute trip round the bay, in order to leave time for questions to the panel.

I want to start with the thing that is most central to my current role – looked after children. What has been very striking since the recent general election, following the establishment in both the DfES and the DCA of teams of ministers who are, in the main, new to the departments, is the further growth of ministerial interest in and concern about looked after children. There is a perception that there has been insufficient progress in achieving improved outcomes for lookedafter children across the eight years that this Government has been in power. The current target, from the Public Service Agreement set in the 2004 Spending Review, is for improved placement stability and educational achievement for looked-after children. The belief is, and it seems reasonable to me, that if children can become more stable other good things, such as better educational attainment and improved life chances, will follow. Progress towards these targets is being made, if more slowly than we would wish. The work in pursuit of this target, in which I have been involved in this year, has benefited from the supportive input of the Association of Directors of Social Services (ADSS), which is extremely interested to learn more from a central government-led secondary data analysis of placement stability, which they themselves would find hard to undertake. This has highlighted various factors which contribute to explaining why it is that there is such variable performance across England. I had, until this conference, been unaware of June Thoburn's comparative international work, and my work has been domestically focused, looking at different rates of court-mandated care across local authorities over the past few years. What is particularly fascinating is that it appears that the variations cannot readily be explained in terms of any specific identifiable factor, including differential rates of deprivation between different local authority areas, which might have been expected. Thus, the explanation appears to lie in the area of variations in practice at local level.

Now, it might be assumed that this variation has much to do with the courts, or the judges, or the lawyers, or CAFCASS. But, of course, these variations in practice arise before the children's cases are brought, or not brought, before the courts. It is generally accepted that the processes preceding the making of applications for care orders are broadly consistent across the country, and have been for many years. Around 75% of the section 31 applications that reach the courts result in care orders being made. So that does beg the question as to whether sufficient applications are being made. We've never experienced the problem, have we, whereby in parts of the country courts are asking a local authority 'why are you bringing me these cases? My court is only making a care order for a quarter of the cases. You are bringing footling matters before the courts that are not properly dealt with here by means of section 31 proceedings.' Thus, we need to consider what it is about pre-court practice that causes differential rates in the numbers of children who are being brought forward to the courts, with local authority applicants seeking care orders.

The 2004 Spending Review addressed the thorny issue of delay. We are now about two years into a programme of wide-ranging endeavour on all of our parts. I think that the most important piece of the jigsaw has been the *Protocol for Judicial Case Management in Public Law Children Act Cases*, which defies all my efforts to create an acronym. Although it has been argued that the DCA's Public Service Agreement target to increase the percentage of care cases completed in 40 weeks is not over-stretching and, indeed, is now being reached in some courts, it is important to recall that there is a ministerial aspiration to go beyond the formal target and to reach 70% of cases completed. Of course, there are elements of work in the delay programme aimed at general improvements in case management practices: the availability of an increased number of sitting days, better court rooms and, of course, the outstanding question of the competence and supply of experts, in particular medical experts. I think it is now two years since the former President first wrote to the Chief Medical Officer, Sir Liam Donaldson, setting out her concerns about those issues. We understand that the his report on this issue is due by the end of the year, and I look forward to it.

We have travelled during the two days of our conference across the whole of the private and public law domain, There are two other 'hot' issues on which I should also touch: the private law initiatives, with the current spotlight on the Children and Adoption Bill, while in public law the main focus is on the Review of Child Care Proceedings, with the last two years having seen at times almost frenetic activity in both areas. I think that the private law developments have much less to do with the stunts of certain fathers' rights lobbyists and a great deal more to do with the earlier careful work of the Children Act Sub Committee. It was being said that Government was not moving quickly enough in producing either its initial or its final response to this report. More recently, however, things have sped up, to the extent that there was a mere six months between the July 2004 Green Paper *Parental Separation: Children's Needs and Parents' Responsibilities* and the January 2005 *Next Steps* White Paper, with legislation – the Children and Adoption Bill – introduced a few months later. During these few months, the opportunity was taken to publish for scrutiny a draft Bill, which was able to take place in advance of the then anticipated general election. The scrutiny process has resulted in some improvements to the Bill and some additions, which are now being considered by Parliament. The Grand Committee stage in the House of Lords, commencing on 11 October, will enable further detailed scrutiny to take place. Amendments relating to presumptions of contact, parenting time and domestic violence will all be considered as part of this process. I think there is a growing concern, reflected particularly by Cathy Humphreys' talk today, partly about the primary legislation but also about underpinning guidance and actual practice. Of course, one can have the best legislation in the world, and often we claim that we do, but practice is equally important and there is growing evidence, which has been available for a while and which continues to come forward, that we lack consistent realisation in practice of the ambitions of current legislation and guidance. It is not surprising, therefore, that some are seeking to use the opportunity offered by new legislation to seek, as they would see it, to raise the game and to improve consistency.

Now, we have the President's private law programme, a sort of practice direction in all but name, and though I think there was initial concern about whether both the judiciary and CAFCASS would do their part in lightening the burden of section 7 reporting requirements in order to create the space for more and better alternative dispute resolutions, judged by CAFCASS' latest statistics the judiciary, in general, are clearly playing their part. A reduction of 7%, in the year to date, in the number of section 7 reports ordered, is a very tangible representation of the keeping of the judicial side of the bargain. Of course, at the same time we have also seen the doubling of the rate of rule 9.5 appointments, following the April 2004 Practice Direction. As someone who is responsible for the financial sponsorship of CAFCASS, I have worried a little about this growth: but the fact of the matter is, whether one looks at the previous work from the Leeds judges or the work by NYAS, or indeed an internal study by CAFCASS itself, there seems to be growing evidence that where rule 9.5 appointments are made, the more intensive intervention undertaken by a guardian is helpful for children. Given this, it becomes more difficult to object to this growth.

The Family Resolutions Pilot Project was presented by Nick Crichton yesterday, with his view from the Wells Street perspective. Liz Trinder has been very dutiful, I think, in not describing the outcome of the evaluation before she has completed her analysis. But let me share with you my impressions, sight unseen of the evaluation report. What the experience of the pilot's participation levels tells me is that you can take a horse to water but it cannot be made to drink. And I am not sure that I am talking about parties so much as practitioners, whether indeed of a CAFCASS or a legal or other variety. There has been much diffidence about the appropriateness of compulsion in the English and Welsh system. We have looked across the pond to the United States, perhaps thinking that it is different here, and that our citizens will not stand for being told what to do about their private and family lives. However, the mood is changing here. Nick Crichton has mentioned the desire to remove the consent requirement from Family Assistance

Orders. National Family Mediation is prepared to say to the Select Committee that it no longer sees initial voluntarism as being essential for successful mediation interventions. Both of these instances suggest to me there is growing support for greater compulsion in the private law domain. I am struck by this toughening of stance, in which we seem more prepared to say that 'if people choose to bring their family affairs before public bodies, they will play by our rules and we don't apologise for that. So bear this in mind if you choose to come before the courts.'

Let me talk a bit about resources. Some people say that CAFCASS was not adequately resourced following its vesting on 1 April 2001. While not commenting on that, I will say that I have been struck by the 50% increase from the first year's budget in 2001/02 of £72m to £107m in 2005/06. That is a 50% cash growth in a four-year period of low inflation – this growth is important to bear in mind before repeating the oft-made assertion that CAFCASS has been starved of resources. Whether it was or was not underfunded on its inception, it has seen marked increases by successive government departments and ministers, in part in response to the concerns of practitioners. But the question, whatever the quantum of CAFCASS resources might be, is what is done with the available money. CAFCASS, under its new leadership, is in a very different place from the situation of two years ago. In that time, we have seen the renewal of the entire senior management team and the board. We no longer hear, at least in fairness, the adjective 'failing' routinely preceding the name CAFCASS. What one hears instead is the adjective 'improving'. The current question for CAFCASS, as it considers what to do next in terms of its professional strategy, is to look at what it is doing, in both its private and public law work. It recognises the need to attend to its in-court conciliation interventions not least because, as the Magistrates' Courts Service Inspectorate's Report *Seeking Agreement* showed, many different models of pre-court interventions were being used by CAFCASS. This report heralded CAFCASS' critical self-examination, in looking at what works best by way of those interventions. Is it better to use the more resource intensive interventions or is the brief 'in corridor' intervention equally effective?

One of the things that I expected to be of interest this weekend, and I have not been disappointed, is the range of views that have been expressed about the jointly-led DCA/DfES Review of Child Care Proceedings. I think perhaps not all of us would have been aware of the Fundamental Legal Aid Review that reported to DCA ministers before the general election. There were discussions between the government departments, at least at that time, and a couple of ideas, including those from both the judiciary and from the DfES, were carried forward. Among them was the idea of 'pre-hearing hearings', informed from the first directions idea in private law, and of whether there should be earlier access to advocacy for parents, prior to commencement of formal proceedings. This might be based on the family group conference model or build on the provision of advocacy for parents involved in child protection proceedings. Those ideas were then carried forward to *A Fairer Deal for Legal Aid*, published on 5 July 2005. The focus of the Review is very clearly on improving outcomes for children, despite the associations that have been made with the level of legal aid. What I would say about resources is this. Whether or not the expenditure on public law legal aid has increased by 77%, during a period in which the number of cases has increased by only 37%, as is the case, the fact is that the Government and those responsible for operating the system have an ongoing responsibility for looking at the use of resources and ensuring that they are producing the best possible outcomes for their application. However, beyond the narrower debate about the costs of legal aid, the interests of my department are rather wider. Our concerns relating to outcomes for the children relates not just to the 40-week, or less we hope, period that children are involved in proceedings. We are equally interested in the five- to six-year, on average, 'care career' that will follow the making of an order. I recognise that there is a view that local authorities will be worried about the £35,000 that is spent on average, on proceedings. However, in terms of the money issues, local authorities would be more likely to be concerned about the quarter to a third of a million pounds that public services will be likely to spend on the care of a child who is the subject of a care order in the years that follow.

Currently, the Review Team is working hard to increase the active engagement of a wide range of stakeholders, with a major event now planned for 10 November. We have now established the usual panoply of advisory, working and steering groups. In addition to the development of more immediate proposals for presentation to ministers by January 2006, a view is already emerging that there may be need for ongoing work and further consultation. This is not surprising, if one looks at the history of successive studies of what is happening in public law. Whether it is Dame Margaret Booth's study, the subsequent scoping study on delay or the more recent Fundamental Legal Aid Review, it seems hard for any individual review exercise to encompass everything that might need to be considered which, perhaps, is why we keep coming back to the issue.

I won't say much about the Adoption and Children Act 2002. It is a staggering achievement that, in five short years, we have recast the entire code of adoption legislation, giving it the focus of the paramountcy of the child's welfare focus, borrowed from the 1989 Act. I know that there has been a comment on the six kilograms of guidance during this weekend. I hope that part of this 'burden' is the cracking 200-page read that is the Adoption and Children Act section 7 guidance that was issued earlier in the autumn, which I commend to you without reservation.

We are now in the training phase, with 75 two-day workshops being delivered to 2,000 social work practitioners, trainers and managers up and down the country. I understand that the Judicial Studies Board awareness events were well received by those who attended them. We are moving speedily to produce the transitional guidance, regulations and orders, in particular because of anxieties about how cases that are already in train should be handled. Naturally, we are applying the lessons that we learned in 1991 at the time of commencement of the Children Act 1989, in relation to the transitional arrangements that were made at that time.

I would also like to touch on the issue of the impact of targets in the adoption sphere. It is true that there has been a 37% increase, up to 2004, towards the Public Service Agreement target of 40%, and the latest figures are due to be published next month. Thus, we do not yet know if the target will be missed, achieved or exceeded. I have been interested to learn that some local authorities, through their local Public Service Agreements, have sought to 'stretch' themselves by developing more challenging local targets, though it is important to understand that reports that they will be 'fined', if they do not reach these targets, are inaccurate. What these local authorities have done is to choose to emphasise this area, above and beyond that which would in any case be expected. It is, of course, important to be sensitive to the possibility of perverse incentives associated with the use of targets, whether national or local. This is why central government has resisted proposals by individual local authorities that they should set targets to reduce the number of looked-after children or the number of children on their Child Protection Register. There are potential risks in such targets.

Finally, I wish to address the issue of disclosure. Early in 2004, it was feared that there would be a seismic impact on public law work arising from the Court of Appeal judgment in *R v Cannings*. In large part, these fears were not realised. I think that the Court of Appeal judgments in the cases of *Re B* and *Re U* were timely and informative, in terms of making clear the proper extent of the read-across from the criminal jurisdiction. An important, related development was Munby J's judgment, in the case of *B*, in relation to the disclosure of material in this case. This has been followed by prompt Government action to fill the identified gap. The case served to amplify the long-standing concerns of Families Need Fathers about the hampering of their ability lawfully and effectively to act as McKenzie Friends to unrepresented parties in private law cases. The revised court rules come into force at the end of October 2005. As with adoption, the emphasis is again placed on paramountcy.

The Government is now turning to consider the rather wider issues of transparency and openness. I think that some of the reporting of the 'forcible adoption' cases revealed the risks that exist when one side of the story is proclaimed very clearly but where the other side remains substantially untold. I think it is without precedent that the Essex County Council placed a link on its website to Pauffley J's judgment, and the reading of it provided a marked contrast to much of the media reporting. The challenge, as we take forward this work, debating how or whether to publish transcripts or reasons for the making of orders, and as we look at other jurisdictions, particularly Australia and New Zealand, is how best we can ensure that justice is not only done but that it is also clearly perceived to be done.

SMALL GROUP DISCUSSIONS: PLENARY 8

SMALL GROUP B

PLENARY 8: HELPING TO ENSURE SOLUTIONS WORK FOR CHILDREN IN THE LONGER TERM.

There is a significant lack of services available for parents following the conclusion of public law proceedings, where their children have been permanently placed in substitute homes secured by final care orders and adoption.

SMALL GROUP C

PLENARY 8: HELPING TO ENSURE SOLUTIONS WORK FOR CHILDREN IN THE LONGER TERM

Discussion focused on patchy availability and differences between advocacy and support services. Local authorities are required to assess need but not to provide services to meet it. It is too soon to draw conclusions, but the assessment of need through the adoption support proposals can inform the development of services.

The Children and Adoption Bill

Family assistance order: the ability to enforce these is supported by the group. The wording 'advice and assist' is appropriate but the word 'befriend' should be removed.

In relation to applications in private law, the tenet 'You come to our courts, you play by our rules' was seen as an important and significant change in approach.

The FAO should provide an exit from court proceedings, a listening, supportive ear, more likely to resolve differences than a lawyer.

The option for the Court to allocate FAO to CAFCASS or the LA should be retained, although usually it will be more appropriate for CAFCASS to undertake the work.

SMALL GROUP D

1.   PRIVATE LAW CHILDREN DISPUTES – DEVELOPING THE CURRENT SYSTEM

(1) We wish to recognise the strengths of the current system with its emphasis on early identification of issues and encouragement of negotiated arrangements. There is a wide range of dedicated professionals, both within and outside the immediate family justice system, who are committed to helping families find solutions for children on family breakdown. However…

(2) Existing schemes (typically in-court conciliation) do not offer:

- any real assessment of risk;

- any significant way of addressing issues about relationships within the family;

- any opportunity for education about or helping understanding of parenting skills or managing conflict.

(3) The Family Resolutions pilot contained elements of these features – particularly through group work and the information video and role-play: it was a 'step in the right direction'. These elements could be built on and incorporated into an initial information/triage process.

(4) There needs to be encouragement for parents to see 'what they are doing wrong' and to acquire new skills.

(5) A system of differential case management is needed, to identify the family's needs and appropriate resources – a 'diagnostic tool'.

(6) A possible model would be to provide CAFCASS intervention at the outset of the court process; ideally such help should be available earlier, but there is then an issue about how and when the difficulties are identified and CAFCASS accessed. The scheme would involve a referral to CAFCASS on issue of an application and several sessions (2–3?) with an officer before or around the first court hearing; the officer could undertake an initial assessment of risk and of the nature and extent of the dispute and give information and advice on basic skills for managing family relationships and understanding change and behaviour.

2.   EDUCATION AND SUPPORT – A CONTINUUM.

(1) The question of relationships and of managing conflict and family breakdown raises much wider issues about adults' understanding of family life and child development. Parents need to have the 'building blocks' of understanding both to enable healthy relationships while together and to manage difficulties in the event of breakdown.

(2) This involves education from an early stage. While many may not be receptive at the time of the birth of a child, such work could be provided in the context of the child's education (analogous with drugs and sex education, with which parents are often expected to engage). Local authority children's services could be involved in this process though the provision of a package of parenting skills material; the development of a strategic approach to parenting support in some authorities could underpin this.

(3) There would remain a need for support and advice at and around the time of breakdown, but parents would be better equipped. Equally, there might be some form of review or follow-up of arrangements agreed or ordered on breakdown, to facilitate flexibility and durability.

This may be an appropriate role for a CAFCASS officer. Thus there would be a continuum of support and advice available for the family before, during and after any breakdown.

(4) Any programme of education or support would need to recognise and be attuned to different cultural mores within the various elements of the population.

3. A NEW APPROACH?

(1) A more radical solution to intervention would be to establish a specialist court focusing on private law disputes, offering (relatively low level) judicial input and continuity, with the ability for the court to refer the family directly to appropriate resources; these might include:

- advice and information on parenting in the context of family breakdown (CAFCASS?);

- initial assessment of need and risk;

- specialist contact centres offering guidance and support in parenting skills;

- access to counselling/therapeutic work;

- specialist mental health/ therapeutic services for high conflict cases.

(2) Additional enforcement powers are of limited benefit, as the aim should be to assess each case and tailor the approach to the needs of and risks posed by the particular family.

(3) Local family justice councils may have a role in developing and supporting strategic interagency partnership to improve access to local services.

(4) But there are limits to the capacity of the family justice system to effect change for families. Is there a case for saying that the high cost of trying to seek solutions for the intractable cases is not merited in terms of outcome and that resources would be best directed at lower-level intervention in a larger number of cases of moderate difficulty, eg in entry-level parenting groups?

(5) Whatever the form or level of intervention, there is a pressing need for impartial explanation of the outcome to the child.

SMALL GROUP E

PRACTICE, POLICY AND RESEARCH

(1) There is a need for cultural change among professionals and public:

(a) to redefine problems in families as public health and / or educational issues rather than solely as legal issue;

(b) to understand that a parent's relationship ideally needs to be sustained throughout their child's life;

(c) that wider family members, particularly grandparents, also need to understand and take on board this concept and be supportive of both parent's continuing involvement following parental separation;

(d) the role of the father and his importance to his child (eg Australian CSA doing workplace seminars and workshops).

(2) Services need to be available to enable parents / other significant adults to:

(a) be able to communicate about the child;

(b) be able to work in collaboration, without conflict;

(c) ensure quality contact is provided;

(d) to help the child and to provide him/her with skills and understand their role in the process.

The workers need the skills to deal with the complexity of the disentanglement process and help parents to reunite the (new) parenting contract and broker a relationship if the child born outside of one. The views and influences of the wider family also need to be addressed and worked on and with.

(3) These services need to be available and delivered at multiple entry points and through self referral as well as teachers, GPs, lawyers, courts etc

- would include support and befriending, parenting classes and relationship issues as in (2) above. The group felt that such referrals should be **compulsory** in certain circumstances.

(4) The group identified a need generally, or at least when an application is made to court, to provide a triage system, ie effective screening of adults involved, to enable the case to proceed and be referred to appropriate services (as above). The screening would be (a) risk assessment for domestic violence (b) for the presence of conflict

Research findings can inform how, by whom and how soon in the process this screening should be undertaken, and what use would be made of the information gathered. The group anticipated the results would divide cases into three categories: (1) cases which could proceed; (2) middle group who would be helped by appropriate interventions; (3) intractable and/or dangerous group.

PUBLIC LAW

(1) Issues are apparent for local authorities on their approach to contact. Some local authorities seem to show a lack of flexibility in their approach.

(2) The group was concerned about lack of separate funding for independent reviewing officers, and the fact that the independent reviewing officer is located within local authorities. The group questioned whether this function should be transferred to CAFCASS. There is a need to ensure a consistency of approach through England and Wales and an evaluation of the service being provided by the independent reviewing officer to see if local authority practice has improved.

(3) The group saw a need for feedback systems to courts from local authorities to improve practice and queried whether there was a role for Local Family Justice Councils in achieving this.

(4) There is a need for proper induction and training for social workers on statutory responsibilities and court based activity such as giving evidence.

(5) Finally, law and policy need to follow evidence and research.

IDEAS AND PROPOSALS

(1) The court should have power in private law proceedings not only to make a s.37 direction but also to 'direct' a local authority to commence care proceedings.

(2) In public law proceedings, the court should remain as the forum to resolve child protection and public law issues.

(3) In private law the court's role should be linked to other 'services' to include:

- private law programmes which directly involve children and lead to 'diversion' or conclusion of care;

- a role for CAFCASS / guardian / co-ordinator being accessible to parties to provide 'practical' help and advice to move situation on. The group discussed whether telephone contact could play a role in this and whether this would require availability 24 hours per day;

- mental health and skilled social workers in an integrated system dealing with those with mental health difficulties, including identifying early on in the process those adults using the court process as a manifestation of their 'illness';

- 'professionalisation' of contact / mediation processes in contact centres.

(4) There needs to be public understanding of the role of the social worker including an improved status and respect for their role. Consideration needs to be given to social workers' training and the support they receive during employment to review if this is adequate and equips them for their difficult job.

(5) There is an ongoing need in all professional practice for the professionals to consider what language and jargon is being used in dealings with families.

SMALL GROUP F

There was support for an amendment to the Children (Contact) and Adoption Bill for the routine provision of information that related to violence, for example information the police held on DV call outs.

The group discussed whether there should be a presumption that the child should be represented in enforcement proceedings. One option might be to make enforcement proceedings 'specified' proceedings. A better option would be to have a requirement that the court should consider whether the child should be separately represented before it exercised its powers.

Whether it should be possible to make family assistance orders without the agreement of adult parties was an issue. The FAO was a potentially useful order but there were very limited services especially for contact cases. The danger if FAOs could be made without agreement cases would quickly be channelled down the compulsory route in order to access services. On the other hand there were cases in which one party was being awkward and the only way progress could be made was to introduce a measure of compulsion.

There were severe reservations about the current DCA/DfES Review of Care proceedings – the way it was being conducted, the timetable and the terms of reference. The comparison with the Child Care Law Review in the 1980s was stark.

- *Domestic violence* – Before the court exercises its powers of enforcement, there should be further consideration of whether the child should be separately represented.

- *Review of care* – Acknowledge that there could be improvement in care proceedings and be willing to engage in a constructive process to achieve it.

- We deplore the approach taken in the current review of care proceedings with:

  - loaded terms of reference

  - without open consultation

  - by a team lacking in any relevant experience

This is in marked contrast to the careful process for child care law reform in the 1980s which provides a model for this type of activity.

ISSUES RAISED IN SMALL GROUPS AND DISCUSSIONS

Thorpe LJ opened the final plenary session by detailing his expectations. The conference was not in a position to approve perfectly crafted resolutions – this would have required a drafting team working into the night. This had not been the case and it may be that the conference would not be in a position to approve any resolutions. Thorpe LJ had hoped that the resolution proposed by Wall LJ would be unanimously approved, but given the discussions earlier in the day this seemed unlikely.

PLENARY 9

Resolution

A resolution in relation to Domestic Violence and the Children and Adoption Bill

This is that amendments are added to the current bill to ensure that child risk and safely assessment are undertaken in relation to all applications for enforcement – this includes cases where there were consent orders

- Dr Cathy Humphreys informed the conference that, if this was approved, the amendments had been drafted.

- Thorpe LJ commented that if there was a consensus from the conference, we did not need to explore the details of the drafting at this stage.

- Black J thought it too simple to say that this should apply to every application for enforcement. It is more complicated than this and there needs to be a risk assessment.

- Thorpe LJ canvassed reducing this to all applications for enforcement following consent orders.

- Professor Judith Masson thought this too narrow, but it would be possible to define the appropriate applications to which it would apply. Her concern was to join up the information held by the various agencies in relation to the children. It was of concern that the court did not have all the information that other agencies do.

- Black J would add her consent if this information was obtained at the beginning of the s 8 process.

- Jane Booth voiced her agreement that it must be the case that a public body makes use of all the information that it can. It is not only about enforcement. Some CAFCASS officers have long-standing arrangements that ignore the current laws. She asked why we would not want to know all the information that is available and supported broader information than simply enforcement.

- Professor Corrine May-Chahal urged caution about putting the work 'risk' before the word 'safety' in the proposals. Her view was that assessment should be safety first or safety alone.

- Thorpe LJ reminded the conference of the need to avoid drafting points. These could be consulted upon later and asked whether there was a broad consensus on the simple concepts.

- There was a consensus.

The wording proposed was not put in detail before the conference but was:

New clause after s 8

8A Child Safety

(1) On receipt of any application for a section 8 order the court shall obtain a child risk and safety assessment

(2) The court may direct CAFCASS to provide a child risk and safety assessment

(3) Where the court directs CAFCASS to provide a child risk and safety assessment under subsection (2) CAFCASS must provide the information

(4) A Court shall not normally make a section 8 order unless it has considered a child risk and safety agreement.

(5) No court may enforce a section 8 order or any condition under a section 11(7) unless

(a) it has considered an assessment of the safety of the child and of any person with whom the child is living, and

(b) it is satisfied that the safety of the child or any person with whom the child is living will not be compromised by such enforcement

Resolution

This conference urges the Government to reconsider its opposition to the recommendation made by the joint committee scrutinising the draft Adoption and Child Bill that the final Bill should remove the need to obtain the consent of all those who are to be named in a Family Assistance Order under s 16 of the Children Act 1989 as amended.

- This was proposed by Wall LJ and as there had been discussion in a previous session it was voted upon. The vote was all in favour save two 'no's and three 'don't know's'.

- The resolution was therefore adopted with some dissent.

- The President pointed out that the resolution only urged the Government to reconsider.

Resolution

Parents who reach agreement at conciliation appointments in private law proceedings be offered a limited and focussed follow up service to reduce the current level of dissatisfaction or breakdown.

- Thorpe LJ commented that this resolution came from Dr Liz Trinder's work in relation to the Conciliation Service.

- There was general support for this resolution.

- Jane Booth raised the question of resources.

Resolution

Social workers should be better trained and remunerated to increase the level of respect for their work and experience.

- Thorpe LJ summarised the resolution.

- It was proposed that this be sent to the Social Work Development Unit.

- It was further commented that this was a sensible place to say something so wonderfully aspirational.

Resolution

The allocation of resources dependent upon the achievement of adoption targets is not in the best interest of children and should be abandoned

- Bruce Clark indicated that this was likely to be stopped anyway and in that sense was not a real issue.

- Professor June Thoburn commented if that was the case, there was no difficulty with leaving the resolution in place. Even if Bruce knows it is not a real issue, there are others who do not.

- Martha Cover was of the view that social workers do feel under pressure. There should be incentives rather than penalties as to placements for adoption.

- Margaret McGlade suggested a performance target without a financial reward. Derby had missed their performance target as did several others. She proposed a general resolution as to targets in child care.

- Thorpe LJ suggested this resolution was dropped as it was offending some and pleasing others.

Resolution

The independence of the Reviewing Officer should be better demonstrated by the severance of current ties to the local authority. Consideration should be given to transferring the function to CAFCASS.

- Jane Booth pointed out that we do not yet know what the problems are. She thought it was premature to scrap the present system and start again. There are pressures which external scrutiny involves and advantages of internal scrutiny. If the reviewing officer is taken out, local authorities would only need to put something else back in its place.

- Professor Mervyn Murch considered that if 'independent' simply meant 'independent of the line of management', that is something that should be made clear in the title. Further, he felt that the Reviewing Officer must be fully independent.

- Bruce Clark confirmed that 'independent' did mean 'independent of the line of management' in the case. Wholly independent people are brought in at stages two and three of the complaints procedure so there is independence later in the process.

- Thorpe LJ suggested this resolution be reduced to an expression of concern and the need for investigation.

Resolution

In all s 8 applications the court should be provided with safeguarding checks including:

(a) any previous convictions of the parties
(b) any relevant police computer records
(c) any risk assessment (ie OASIS, MAPPA) available to the police

Where any significant child protection issue is revealed, CAFCASS to refer to SST.

- Thorpe LJ summarised this resolution as confirming that the court should have checks. He pointed out this is not an untried practice but this is what happens in Manchester.

- Jane Booth said the process is taken further in Manchester to provide a full interagency picture to include any information as to psychiatric problems that the police might not be aware of.

- DJ Waller confirmed that he was not against this resolution but concerned as to the issue of resources. He was anxious as to the resolution of cases. The Principal Registry lists 2,500 private law Children Act applications each year. This resolution may mean that the police require extra resources. If this means taking CAFCASS officers away from their other work, this should be thought through.

- Thorpe LJ replied that this had not caused difficulties for the team in Manchester but recognised that it might for other regions.

- Jane Booth gave information that it takes five days for this information to be supplied in Manchester.

- DJ Waller commented that there are practical issues in some cases.

- Professor Mervyn Murch stated that this may deter people from applying for s 8 applications. Further in applications where lawyers are publicly funded this may affect lawyers' legal aid remuneration. Issues may arise as to privacy for adults in mental health cases: there may be an issue as to whether this information should be disclosed to the other party and to the court.

- Professor Judith Masson suggested that guidance could be provided as to how far back the information had to be provided. It could be done as a stage-by-stage process. However, the court should have available to it the same information that is available to the NHS etc.

- Thorpe LJ thought we could be optimistic as this system was currently being used in Manchester.

- David Spicer raised the concern that we do not keep records of factual findings made against parties in care proceedings and that a record of these findings should be kept. This was already causing problems in appeals to Care Standards Tribunals.

- Yvonne Brown explained that our priority must be to protect children. Information must be provided where this would safeguard children's well-being, but questioned whether criminal records are relevant if they have nothing to do with the assessment of risk in relation to the child.

- Thorpe LJ replied that it could be left to the court to determine what is relevant.

- Professor Judith Masson suggested adopting only the first lines of the resolution and not the subsequent sub-paragraphs. This could be provided as guidance rather than legislation as to what those safeguard checks should be in light of evidence from Manchester etc.

[Each small group produced a number of resolutions to put to the conference. However, there was not sufficient time for all the proposals to be considered during the conference. Where the resolution was discussed at the conference the discussion is recorded below. After the conference, a draft version of this document was circulated among the conference delegates and speakers for their further comments. These are included below.]

GROUP A

Resolution

> *The DFES should:*
>
> *(1) compile a publicly available directory of the location and nature of the contact services presently available nationally;*
> *(2) develop a strategic approach to the commissioning of contact services facilities and activities within a clear framework of standards concerned with safety and quality of support.*

- Bruce Clark stated that there already was such a directory.

- Group A explained that the first part of the resolution was intended to do more than list the contact centres available – list all the services that were available to support and enable contact itself and those involved in the contact process.

- Professor Corrine May-Chahal clarified the resolution as looking at the plan. It may be a costly exercise to provide these services and facilities. This should be designed to support all parents and children, including those in the public law system.

- Bruce Clark agreed.

GROUP B

Resolution

Our authors of research papers be commissioned to distil the messages into a guide to be offered to the JSB and other trainers to assist practitioners and judges in their assessment of the welfare of children.

- Thorpe LJ clarified this resolution as an opportunity to pick up the sum of the research papers, to question some of the assumptions which are currently held. This is to assist practitioners and judges. There was a suggestion that Joan Hunt had already done some of this work. However, there seems to be a gap or risk of a gap between the highly relevant information coming out of the research papers and the assumptions that people are making on a case-by-case basis. Principles regarding contact should change in relation to information that is coming out of current research, including academic research, to ensure there is good communication between those that are discovering relevant statistics and those who have to make decisions about children.

- Joan Hunt confirmed this was a bigger issue as to the dialogue between researchers and reviews and whether the two require something separate.

- Bruce Clark clarified that research needs to come from members and not from the Government.

- Dr Cathy Humphreys suggested that research was needed into the application of research in practice, particularly in the social care and health sector.

- Professor Judith Masson suggested research needed to be brought to the Family Justice Council. Further, there needed to be wider access to research. CAFCASS research needed to be made available publicly through the website. The Institute for Excellence had some material which could be transferred into data and made available more widely.

GROUP C

Resolution

(1) We propose that the needs of vulnerable children caught up in parental separation and conflict should be highlighted within the 'Every Child Matters' arrangements.

(2) We propose that Independent Reviewing Officers should be employed and funded independently of the local authority.

(3) We propose that performance targets and financial penalties which favour one form of permanent placement for looked after children (presently adoption) should be removed and the paramouncy of the child's welfare should be the deciding principle.

(4) We propose that the information required for inclusion on the form C1 should include ethnicity.

(5) We propose that research should be undertaken into contact orders made either by consent or imposed by the courts in cases involving allegations of domestic violence; firstly the number of such orders needs to be established, and then whether any such orders are putting children at risk.

- In correspondence following the conference, Dr Claire Sturge emphasised the importance that Group C had attached to ethnic monitoring as there had been little emphasis during the conference on the particular needs of some ethnic groups.

- Arran Poyser agreed commenting that the group recognised that the question of ethnic monitoring deserved urgent attention in order that those providing services within the wider family justice system are able to do so with increased understanding, sensitivity and appropriateness for the whole diversity of court users, of which race is but one important aspect.

- Malcolm Richardson JP proposed that any further discussion on this issue should take account of the research published by Dr Julia Brophy on the subject of child protection litigation in a multi-cultural setting.

- Yvonne Brown agreed and requested that the Family Justice Council members pursue this matter with the DFES.

- This was endorsed by Liz Goldthorpe who believes the DCA to be in breach of the Race Relations (Amendment) Act 2000, as Dr Julia Brophy pointed out in her recent research.

- Although Dr Julia Brophy did not attend the conference, she has confirmed that her research will be passed to the Family Justice Council.

GROUP D

Resolution

Private law children disputes – developing the current system

> *To provide CAFCASS intervention at the outset of the court process. The scheme would involved a referral to CAFCASS on issue of an application and several sessions (2–3) with an officer before or around the first court hearing; the officer could undertake an initial assessment of risk and of the nature and extent of the dispute and give information and advice on basic skills for managing family relationships and understanding change and behaviour.*

Education and support – a continuum

> *Education from an early state. While many may not be receptive at the time of the birth of a child, such work could be provided in the context of the child's education (analogous with drugs and sex education, with which parents are often expected to engage). Local authority children's services could be involved in this process, through the provision of a package of parenting skills material; the development of a strategic approach to parenting in some authorities could underpin this.*

A new approach?

> - *A more radical solution of intervention would be to establish a specialist court focusing on private law disputes, offering (relatively low level) judicial input and continuity, with the ability for the court to refer the family directly to appropriate resources; these might include:*
>   - *advice and information on parenting in the context of family breakdown (CAFCASS?);*
>   - *initial assessment of need and risk;*
>   - *specialist contact centres offering guidance and support in parenting skills;*
>   - *access to counselling/therapeutic work;*
>   - *specialist mental health/therapeutic services for high conflict cases.*
> - *The aim should be to assess each case and tailor the approach to the needs of and risks posed by the particular family.*
> - *Local Family Justice Councils may have a role in developing and supporting strategic interagency partnership to improve access to local services.*
> - *Whatever the form or level of intervention, there is a pressing need for impartial explanation of the outcome to the child.*
> - *There might be some form of review or follow-up of arrangements agreed or ordered on breakdown, to facilitate flexibility and durability. This may be an appropriate role for a CAFCASS officer. Thus there would be a continuum of support and advice available for the family before, during and after any breakdown.*

- Thorpe LJ commented that he was not sure these ideas could be put forward as resolution material but rather to promote on-going debate.

- Jane Booth replied that there is a private law framework rolling out and it is helpful to say that people should be debating this. This is on the agenda and we did not wish to make prescription for this. These suggestions were not cost neutral and it is not unhelpful that the conference should support an active debate.

- Bruce Clark thought that the private law programme envisages this. In Manchester, CAFCASS are involved from the date that the application is issued. CAFCASS carry out the safety checks. He expressed surprise that it was only in Manchester that this was happening. Intervention might be viewed as fitting the bill.

GROUP E

Resolution

(1) *To raise the status and experience of social workers to restore their skills in working with people by addressing:*
- *qualifications at entry*
- *training*
- *skills*
- *remuneration.*

(2) *Measures should be put in place to enable 'services' to be delivered and to parents to assist them to deal with family breakdown and contact issues **before** they reach court – with 'referrals' via schools, GPs, health visitors, lawyers etc.*

(3) *In any case which reaches a court, the court should be able to compel parties to participate/accept services.*

(4) *In every case there should be an initial 'screening'/risk assessment of adult parties, by CAFCASS with the results being filed with the court.*

GROUP F

Resolution

We deplore the approach taken to the current review of care proceedings with:

- *loaded terms of reference*
- *without open consultation*
- *by a team lacking in any relevant experience.*

This is in marked contrast to the careful process for child care law reform in the 1980s which provides a model for this type of activity.

The conference applauded.

Resolution

Children Contact Bill

Before the court exercises its powers of enforcement, there should be further consideration of whether the child should be separately represented.

Review of care

Acknowledge that there could be improvement in care proceedings and willing to engage in a constructive program to achieve it.

THE CONCLUSION OF THE CONFERENCE

Thorpe LJ stated that the conference had maintained extremely high standards. The conference had been overstretched by the quality and quantity of the research which had been put before it. The conference risked indigestion or weight gain but this was better than being undernourished.

The Council's thanks were due to all those who had generously given up their time to prepare papers, to the planning group who had pursed their objectives and ideals with enthusiasm, imagination and persistence and to Malcolm Welsh, the conference administrator, who had ensured that all went smoothly in the run up to and at Dartington.